STUDY GUIDE

Social Psychology

Social Psychology

Gilovich, Keltner, and Nisbett

Connie Wolfe

MUHLENBERG COLLEGE

 W • W • NORTON & COMPANY • NEW YORK • LONDON

Copyright © 2006 by W. W. Norton & Company, Inc.

Printed in the United States of America

First Edition

Composition and layout by R. Flechner Graphics

ISBN 13: 978-0-393-92807-5

ISBN 10: 0-393-92807-1

W. W. Norton & Company, Inc., 500 Fifth Avenue, New York, NY 10110
www.wwnorton.com

W. W. Norton & Company Ltd., Castle House, 75/76 Wells Street, London W1T 3QT

1 2 3 4 5 6 7 8 9 0

CONTENTS

Tips for Effective Studying

Finding an effective study strategy is largely an individual task of trial and error. Some students find it useful to outline a chapter; others would rather take notes on it. Some students like to study with music on, and others do better in silence. Some students like flashcards; others find them a waste of time. Social and cognitive research on learning and memory, however, does offer some suggestions that should be helpful to most people.

Elaborative rehearsal is better than rote repetition.

Many students mistakenly believe that if they repeat something enough times they will or should know it. Simply repeating a definition (out loud or otherwise) over and over is called *rote repetition*. While this kind of repetition is sometimes sufficient to memorize a concept, more often than not, people forget the information shortly after stopping the repetition. (Have you ever looked up a phone number, then repeated it several times, only to forget it once you reached the phone?)

A better strategy is to engage in what is sometimes called *elaborative rehearsal.* Elaborative rehearsal also involves rehearsing or repeating the information you desire to learn. But with elaborative rehearsal, instead of repeating the same information over and over, you find multiple ways to elaborate on the information. For example, imagine you are trying to remember the definition of the fundamental attribution error. With rote repetition you would simply repeat the definition over and over again: "underestimating situational causes for behavior and overestimating personal causes." With elaborative rehearsal, you would expand on or provide new information about the concept with each repetition.

There are several ways to elaborate on any given piece of information. For example: (1) repeat the definition; (2) put the definition in your own words; (3) provide a generic example; (4) provide a personal example from your own life; (5) provide a real-world example from sports, politics, world events, and so on; (6) answer one or more practice exam questions about the concept; (7) explain how the concept relates to one or more other concepts you are learning. In short, the more ways you *actively* work with the material, the easier it will be to remember it and the more likely you will have an in-depth understanding of the information.

The reason this works is because elaborative rehearsal creates a richer network of associations so that when you need to retrieve the information, you have more retrieval cues. As depicted in Figure 1, rote repetition essentially re-

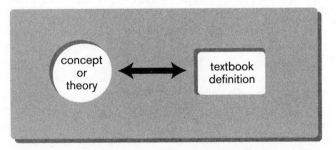

Figure 1. Associative network created by rote repetition

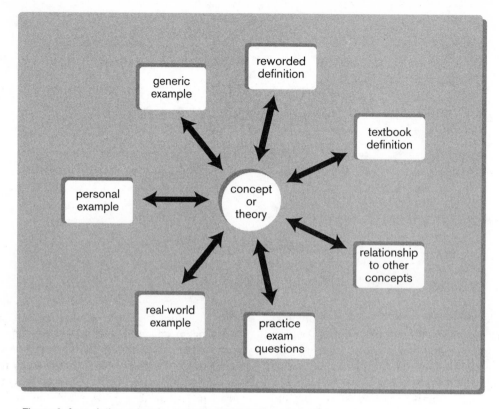

Figure 2. Associative network created by elaborative rehearsal

sults in just one association to the concept: the definition. On the other hand, as shown in Figure 2, elaborative rehearsal provides lots of associations. So, when you try to remember the concept, you have seven chances instead of just one. And, when you do remember the concept, all the other associations also come to mind. Thus, you have a fuller, richer representation of the concept active in your mind.

Self-relevant information is easier to remember.

As you'll learn in Chapter 5, the self has incredibly important influences on our thoughts and behaviors. This influence extends to basic memory processes. We tend to better remember information that is relevant to the self. So, any instance in which you can relate a concept or theory to your own life increases the chances that you will better remember the information. Think of it as creating an association to one of the most easily accessible associative networks there is: the self (see Figure 3). This is why, in the section on elaborative rehearsal, key suggestions were to put definitions in your own words and come up with your own examples (especially examples from your own life).

More distributed study sessions are better than fewer mass sessions.

Research suggests that, when memorizing a list of information, people will often better remember information at the beginning and end of the list and will often forget information in the middle of the list. This is known as the serial-position effect. Extrapolating to more complex tasks, this effect suggests that we will better remember information at the beginning and end of a study session. This is one reason why it is much more effective to have more, shorter study sessions as opposed to fewer "cram" sessions.

Another reason to engage in more frequent (though shorter) study sessions is that you will better understand the material. Students often mistakenly believe that if they read information in a textbook and understand it, then they know it and only need to review it before the exam to retain it. Not only does this sort of study strategy usually lead students to draw a blank on an exam, students using this strategy also overestimate their deep understanding of a concept. One way to understand this is to refer back to the associative network model. It is incredibly difficult to create the placeholders for a brand new concept *and* fill in those placeholders in

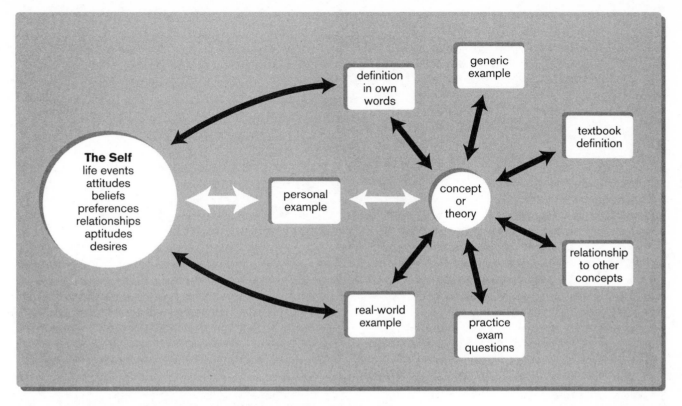

Figure 3. Associating new information with existing information about the self

a single step. Reading something once will, at best, alert your brain to the existence of new concepts (creating the placeholders). You need to engage in elaborative rehearsal (over several study sessions) to nail down what the concept is all about (filling in the placeholders). If you follow the exercises in this Study Guide, you will be building up and layering information so that you can better understand and retain the concepts.

CHAPTER 1 | Introduction

The goals of this chapter are to define, in a comprehensive way, the discipline of social psychology, to explain some of the major themes in social psychology—the power of the situation, construals, automatic versus controlled processing, evolution, and culture, and to provide an overview of the primary methods by which social psychologists test their hypotheses—through experiments and correlational studies.

ANNOTATED CHAPTER OUTLINE

After first reading through the chapter quickly, create a comprehensive framework for the information in the chapter by reading the outline below and filling in the missing information. Instead of simply re-copying information from the textbook, try to use your own words wherever possible; you can check your answers against the completed outline in the Answer Key section at the end of the chapter.

I. Characterizing Social Psychology
   A. Social psychology can be defined as

   _____
   _____
   _____

   B. Explaining Behavior
      1. Social psychologists study how people (real, imagined, encountered today or in the past, face-to-face or through the media) influence our thoughts, feelings, and behaviors.
      2. Social psychologists study how we understand and make sense of our social worlds.
      3. Social psychology differs from folk wisdom because _____

      _____

_____
_____

   C. Comparing Social Psychology to Related Disciplines
      1. Personality psychology vs. social psychology
         a. Personality psychology stresses

         _____
         _____
         _____
         _____

         b. Social psychology stresses

         _____
         _____
         _____
         _____

      2. Cognitive psychology vs. social psychology
         a. Cognitive psychologists study

         _____
         _____
         _____

         b. Social psychologists, or social-cognitive psychologists, study

         _____
         _____
         _____

      3. Sociology vs. social psychology
         a. Sociologists study macro characteristics of populations (e.g., institutions, subgroups).
         b. Social psychologists study

         _____
         _____
         _____
         _____

D. Proximal vs. Distal Influences in Social Psychology
1. Proximal factors are those factors that exist in the here-and-now or that immediately precede what the individual does.
   a. Situation
   b. Construal of situation
   c. Automatic or controlled perceptions and reactions to a situation
2. Distal factors are those factors that are more removed in time from a given context or episode, such as:
   a. _____
   _____
   _____

   b. _____
   _____
   _____
   _____

II. The Power of the Situation
A. Kurt Lewin (the founder of modern social psychology) thought that the behavior of people is always a function of the field of forces in which they find themselves.
B. The Milgram Experiment
1. Stanley Milgram (1963) illustrated the power of the situation in his experiment on obedience.
2. Milgram found that
   _____
   _____
   _____
   _____

3. Features of the situation that exert power over the participants' behavior include:
   a. The experiment was presented as an official scientific investigation.
   b. _____
   c. _____
   d. _____
   e. _____
   f. _____
C. Seminarians as Good Samaritans
1. Darley and Batson (1973) illustrated the power of the situation in their Good Samaritan study.
2. Darley and Batson found that
   _____
   _____
   _____
   _____

3. The basis of their religious calling—that is, whether students were oriented toward religion for spiritual reasons or personal gains—did not predict their behavior toward the man in the doorway.

D. Channel Factors
1. In a 1952 study, Lewin said that channel factors help explain the power of the situation.
2. Channel factors can be defined as
   _____
   _____
   _____
   _____

3. Leventhal, Singer, and Jones (1965) did a study that examined channel factors.
   a. Students were warned about the dangers of getting tetanus, and they were encouraged to go to the health center for an inoculation.
   b. All students formed the intention to get the inoculation.
   c. Only 3 percent of students in the control condition actually got the inoculation.
   d. In contrast, 27 percent of students in the experimental condition got the inoculation.
   e. The experimental condition included the channel factors of
   _____
   _____
   _____
   _____

E. The Fundamental Attribution Error
1. The fundamental attribution error can prevent people from realizing the power of the situation.
2. Dispositions can be defined as
   _____
   _____
   _____

3. The fundamental attribution error can be defined as
   _____
   _____
   _____
   _____

III. The Role of Construal
A. Construal is defined as
   _____
   _____
   _____

B. Interpreting Reality
1. Gestalt psychology maintains that objects are perceived, not by means of some automatic registering device, but by active, usually unconscious interpretation of what the object represents as a whole.
2. What is true for object perception is even more true for the social world.

3. Liberman, Samuels, and Ross (2002) conducted a study that used the prisoner's dilemma game to show how construal influenced behavior.
   a. The prisoner's dilemma can be defined as a situation involving payoffs to two people in which trust and cooperation lead to higher payoffs than mistrust and defection.
   b. Participants who were told the game was called the "Wall Street game" were more likely to play

   _____
   _____
   _____
   _____

C. Schemas
   1. Schemas can be defined as

   _____
   _____
   _____
   _____

   2. Asch (1940) conducted a study showing how schemas influence judgments.
      a. Participants were asked to rate the profession of "politician."
      b. Half of the participants were told that others had rated politicians as near the top in prestige; the other half were told that others had rated politicians near the bottom in prestige.
      c. Participants in the first group

      _____

      _____;

      participants in the second group

      _____
      _____

      d. Asch concluded that peer ratings helped define the object of interest (politicians), calling up schemas about politicians as either statesmen or corrupt hacks.
D. Stereotypes
   1. Stereotypes can be defined as

   _____
   _____
   _____
   _____

   2. Stereotypes can help us to function efficiently, but they may also be wrong or given too much weight.
IV. Automatic and Controlled Processing
   A. Distingishing Automatic Processing and Controlled Processing.
      1. Automatic processing can be defined as

      _____
      _____
      _____
      _____

      2. Controlled processing can be defined as

      _____
      _____
      _____
      _____

      3. Patricia Devine and her colleagues conducted a study that showed that white participants, even those who expressed controlled attitudes of low prejudice, may automatically associate hostility with African Americans.
      4. Greenwald, McGhee, and Schwartz (1998) demonstrated that

      _____
      _____
      _____
      _____

   B. Types of Unconscious Processing
      1. As skills are learned and then overlearned, they can then be carried out without awareness (e.g., driving a car).
      2. Beliefs and behaviors can be presented without awareness of the cognitive processes that generated them. Visual stimuli, presented so quickly that people cannot even report having seen them, can still exert an influence on beliefs and behavior.
   C. Functions of Unconscious Processing
      1. Conscious processes are slow and can only operate serially.
      2. Automatic processes are

      _____
      _____
      _____
      _____

      3. To study unconscious, automatic processes, social psychologists craft careful experiments to isolate the causes of people's behavior.
         a. Cacioppo, Priester, and Berntson (1993) conducted a study that illustrated unconscious influences on our attitudes.
            (1) Because of a lifetime of embracing positive stimuli and pushing negative stimuli away, people who encounter a novel stimuli with their arm flexed toward the body report more positive reactions than people who have their arm extended away from the body.
            (2) People are unaware of arm position influencing their judgments.
         b. Bargh, Chen, and Burrows (1996) conducted a study in which college students primed to think about words associated with being elderly walked down a hallway more slowly than students with no such priming.

V. Evolution and Human Behavior: How We Are the Same

A. Natural selection can be defined as

_____

_____

_____

B. Social Darwinism was a distorted application of Darwin's theory in which people incorrectly believed that "survival of the fittest" meant the survival of one human group over another.

C. Human Universals
1. Evolutionary psychology suggests that many human behaviors and institutions are universal.
2. We share some of our human practices and institutions with animals, but not most of them.

D. Group Living, Language, and Theory of Mind
1. Humans lived in groups and acquired language, both of which contributed to survival and reproduction.
2. Survival may also have been promoted by a theory of mind, which can be defined as

_____

_____

_____

_____

3. The candy box study provides evidence for a theory of mind.
   a. Children were shown a candy box and asked what they thought was in it; children responded "candy"; they were then shown that the box actually contained something other than candy.
   b. Most non-autistic children with a mental age of at least four then predicted that the next child who was asked the same question would say

_____

_____

_____

_____

   c. Non-autistic children appear to have learned that a person's behavior can be predicted by a person's beliefs—even if those beliefs are incorrect.

E. Parental Investment
1. Women can only bear a limited number of offspring, while men theoretically can produce a nearly unlimited number of offspring.
2. Concerns about the survival of one's genetic material push women to be more invested than men in the care and well-being of each child.
3. Many gender differences are traced back to this asymmetry.

F. Avoiding the Naturalistic Fallacy
1. It is easy to make incorrect claims or conclusions on the basis of evolutionary reasoning, such as faulty assertions legitimizing male privilege or white privilege. But people should resist making such claims.
2. The naturalistic fallacy can be defined as

_____

_____

_____

_____

VI. Culture and Human Behavior: How We Are Different

A. Cultural differences exist even in fundamental forms of social existence, self-conceptions, and in perceptual and cognitive processes underlying new thoughts and beliefs.

B. Cultural Differences in Self-Definition
1. Individualistic (independent) cultures can be defined as

_____

_____

_____

2. Collectivistic (interdependent) cultures can be defined as

_____

_____

_____

_____

C. Individualism versus Collectivism in the Workplace
1. Middle managers from countries of British heritage are the most independent, followed by those from countries in continental Europe, South Asia, Asia Minor, and Latin America.
2. Middle managers from East Asia tend to value interdependence, while middle managers from British and former British colonies tend to value independence. Middle managers from continental Europe valued a mix of independence and interdependence.

D. Dick and Jane, Deng and Janxing
1. Readers for American children tend to orient the children toward

_____

_____

_____

2. Readers for Chinese children tend to teach the children

_____

_____

_____

_____

E. Who Are You?
1. Kuhn and McPartland (1954) developed the "Who Am I" test.
2. Ma and Schoeneman (1997) found that Kenyan students exposed to Western culture were more individualistic than traditional peoples in Kenya.

F. Some Qualifications
1. Individualism and collectivism differ by

_____
_____
_____
_____

2. Socialization within a given society of particular individuals may be oriented more toward independence or more toward interdependence.

G. Culture and Evolution as Tools for Understanding Situations
1. Culture and evolution play a role, together, in creating social systems and construals.
2. Evolutionary pressures create pre-wired inclinations, but cultural pressures modify, amplify, or suppress those inclinations.

VII. Doing Research
A. Theories and Hypotheses
1. Testable theories about human behavior come from almost anywhere, including folk wisdom, plays, novels, observation, and published research.
2. Early social psychological research was motivated by the desire to understand the effectiveness of Nazi propaganda.
3. Research on prejudice and discrimination was fueled by the desire to understand observed intergroup enmity and violence.

B. Correlational and Experimental Research
1. Correlational research can be defined as

_____
_____
_____
_____

2. Experimental research can be defined as

_____
_____
_____
_____
_____

3. Correlational Research
a. There are three possible causal explanations for an observed correlation.
(1) A could cause B, leading to a correlation between A and B.
(2) B could cause A, leading to a correlation between A and B.
(3) Some third variable could cause both A and B, leading to a correlation between A and B.

b. Correlations range in value from 0 (no relationship) to 1 (perfect relationship).
c. People who watch the news see more danger in the world than people who do not. Apply the three possible causal explanations to this example of correlation:
(1) _____
(2) _____
(3) _____
d. A study can be designed to eliminate one possible causal option. For example, one study examined whether people who watched violent TV at age eight were more likely to be incarcerated for violent behavior in adulthood.
(1) Researchers examined the hypothesis that watching violent TV as a kid causes violent tendencies to develop in adulthood.
(2) A longitudinal study logically rules out the reverse possibility that violent tendencies in adulthood cause violent TV watching in childhood.
(a) Longitudinal studies can be defined as studies conducted over a long period of time with the same population, which is periodically assessed regarding particular behaviors or other measures.
(b) Such a study suffers from self-selection effects—investigaters have no control over who chooses to watch a lot of TV and who chooses to watch a little.
(3) An initial attraction to violence may lead both to violent TV preferences and to later violent behavior.

4. Experimental Research
a. An independent variable can be defined as

_____
_____
_____

(1) The researcher determines the levels for the independent variable.
(2) In the Good Samaritan study, the participants were told they were late, needed to hurry, or had plenty of time.
b. A dependent variable can be defined as

_____
_____
_____

(1) The dependent variable is measured by verbal reports, behavior, or physiological measures.

(2) In the Good Samaritan study, the researchers measured whether participants stopped to help the man in the doorway or not.

c. Random assignment can be defined as

_____

_____

_____

(1) With random assignment, there should be no differences across experimental groups.

(2) In the Good Samaritan study, the seminary students were assigned randomly to one of the three conditions; each of the three groups of students was essentially equivalent except for the influence of the independent variable.

d. The control group can be defined as

_____

_____

_____

_____

e. Natural experiments can be defined as

_____

_____

_____

_____

5. Evaluating Research
   a. Validity
      (1) External validity can be defined as

_____

_____

_____

(2) External validity is critical when the purpose of the research is to generalize the results of the experiment directly to the outside world.

   b. Reliability
      (1) Reliability can be defined as

_____

_____

_____

_____

(2) There is reliability if the same result is obtained when testing is repeated on another occasion.

   c. Statistical Significance
      (1) Statistical significance can be defined as

_____

_____

_____

(2) Statistical significance is a function of the size of the participant sample and how big an effect one variable actually has on the other.

(3) All results presented in the textbook are statistically significant, though not all studies necessarily reflect large effects.

(a) The size of an effect is defined as how big an impact one variable has on another.

(b) If someone punches you in the nose, that will have a large (negative) effect on your mood; if you find a nickel on the ground that will have a small (positive) effect on your mood.

C. Other Kinds of Research
   1. Demonstrations
      a. Demonstration studies can be defined as

_____

_____

_____

      b. Milgram's obedience studies are examples of demonstration studies.
   2. Observational Studies
      a. Observational studies can be defined as

_____

_____

_____

_____

      b. Anthropologists conduct observational studies more often than psychologists do.
   3. Surveys
      a. Surveys can be defined as

_____

_____

_____

      b. Experiments can be conducted within the context of a survey.
   4. Field Experiments
      a. Field experiments can be defined as

_____

_____

_____

      b. An example of a field experiment is asking a person to give up a seat on an uncrowded bus or train and seeing how he or she reacts.
   5. Findings of real importance are often studied using multiple studies and multiple methods, providing triangulation of the results.

TESTING YOUR BASIC KNOWLEDGE

After studying the information in the chapter by filling in the outline above, test your basic knowledge with the following multiple-choice test. Answers are provided in the Answer Key section at the end of the chapter. If you find that you have gotten an answer wrong, it is important that you understand why it is wrong (as well as understanding why the correct answer is the better choice). Talk with peers, your tutor, or your professor if you need help.

Multiple-Choice Questions

1. Social psychology differs from folk wisdom (or everyday knowledge) in what important way?
   a. Social psychologists test their hypotheses using carefully crafted empirical studies.
   b. A social psychologist has special training that makes him or her more insightful than the everyday person.
   c. Social psychology is a legitimate enterprise while folk wisdom has no value.

2. Which of the following research questions is a social psychologist most likely to pursue?
   a. To what extent does extraversion influence a person's tendency to obey authority figures?
   b. The greatest voter participation in the last election came from members of which socioeconomic class?
   c. To what extent does the attractiveness of a speaker influence the persuasiveness of that speaker's message?

3. Which of the following is one reason why participants in the Milgram studies are thought to have obeyed the experimenter?
   a. Their personalities predisposed them to obedience.
   b. The experimenter took responsibility for the participants' actions.
   c. Participants were afraid the experimenter would hurt them if they didn't obey.

4. According to Darley and Batson's 1973 Good Samaritan study, the factor that best predicted whether or not the students would help the man in the doorway was
   a. how late they thought they were for their talk.
   b. their personal beliefs about the importance of a religious life.
   c. whether the topic of their talk was the parable of the Good Samaritan or not.

5. According to Kurt Lewin, which of the following people would be most likely to volunteer their time collecting food for a hunger drive?
   a. Beth, who is extremely altruistic.
   b. Janine, who enthusiastically agreed to a request to "come to the YMCA and help out anytime on Saturday."
   c. Lane, who agreed to meet volunteers at 10 A.M. on Saturday and was given directions to the YMCA.

6. Charles has just seen a play in which Troy portrayed the villain. Troy's performance was brilliant and quite convincing. Despite knowing that Troy was just acting, Charles insists that Troy must have a mean, devious, and villainous side to his personality. This belief is being influenced by
   a. the fundamental attribution error.
   b. automatic processing.
   c. channel factors.

7. Carol believes that all blondes are dumb. This belief could best be described as a
   a. schema.
   b. stereotype.
   c. naturalistic fallacy.

8. Joey meets Monica for the first time in the hallway outside of their respective apartments. They flirt with each other for a few minutes, and then Monica invites Joey in for a glass of lemonade. While she is making the lemonade in the kitchen, Joey takes off all his clothes and prepares for a romantic encounter. Monica arrives with the lemonade and is shocked!! A social psychologist would say that Joey and Monica have very different _____ regarding this situation.
   a. construals
   b. theories of mind
   c. stereotypes

9. Studies indicate that visual stimuli can still exert an influence on beliefs and behavior, even when the stimuli are presented so quickly that people cannot even report having seem them. This is evidence for the existence of
   a. automatic processing.
   b. controlled processing.
   c. schemas.

10. Greenwald, McGhee, and Schwartz (1998) found that some of their participants denied being prejudiced toward blacks in a survey, but that these same participants were slower to identify pleasant words when they were paired with a black versus a white face in a computer task. Denying prejudice in a survey is a consequence of a(n) _____ process, while slower identification of words reflects a(n) _____ process.
   a. automatic; controlled
   b. controlled; automatic
   c. universal; stereotyped

11. What is a benefit of automatic processing?
    a. it is faster than controlled processing and can be conducted with limited cognitive resources.
    b. it is easier for researchers to study automatic processing than controlled processing.
    c. it always produces more accurate results than controlled processing.

12. According to evolutionary theory, humans tend to live in groups because
    a. groups provide important forms of emotional and social support.
    b. larger groups lead to healthier industrial economies.
    c. living in groups afforded our ancestors benefits that aided in survival and reproduction.

13. The textbook authors suggest that evolution may also have left humans with an awareness that other people have beliefs and that those beliefs may predict their actions. This is called
    a. a theory of mind.
    b. natural selection.
    c. parental investment.

14. Construals represent _____ influences on our thoughts, feelings, and behaviors, while evolution represents a _____ influence.
    a. distal; proximal
    b. proximal; distal
    c. social psychological; sociological

15. Which of the following would best explain why men are more attracted to young, physically healthy women, and women are more attracted to rich, powerful men?
    a. parental investment
    b. theory of mind
    c. the fundamental attribution error

16. Jeff believes that monogamy is impossible for men. He believes that, because evolution favored the genes of men who had as many children as possible, it is inevitable (and therefore morally acceptable) that men should have sex with as many partners as possible. This reasoning represents
    a. the fundamental attribution error.
    b. the influence of channel factors.
    c. the naturalistic fallacy.

17. According to Hofstede, people in individualistic cultures are more likely to want which of the following in their work environment?
    a. to get the recognition deserved for a job well done
    b. to work in a friendly atmosphere
    c. to work with managers who have been with the company for the longest time

18. Business managers were asked how one should deal with an employee who had performed well for fifteen years but had recently become unproductive. Who would be more likely to give the following response: "[it is] wrong to disregard the fifteen years the employee has been working for the company. One has to take into account the company's responsibility for his life"?
    a. a manager from an independent culture
    b. a manager from an interdependent culture
    c. a manager from an individualistic culture

19. Even children's earliest books (e.g., "Dick and Jane") communicate cultural values. Chinese children learn from their reading primers
    a. to value personal choice.
    b. to ready themselves to take action.
    c. to be attuned to interpersonal relationships.

20. Generally speaking, women in America are more likely to be socialized to be _____, while men are more likely to be socialized to be _____.
    a. interdependent; independent.
    b. independent; interdependent.
    c. dependent; independent.

21. If we know that the number of bars in a town is positively correlated with the number of churches in a town, which of the following can we conclude with certainty?
    a. Drinking causes people to turn to religion.
    b. Towns with larger populations are more likely to have more bars and more churches.
    c. There is a relationship between the variables, such that more bars predict more churches, and more churches predict more bars.

22. Wanda reads a research report that says that a recent study found a correlation between oatmeal and cancer: the more oatmeal a person eats, the greater the risk of being diagnosed with cancer. Wanda immediately concludes that she needs to stop eating oatmeal for breakfast. What is wrong with this conclusion?
    a. It represents the naturalistic fallacy.
    b. It is a consequence of the fundamental attribution error.
    c. It reflects the erroneous belief that a correlation establishes causality.

23. Researchers are interested in whether feedback on one math test influences motivation for a second test. Middle school students meet individually with an experimenter and are given a math test. After grading the test, the experiment gives every student positive feedback by saying "you did well on the test." Half the students are also told "you must have worked very hard," and the other half of the students are told "you

must be very smart." Experimenters found that students who had been told they must be smart were reluctant to do a second math test and were more likely to choose a test they knew would be easier. Participants who were told they must have worked hard were eager to take a second test and happy to choose a challenging test. What is the independent variable in this study?
   a. positive or negative feedback
   b. "smart" versus "worked hard" comment
   c. the difficulty of the second math test

24. What type of study is the one described in question 23?
   a. an experiment
   b. a field experiment
   c. an observational study

25. A study that has high external validity is one that
   a. makes accurate conclusions.
   b. yields results unlikely to be due to chance.
   c. has an experimental setup that resembles a real-life situation.

Essay Questions

After you have mastered the multiple-choice questions, try testing your basic understanding by thoroughly answering each of the broad essay questions below. Because it is critical that you think through this information on your own, we have not provided any answers to these questions. Your learning and retention of this material will be greatly enhanced if you do one or more of the following to check your answers: carefully review the textbook information; compare your responses to your class lecture notes; talk over your answers with a peer; ask your professor to review your answers or review any information that is unclear to you.

1. In your own words, provide a thorough definition of social psychology. In your definition, be sure to give examples of how social psychology differs from other disciplines, and then describe major themes that help to define social psychology.

2. Discuss what social psychologists mean by "the power of the situation" and provide empirical examples (i.e., research studies) of how the power of the situation can influence people's behavior.

3. Distinguish between automatic and controlled processing, and explain how or why these two modes of processing are relevant to the study of social psychology.

4. From an evolutionary perspective, how are people "the same," and what processes have led us to be similar?

5. Explain one major cultural difference in self-definition that social psychologists have studied. How is this difference manifested in thoughts, feelings, and behaviors, and what factors are thought to be responsible for the creation of this difference?

6. Distinguish between correlational research and experimental research, and provide an example of each kind of study.

TESTING YOUR IN-DEPTH UNDERSTANDING

Test your in-depth understanding of the material by working through the Critical Thinking Exercises provided at the end of each textbook chapter. To maximize this learning opportunity, work together with a tutor, study group, or your professor. Alternatively, write down your thoughts and responses.

Guided questions for one of the exercises are provided below. While there are multiple ways to answer these questions, short answers are given in the Answer Key at the end of the chapter. Note that the valuable part of this exercise is not simply knowing the answer but working with the material to come up with the answer.

Guided Questions for Critical Thinking Exercise #2

Suppose you are making "get out the vote" calls for a political party the night before the election. What would you say to increase the likelihood that voters would actually make it to the polls?

1. Consider proximal factors first.
   a. What are all the different construals a person might have about voting, elections, and politicians?
      (1) What construals would you want a person to have in order to get him or her to vote?
      (2) What does the Liberman, Samuels, and Ross (2002) study (see pp. 15–17 of the text) suggest about what you could say to influence his or her construals?
      (3) What does the Asch (1940) study (see pp. 17–18 of the text) suggest about what you could say to influence his or her schemas?
   b. What are channel factors? What channel factors could you provide to increase the likelihood that someone will vote (see Leventhal, Singer, and Jones 1965, pp. 12–13 of the text)?
   c. Imagine someone you speak with refuses to vote and/or is rude to you.
      (1) According to the fundamental attribution error (see p. 13 of the text), what conclusion would most people reach about this rude person?
      (2) What are some other explanations for the rude person's behavior?
   d. Can you think of any subtle way to influence automatic processing of the person you are calling?

2. Now consider distal factors.
   a. Keeping evolutionary theory in mind, would you appeal to a female voter differently than you would appeal to a male voter? If yes, how so and why?
   b. Keeping cultural differences in mind, would you appeal to voters in individualistic cultures differently than those in collectivistic cultures? If yes, how so and why?

3. Pretend you are a social psychologist, and choose different "manipulations" (that is, different ways of talking to potential voters) to set up an experiment.
   a. How could you design an experiment to test whether your manipulation worked?
   b. What would be the independent variable in the study?
   c. What would be the dependent variable in the study?
   d. How could you accomplish random assignment?
   e. Would this study have high or low external validity?
   f. This study would be an example of a field experiment—why?

Enhance your understanding of the chapter by trying to break down the remaining two Critical Thinking Exercises into smaller sub-questions, and then answering those questions. Discuss your answers with your peers, study group, tutor, or professor.

Critical Thinking Exercise #1

It's a serious problem for expensive restaurants in Manhattan when reservation holders don't show up. The restaurants lose a considerable amount of overhead for each no-show. Many restaurants have made it a custom to ask patrons to "Please call us if you won't be able to make it." Recently, some restaurants have started asking instead, "Will you call us if you're not able to make it?" Would you think this would be more effective than the standard request, or less? Why?

Critical Thinking Exercise #3

Aristotle's moral philosophy was based on what has come to be called "virtue ethics." He encouraged people to strive to develop all the character traits of a virtuous person. Do you see limits to how much can be achieved by such a moral philosophy? How could it be profitably supplemented?

SOCIAL PSYCHOLOGY IN THE POPULAR MEDIA

You might be interested in the following popular media references, each of which relates in some way to information in this chapter.

Books

Blass, Thomas. (2004). *The Man Who Shocked the World: The Life and Legacy of Stanley Milgram.* New York: Basic Books.

Sabini, John, & Silver, Maury (1992). *The Individual in a Social World: Essays and Experiments by Stanley Milgram.* New York: McGraw-Hill.

Song

Gabriel, Peter. (1986). "We Do What We're Told (Milgram's 37)." From the album: *So.* Recommended for Peter Gabriel fans. A fun reference to Milgram's research.

Film

Das Experiment (*The Experiment;* 2001; German with English subtitles; directed by Oliver Hirschbiegel; starring Moritz Bleibtrau Christian Berkel, Oliver Stokowski). This film is based on the setup of Zimbardo's Stanford Prison Experiment, but note that this is a *fictional* drama/thriller, and that most of the events in this film did not happen in the Zimbardo study.

Web Sites

Milgram Obedience Studies—http://www.stanleymilgram.com/main.html. This Web site provides information about Stanley Milgram and his famous studies.

Social Psychology Network—http://www.socialpsychology.org. This Web site has the largest collection of links and information about the discipline of social psychology on the Internet. Learn more about what a social psychologist is and the types of topics social psychologists study.

Zimbardo Prison Study—http://www.prisonexp.org. The Stanford Prison Experiment Web site features an extensive slide show and information about this classic psychology experiment.

ANSWER KEY

Annotated Chapter Outline

I. Characterizing Social Psychology
   A. Social psychology can be defined as the scientific study of the feelings, thoughts, and behaviors of individuals in situations.
   B. Explaining Behavior
      1. Social psychologists study how people (real, imagined, encountered today or in the past,

face-to-face or through the media) influence our thoughts, feelings, and behaviors.

    2. Social psychologists study how we understand and make sense of our social worlds.

    3. Social psychology differs from folk wisdom because social psychologists test intuitions with carefully crafted research studies.

C. Comparing Social Psychology to Related Disciplines

    1. Personality psychology vs. social psychology

      a. Personality psychology stresses individual traits and characteristics within persons (e.g., extraversion).

      b. Social psychology stresses how the "average" person would respond to various types of situational pressures.

    2. Cognitive psychology vs. social psychology

      a. Cognitive psychologists study nonsocial processes.

      b. Social psychologists, or social-cognitive psychologists, study perception, cognition, and memory for social processes (such as beliefs about other people).

    3. Sociology vs. social psychology

      a. Sociologists study macro characteristics of populations (e.g., institutions, subgroups).

      b. Social psychologists study individuals within those macro structures.

D. Proximal vs. Distal Influences in Social Psychology

    1. Proximal factors are those factors that exist in the here-and-now or that immediately precede what the individual does.

      a. Situation

      b. Construal of situation

      c. Automatic or controlled perceptions and reactions to a situation

    2. Distal factors are those factors that are more removed in time from a given context or episode, such as:

      a. Evolution

      b. Culture

II. The Power of the Situation

A. Kurt Lewin (the founder of modern social psychology) thought that the behavior of people is always a function of the field of forces in which they find themselves.

B. The Milgram Experiment

    1. Stanley Milgram (1963) illustrated the power of the situation in his experiment on obedience.

    2. Milgram found that 62.5 percent of all participants obeyed an experimenter's request to (supposedly) shock a fellow subject despite hearing agonized screams from the subject.

    3. Features of the situation that exert power over the participants' behavior include:

      a. The experiment was presented as an official scientific investigation.

      b. Participants probably had never before been in a situation in which they had to do serious physical damage to another person.

      c. Participants were not given an easy way to step out of the vaguely defined situation.

      d. The experimenter explicitly took responsibility for the consequences of the participants' actions.

      e. The participants were unprepared to resist the demands of the experimenter.

      f. The shocks were administered in a step-by-step fashion.

C. Seminarians as Good Samaritans

    1. Darley and Batson (1973) illustrated the power of the situation in their Good Samaritan study.

    2. Darley and Batson found that seminary students who were told they were already late for a talk they had to give were less likely to stop to help an apparently ill man in a doorway than seminary students who were told they had plenty of time before their talk.

    3. The basis of their religious calling—that is, whether students were oriented toward religion for spiritual reasons or personal gains—did not predict their behavior toward the man in the doorway.

D. Channel Factors

    1. In a 1952 study, Lewin said that channel factors help explain the power of the situation.

    2. Channel factors can be defined as certain situational circumstances that appear unimportant on the surface but that can have great consequences for behavior, either facilitating or blocking it or guiding behavior in a very particular direction.

    3. Leventhal, Singer, and Jones (1965) did a study that examined channel factors.

      a. Students were warned about the dangers of getting tetanus, and they were encouraged to go to the health center for an inoculation.

      b. All students formed the intention to get the inoculation.

      c. Only 3 percent of students in the control condition actually got the inoculation.

      d. In contrast, 27 percent of students in the experimental condition got the inoculation.

      e. The experimental condition included the channel factors of a map to the health center and a request to choose a time and route to get to the center.

E. The Fundamental Attribution Error
   1. The fundamental attribution error can prevent people from realizing the power of the situation.
   2. Dispositions can be defined as internal factors such as beliefs, values, personality traits, or abilities—real or imagined—that guide a person's behavior.
   3. The fundamental attribution error can be defined as the failure to recognize the importance of situational influences on behavior, together with the tendency to overemphasize the importance of dispositions or traits on behavior.

III. The Role of Construal
   A. Construal is defined as the interpretation and inference about people's behavior and the situations in which they find themselves.
   B. Interpreting Reality
      1. Gestalt psychology maintains that objects are perceived, not by means of some automatic registering device, but by active, usually unconscious interpretation of what the object represents as a whole.
      2. What is true for object perception is even more true for the social world.
      3. Liberman, Samuels, and Ross (2002) conducted a study that used the prisoner's dilemma game to show how construal influenced behavior.
         a. The prisoner's dilemma can be defined as a situation involving payoffs to two people in which trust and cooperation lead to higher payoffs than mistrust and defection.
         b. Participants who were told the game was called the "Wall Street game" were more likely to play in a competitive fashion than those told the game was called "the community game."
   C. Schemas
      1. Schemas can be defined as generalized knowledge about the physical and social world and how to behave in particular situations and with different kinds of people.
      2. Asch (1940) conducted a study showing how schemas influence judgments.
         a. Participants were asked to rate the profession of "politician."
         b. Half of the participants were told that others had rated politicians as near the top in prestige; the other half were told that others had rated politicians near the bottom in prestige.

         c. Participants in the first group had a higher opinion of politicians and were thinking about great statesmen; participants in the second group had a lower opinion of politicians and were thinking about corrupt politicians.
         d. Asch concluded that peer ratings helped define the object of interest (politicians), calling up schemas about politicians as either statesmen or corrupt hacks.
   D. Stereotypes
      1. Stereotypes can be defined as schemas that we have for people of various kinds that can be applied and misapplied so as to facilitate, and sometimes derail, the course of interaction.
      2. Stereotypes can help us to function efficiently, but they may also be wrong or given too much weight.

IV. Automatic and Controlled Processing
   A. Distingishing Automatic Processing and Controlled Processing
      1. Automatic processing can be defined as unconscious processing, often based on emotional factors.
      2. Controlled processing can be defined as conscious, systematic processing that is more likely to be controlled by careful thought.
      3. Patricia Devine and her colleagues conducted a study that showed that white participants, even those who expressed controlled attitudes of being low in prejudice, may automatically associate hostility with African Americans.
      4. Greenwald, McGhee, and Schwartz (1998) demonstrated that even overtly nonprejudiced participants took longer to identify pleasant words when those words were presented along with black faces compared to when they were presented along with white faces.
   B. Types of Unconscious Processing
      1. As skills are learned and then overlearned, they can then be carried out without awareness (e.g., driving a car).
      2. Beliefs and behaviors can be produced without awareness of the cognitive processes that generated them. Visual stimuli, presented so quickly that people cannot even report having seen them, can still exert an influence on beliefs and behavior.
   C. Functions of Unconscious Processing
      1. Conscious processes are slow and can only operate serially.
      2. Automatic processes are faster and can operate in parallel.

3. To study unconscious, automatic processes, social psychologists craft careful experiments to isolate the causes of people's behavior.
   a. Cacioppo, Priester, and Berntson (1993) conducted a study that illustrated unconscious influences on our attitudes.
      (1) Because of a lifetime of embracing positive stimuli and pushing negative stimuli away, people who encounter a novel stimuli with their arm flexed toward the body report more positive reactions than people who have their arm extended away from the body.
      (2) People are unaware of arm position influencing their judgments.
   b. Bargh, Chen, and Burrows (1996) conducted a study in which college students primed to think about words associated with being elderly walked down a hallway more slowly than students with no such priming.

V. Evolution and Human Behavior: How We Are the Same
   A. Natural selection can be defined as an evolutionary process that operates to mold animals and plants so that traits that enhance the probability of survival and reproduction are passed on to subsequent generations.
   B. Social Darwinism was a distorted application of Darwin's theory in which people incorrectly believed that "survival of the fittest" meant the survival of one human group over another.
   C. Human Universals
      1. Evolutionary psychology suggests that many human behaviors and institutions are universal.
      2. We share some of our human practices and institutions with animals, but not most of them.
   D. Group Living, Language, and Theory of Mind
      1. Humans lived in groups and acquired language, both of which contributed to survival and reproduction.
      2. Survival may also have been promoted by a theory of mind, which can be defined as the understanding that other people have beliefs and desires.
      3. The candy box study provides evidence for a theory of mind.
         a. Children were shown a candy box and asked what they thought was in it; children responded "candy"; they were then shown that the box actually contained something other than candy.
         b. Most non-autistic children with a mental age of at least four then predicted that the next child who was asked the same question would say (incorrectly) that the box has candy in it based on their false belief.
         c. Non-autistic children appear to have learned that a person's behavior can be predicted by a person's beliefs—even if those beliefs are incorrect.
   E. Parental Investment
      1. Women can only bear a limited number of offspring, while men theoretically can produce a nearly unlimited number of offspring.
      2. Concerns about the survival of one's genetic material push women to be more invested than men in the care and well-being of each child.
      3. Many gender differences are traced back to this asymmetry.
   F. Avoiding the Naturalistic Fallacy
      1. It is easy to make incorrect claims or conclusions on the basis of evolutionary reasoning, such as faulty assertions legitimizing male privilege or white privilege. But people should resist making such claims.
      2. The naturalistic fallacy can be defined as the claim that the way things are is the way they should be (biology is destiny).

VI. Culture and Human Behavior: How We Are Different
   A. Cultural differences exist even in fundamental forms of social existence, self-conceptions, and in perceptual and cognitive processes underlying new thoughts and beliefs.
   B. Cultural Differences in Self-Definition
      1. Individualistic (independent) cultures can be defined as cultures in which people tend to think of themselves as distinct social entities, tied to each other by voluntary bonds of affection and organizational memberships, but essentially separate from other people and having attributes that exist in the absence of any connection to others.
      2. Collectivistic (interdependent) cultures can be defined as cultures in which people tend to define themselves as part of a collective, inextricably tied to others in their group, and in which they have relatively little individual freedom or personal control over their lives, but do not necessarily want or need these things.

C. Individualism versus Collectivism in the Workplace
   1. Middle managers from countries of British heritage are the most independent, followed by those from countries in continental Europe, South Asia, Asia Minor, and Latin America.
   2. Middle managers from East Asia tend to value interdependence, while middle managers from British and former British colonies tend to value independence. Middle managers from continental Europe valued a mix of independence and interdependence.
D. Dick and Jane, Deng and Janxing
   1. Readers for American children tend to orient the children toward action and individual choice.
   2. Readers for Chinese children tend to teach the children to be attuned to relationships.
E. Who Are You?
   1. Kuhn and McPartland (1954) developed the "Who Am I" test.
   2. Ma and Schoeneman (1997) found that Kenyan students exposed to Western culture were more individualistic than traditional peoples in Kenya.
F. Some Qualifications
   1. Individualism and collectivism differ by region, subculture, gender, and situation.
   2. Socializatoin within a given society of particular individuals may be oriented more toward independence or more toward interdependence.
G. Culture and Evolution as Tools for Understanding Situations
   1. Culture and evolution play a role, together, in creating social systems and construals.
   2. Evolutionary pressures create pre-wired inclinations, but cultural pressures modify, amplify, or suppress those inclinations.

VII. Doing Research
   A. Theories and Hypotheses
      1. Testable theories about human behavior come from almost anywhere, including folk wisdom, plays, novels, observation, and published research.
      2. Early social psychological research was motivated by the desire to understand the effectiveness of Nazi propaganda.
      3. Research on prejudice and discrimination was fueled by the desire to understand observed intergroup enmity and violence.
   B. Correlational and Experimental Research
      1. Correlational research can be defined as research in which there is not random assignment to different situations or conditions, and from which psychologists can just see whether or not there is a relationship between two or more variables.
      2. Experimental research can be defined as research in which people are randomly assigned to different situations (or conditions) and from which it is possible to make very strong inferences about how these different situations or conditions affect people's behavior.
      3. Correlational Research
         a. There are three possible causal explanations for an observed correlation.
            (1) A could cause B, leading to a correlation between A and B.
            (2) B could cause A, leading to a correlation between A and B.
            (3) Some third variable could cause both A and B, leading to a correlation between A and B.
         b. Correlations range in value from 0 (no relationship) to 1 (perfect relationship).
         c. People who watch the news see more danger in the world than people who do not. Apply the three possible causal explanations of this example of correlation:
            (1) Watching the news may cause people to feel more risk of danger.
            (2) Feeling more risk of danger may cause people to watch the news.
            (3) Elderly people may have more time to watch TV, and they may be more anxious about crime.
         d. A study can be designed to eliminate one possible causal option. For example, one study examined whether people who watched violent TV at age eight were more likely to be incarcerated for violent behavior in adulthood.
            (1) Researchers examined the hypothesis that watching violent TV as a kid causes violent tendencies to develop in adulthood.
            (2) A longitudinal study logically rules out the reverse possibility that violent tendencies in adulthood cause violent TV watching in childhood.
               (a) Longitudinal studies can be defined as studies conducted over a long period of time with the same population, which is periodically assessed regarding particular behaviors or other measures.

(b) Such a study suffers from self-selection effects—investigaters have no control over who chooses to watch a lot of TV and who chooses to watch a little.

(3) An initial attraction to violence may lead both to violent TV preferences and to later violent behavior.

4. Experimental Research
   a. An independent variable can be defined as the variable about which a prediction is made and that is manipulated in experimental research.
      (1) The researcher determines the levels for the independent variable.
      (2) In the Good Samaritan study, the participants were told they were late, needed to hurry, or had plenty of time.
   b. A dependent variable can be defined as the variable that is presumed to be affected by the independent variable manipulation and that is measured in experimental research.
      (1) The dependent variable is measured by verbal reports, behavior, or physiological measures.
      (2) In the Good Samaritan study, the researchers measured whether participants stopped to help the man in the doorway or not.
   c. Random assignment can be defined as assigning participants in experimental research to different groups randomly, such that they are as likely to be assigned to one condition as another.
      (1) With random assignment, there should be no differences across experimental groups.
      (2) In the Good Samaritan study, the seminary students were assigned randomly to one of the three conditions; each of the three groups of students was essentially equivalent except for the influence of the independent variable.
   d. The control group can be defined as the group of participants that does not receive the experimental manipulation.
   e. Natural experiments can be defined as naturally occurring phenomena having somewhat different conditions that can be compared with almost as much rigor as in experiments where the investigator manipulates the conditions.

5. Evaluating Research
   a. Validity
      (1) External validity can be defined as an experimental setup that closely resembles real-life situations.
      (2) External validity is critical when the purpose of the research is to generalize the results of the experiment directly to the outside world.
   b. Reliability
      (1) Reliability can be defined as the degree to which the particular way one measures a given variable is likely to yield consistent results.
      (2) There is reliability if the same result is obtained when testing is repeated on another occasion.
   c. Statistical Significance
      (1) Statistical significance can be defined as a measure of the probability that a given result would not have been obtained by chance.
      (2) Statistical significance is a function of the size of the participant sample and how big an effect one variable actually has on the other.
      (3) All results presented in the textbook are statistically significant, though not all studies necessarily reflect large effects.
         (a) The size of an effect is defined as how big an impact one variable has on another.
         (b) If someone punches you in the nose, that will have a large (negative) effect on your mood; if you find a nickel on the ground that will have a small (positive) effect on your mood.

C. Other Kinds of Research
   1. Demonstrations
      a. Demonstration studies can be defined as research in which no variable is correlated with any other variable and in which nothing is manipulated.
      b. Milgram's obedience studies are examples of demonstration studies.
   2. Observational Studies
      a. Observational studies can be defined as research involving observation of and often participation in the lives of people in some group or situation with the intention of studying aspects of group beliefs, values, or behavior.

b. Anthropologists conduct observational studies more often than psychologists do.

3. Surveys

   a. Surveys can be defined as a series of questions asked of people, sometimes students in laboratories and sometimes citizens in the community, to ascertain their attitudes or beliefs.

   b. Experiments can be conducted within the context of a survey.

4. Field Experiments

   a. Field experiments can be defined as experiments that are set up in the real world, usually under circumstances in which participants are not aware that they are in a study of any kind.

   b. An example of a field experiment is asking a person to give up a seat on an uncrowded bus or train and seeing how he or she reacts.

5. Findings of real importance are often studied using multiple studies and multiple methods, providing triangulation of the results.

Testing Your Basic Knowledge

ANSWERS TO MULTIPLE-CHOICE QUESTIONS

1. a	14. b
2. c	15. a
3. b	16. c
4. a	17. a
5. c	18. b
6. a	19. c
7. b	20. a
8. a	21. c
9. a	22. c
10. b	23. b
11. a	24. a
12. c	25. c
13. a	

Testing Your In-Depth Understanding

EXAMPLE ANSWERS TO THE GUIDED QUESTIONS FOR CRITICAL THINKING EXERCISE #2

1. Consider proximal factors first.

   a. People might construe voting as a civic duty, or they might construe voting as a useless endeavor. They might construe elections as a real selection process, or (thinking back to the 2000 Presidential elections) they might think of elections as "fixed" or "shams."

      (1) We would want people to see elections as meaningful, and their vote as valuable.

      (2) Using words like "civic duty" and "democratic process" (as opposed to saying something that sounded manipulative like "we want your vote") might lead to the construal we want.

      (3) One could note that the potential voter is a neighbor and that this calling campaign is about a community coming together for an important decision.

   b. Channel factors are seemingly unimportant characteristics that might actually make a big difference. For example, we might ask if the potential voter knows where his or her polling place is, if he or she has a way to get there, if he or she needs a ride or needs directions. We might also ask the person to think about his or her schedule on election day and to think about whether he or she will vote before work or after work.

   c. Imagine someone you speak with refuses to vote and/or is rude to you.

      (1) Most people would quickly reach the conclusion that the person had a nasty or uncaring personality.

      (2) There are many situational factors that we may not know about. For example, we may have called the person right in the middle of a fight with his or her spouse or a discipline battle with his or her child. Keeping these factors in mind may help us to be more patient and kind to the potential voter.

   d. One way to influence automatic processing might be to ask the person his or her nationality at the beginning of the phone call to unconsciously invoke patriotism.

2. Now consider distal factors.

   a. According to the theory of parental investment, women may be genetically inclined to care more about the rearing of their children than men. Thus, if the potential voter is a female and has a child, linking the outcome of the upcoming election to outcomes for her children might be effective.

   b. For potential voters who are individualistic, effective calls might appeal to the choice the potential voter has, and to the idea that a "smart" or "right" choice is to vote. For potential voters who are more collectivistic, effective calls might appeal to the way in which voting is required to be a loyal member of the collective and to the point that voting is an important responsibility toward the well-being of loved ones.

3. Pretend you are a social psychologist, and choose different manipulations (that is different ways of talking to potential voters) to set up an experiment.

a. The experiment would need to compare a group of people who are asked their nationality to a group of people who are not asked their nationality.
b. The presence or absence of the nationality question would be the independent variable.
c. Ideally, the dependent variable would be whether the person actually voted or not. Alternatively, the dependent variable could be the person's stated intention to vote at the end of the phone call.
d. Assuming we are calling potential voters in a relatively random order, we could simply vary the nationality question every other call. If we are not calling voters in a random order, we can flip a coin or roll a die before each phone call to determine the condition.
e. This study would have high external validity.
f. This study would be taking place as part of a real-life activity (calling voters), and the participants would be unaware they were taking part in a study.

CHAPTER 2 | Groups

The goal of this chapter is to explain some of the consequences of being a member of a group. The chapter addresses classic social psychological theories and findings, including social facilitation, deindividuation, decision-making in groups, and group polarization.

ANNOTATED CHAPTER OUTLINE

After first reading through the chapter quickly, create a comprehensive framework for the information in the chapter by reading the outline below and filling in the missing information. Instead of simply re-copying information from the textbook, try to use your own words wherever possible; you can check your answers against the completed outline in the Answer Key section at the end of the chapter.

I. The Nature and Purpose of Group Living
  A. Reasons for Group Living
    1. Groups afforded evolutionary benefits such as

    _____

    _____

    _____

    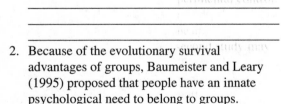

    2. Because of the evolutionary survival advantages of groups, Baumeister and Leary (1995) proposed that people have an innate psychological need to belong to groups.
  B. Defining Groups
    1. Cartwright and Zander (1968) defined a group as

    _____

    _____

    _____

    _____

    2. Just as interdependence varies on a continuum, so does the decision about how much of a group a collection of people represents.
      a. The members of a family are more of a group than are students in a large class.
      b. A nation's citizens make up a group but less so than do members of a tribe.

II. Social Facilitation
  A. The presence of other people appears to influence the performance of individuals.
  B. Initial Research
    1. Triplett (1898) was the first researcher to study this topic and also conducted what is usually thought of as the first social psychological laboratory experiment.
      a. Triplett noticed that the fastest times among cyclists were when the cyclists competed against other people, rather than racing alone against the clock.
      b. Triplett conducted a lab investigation to test the general hypothesis that the presence of others facilitates performance.
        (1) Experimental design:

        _____

        _____

        _____

        _____

        (2) Independent variable:

        _____

        _____

        _____

        _____

        (3) Findings:

        _____

_____

_____

_____

c. Social facilitation can be defined as

_____

_____

_____

_____

2. Triplett's findings were extended in two important ways by other researchers.
   a. Researchers showed that

   _____

   _____

   _____

   _____

   b. Researchers observed social facilitation in many types of animals, suggesting that the phenomenon is very general and fundamental (i.e., evidence for evolutionary roots).

3. Other researchers also found a troubling number of exceptions to social facilitation—instances where the presence of other people inhibited or worsened performance.
   a. Allport (1920) found that students at Harvard and Radcliffe provided higher quality philosophical arguments when working alone than when working in the presence of another student.
   b. The presence of others can inhibit performance on

   _____

   _____

   _____

   _____

C. Resolving the Contradictions
   1. Zajonc (1965) proposed a theory that would explain both the facilitation and the inhibition study results.
      a. Zajonc's (1965) theory has three parts:
         (1) _____

         _____

         _____

         (2) _____

         _____

         _____

         (3) _____

         _____

         _____

      b. The gist of his theory is that the mere presence of other people is likely to

facilitate performance on easy tasks and to inhibit performance on complex and/or unfamiliar tasks.

2. Testing the Theory
   a. Zajonc, Heingartner, and Herman (1969) set up an experiment to test the theory using cockroaches.
      (1) The researchers had the cockroaches run through mazes toward a goal box.
      (2) Independent variable #1:

      _____

      _____

      _____

      (3) Independent variable #2:

      _____

      _____

      _____

      (4) Dependent variable: length of time it took the cockroach to reach the darkened goal box.
      (5) Findings:

      _____

      _____

      _____

      _____

   b. The same results were found when the other cockroaches were in a little "grandstand" observing the cockroach run the maze, indicating that even a passive audience leads to facilitation of easy tasks, but hinders performance on complex tasks.

3. A Methodological Aside: External Validation and Theory Testing
   a. The results of Zajonc's social facilitation studies lacked external validity.
   b. Yet, when testing a theory, the goal is to understand and test the *theory* and apply the theory to the real world, not to apply specific *findings* to the real world.
      (1) If you drop a bowling ball and a feather inside a perfect vacuum, they will hit the ground at the same time. By definition, this study lacks external validity, since there aren't many naturally occurring perfect vacuums here on Earth.
      (2) The theory that prompted the study is supported, leading to important advances in the understanding of physics and our world.

c. The highly controlled (and, thus somewhat strange nature) of the cockroach study allowed for a rigorous experimental test. There were two factors that made the cockroach studies precise and controlled:

(1) _____

_____

_____

(2) _____

_____

_____

D. Mere Presence or Evaluation Apprehension?

1. One aspect of Zajonc's theory that was disputed was whether mere presence created arousal, or whether arousal was a consequence of evaluation apprehension.

2. Evaluation apprehension can be defined as

_____

_____

_____

_____

3. Testing for Evaluation Apprehension

a. Cottrell, Wack, Sekerak, and Rittle (1968) set up an experiment to determine whether evaluation apprehension is the critical element underlying social facilitation effects.

(1) Participants were given a list of nonsense words.

(2) Independent variable #1: type of nonsense word—words repeated once, twice, five, ten, or twenty-five times.

(3) Independent variable #2:

_____

_____

_____

b. Findings:

_____

_____

_____

_____

c. This finding highlights the importance of evaluation apprehension because the presence of others only had an impact when others could watch and therefore evaluate the proceedings.

d. Initially, these findings seemed to suggest that mere presence does not have an influence since the results were the same for the alone condition and for the blindfolded observer condition.

4. Testing for Mere Presence

a. In the Cottrell, Wack, Sekerak, and Rittle (1968) study, the alone condition may have

been tainted by participants' psychological sense of being observed somehow by an experimenter.

b. If this was the case, then participants in the "alone" condition would have had their dominant responses increased by social facilitation effects—thus, the fact that the participants in the blindfolded observer condition performed similarly to those in the alone condition does not necessarily refute the influence of mere presence.

c. Markus (1978) conducted an experiment with a "true" alone condition.

(1) The setup of the experiment:

_____

_____

_____

(2) Independent variable #1: complexity of dressing task (putting on the UNFAMILIAR clothes vs. putting back on their own FAMILIAR clothes).

(3) Independent variable #2:

_____

_____

_____

_____

(4) Dependent variable:

_____

_____

_____

(5) Findings: participants put on their own clothes more quickly than the unfamiliar clothes in the presence of another person compared to when they were alone. Thus, mere presence is supported.

(6) The facilitation and inhibition results were even stronger in the condition with the attentive audience. Thus, evaluation apprehension does play a role in that it adds to the influence of mere exposure.

E. Current Perspectives

1. Experimental evidence suggests that mere presence increases arousal and encourages the dominant response on easy and difficult tasks.

2. What is it about the awareness of another person's presence that increases arousal?

a. Distraction-conflict theory can be defined as

_____

_____

_____

_____

b. Some evidence suggests that nonsocial distractions can produce facilitation effects, but not enough evidence has been gathered to confidently accept this theory.

3. Evaluation apprehension enhances mere presence effects.

4. Some norms (for example, norms in work settings against working harder than the established group norm) encourage poor performance.

5. Social loafing hides mere presence effects.
   a. Social loafing can be defined as

   _____

   _____

   _____

   _____

   b. People may engage in social loafing because they believe that their efforts are not crucial to the task.

F. Practical Applications
   1. People should study complex material alone, but they should rehearse or practice well-learned material in a group.
   2. Employers should arrange workplace settings so that workers are in contact with one another if they are doing repetitive, simple tasks, but they should give workers privacy if they are doing complex tasks.

III. Deindividuation and the Psychology of Mobs
   A. Real-world experiences illustrate that individuals can engage in destructive acts that are contrary to their character when in large groups of people. The question is why.
   B. Emergent Properties of Groups
      1. Emergent properties of groups can be defined as

      _____

      _____

      _____

      _____

      2. Studying group behavior in a laboratory setting is more difficult than studying social facilitation in a lab because:
         a. _____

         _____

         _____

         _____

         b. _____

         _____

         _____

         _____

c. _____

_____

_____

_____

d. _____

_____

_____

_____

e. _____

_____

_____

3. Most research on the psychology of the mob takes place in the "real world."

C. Deindividuation and the Group Mind
   1. Social psychologists have expanded on work by sociologist LeBon (1895) and studied how being in a group changes an individual's general orientation to the world.
   2. Individuals may act differently in a group because of deindividuation, which can be defined as

   _____

   _____

   _____

   _____

   a. Most of the time we feel identifiable by others, individually responsible for our actions, and concerned about the consequences of our actions.
   b. When in a crowd, under certain conditions, we can feel "lost in the crowd."

   3. A Model of Deindividuation
      a. Zimbardo (1970) proposed a model of deindividuation that specified:
         (1) Certain antecedent conditions create a psychological state that promotes deindividuation:
             (a) _____

             _____

             _____

             (b) _____

             _____

             _____

             (c) _____

             _____

             _____

             (d) _____

             _____

             _____

(e) _____

_____

_____

_____

  (2) Deindividuation is characterized by three important psychological features (all three are required to be considered deindividuated):

    (a) _____

_____

_____

_____

    (b) _____

_____

_____

_____

    (c) _____

_____

_____

_____

  (3) A deindividuated person will be more responsive to the behavioral cues of those around him or her.

  (4) Deindividuated behavior can be irrational, emotional, and less responsive to attempts to stop it.

  (5) This model predicts impulsive behavior, although such impulsivity often turns into destructive behavior.

 b. People often find impulsivity liberating, and societies try to safely channel its expression.

4. Testing the Model

 a. Because the tests of the model described here involve an examination of archival (existing real world) data, one must be cautious in interpreting the data.

  (1) Alternative interpretations for the patterns found in the data have not been ruled out by experimental control.

  (2) Although one study may be flawed in one way and leave one alternative explanation open, a second study may eliminate that alternative explanation.

  (3) A series of studies together will provide stronger support.

 b. Correlation does not imply causation.

5. Suicide Baiting

 a. Suicide baiting can be defined as

_____

_____

_____

_____

 b. Mann (1981) examined fifteen years of newspaper accounts of suicidal jumps and averted jumps.

  (1) Data:

_____

_____

_____

_____

  (2) Variables associated with deindividuation that were present:

_____

_____

_____

_____

6. The Conduct of War

 a. Watson (1981) studied the war practices of twenty-three non-Western cultures.

 b. Findings: 80 percent of cultures that deindividuated themselves (e.g., with war paint) before battle were judged especially aggressive; only 13 percent of nondeindividuating cultures were judged especially aggressive.

7. Halloween Mayhem

 a. Diener, Fraser, Beaman, and Kelem (1976) conducted a "Halloween study" to examine the role of deindividuation in antisocial behavior.

  (1) They set up a field experiment in twenty-seven homes throughout Seattle on Halloween.

  (2) Over 1,000 children were told they could take a single piece of candy from a large bowl outside the house.

  (3) There was also a bowl filled with coins present.

  (4) (Correlational) Variable #1: the children arrived individually or in groups (children in groups would feel more anonymous).

  (5) (Experimental) Variable #2:

_____

_____

_____

_____

  (6) Findings:

    (a) _____

_____

_____

_____

    (b) _____

_____

_____

_____

(c) _____
_____
_____
_____

8. Summary of the Evidence
   a. The results are very supportive of deindividuation, but most are correlational findings.
   b. A group may make people feel deindividuated, but perhaps rowdier people like being in groups.
   c. Variable #2 in the Halloween study is a true experimental variable because children were randomly assigned to one condition or another.
     (1) Random assignment allows us to assume that the two groups of children (anonymous or individuated) were (on average) equivalent in terms of how likely they would be to transgress.
     (2) Any increase in transgression can be confidently attributed to the anonymity of the children, not to the kind of person who would seek out anonymity.

D. Self-Awareness and Individuation
  1. Individuation can be defined as
_____
_____
_____
_____

  2. Self-awareness theory can be defined as
_____
_____
_____
_____

  3. Studies of Self-Awareness
   a. Many studies support self-awareness theory.
   b. Diener and Wallbom (1976) conducted a study on the effect of self-awareness on cheating.
     (1) Experimental setup:
_____
_____
_____
_____

     (2) Control condition:
_____
_____
_____
_____

     (3) Experimental condition:
_____
_____

_____
_____
     (4) Findings:
_____
_____
_____
_____

4. Self-Consciousness and the Spotlight Effect
   a. Individual differences aside, there is evidence that typical levels of self-consciousness among people under ordinary circumstances may be high.
   b. Baumeister (1991) argues that alcoholism, binge eating, and other destructive behaviors may be ways of escaping self-consciousness.
   c. Hull and colleagues found that students who drank gin and tonic were less likely to use first-person pronouns (e.g., "I" and "me") than students given plain tonic water.
   d. The spotlight effect can be defined as
_____
_____
_____
_____

   e. Gilovich, Medvec, and Savitsky (2000) conducted a study to demonstrate the spotlight effect.
     (1) Participants arrived individually for a study and were asked to put on a Barry Manilow T-shirt (a potentially embarrassing action).
     (2) Participants then went into another room where a group of people were filling out questionnaires.
     (3) After leaving the room, participants were asked to estimate how many members of the group would be able to recall that it was Barry Manilow pictured on the T-shirt.
     (4) Findings:
_____
_____
_____
_____

IV. Group Decision Making
  A. For tasks that have factual and precise answers, a group often produces more accurate answers than any one individual.
  B. Groups may perform more poorly than individuals, particularly when individual concerns override a group goal to arrive at the best solution.

C. Groupthink
1. Irving Janis studied several (bad) decisions made by the government through history, claiming that these disasters happened as a consequence of groupthink.
   a. Cuban Bay of Pigs, in which the U.S. planted CIA-trained Cuban refugees back in Cuba to help overthrow Castro, but failed to provide adequate military support, leading to the capture of the refugees.
   b. Johnson administration's decision to send more troops to Vietnam, which did not advance U.S. objectives but resulted in more lives lost.
   c. Pearl Harbor, in which the U.S. naval high command decided it did not need to take extra precautions in the face of warnings about an imminent attack on Pearl Harbor.
2. Groupthink can be defined as

   _____

   _____

   _____

   _____

3. Symptoms and Sources of Groupthink
   a. Janis argued that a certain set of conditions were necessary to create groupthink:
      (1) _____

      _____

      _____

      (2) _____

      _____

      _____

      (3) _____

      _____

      _____

      (4) _____

      _____

      _____

      (5) _____

      _____

      _____

   b. There is mixed empirical evidence that these conditions are all essential and/or that they combine into groupthink per se rather than operating on their own.
   c. Janis's research on groupthink can help identify factors that have been present in real-world poor decisions.

   (1) Strong leaders and a need for consensus can lead to self-censorship.
   (2) Self-censorship can be defined as

   _____

   _____

   _____

   _____

4. Preventing Groupthink
   a. Janis's suggestions to avoid groupthink have been shown to have merit:
      (1) _____

      _____

      _____

      (2) _____

      _____

      _____

      (3) _____

      _____

      _____

   b. During the Cuban Missile Crisis, the Kennedy administration actively worked to avoid another Bay of Pigs situation:
      (1) _____

      _____

      _____

      (2) _____

      _____

      _____

      (3) _____

      _____

      _____

5. Groupthink in Other Cultures
   a. The drive for harmony is greater in East Asian cultures than it is in Western cultures.
   b. Groupthink appears to be very common in East Asian cultures.
   c. Japanese corporations manage to avoid groupthink because

   _____

   _____

   _____

   _____

D. Group Decisions: Risky or Conservative?
1. Stoner (1961) conducted a study of group decision making.
   a. Participants were given twelve different dilemmas and asked to decide the extent of

risk the hypothetical individual should take in order to possibly attain a desired outcome.

b. Participants responded to the scenarios alone first, and then in a group discussion setting.

c. Stoner found support for a risky shift.

d. Risky shift can be defined as

_____

_____

_____

_____

2. Follow-up studies suggested that sometimes people in groups will make more cautious decisions than individuals, and sometimes they will make more risk-averse decisions than individuals.

3. Researchers investigated what conditions led to risky shift versus more conservative decisions.

E. Group Polarization

1. Research suggests that individuals in groups will endorse whatever opinion they were predisposed to prior to discussion, but that the group discussion makes that predisposition more intense.

2. Group polarization can be defined as

_____

_____

_____

_____

3. Explanations of group polarization show that there is no overall risky shift.

4. Moscovici and Zavalloni (1969) conducted a study in which they found that French students' initially positive views of Charles DeGaulle and their initially negative views of America became stronger after group discussion.

5. The "Persuasive Arguments" Account

a. The persuasive arguments account explains group polarization by saying that

_____

_____

_____

_____

b. This explanation is supported by research that shows that participants exhibit group polarization effects even after *reading* novel arguments.

6. The "Social Comparison" Interpretation

a. Festinger's social comparison theory explains group polarization by maintaining that

_____

_____

_____

b. People like to think of themselves as having more than an average amount of a valued trait.

(1) In situations in which a risky decision is favored, an individual will want to seem

_____

_____

_____

_____

(2) In situations in which a conservative decision is favored, an individual will want to seem

_____

_____

_____

_____

c. When individuals are exposed to others' stances on a position (but not their arguments supporting their stance) group polarization effects occur.

7. Valuing Risk

a. In many studies, risk is valued.

b. Risk appears to be culturally valued by Americans because:

(1) _____

_____

_____

(2) _____

_____

_____

F. Polarization in Modern Life

1. Group polarization can be relevant to even contentious issues for which no initial, common predisposition appears to exist.

2. If people only associate with those with the same perspectives, concerns, and general preferences, group polarization is likely to occur.

a. People tend to discuss difficult issues with people who share their perspectives.

b. Although the country is more multicultural than ever, people also have modern ways of screening the information they take in (e.g., biased television news, partisan Internet sites).

TESTING YOUR BASIC KNOWLEDGE

After studying the information in the chapter by filling in the outline above, test your basic knowledge with the following multiple-choice test. Answers are provided in the Answer Key section at the end of the chapter. If you find that you have gotten an answer wrong, it is important that you understand why it is wrong (as well as understanding why the correct answer is the better choice). Talk with peers, your tutor, or your professor if you need help.

Multiple-Choice Questions

1. According to Cartwright and Zander's (1968) definition, which of the following would be the best example of a group?
   a. a group of students in a lecture hall during a social psychology class
   b. a group of coworkers collaborating on a team project
   c. a group of cousins who are meeting each other for the first time at a large family reunion

2. In what is typically regarded as the first social psychological experiment, Triplett (1898) found which of the following social facilitation results?
   a. Children reeled in a fishing line faster when in the presence of another child engaged in the same activity than when alone.
   b. Children reeled in a fishing line more slowly when in the presence of another child engaged in the same activity than when alone.
   c. All bicyclists recorded faster times when in direct competition with one another, as opposed to competing alone on the track against the clock.

3. Connie and her friend Izumi went out with a group of people for Japanese food and ate with chopsticks. Izumi grew up in Japan and has used chopsticks her whole life. Connie grew up in the Midwestern U.S. and has only used chopsticks a few times. Compared to how effectively they use chopsticks in private, what will happen to Connie's and Izumi's chopstick performance when all their dinner companions are gathered around and looking on?
   a. Izumi's performance will get worse, but Connie's will get better.
   b. Izumi's performance will get better, Connie's will get worse.
   c. They will both get better.

4. Zajonc and his colleagues (1969) found that cockroaches
   a. are immune to social facilitation effects.
   b. run a simple maze more quickly in the mere presence of other cockroaches.

c. run a complex maze more quickly in the mere presence of other cockroaches.

5. Zajonc's research involved cockroaches, not people. Taken as a whole, these studies
   a. lack external validity, and the findings have very little psychological value.
   b. have high external validity.
   c. lack external validity, but provide valuable information about the theory of social facilitation.

6. Markus's (1978) study in which she had participants put on an unfamiliar set of clothes and then change back into their own clothes provided support for which of the following?
   a. mere presence
   b. evaluation apprehension
   c. Both a and b are supported by the findings.
   d. None of the above.

7. According to distraction-conflict theory, the mere presence of another person has an effect on our behavior because
   a. the self-consciousness we feel around other people is distracting.
   b. we are physiologically aroused because our attention is split between the other person and the task at hand.
   c. we are evolutionarily wired to anticipate a conflict with the other person.

8. Jozmell, Christina, Jordan, and Melissa have been assigned to complete a group project for a class. Over the three weeks they developed and completed the project, Jozmell, Christina, and Jordan did most of the work. Melissa missed meetings, turned in inferior summaries of her assigned readings, and was quiet during brainstorming sessions. On the day of the project presentation, Melissa did a good job delivering her part of the presentation. For most of the project, Melissa was engaging in which of the following group processes?
   a. social loafing
   b. groupthink
   c. deindividuation

9. In the scenario presented in #8, what can explain Melissa's sudden burst of good work during her portion of the graded presentation?
   a. The guilt she experienced from having previously done a poor job motivated her.
   b. She was physiologically aroused by the situation, which facilitated her performance.
   c. Because she was the presenter, her work was individuated and her efforts were identifiable.

10. A large group of people gather outside of a corporation for a peaceful protest. Suddenly, a few people begin shoving each other and violence erupts. David, a normally peaceful and gentle-natured person finds himself participating in the shoving match. What psychological condition is likely to have led to David's behavior?
    a. social loafing
    b. groupthink
    c. deindividuation

11. Suzanne finds herself in the middle of a confusing uproar outside a closed appliance store. Someone has broken the front window, and a crowd has gathered around looking at the damage. Suddenly, a few members of the crowd snatch small televisions and run away. Suzanne reflects on how much she would like a new MP3 player. She figures that if she slips through the side edge of the crowd she can get a player and slip it in her pocket without anyone noticing. She does so and calmly walks home. Can deindividuation explain Suzanne's behavior?
    a. yes, because she was going along with the crowd
    b. no, because she was aware of herself and planned out how to avoid being caught
    c. maybe, there isn't enough information given to tell

12. Diener and his colleagues conducted a study in 1976 on trick-or-treating on Halloween night. They found that
    a. children who were in a group and not identified took more candy than they were allowed, compared to children who were alone and identified.
    b. children in costumes that covered their faces were more likely to steal money than children whose faces could be seen.
    c. children who were identified by name by the experimenter behaved in a more deindividuated manner.

13. According to self-awareness theory, professors could discourage cheating by doing which of the following?
    a. leave an answer key available and demonstrate trust in students by having them grade their own exams
    b. have students take their exams in front of a mirror
    c. recruit more exam proctors to more carefully observe students during the exam period

14. Niles is asked to wear the ugly sweater his Aunt Lisa gave him the day she is visiting the family. When going out to dinner, Niles runs into a group of people from his school. The next day at school he expects to be teased about the sweater but, in fact, no one remembers the sweater. Niles' mistaken conviction that everyone would notice his sweater is a good example of

    a. self-awareness theory.
    b. individuation effects.
    c. the spotlight effect.

15. During the Cuban Missile Crisis, President Kennedy deliberately excused himself from deliberations several times, invited outside experts to give their views, and assigned two people to argue against any solution that was raised. Taking these steps likely avoided
    a. groupthink.
    b. group polarization.
    c. social loafing.

16. Which of the following is the best example of groupthink?
    a. Sally enthusiastically presents a new software program to her employees at the monthly meeting and asks for their feedback. She notes that a decision needs to be made within the hour. One employee voices strong support and quickly the others follow suit.
    b. Lauren, the captain of the cheerleading squad, shows her fellow teammates three design ideas for their new uniforms. She asks the women to take a day or two to consider the new ideas, and tells them that they will vote on the uniform design at their next meeting.
    c. Henry is a juror at a murder trial. During deliberations, the eleven other jurors indicate that they think the defendant is guilty. Henry stubbornly refuses to vote "guilty" and explains his reasoning over and over until convincing everyone else. In the end, the defendant is found not guilty.

17. Mr. X, a thirty-five-year-old, single man, has a chance to double his retirement nest egg by investing it in a new company. If the new company fails, however, Mr. X will lose his retirement funds entirely. When presented with this scenario, Americans are more likely than people in non-Western cultures to
    a. engage in a conservative shift rather than a risky shift.
    b. discourage Mr. X from taking the investment risk.
    c. encourage Mr. X to take the investment risk.

18. The psychology department at a college is trying to decide whether or not to take a chance and hire Dr. Amanda Cole. Amanda is young and inexperienced, but she is enthusiastic and very well liked by her students. Every member of the department is initially leaning toward taking the chance and hiring Amanda. According to group polarization, a meeting to discuss the issue is likely to have what result?

a. A discussion will reinforce initial views because each professor will hear novel arguments in favor of hiring Amanda.

b. A discussion will allow Amanda's strengths and weaknesses to be fairly discussed and the department will be able to reach a reasoned conclusion.

c. Face-to-face discussions will result in group polarization, but a discussion conducted by exchanging e-mails will prevent group polarization.

19. What explanation does social comparison theory give for group polarization?

a. People compare their views to others and conform to the group's inclination in order to be accepted.

b. An individual will strengthen his or her initial attitude in order to seem more risky or conservative than the other people in the group.

c. Changing one's opinion to be contrary to that of the social reference group helps boost self-esteem.

20. In the military, soldiers are asked to wear matching uniforms and to have similar hairstyles. In what way would this uniform appearance encourage deindividuation?

a. Soldiers will feel more anonymous and less self-aware.

b. Soldiers will feel pride in their organizational membership.

c. By feeling a sense of group belonging, the soldiers will develop more trust.

21. According to research on groupthink, one disadvantage of a strong and directive leader is that he or she may

a. paralyze a group by encouraging never-ended discussions of the pros and cons of every decision.

b. demoralize group members by preventing them from making independent decisions.

c. unknowingly encourage group members to engage in self-censorship.

22. Research studies supported the "persuasive arguments" reasoning for group polarization by showing that participants intensified their initial opinions on a topic after

a. reading a set of arguments about the issue.

b. hearing the "yes" or "no" votes of fellow group members.

c. spending time alone contemplating their opinion.

23. Behaviors that surface only when a person is in a group are called

a. dominant responses.

b. emergent properties of groups.

c. spotlight effects.

24. Research suggests that "suicide baiting" is more likely to occur among

a. large crowds of people at night.

b. young adults in cities.

c. non-Western cultures.

25. Which of the following is *not* an antecedent to groupthink?

a. concern with generating consensus

b. knowledge of the leader's opinion

c. similarity of opinions among the group members

Essay Questions

After you have mastered the multiple-choice questions, try testing your basic understanding by thoroughly answering each of the broad essay questions below. Because it is critical that you think through this information on your own, we have not provided any answers to these questions. Your learning and retention of this material will be greatly enhanced if you do one or more of the following to check your answers: carefully review the textbook information; compare your responses to your class lecture notes; talk over your answers with a peer; ask your professor to review your answers or review any information that is unclear to you.

1. In your own words, explain what a group is and why humans have a predisposition toward living in groups.

2. Social facilitation research suggests that the presence of other people sometimes makes us perform better and sometimes makes us perform worse. Discuss the research that resolved this contradiction, and explain the role of mere presence and evaluation apprehension.

3. Explain the antecedents and consequences of deindividuation, and explain how deindividuation can explain suicide baiting and Diener, Fraser, Beaman, and Kelem's (1976) "Halloween study" results.

4. Using your own words, explain self-awareness theory and discuss one study that illustrates the theory.

5. Groupthink and group polarization are influences that often cause groups to reach different solutions to a problem than individuals. Explain each concept and discuss the antecedent conditions that are thought to lead to each.

TESTING YOUR IN-DEPTH UNDERSTANDING

Test your in-depth understanding of the material by working through the Critical Thinking Exercises provided at the end of each textbook chapter. To maximize this learning opportunity, work together with a tutor, study group, or your professor. Alternatively, write down your thoughts and responses.

Guided questions for one of the exercises are provided below. While there are multiple ways to answer these questions, short answers are given in the Answer Key at the end of the chapter. Note that the valuable part of this exercise is not simply knowing the answer but working with the material to come up with the answer.

Guided Questions for Critical Thinking Exercise #2

In light of what you've learned about the presence of others on performance, what activities can you think of that (a) are typically performed with people working side-by-side but would be better performed by people working alone, and (b) are typically performed by people working alone but would be better performed by people working side-by-side?

1. First, review the major processes you learned about. How do each of the following generally influence behavior? Also, what conditions lead to the process and/or what additional factors influence the process?
   a. Deindividuation
      (1) Self-awareness
      (2) Spotlight effect
   b. Zajonc's social facilitation theory
      (1) Mere presence
      (2) Evaluation apprehension
      (3) Distraction-conflict theory
      (4) Social loafing
   c. Groupthink
   d. Group polarization
      (1) Persuasive arguments
      (2) Social comparison

2. Reviewing the notes you generated above, create a list of general circumstances for which being alone would promote optimal performance, and a list for which being in a group would produce optimal performance. Also make note of any additional suggestions that come out of an examination of these processes (e.g., if you are going to meet in a group, then do x, y, and z).

3. Think about your own life, college life, politics, your job, and other settings in order to generate as many examples for each case as you can.

4. Pretend you are a social psychologist and choose one of the suggestions from the ideas you generated above.
   a. How could you design an experiment to test whether your suggestion to switch the task to one in which a person is alone versus in a group (or vice versa) is a good one? Try to design a highly controlled study, even if that means sacrificing external validity.

   b. What would be the independent variable in the study?
   c. What would be the dependent variable in the study?
   d. How could you accomplish random assignment?
   e. What field study could you do in order to apply the findings (not just the theory) to the "real" world?

Enhance your understanding of the chapter by thinking about and doing the remaining three Critical Thinking Exercises. Discuss your answers with your peers, study group, tutor, or professor.

Critical Thinking Exercise #1

What experiments can you think of from this chapter that: (a) lack external validity, and this lack represents a serious shortcoming of the research; (b) lack external validity, but this lack does not represent a shortcoming at all; and (c) do not lack external validity?

Critical Thinking Exercise #3

Research on the spotlight effect indicates that people tend to overestimate the extent to which others take note of them and their behavior. But as with nearly all psychological phenomena, there are exceptions. Can you think of any examples of circumstances or instances in which people systematically *under*estimate the extent to which others take note of them?

Critical Thinking Exercise #4

Copy the "Mr. A., the electrical engineer" example from page 77 (in the text) and give it to four of your friends. Have them render a decision individually and then bring them together and have them discuss the case and arrive at a consensus opinion. Finally, compare the joint opinion with the average individual recommendation. Is the group's recommendation riskier than the average individual recommendation?

SOCIAL PSYCHOLOGY IN THE POPULAR MEDIA

You might be interested in the following popular media references, each of which relates in some way to information in this chapter.

Book

McCain, John, & Salter, Mark (2000). *Faith of My Fathers: A Family Memoir.* New York: Perennial. This book is about John McCain's life up to and including his time as a prisoner of war.

Songs

Dead Kennedys (2004). "Riot." From the album *Mutiny on the Bay*. Commentary (using explicit language) on the conditions leading to a riot and the feelings a person may have when part of a riot.

Whitney Houston (2002). "Whatchulookinat." From the album *Just Whitney*. Whitney Houston reacts to the feelings of always being observed in the spotlight.

Film

Thirteen Days (2000; directed by Roger Donaldson; starring Kevin Costner). Based closely on the events of the Cuban Missile Crisis, this film will give you greater insight into the decision-making processes described briefly in the textbook.

Web Sites

Deindividuation—http://www.ex.ac.uk/%7Epostmes/deindividuation.html. This Web site by Dr. Postmes at Exeter University gives detailed text-only information about deindividuation.

Social Facilitation—http://samiam.colorado.edu/%7Emcclella/expersim/introsocial.html. This Web site provides an explanation and interactive exercise about social facilitation. You set the experimental conditions, and the Web site produces statistical data about ten participants.

ANSWER KEY

Annotated Chapter Outline

I. The Nature and Purpose of Group Living
   A. Reasons for Group Living
      1. Groups afforded evolutionary benefits such as help in survival, reproduction, and child rearing.
      2. Because of the evolutionary survival advantages of groups, Baumeister and Leary (1995) proposed that people have an innate psychological need to belong to groups.
   B. Defining Groups
      1. Cartwright and Zander (1968) defined a group as "a collection of individuals who have relations to one another that make them interdependent to some significant degree."
      2. Just as interdependence varies on a continuum, so does the decision about how much of a group a collection of people represents.
         a. The members of a family are more of a group than are students in a large class.
         b. A nation's citizens make up a group, but less so than do members of a tribe.

II. Social Facilitation
   A. The presence of other people appears to influence the performance of individuals.
   B. Initial Research
      1. Triplett (1898) was the first researcher to study this topic and also conducted what is usually thought of as the first social psychological laboratory experiment.
         a. Triplett noticed that the fastest times among cyclists were when the cyclists competed against other people rather than racing alone against the clock.
         b. Triplett conducted a lab investigation to test the general hypothesis that the presence of others facilitates performance.
            (1) Experimental design: forty children were asked to reel in fishing lines as fast as they could six separate times.
            (2) Independent variable: whether the child was alone or with another child engaged in the same task.
            (3) Findings: children reeled the fishing line faster in the presence of another child.
         c. Social facilitation can be defined as enhanced performance in the presence of others.
      2. Triplett's findings were extended in two important ways by other researchers.
         a. Researchers showed that participants performed better in the presence of others, even if those others were passive observers (rather than co-actors).
         b. Researchers observed social facilitation in many types of animals, suggesting that the phenomenon is very general and fundamental (i.e., evidence for evolutionary roots).
      3. Other researchers also found a troubling number of exceptions to social facilitation—instances where the presence of other people inhibited or worsened performance.
         a. Allport (1920) found that students at Harvard and Radcliffe provided higher quality philosophical arguments when working alone than when working in the presence of another student.
         b. The presence of others can inhibit performance on arithmetic problems, memory tasks, and maze learning.
   C. Resolving the Contradictions
      1. Zajonc (1965) proposed a theory that would

explain both the facilitation and the inhibition study results.

  a. Zajonc's (1965) theory has three parts:

    (1) The mere presence of others leads to physiological arousal (there is a need to be alert to respond to others' behavior).

    (2) Arousal makes a person more likely to engage in his or her dominant response, which can be defined as the response you are most likely to make in a hierarchy of responses.

    (3) For easy/familiar tasks, the dominant response will be to perform well; for complex/unfamiliar tasks, the dominant response will be to perform poorly.

  b. The gist of his theory is that the mere presence of other people is likely to facilitate performance on easy tasks and to inhibit performance on complex and/or unfamiliar tasks.

2. Testing the Theory

  a. Zajonc, Heingartner, and Herman (1969) set up an experiment to test the theory using cockroaches.

    (1) The researchers had the cockroaches run through mazes toward a goal box.

    (2) Independent variable #1: alone or with another cockroach.

    (3) Independent variable #2: simple maze or complex maze.

    (4) Dependent variable: length of time it took the cockroach to reach the darkened goal box.

    (5) Findings: support for Zajonc's theory; the presence of another cockroach in the maze facilitated performance on the simple maze, but hindered performance on the complex maze.

  b. The same results were found when the other cockroaches were in a little "grandstand" observing the cockroach run the maze, indicating that even a passive audience leads to facilitation of easy tasks, but hinders performance on complex tasks.

3. A Methodological Aside: External Validation and Theory Testing

  a. The results of Zajonc's social facilitation studies lacked external validity.

  b. Yet, when testing a theory, the goal is to understand and test the *theory* and apply the theory to the real world, not to apply specific *findings* to the real world.

    (1) If you drop a bowling ball and a feather inside of a perfect vacuum, they will hit the ground at the same time. By definition, this study lacks external validity since there aren't many naturally occurring perfect vacuums here on Earth.

    (2) The theory that prompted the study is supported, leading to important advances in the understanding of physics and our world.

  c. The highly controlled (and, thus somewhat strange nature) of the cockroach study allowed for a rigorous experimental test. There were two factors that made the cockroach studies precise and controlled:

    (1) Running away from light is unambiguously a dominant response among cockroaches.

    (2) It was easy to create multiple conditions (e.g., simple vs. complex maze) to make relevant comparisons.

D. Mere Presence or Evaluation Apprehension?

1. One aspect of Zajonc's theory that was disputed was whether mere presence created arousal, or whether arousal was a consequence of evaluation apprehension.

2. Evaluation apprehension can be defined as a concern about how one appears in the eyes of others—that is, about being evaluated.

3. Testing for Evaluation Apprehension

  a. Cottrell, Wack, Sekerak, and Rittle (1968) set up an experiment to determine whether evaluation apprehension is the critical element underlying social facilitation effects.

    (1) Participants were given a list of nonsense words.

    (2) Independent variable #1: type of nonsense word—words repeated once, twice, five, ten, or twenty-five times.

    (3) Independent variable #2: participants completed the false recognition task alone, in the presence of two other students watching the proceedings carefully, or in the presence of blindfolded observers.

  b. Findings: individuals performing in front of an observing audience guessed more "dominant" words (words repeated twenty-five times) during the false recognition task than those performing alone; individuals performing in front of a blindfolded audience did not guess more dominant words.

c. This finding highlights the importance of evaluation apprehension in that the presence of others only had an impact when others could watch and therefore evaluate the proceedings.

d. Initially, these findings seemed to suggest that mere presence does not have an influence since the results were the same for the alone condition and for the blindfolded observer condition.

4. Testing for Mere Presence

a. In the Cottrell, Wack, Sekerak, and Rittle (1968) study, the alone condition may have been tainted by participants' psychological sense of being observed somehow by an experimenter.

b. If this was the case, then participants in the "alone" condition would have had their dominant responses increased by social facilitation effects—thus, the fact that the participants in the blindfolded observer condition performed similarly to those in the alone condition does not necessarily refute the influence of mere presence.

c. Markus (1978) conducted an experiment with a "true" alone condition.

(1) The setup of the experiment:

(a) Participants were initially asked to go into a separate room and get dressed in the required outfit for the study.

(b) After ten minutes, they were told the other participants were not coming and the study was cancelled.

(c) Participants were told to change back into their own clothes.

(d) They were asked to wait in that room until other participants arrived and the study could start.

(2) Independent variable #1: complexity of dressing task (putting on the UNFAMILIAR clothes vs. putting back on their own FAMILIAR clothes).

(3) Independent variable #2: participants were alone, with another person who was watching them, or with a repairman who had his back to the participants.

(a) This alone condition is better that Cottrell et al.'s condition because participants did not believe the study had even started yet.

(b) Since they thought they were alone, they did not think of changing clothes as a task they were being evaluated on.

(4) Dependent variable: speed with which they changed clothes.

(5) Findings: participants put on their own clothes more quickly and put on the unfamiliar clothes more slowly in the presence of another person compared to when they were alone. Thus, mere presence is supported.

(6) The facilitation and inhibition results were even stronger in the condition with the attentive audience. Thus, evaluation apprehension does play a role in that it adds to the influence of mere exposure.

E. Current Perspectives

1. Experimental evidence suggests that mere presence increases arousal and encourages the dominant response on easy and difficult tasks.

2. What is it about the awareness of another person's presence that increases arousal?

a. Distraction-conflict theory can be defined as a theory that says that being aware of another person's presence creates a conflict between attending to that person and attending to the task at hand, and that it is this attentional conflict that is arousing and that produces social facilitation effects.

b. Some evidence suggests that nonsocial distractions can produce facilitation effects, but not enough evidence has been gathered to confidently accept this theory.

3. Evaluation apprehension enhances mere presence effects.

4. Some norms (for example, norms in work settings against working harder than the established group norm) encourage poor performance.

5. Social loafing hides mere presence effects.

a. Social loafing can be defined as the tendency to exert less effort when working on a group task in which individual contributions cannot be monitored.

b. People may engage in social loafing because they believe that their efforts are not crucial to the task.

F. Practical Applications

1. People should study complex material alone, but they should rehearse or practice well-learned material in a group.

2. Employers should arrange workplace settings so that workers are in contact with one another if they are doing repetitive, simple tasks, but they should give workers privacy if they are doing complex tasks.

III. Deindividuation and the Psychology of Mobs
   A. Real-world experiences illustrate that individuals can engage in destructive acts that are contrary to their character when in large groups of people. The question is why.
   B. Emergent Properties of Groups
      1. Emergent properties of groups can be defined as those behaviors that only surface ("emerge") when people are in groups.
      2. Studying group behavior in a laboratory setting is more difficult than studying social facilitation in a lab because:
         a. People are motivated to perform their best in a laboratory setting.
         b. It is easy to set up a situation in which an audience is present or not present.
         c. There are many different ways to easily and clearly measure "performance."
         d. It is difficult to get a person to act destructively in a laboratory setting.
         e. It is unethical to put people in experimental situations in which aggression is likely.
      3. Most research on the psychology of the mob takes place in the "real world."
   C. Deindividuation and the Group Mind
      1. Social psychologists have expanded on work by sociologist LeBon (1895) and studied how being in a group changes an individual's general orientation to the world.
      2. Individuals may act differently in a group because of deindividuation, which can be defined as a reduced sense of individual identity accompanied by diminished self-regulation that comes over a person when he or she is in a large group.
         a. Most of the time we feel identifiable by others, individually responsible for our actions, and concerned about the consequences of our actions.
         b. When in a crowd, under certain conditions, we can feel "lost in the crowd."
      3. A Model of Deindividuation
         a. Zimbardo (1970) proposed a model of deindividuation that specified:
            (1) Certain antecedent conditions create a psychological state that promotes deindividuation:
               (a) Anonymity
               (b) Diffusion of responsibility—more people present allows blame to be spread out more
               (c) Physiological arousal
               (d) Heightened activity
               (e) Sensory overload
            (2) Deindividuation is characterized by three important features (all three are required to be considered deindividuated):
               (a) Diminished self-observation
               (b) Diminished self-evaluation
               (c) Diminished concern with how others view and judge you
            (3) A deindividuated person will be more responsive to the behavioral cues of those around him or her.
            (4) Deindividuated behavior can be irrational, emotional, and less responsive to attempts to stop it.
            (5) This model predicts impulsive behavior, although such impulsivity often turns into destructive behavior.
         b. People often find the impulsivity liberating, and societies try to safely channel its expression.
      4. Testing the Model
         a. Because the tests of the model described here involve an examination of archival (existing real world) data, one must be cautious in interpreting the data.
            (1) Alternative interpretations for the patterns found in the data have not been ruled out by experimental control.
            (2) Although one study may be flawed in one way and leave one alternative explanation open, a second study may eliminate that alternative explanation.
            (3) A series of studies together will provide stronger support.
         b. Correlation does not imply causation.
      5. Suicide Baiting
         a. Suicide baiting can be defined as urging a person who is on the verge of committing suicide to jump to his or her death.
         b. Mann (1981) examined fifteen years of newspaper accounts of suicidal jumps and averted jumps.
            (1) Data: Mann found that suicide baiting occurred in the ten out of twenty-one instances of attempted suicide.
            (2) Variables associated with deindividuation that were present: deindividuation, darkness, and a large group.

6. The Conduct of War
   a. Watson (1981) studied the war practices of twenty-three non-Western cultures.
   b. Findings: 80 percent of cultures that deindividuated themselves (e.g., with war paint) before battle were judged especially aggressive; only 13 percent of nondeindividuating cultures were judged especially aggressive.
7. Halloween Mayhem
   a. Diener, Fraser, Beaman, and Kelem (1976) conducted a "Halloween study" to examine the role of deindividuation in antisocial behavior.
      (1) They set up a field experiment in twenty-seven homes throughout Seattle on Halloween.
      (2) Over 1,000 children were told they could take a single piece of candy from a large bowl outside the house.
      (3) There was also a bowl filled with coins present.
      (4) (Correlational) Variable #1: the children arrived individually or in groups (children in groups would feel more anonymous).
      (5) (Experimental) Variable #2: the experimenter answering the door asked each child his/her name and address and then repeated it (identifying the children should individuate them and lead to less anonymity).
      (6) Findings:
          (a) Children who were in groups were more likely to take coins and more than one piece of candy than children who were alone, regardless of whether they were anonymous.
          (b) Children who were anonymous were more likely to transgress than children who were individuated, regardless of whether they were alone or in a group.
          (c) Children who were both in groups and who remained anonymous were more likely to transgress than those in any other group.
8. Summary of the Evidence
   a. The results are very supportive of deindividuation, but most are correlational findings.
   b. A group may make people feel deindividuated, but perhaps rowdier people like being in groups.

c. Variable #2 in the Halloween study is a true experimental variable because children were randomly assigned to one condition or another.
   (1) Random assignment allows us to assume that the two groups of children (anonymous or individuated) were (on average) equivalent in terms of how likely they would be to transgress.
   (2) Any increase in transgression can be confidently attributed to the anonymity of the children, not to the kind of person who would seek out anonymity.
D. Self-Awareness and Individuation
   1. Individuation can be defined as emphasizing individual identity by focusing attention on the self, which will generally lead a person to act carefully and deliberately and in accordance with his or her sense of propriety and values.
   2. Self-awareness theory can be defined as a theory that predicts that when people focus their attention inward on themselves, they become concerned with self-evaluation and how their current behavior conforms to their internal standards and values.
   3. Studies of Self-Awareness
      a. Many studies support self-awareness theory.
      b. Diener and Wallbom (1976) conducted a study on the effect of self-awareness on cheating.
         (1) Experimental setup: participants were asked to solve a series of anagrams and stop when a bell rang.
         (2) Control condition: one-third of the participants "cheated" by continuing to work past the bell.
         (3) Experimental condition: participants did the task by working in front of a mirror.
         (4) Findings: fewer than 10 percent of participants who worked in front of a mirror cheated.
   4. Self-Consciousness and the Spotlight Effect
      a. Individual differences aside, there is evidence that typical levels of self-consciousness among people under ordinary circumstances may be high.
      b. Baumeister (1991) argues that alcoholism, binge eating, and other destructive behaviors may be ways of escaping self-consciousness.
      c. Hull and colleagues found that students who drank gin and tonic were less likely to

use first-person pronouns (e.g., "I" and "me") than students given plain tonic water.

d. The spotlight effect can be defined as people's conviction that other people are attending to them—to their appearance and behavior—more than is actually the case.

e. Gilovich, Medvec, and Savitsky (2000) conducted a study to demonstrate the spotlight effect.

   (1) Participants arrived individually for a study and were asked to put on a Barry Manilow T-shirt (a potentially embarrassing action).

   (2) Participants then went into another room where a group of people were filling out questionnaires.

   (3) After leaving the room, participants were asked to estimate how many members of the group would be able to recall that it was Barry Manilow pictured on the T-shirt.

   (4) Findings: participants overestimated the percentage of group members who would remember the T-shirt (46 percent) when actually only 23 percent actually did remember who was on the T-shirt.

IV. Group Decision Making

A. For tasks that have factual and precise answers, a group often produces more accurate answers than any one individual.

B. Groups may perform more poorly than individuals, particularly when individual concerns override a group goal to arrive at the best solution.

C. Groupthink

1. Irving Janis studied several (bad) decisions made by the government through history, claiming that these disasters happened as a consequence of groupthink.

   a. Cuban Bay of Pigs, in which the U.S. planted CIA-trained Cuban refugees back in Cuba to help overthrow Castro, but failed to provide adequate military support, leading to the capture of the refugees.

   b. Johnson administration's decision to send more troops to Vietnam, which did not advance U.S. objectives but resulted in more lives lost.

   c. Pearl Harbor, in which the U.S. naval high command decided it did not need to take extra precautions in the face of warnings about an imminent attack on Pearl Harbor.

2. Groupthink can be defined as a kind of faulty thinking on the part of highly cohesive groups in which the critical scrutiny that should be devoted to the issues at hand is subverted by social pressures to reach consensus.

3. Symptoms and Sources of Groupthink

   a. Janis argued that a certain set of conditions were necessary to create groupthink:

      (1) A strong leader who states his or her favored opinion

      (2) Strong group cohesiveness

      (3) Stressful or important decision

      (4) Insulation of the group

      (5) Lack of procedures for information search and appraisal

   b. There is mixed empirical evidence that these conditions are all essential and/or that they combine into groupthink per se rather than operating on their own.

   c. Janis's research on groupthink can help identify factors that have been present in real-world bad decisions.

      (1) Strong leaders and a need for consensus can lead to self-censorship.

      (2) Self-censorship can be defined as the decision to withhold information or opinions in order to promote consensus within a group and not to offend one another.

4. Preventing Groupthink

   a. Janis's suggestions to avoid groupthink have been shown to have merit:

      (1) The leader should refrain from making his or her opinions known at the beginning of deliberation.

      (2) The group should make sure that it has access to outside input.

      (3) The group should designate one person to play "devil's advocate" to point out any weaknesses in the group's plan.

   b. During the Cuban Missile Crisis, the Kennedy administration actively worked to avoid another Bay of Pigs situation:

      (1) Kennedy frequently excused himself from the group to allow for more free discussion.

      (2) Kennedy brought in outside experts to critique the group's analysis and plans.

      (3) Kennedy appointed specific individuals to play devil's advocate.

5. Groupthink in Other Cultures
   a. The drive for harmony is greater in East Asians cultures than it is in Western cultures.
   b. Groupthink appears to be very common in East Asian cultures.
   c. Japanese corporations manage to avoid groupthink because, prior to a large group meeting in which consensus is stressed, managers will have discussed the problem with each group member individually, allowing for frank one-on-one exchanges.

D. Group Decisions: Risky or Conservative?
   1. Stoner (1961) conducted a study of group decision making.
      a. Participants were given twelve different dilemmas and asked to decide the extent of risk the hypothetical individual should take in order to possibly attain a desired outcome.
      b. Participants responded to the scenarios alone first, and then in a group discussion setting.
      c. Stoner found support for a risky shift.
      d. Risky shift can be defined as the tendency for groups to make riskier decisions than individuals.
   2. Follow-up studies suggested that sometimes people in groups will make more cautious decisions than individuals, and sometimes they will make more risk-averse decisions than individuals.
   3. Researchers investigated what conditions led to risky shift versus more conservative decisions.

E. Group Polarization
   1. Research suggests that individuals in groups will endorse whatever opinion they were predisposed to prior to discussion—but that the group discussion makes that predisposition more intense.
   2. Group polarization can be defined as the tendency for group decisions to be more extreme than those made by individuals; whatever way the individuals are leaning, group discussion tends to make them lean further in that direction.
   3. Explanations of group polarization show that there is no overall risky shift.
   4. Moscovici and Zavalloni (1969) conducted a study in which they found that French students' initially positive views of Charles DeGaulle and their initially negative views of America became stronger after group discussion.

5. The "Persuasive Arguments" Account
   a. The "persuasive arguments" account explains group polarization by saying that no one individual is likely to think of every argument that supports his or her initial opinions, but that when in a group, each individual may hear new arguments that support and intensify his or her predispositions.
   b. This explanation is supported by research that shows that participants exhibit group polarization effects even after just *reading* novel arguments.

6. The "Social Comparison" Interpretation
   a. Festinger's social comparison theory explains group polarization by maintaining that when there is not an objective standard of evaluation or comprehension, people will evaluate their opinions and abilities by comparing themselves to others.
   b. People like to think of themselves as having more than an average amount of a valued trait.
      (1) In situations in which a risky decision is favored, an individual will want to seem more willing to take risks than fellow group members.
      (2) In situations in which a conservative decision is favored, an individual will want to seem more conservative than fellow group members.
   c. When individuals are exposed to others' stances on a position (but not their arguments supporting their stance) group polarization effects occur.

7. Valuing Risk
   a. In many studies, risk is valued.
   b. Risk appears to be culturally valued by Americans because:
      (1) Capitalism encourages risk
      (2) Immigrants who populated America passed on their risk-taking, adventurous genes (this is a highly shaky contention).

F. Polarization in Modern Life
   1. Group polarization can be relevant to even contentious issues for which no initial, common, predisposition appears to exist.
   2. If people only associate with those with the same perspectives, concerns, and general preferences, group polarization is likely to occur.
      a. People tend to discuss difficult issues with people who share their perspectives.

b. Although the country is more multicultural than ever, people also have modern ways of screening the information they take in (e.g., biased television news, partisan Internet sites).

TESTING YOUR BASIC KNOWLEDGE

Answers to Multiple-Choice Questions

1. b	14. c
2. a	15. a
3. b	16. a
4. b	17. c
5. c	18. a
6. c	19. b
7. b	20. a
8. a	21. c
9. c	22. a
10. c	23. b
11. b	24. a
12. a	25. c
13. b	

Testing Your In-Depth Understanding

EXAMPLE ANSWERS TO THE GUIDED QUESTIONS FOR CRITICAL THINKING EXERCISE #2

1. First review the major processes you learned about. How do each of the following generally influence behavior? Also, what conditions lead to the process and/or what additional factors influence the process?
   a. Deindividuation—when a person feels anonymous, is too cognitively overloaded to think about his or her own values, and is physiologically aroused, he or she will be susceptible to impulsive behavior, even destructive behavior, if that is what the "crowd" is doing.
      (1) Self-awareness—being in front of a mirror or otherwise made to feel very aware of one's own personal identity will make a person act in strict accordance with his or her values, even in the face of temptation.
      (2) Spotlight effect—people tend to overestimate the extent to which others are evaluating or even noticing their behavior.
   b. Zajonc's social facilitation theory
      (1) Mere presence—having other people around (whether they are observing or not) will lead people to perform better on easy tasks and worse on hard tasks.
      (2) Evaluation apprehension—having other people around facilitates easy tasks and inhibits hard tasks when those other people are in a position to evaluate one's performance.
      (3) Distraction-conflict theory—having another person around will lead to a conflict between paying attention to the person or to the task.
      (4) Social loafing—having other people participating in the same task together leads each individual to slack off (assuming his or her individual contribution cannot be identified).
   c. Groupthink—when there is pressure to reach a consensus in a group (because of a directive leader, strong group cohesion, and/or a high-pressure situation), groups may often end up having shallow discussions of only a few narrow alternatives. Individuals in the group may end up self-censoring and not sharing vital information.
   d. Group polarization—when people make a decision as a member of group, the decision tends to be more extreme than one made by an individual (either riskier or more conservative).
      (1) Persuasive arguments—hearing novel arguments that support one's predisposition leads to an even stronger endorsement of that view.
      (2) Social comparison—a desire to have the greatest amount of a situationally favored trait (conservatism or risk) may lead one to more strongly endorse a view shared by the group.

2. Reviewing the notes you generated above, create a list of general circumstances for which being alone would promote optimal performance, and a list for which being in a group would produce optimal performance. Also make note of any additional suggestions that come out of an examination of these processes (e.g., if you are going to meet in a group, then do x, y, and z).
   a. Better Alone:
      (1) For ethical and honest behavior, the person should be alone or highly identifiable, given the findings about deindividuation and self-awareness.
      (2) Complex or unfamiliar tasks should be done alone.
      (3) When an important decision needs to be made, individual members of a group should be encouraged to think through their positions while alone, before meeting with a group. According to groupthink and group polarization, the more carefully thought out the individual's position is before meeting with the group, the better the information will flow.
   b. Better in a Group:
      (1) If you want a person to go along with the crowd without pausing to think about his or her own

needs or values, deindividuation and the spotlight effect suggest the person should be in a group and/or otherwise made anonymous.

(2) Easy or familiar tasks should be done in a group.

c. General Advice:

(1) Tasks for which the overall result will be better if every member of a group gives 100 percent should include a way to identify each individual's contribution (to discourage social loafing).

(2) When an important decision needs to be made in a group meeting, someone should be assigned to be a devil's advocate (breaking the "persuasive arguments" influence and groupthink), and all views should be heard before the leader of a group shares his or her views.

3. It would defeat the purpose of the exercise to give you examples here. If you are feeling "stuck" for ideas, try brainstorming for group activities in general (e.g., team sports, the military, a decision about where to go for dinner, group projects for a class, team generation of ideas at an advertising agency or other creative activity, writing a group paper, etc.). Also try brainstorming for ideas about solitary activities (studying, library searches, being a toll booth attendant, accounting, driving a bus or train, analyzing data, practicing a musical instrument or athletic skill, coming up with an idea for a paper, etc.)

4. Pretend you are a social psychologist, and choose one of the suggestions from the ideas you generated above.

a. To design a highly controlled study, I would have to isolate the task as much as possible. For example, if I chose the task of practicing the flute, I would want to bring participants into the lab and choose something specific for them to play. If I chose the task of driving a bus, I could isolate the skill of reaction time and ask participants to do a reaction time task.

b. At least one of my independent variables would be performing the task alone or in a group. I might have other independent variables (for example, an easy and a hard version of the task).

c. My dependent variable would be some measure of performance.

d. As with any study, I could flip a coin, roll a dice, or assign random numbers to be sure my participants are randomly placed into different conditions.

e. A field study is one done in conditions that represent "real-life" conditions. Thus, I might observe the flute player in the practice hall or the bus driver actually driving a bus (or maybe a simulator).

CHAPTER 3 | Attraction

The goal of this chapter is to explore what variables influence interpersonal attraction. The chapter focuses on the three biggest influences on attraction: propinquity, similarity, and physical attractiveness. A large portion of the chapter is devoted to an examination of why physical attractiveness is so important to interpersonal attraction, and to a close examination of the prevailing evolutionary logic underlying research on gender differences in mate preferences. The chapter concludes with a brief presentation of three theoretical perspectives on what a person values in a relationship: reward theory, social exchange theory, and equity theory.

ANNOTATED CHAPTER OUTLINE

After first reading through the chapter quickly, create a comprehensive framework for the information in the chapter by reading the outline below and filling in the missing information. Instead of simply re-copying information from the textbook, try to use your own words wherever possible; you can check your answers against the completed outline in the Answer Key section at the end of the chapter.

I. Studying Attraction
  A. The research that will be presented will mostly confirm our intuitions.
  B. Research will also yield some surprises, especially regarding the strength with which certain variables influence attraction.

II. Propinquity
  A. Propinquity can be defined as

  _____

  _____

  _____

  _____

B. Studies of Propinquity and Attraction
  1. Festinger, Schachter, and Back (1950) studied the friendship patterns in a married student housing project in which incoming students were randomly assigned to their residences.
    a. A sociometric survey can be defined as

    _____

    _____

    _____

    _____

    b. Briefly describe two of the findings of the Festinger study at Westgate West:
      (1) _____

    _____

    _____

      (2) _____

    _____

    _____

    _____

  2. Functional distance can be defined as

  _____

  _____

  _____

  _____

    a. Residents who lived near the stairs on the bottom floor had more chance encounters with upstairs neighbors than did residents of middle apartments.
    b. Festinger found that residents who were functionally closer to one another (e.g., met in the stairwells) were much more likely to become friends than those who were physically close but functionally more distant.

3. Segal (1974) studied forty-five police academy trainees assigned to quarters alphabetically.
   a. Segal found that

   _____

   _____

   _____

   _____

   b. Minor differences in propinquity led to major differences in friendships.
   c. The correlation between location and friendship was remarkably high: .90.
4. Similarity matters, too, but it does not override propinquity.
   a. Nahemow and Lawton (1975) studied friendships in an age- and race-diverse housing project.
   b. They found that both proximity and similarity had strong effects on friendships:
      (1) _____

      _____

      _____

      (2) _____

      _____

      _____

C. Explanations of Propinquity Effects
   1. Availability and Propinquity
      a. Proximity allows for the passive and frequent contacts necessary to develop a dialogue and, subsequently, friendship.
      b. Proximity not only makes friendship possible; it also encourages it.
   2. The Effect of Anticipating Interaction
      a. Darley and Berscheid (1967) found that participants, after reading personality descriptions, indicated that they liked the person they thought they were going to meet more than the person they did not think they were going to meet.
         (1) Counterbalancing can be defined as

         _____

         _____

         _____

         (2) The initial positive stance toward the other person

         _____

         _____

         _____

         (3) When we live near another person, we make an effort to have our initial encounters with him or her go well.

   b. Insko and Wilson (1977) crafted a study in which participants A and C interacted with participant B, but not with each other.
      (1) Insko and Wilson found that

      _____

      _____

      _____

      (2) The results supported the idea that

      _____

      _____

      _____

3. The Mere Exposure Effect
   a. The mere exposure effect can be defined as

   _____

   _____

   _____

   b. There is a great deal of *correlational* evidence supporting the idea that familiarity with stimuli breeds liking.
      (1) Commonly mentioned flowers, trees, fruits, vegetables, countries, and cities are liked more than uncommon ones.
      (2) An alternative explanation is that causality may run the other way—people may mention things they like more often than things they don't like.
      (3) Empirical evidence supports the mere exposure direction of causality.
         (a) People prefer more common letters of the alphabet.
         (b) People prefer letters that are found in their names.
   c. There is also sufficient *experimental* evidence for mere exposure.
      (1) Zajonc (1968) exposed participants to unfamiliar Turkish words.
         (a) Independent variable:

         _____

         _____

         _____

         (b) Dependent variable:

         _____

         _____

         _____

         (c) Findings:

         _____

         _____

         _____

(2) Zajonc also replicated the experiment with Chinese pictographs and college yearbook photos as stimuli to see how greater exposure affected liking.

(3) An alternative explanation is that repeated exposure may matter because of repeated associations with the pleasant experimental surroundings.

(a) Saegert, Swap, and Zajonc (1973) had participants do a study that was described as a taste test.

   i. Independent variable #1:

_____

_____

_____

_____

   ii. Independent variable #2:

_____

_____

_____

_____

   iii. Dependent variable: liking for the other participants.

   iv. Findings: regardless of whether encountered while tasting pleasant or unpleasant stimuli, participants who were encountered more often were liked more.

(4) Mita, Dermer, and Knight (1977) found that people prefer photographs depicting their mirror image, while their friends prefer their true image.

(5) Cross, Halcomb, and Matter (1967) used albino rats and music in their study of the mere exposure effect.

(a) Independent variable: exposure to the music of either Mozart or Schoenberg.

(b) Dependent variable: which side of the cage the rats stepped on (activating either Mozart's music or Schoenberg's music).

(c) Findings:

_____

_____

_____

_____

d. What explains mere exposure?

(1) Zajonc hypothesized that every encounter with a stimulus that does not result in an aversive consequence classically conditions us to favor that stimulus over other stimuli.

(2) Repeated exposure and absence of aversive consequences leads to positive associations; mere repeated exposure leads to attraction because it is reinforcing.

III. Similarity

A. Similarity of interests, beliefs, values, worldviews, background, ethnicity, and religion predicts liking.

B. Studies of Similarity and Attraction

1. Whyte (1956) conducted a classic study showing that proximity predicted inclusion in social events in a neighborhood, but so did similarity.

2. Studies like that of Burgess and Wallin (1953) have found that people who intend to marry one another are similar on a variety of dimensions.

a. Members of engaged couples

_____

_____

_____

b. Similarity was strongest for

_____

_____

_____

3. Other studies on the link between similarity and attraction have examined strangers who were thrown together for an extended period of time.

a. Newcomb (1956, 1961) offered transfer students free rent for one year if they lived in a house with strangers and filled out weekly questionnaires.

b. Finding:

_____

_____

_____

4. Some experimental studies supporting the theory that people are more attracted to those whom they believe to be similar use the "bogus stranger" paradigm, in which participants are given responses to attitude or personality questionnaires supposedly filled out by another participant.

a. Independent variable: the extent to which the questionnaire depicts this (bogus) other person as similar to the participant.

b. Dependent variable:

_____

_____

_____

_____

c. Finding:

_____

_____

_____

C. But Don't "Opposites Attract"?
   1. Complementarity can be defined as

   _____

   _____

   2. Logically, we would only expect complementarity when the differences between the two people fulfill one another's needs (rather than creating conflict).
   3. Studies do not support complementarity, even in the above-mentioned cases.
D. Why Does Similarity Promote Attraction?
   1. Similar others validate our beliefs and orientations.
      a. Similar others reinforce rather than challenge our beliefs, outlooks, ideologies, and personal strivings.
      b. Clore and Gormly (1974) found that

      _____

      _____

   2. Similarity facilitates smooth interactions.
      a. Those who share similar views and beliefs and orientations with us enable us to interact without conflict over our views.
      b. Davis (1981) found that

      _____

      _____

   3. We expect similar others to like us.
      a. People who are similar to us may share our worldviews as well as our self-views (i.e., see us the way we see ourselves).
      b. We like people who like us.
   4. Similar others have qualities we like.
      a. People who are similar to us hold beliefs and values that are, from our perspective, "correct."
      b. We tend to think that our personality characteristics are the appropriate ones to have, and so we value others who

      _____

      _____

      _____

IV. Physical Attractiveness
   A. Physical attractiveness is one of the most powerful determinants of interpersonal attraction.
   B. There are some important caveats to remember when reading the research on attractiveness:
      1. _____

_____

_____

2. _____

_____

_____

3. _____

_____

4. _____

_____

_____

C. Impact of Physical Attractiveness
   1. Many studies have found evidence that being judged physically attractive has a wide variety of positive benefits, including:
      a. _____

      _____

      _____

      b. _____

      _____

      _____

      c. _____

      _____

      _____

      d. _____

      _____

      _____

      e. _____

      _____

      _____

   2. The Halo Effect
      a. The halo effect can be defined as

      _____

      _____

      _____

      b. Studies have found that good-looking people are consistently thought to be happier, more intelligent, more popular, and to have better personalities and higher salaries.
      c. Culturally valued characteristics are believed to be held by attractive people.
         (1) Individualistic cultures find attractive people to be

         _____

         _____

    (2) Collectivistic cultures find attractive
       people to be

_____

_____

_____

d. Validity of these beliefs
    (1) Attractive people are not more
       intelligent than unattractive people but
       are (to a small extent) happier, less
       stressed, more satisfied, and perceive
       themselves to have more control over
       their outcomes.
    (2) Goldman and Lewis (1977) found that

_____

_____

_____

_____

e. Creating the truth
    (1) A self-fulfilling prophecy can be
       defined as

_____

_____

_____

_____

    (2) Snyder, Tanke, and Berscheid (1977)
       conducted a study in which they asked
       undergraduate men to have a phone
       conversation with undergraduate
       women. The men were given a
       photograph that they believed was a
       picture of the woman they were talking
       to (it wasn't; the men were actually
       randomly assigned photographs).
      (a) Independent variable:

_____

_____

_____

_____

      (b) Dependent variable: ratings of the
          woman's side of the conversation
          by raters who had not seen the
          photographs.
      (c) Finding: the objective ("blind")
          raters judged the woman who had
          been in the "attractive photo"
          condition as more sociable and
          warmer than the woman in the
          "unattractive photo" condition.
    (3) The women in the attractive photo
       condition were probably more sociable
       because of the effects of the self-

fulfilling prophecy, which would say
that

_____

_____

_____

_____

3. Early Effects of Physical Attractiveness
  a. Attractive infants and children receive more
    positive treatment than do less attractive
    infants and children:
    (1) _____

_____

_____

    (2) _____

_____

_____

    (3) _____

_____

    (4) Dion (1972) found that college students
       rated a transgression committed by a
       seven-year-old as being less serious
       when the child was believed to be
       attractive rather than unattractive.
  b. Very young children also recognize
    different levels of attractiveness.
    (1) Langlois and her colleagues found that
       infants as young as three months
       display a preference (as judged by
       length of gaze) for faces rated by adults
       as relatively attractive.
    (2) By the end of their first year, babies
       will play more contentedly with an
       attractive versus an unattractive adult
       stranger.
4. Gender and the Impact of Physical
  Attractiveness
  a. Attractiveness is more important in
    determining women's life outcomes than
    men's, as in these examples:
    (1) _____

_____

_____

    (2) _____

_____

_____

  b. Fredrickson and Roberts (1997) suggest
    that these external factors encourage
    women to objectify and judge their bodies.

D. Why Does Physical Attractiveness Have Such Impact?

1. Physical appearance is easily and immediately visible.

2. A person may be judged more positively and have more prestige if he or she has an attractive (and, therefore, valued) partner.

   a. Sigall and Landy (1973) had participants enter a waiting room in which two other supposed participants (a man and a woman) were seated.

      (1) Independent variable #1:

_____

_____

_____

      (2) Independent variable #2: whether the woman was described as the man's girlfriend or a stranger to him.

      (3) Dependent variable: the participant's first impressions of the male "participant."

      (4) Finding:

_____

_____

_____

_____

   b. This prestige effect is stronger when judging heterosexual males than females.

   c. The effect impacts perceptions of intelligence, income, or occupation more than impressions of personality, popularity, or happiness.

3. Biology

   a. What do people find attractive?

      (1) There is considerable individual and cultural variability.

      (2) There is also widespread agreement as to which features of the face and body are attractive.

         (a) Within Western culture, people tend to agree as to who is or is not attractive.

         (b) Across other cultures and subcultures, people agree as to which Asian, white, or black faces are attractive.

         (c) Infants seem to agree with adult conceptions of attractiveness, indicating some innate sense of what features are attractive.

   b. What is the basis of agreement?

      (1) Evolutionary psychologists argue that we have evolved to value certain physical characteristics that indicate reproductive fitness.

         (a) Reproductive fitness can be defined as

_____

_____

_____

_____

         (b) An example of reproductive fitness is inheriting a genetic predisposition to like sugar, salt, and fat because our evolutionary ancestors who liked these foods were more likely to live long enough to reproduce successfully.

      (2) We are attracted to features that signify reproductive fitness in others.

         (a) There is evidence that we find anomalous facial features unattractive, as they may have been caused by disease or defect.

         (b) Composite faces generated by computer are judged more attractive than any individual face used in the composite, presumably because the composite face is more "average" and less anomalous.

         (c) Perrett, May, and Yoshikawa (1994) studied the reactions of British and Japanese participants to three different kinds of face composites.

            i. Independent variable:

_____

_____

_____

_____

           ii. Dependent variable: ratings of attractiveness.

           iii. Finding:

_____

_____

_____

_____

         (d) There is evidence that we favor bilateral symmetry, which may indicate health.

           i. Departures from symmetry usually result from *in utero* injuries, and bodily asymmetry correlates with infection and diseases experienced by the mother during pregnancy.

           ii. In a variety of species, bilaterally symmetrical individuals have been shown to have an advantage in sexual competition.

iii. Among humans, facial attractiveness is correlated with symmetry.

E. Sex Differences in Mate Preferences and Perceived Attractiveness

1. Evolutionary psychologists argue that reproductive fitness concerns lead men and women to value different features in a mate.

2. Investment in Offspring

  a. Biologically, women invest more in each child than do men.

    (1) Women are more selective in choosing a mate than are men.

    (2) Men must compete among themselves for access to women; thus, they experience more intrasex competition, which can be defined as

_____

_____

_____

_____

    (3) Typically, men work harder than women for intersex attraction, which can be defined as

_____

_____

_____

_____

    (4) Research has shown that in virtually every society studied, men are ready to have sex more quickly and are less discriminating about their partners than are women.

    (5) Schmitt (2003) found that

_____

_____

_____

_____

  b. Men are attracted to mates who are fertile.

    (1) Men must find fertile women so that they can reproduce successfully.

    (2) Youth (smooth skin, lustrous hair, full lips, and a narrower waist than hips) indirectly signals fertility.

  c. Women need to find mates who can support their hefty investment in the child.

    (1) There is no evolutionary pressure for women to mate with men with youthful characteristics.

    (2) Women seek mates with

_____

_____

_____

_____

  d. Various studies of personal ads in the U.S., Canada, and India support the hypothesis that men will seek youth and beauty in their mates, and women will seek resources and accomplishment in their mates.

  e. Buss's research has supported this hypothesis cross-culturally.

    (1) Kindness and intelligence were rated as most valued in a mate.

    (2) Buss found that men in every culture

_____

_____

_____

_____

    (3) Buss found that women in nearly every culture

_____

_____

_____

_____

3. Critique of Evolutionary Theorizing on Sex Differences in Attraction

  a. Eagly and her colleagues propose an explanation for women's attraction to men with status and material resources that does not involve evolutionary reasoning:

    (1) _____

_____

_____

_____

    (2) Wood and Eagly (2002) reexamined Buss's data and found that the more equality there was between the sexes in a society, the less concerned women were about a mate's earning capacity, but that equality did not influence a man's preference for attractive mates.

  b. Evolutionary reasoning is supported by studies of different species, but within the human species, uniformity can be explained by Eagly's explanation or by Buss's explanation.

  c. Unambiguous support for evolutionary reasoning would come from

_____

_____

_____

_____

    (1) Gangestad and colleagues found that ovulating women demonstrated a greater preference for the scent of attractive men (without seeing the men). This was not the case among nonovulating women.

(2) Women who are ovulating prefer more masculine faces and recognize male faces as being male more quickly than nonovulating women.

V. Theoretical Integration

  A. The Reward Perspective on Interpersonal Attraction

    1. People tend to like those who

      _____

      _____

      _____

      _____

    2. Rewards can be intangible, and they do not need to be immediate or direct.

    3. This perspective can explain the variables featured in this chapter.

      a. Attractive partners are rewarding because

        _____

        _____

        _____

        _____

      b. For heterosexual relationships, evolutionary theory suggests that a particular type of attractive partner offers the ultimate reward of the survival of one's genes.

      c. Similar others are rewarding because

        _____

        _____

        _____

        _____

      d. Proximal others are rewarding indirectly—proximity encourages good behavior, which leads to rewarding and smooth interactions.

    4. This perspective suggests that if you want people to like you, provide them with rewarding interactions.

    5. Some research disputes a strict reward perspective.

      a. Someone who consistently offers praise is sometimes less liked than someone who is initially less positive but later offers more enthusiastic praise.

      b. This contradicts the reward perspective since the person who was always positive gave us more rewards.

    6. The broad perspective is well supported by research.

  B. The Social Exchange Perspective on Interpersonal Attraction

    1. The social exchange perspective encompasses the reward perspective since people seek to maximize their rewards in a relationship.

      a. Social exchange theory can be defined as

        _____

        _____

        _____

        _____

      b. People will seek out rewards in their relationships and will pay costs to obtain them, but they want the rewards to exceed the costs.

    2. Research suggests that, in addition to maximizing one's own satisfaction, people are also concerned about equity.

      a. Equity theory can be defined as

        _____

        _____

        _____

        _____

      b. People see relationships as equitable when

        _____

        _____

        _____

        _____

TESTING YOUR BASIC KNOWLEDGE

After studying the information in the chapter by filling in the outline above, test your basic knowledge with the following multiple-choice test. Answers are provided in the Answer Key section at the end of the chapter. If you find that you have gotten an answer wrong, it is important that you understand why it is wrong (as well as understanding why the correct answer is the better choice). Talk with peers, your tutor, or your professor if you need help.

Multiple-Choice Questions

1. Marissa and Quita were strangers at the beginning of the school year. They were assigned to live in dorm rooms right next door to one another. Now Marissa and Quita are best friends. Based only on this information, which social psychological principle best explains their friendship?
   a. propinquity
   b. similarity
   c. mere exposure
   d. Both a and c could be operating.

2. Jason, Daniel, and Larry live in the same apartment building. Jason lives on the fourth floor, right above Daniel on the third floor and right next to the stairwell. Larry lives next door to Jason and typically takes the elevator at the other end of the hallway. Jason and

Daniel typically take the stairs. Which two of these three men are most likely to become friends?

   a. Jason and Daniel because they have a closer functional distance.
   b. Jason and Larry because they are physically closer to each other.
   c. Daniel and Larry because of the mere exposure effect.
   d. It is impossible to tell from the information given.

3. Anu is an exchange student from India. According to the Nahemow and Lawton (1975) study, under what condition is Anu most likely to become friends with Sally, an American?

   a. Anu and Sally are most likely to become friends if they share similar hobbies.
   b. Anu and Sally are most likely to become friends if they live near each other.
   c. Anu and Sally are unlikely to become friends because they are from different cultures.

4. Ally and Bill chat and get to know each other in the presence of Cathy, who does not take part in the conversation. Later, Cathy and Bill strike up a conversation, which Ally observes but does not participate in. According to the logic of propinquity, which pair is most likely to report liking each other?

   a. Ally and Cathy
   b. Ally and Bill
   c. Bill and Cathy
   d. b and c are equally likely

5. Imagine an experiment in which participants see the following symbols projected one at a time on a screen:

   $$\varphi \iota \varphi \Delta \xi \varphi \theta \varphi \tau \varphi \mu \varphi \pi \varphi \sigma \varphi \varphi \omega \varphi \zeta \varphi$$

   If participants are asked how much they liked each character, which character are they probably going to report liking the most?

   a. φ
   b. ξ
   c. There is no way to tell from the information given.

6. Imagine that, in the above experiment, one of the participants is a member of the Greek organization Delta Zappa Zappa (ΔZZ). This particular participant might favor the symbol Δ. Why?

   a. out of loyalty to his or her organization
   b. because of a greater frequency of exposure to the symbol outside of the study
   c. because of the propinquity effect

7. A researcher conducts a study in which participants are asked to taste test different substances. For half of the participants, these are pleasant tastes, for the other half,

these are unpleasant tastes. In addition, participants are paired with a confederate participant in the tasting cubicles 10 times, 5 times, 2 times, or 1 time. After the taste test, participants are asked to rate their liking for the person they were paired with. According to the research on the mere exposure effect, what are the likely results of this study?

   a. Participants will report more liking the more times they were paired with the confederate, regardless of whether they were tasting pleasant or unpleasant flavors.
   b. Participants will report more liking the more times they were paired with the confederate, but only if they were tasting pleasant flavors.
   c. Participants will report more liking for the confederate in the pleasant flavor condition than in the unpleasant flavor condition, regardless of the number of times they were paired with the confederate.

8. According to the textbook, the marriage between James Carville and Mary Matalin is so surprising because

   a. there is a great functional distance between their two opposing political views.
   b. they do not have similarity on what is often considered a key worldview, politics.
   c. Carville is significantly more physically attractive than Matalin.

9. Similarity does *not* lead to greater liking in which of the following cases?

   a. similarity between two people who intend to marry
   b. similarity between random strangers asked to live together for a specified period of time
   c. similarity breeds liking in both of the above instances

10. The "bogus stranger" paradigm studies generally suggest that

   a. participants give higher likeability ratings to people they are told are similar to them.
   b. participants give higher likeability ratings to people who are similar only after a face-to-face meeting.
   c. participants' likeability ratings are unaffected by reports of similarity.

11. Research suggests that

   a. the complementarity hypothesis is well supported.
   b. the complementarity hypothesis holds true only for personality characteristics.
   c. the complementarity hypothesis has virtually no empirical support.

12. In general, people like to have their beliefs validated by others. This suggests that
    a. those with strong opinions will have a harder time making friends.
    b. people will exhibit more liking for those who hold similar beliefs.
    c. people will exhibit more liking for those who hold complementary beliefs.

13. One of the most powerful determinants of interpersonal attraction is
    a. similarity.
    b. propinquity.
    c. physical attractiveness.

14. Julie is considered by most people to be a very attractive young woman. According to research, she is also likely to be
    a. happier.
    b. more intelligent.
    c. neither of the above.

15. Infants who are shown slides of attractive and unattractive faces
    a. gaze longer at the unattractive faces.
    b. gaze longer at the attractive faces.
    c. do not differentiate between attractive and unattractive faces.

16. Wendy is, regrettably, an unattractive woman as judged by conventional beauty standards. Jim shares her fate in that he is an unattractive man. Which of these two people is more likely to have had a harder time at work (getting turned down for raises and promotions, receiving less respect)?
    a. Wendy
    b. Jim
    c. There is no way to tell from the information given.

17. Nick has been subscribing to an Internet dating site for several months. He has identified two men that he is interested in and, after weeks of exchanging engaging e-mails, has decided to have a phone conversation with each of them to decide whom he likes better. One of the men posted a beautifully composed professional photograph with his profile, and Nick thinks he is very handsome. The other man posted a grainy, low-resolution photo, which leaves Nick with the uncertain impression that he is less handsome. At the end of the conversation, Nick decides the handsome man was more warm and sociable. What psychological effect could have contributed to this result?
    a. self-fulfilling prophecy
    b. complementarity hypothesis
    c. propinquity effect

18. According to the idea of reproductive fitness, our evolutionary ancestors were mostly concerned with
    a. individual survival.
    b. survival of one's genes.
    c. being stronger and more fit than competitors.

19. Physical attractiveness may be such an important factor in interpersonal attraction because
    a. appearance is easily and immediately available for scrutiny.
    b. being with an attractive person confers prestige.
    c. both of the above are true.

20. According to the halo effect, attractive people in individualistic cultures are thought to be _____, while attractive people in collectivistic cultures are thought to be _____.
    a. more intelligent; more emotional.
    b. more dominant; more empathetic.
    c. less altruistic; more altruistic.

21. According to Perrett, May, and Yoshikawa (1994), British and Japanese judges were most attracted to
    a. composites of attractive faces with certain features artificially exaggerated.
    b. composites of attractive faces otherwise unaltered.
    c. composites of a larger number of faces, creating the ideal average.

22. According to evolutionary psychologists, women biologically invest more in any one offspring then men do. Thus, women will seek mates who are _____ and men will seek mates who are _____.
    a. able to provide sufficient material resources; attractive, thus signaling fertility.
    b. attractive, thus signaling good health; intelligent and prepared to care for a child.
    c. attractive, thus signaling fertility; attractive, thus signaling fertility.

23. The evolutionary perspective on gender differences in mate selection
    a. has no empirical support.
    b. has irrefutable empirical support.
    c. has a great deal of empirical support, but much of that support is open to alternative explanations.

24. Wood and Eagly (2002) found that
    a. among societies that had greater gender equality, women placed less importance on a potential mate's earning capacity.
    b. social factors could not account for the gender differences that evolutionary theory predicted.
    c. gender equality resulted in men being less interested in finding a physically attractive mate.

25. Jenny decides to try to quantify the costs and rewards of her relationship with Fred. Jenny believes that she puts in 20 percent effort but gets back 80 percent reward. Further, Jenny believes that Fred puts in 90 percent effort and gets back 30 percent reward. The _____ theory of interpersonal attraction predicts that Jenny will be happy in the relationship, but the _____ theory predicts she might be troubled.
    a. social exchange; equity
    b. equity; social exchange
    c. similarity; propinquity

Essay Questions

After you have mastered the multiple-choice questions, try testing your basic understanding by thoroughly answering each of the broad essay questions below. Because it is critical that you think through this information on your own, we have not provided any answers to these questions. Your learning and retention of this material will be greatly enhanced if you do one or more of the following to check your answers: carefully review the textbook information; compare your responses to your class lecture notes; talk over your answers with a peer; ask your professor to review your answers or review any information that is unclear to you.

1. In your own words, define propinquity, describe one empirical study that supports its influence, and explain why it exerts such a powerful influence on interpersonal attraction.

2. Describe one empirical study that suggests that similarity influences interpersonal attraction, and discuss reasons why similarity breeds liking.

3. Provide several examples of empirical evidence that support the notion that physical attractiveness is an important predictor of interpersonal attraction. What is the evolutionary argument for why men and women find different traits attractive? To what extent does the evidence support this argument?

4. Compare and contrast reward theory, social exchange theory, and equity theory.

TESTING YOUR IN-DEPTH UNDERSTANDING

Test your in-depth understanding of the material by working through the Critical Thinking Exercises provided at the end of each textbook chapter. To maximize this learning opportunity, work together with a tutor, study group, or your professor. Alternatively, write down your thoughts and responses.

Guided questions for one of the exercises are provided below. While there are multiple ways to answer these questions, short answers are given in the Answer Key at the end of the chapter. Note that the valuable part of this exercise is not simply knowing the answer but working with the material to come up with the answer.

Guided Questions for Critical Thinking Exercise #2

In the run-up to the 2004 U.S. presidential election, many households put up "Bush Must Go" signs in their front yards. The motive, clearly, was to influence undecided voters to vote against the incumbent president, George W. Bush. Do any of the ideas presented in this chapter give one reason to believe that the effort might have backfired, and actually *increased* support for Bush?

1. First, review the major processes you learned about in the chapter (as listed below), and consider why the yard signs may have succeeded in their goal of influencing undecided voters.
    a. Similar others validate our beliefs.
    b. Similarity facilitates smooth interactions.
    c. Similar others have qualities we like.
    d. The halo effect and physically attractive people may influence decisions.
    e. Self-fulfilling prophecies can affect decisions.

2. Review the research and major findings on mere exposure.

3. How might mere exposure predict the failure of the yard sign tactic?

4. Pretend you are a social psychologist, and design a study with two variables to test your hypothesis about mere exposure. Describe your independent variable(s), and dependent variable(s) and explain what findings you would predict based on your answer to #3.

Enhance your understanding of the chapter by thinking about and doing the remaining two Critical Thinking Exercises. Discuss your answers with your peers, study group, tutor, or professor.

Critical Thinking Exercise #1

Most (but by no means all) evolutionary psychologists are male. How do you think an evolutionary approach to attraction might be different if it were taken up by many more female researchers? What predictions might we see advanced and tested that are different from those we see now? Are there any "twists" on currently advanced claims that might be made?

Critical Thinking Exercise #3

Evolutionary psychology is the idea that behavioral predispositions, in the same way as anatomy and physiology, are determined by genes and passed on from generation to generation. This idea has been derided by some as "just so" theorizing because it advocates provide evolutionary explanations that fit (just like Rudyard Kipling's "just so" stories) the behavior patterns we observe "just so." Can you think of any examples for which this criticism seems valid? Can you think of any for which it is invalid?

SOCIAL PSYCHOLOGY IN THE POPULAR MEDIA

You might be interested in the following popular media references, each of which relates in some way to information in this chapter.

Books

Carville, James, & Matalin, Mary (1994). *All's Fair: Love, War, and Running for President.* New York: Random House. These political strategists for opposing sides of the 1992 presidential campaign married each other after the election. In their book, they discuss the ups and downs of the battle over the presidency. The book is more about the campaign than their romance, but you can get an idea of the personalities of these two dynamic individuals.

Wolf, Naomi (1991; reissued in paperback 2002). *The Beauty Myth: How Images of Beauty Are Used Against Women.* New York: William Morrow. Wolf discusses the social pressures women face to conform to an unattainable standard of beauty

Song

Jill Sobule (1994). "Supermodel." Featured in the 1995 movie *Clueless,* the song pokes fun at a teenage girl whose main ambition is to become a skinny supermodel.

Films

The Killing Us Softly Series (1979, 1987, 2000). A series of short videos by Jean Kilbourne which discuss in compelling and graphic detail the ways in which women's bodies are portrayed in advertising and the negative impact these portrayals have on women. Your college or university library is likely to have one or more of these videos available.

Closer (2004; directed by Mike Nichols; starring Julia Roberts, Jude Law, Clive Owen, Natalie Portman). A cynical tale of initial attraction, dysfunctional relationships, the power of women versus men in relationships, and betrayal. Prepare to leave the film debating who did what, why, and who (if anyone) is the "good guy" in this story. Rated R for strong language and cyber-sex.

Web Sites

The Human Face—http://tlc.discovery.com/convergence/humanface/humanface.html. Web site to accompany The Learning Channel's program "The Human Face with John Cleese." Information and interesting activities, including a timeline of what has been considered beautiful through the ages.

Sexual Orientation: Science, Policy, and Education—http://psychology.ucdavis.edu/rainbow/index.html. From the Web site: "This site features work by Dr. Gregory Herek, an internationally recognized authority on sexual prejudice (also called homophobia), hate crimes, and AIDS stigma. It provides factual information to promote the use of scientific knowledge for education and enlightened public policy related to sexual orientation and HIV/AIDS." This Web site complements the chapter's focus on heterosexual attraction and relationships.

ANSWER KEY

Annotated Chapter Outline

I. Studying Attraction
   A. The research that will be presented will mostly confirm our intuitions.
   B. Research will also yield some surprises, especially regarding the strength with which certain variables influence attraction.

II. Propinquity
   A. Propinquity can be defined as physical proximity.
   B. Studies of Propinquity and Attraction
      1. Festinger, Schachter, and Back (1950) studied the friendship patterns in a married student housing project in which incoming students were randomly assigned to their residences.
         a. A sociometric survey can be defined as a survey that attempts to measure the interpersonal relationships in a group of people.
         b. The Festinger study found propinquity effects at Westgate West:
            (1) Two-thirds of people listed as friends in the survey lived in the same building as the respondent.

(2) Forty-one percent of those living next door to one another listed each other as friends, compared to 10 percent of those living at opposite ends of the building.

2. Functional distance can be defined as an architectural layout's propensity to encourage or inhibit certain activities, like contact between people.
   a. Residents who lived near the stairs on the bottom floor had more chance encounters with upstairs neighbors than did residents of middle apartments.
   b. Festinger found that residents who were functionally closer to one another (e.g., met in the stairwells) were much more likely to become friends than those who were physically close but functionally more distant.

3. Segal (1974) studied forty-five police academy trainees assigned to quarters alphabetically.
   a. Segal found that those who roomed closer to each other were more likely to become friends, despite the intense and close contact among all the trainees.
   b. Minor differences in propinquity led to major differences in friendships.
   c. The correlation between location and friendship was remarkably high: .90.

4. Similarity matters, too, but it does not override propinquity.
   a. Nahemow and Lawton (1975) studied friendships in an age- and race-diverse housing project.
   b. They found that both proximity and similarity had strong effects on friendships:
      (1) Eighty-eight percent of best friends lived in the same building, and nearly 50 percent lived on the same floor.
      (2) Seventy percent of friendships between people of different ages or races involved people who lived on the same floor as one another, compared to 40 percent of same-race or same-age friendships.

C. Explanations of Propinquity Effects
   1. Availability and Propinquity
      a. Proximity allows for the passive and frequent contacts necessary to develop a dialogue and, subsequently, friendship.
      b. Proximity not only makes friendship possible; it also encourages it.
   2. The Effect of Anticipating Interaction
      a. Darley and Berscheid (1967) found that participants, after reading personality descriptions, indicated that they liked the person they thought they were going to meet more than the person they did not think they were going to meet.
         (1) Counterbalancing can be defined as a methodological procedure whereby an investigator makes sure that any extraneous variable (for example, a stimulus person's name) that might influence the dependent measure (for example, liking) is distributed equally often across the different levels of the independent variable (for example, the stimulus person a participant expects to meet and the stimulus person the participant does not expect to meet).
         (2) The initial positive stance toward the other person creates a positive cycle in which the favorable expectations of one partner are reinforced by the positive behavior of the other partner.
         (3) When we live near another person, we make an effort to have our intitial encounter with him or her go well.
      b. Insko and Wilson (1977) crafted a study in which participants A and C interacted with participant B, but not with each other.
         (1) Insko and Wilson found that Participants A and C rated liking each other less than they liked Participant B.
         (2) The results supported the idea that interactions are rewarding.
   3. The Mere Exposure Effect
      a. The mere exposure effect can be defined as the finding that repeated exposure to a stimulus (for example, an object or person) leads to greater liking of the stimulus.
      b. There is a great deal of *correlational* evidence supporting the idea that familiarity with stimuli breeds liking.
         (1) Commonly mentioned flowers, trees, fruits, vegetables, countries, and cities are liked more than uncommon ones.
         (2) An alternative explanation is that the causality may run the other way—people may mention things they like more often than things they don't like.
         (3) Empirical evidence supports the mere exposure direction of causality.
            (a) People prefer more common letters of the alphabet.

(b) People prefer letters that are found in their names.
c. There is also sufficient *experimental* evidence for mere exposure.
  (1) Zajonc (1968) exposed participants to unfamiliar Turkish words.
    (a) Independent variable: the number of times the participant saw each word.
    (b) Dependent variable: participants' guesses as to whether the word meant something positive or something negative.
    (c) Findings: the more times participants saw the words, the more likely they were to guess that the word referred to something positive.
  (2) Zajonc also replicated the experiment with Chinese pictographs and college yearbook photos as stimuli to see how greater exposure affected liking.
  (3) An alternative explanation is that repeated exposure may matter because of repeated associations with the pleasant experimental surroundings.
    (a) Saegert, Swap, and Zajonc (1973) had participants do a study that was described as a taste test.
      i. Independent variable #1: the number of times a participant shared a cubicle with another participant.
      ii. Independent variable #2: whether the participant was tasting something pleasant or unpleasant.
      iii. Dependent variable: liking for the other participants.
      iv. Findings: regardless of whether encountered while tasting pleasant or unpleasant stimuli, participants who were encountered more often were liked more.
  (4) Mita, Dermer, and Knight (1977) found that people prefer photographs depicting their mirror image, while their friends prefer their true image.
  (5) Cross, Halcomb, and Matter (1967) used albino rats and music in their study of the mere exposure effect.
    (a) Independent variable: exposure to the music of either Mozart or Schoenberg.
    (b) Dependent variable: which side of the cage the rats stepped on (activating either Mozart's music or Schoenberg's music).
    (c) Findings: the Mozart-exposed rats spent more time on the Mozart side of the cage, the Schoenberg-exposed rats spent more time on the Schoenberg side of the cage.
d. What explains mere exposure?
  (1) Zajonc hypothesized that every encounter with a stimulus that does not result in an aversive consequence classically conditions us to favor that stimulus over other stimuli.
  (2) Repeated exposure and absence of aversive consequences leads to positive associations; mere repeated exposure leads to attraction because it is reinforcing.

III. Similarity
  A. Similarity of interests, beliefs, values, worldviews, background, ethnicity, religion predicts liking.
  B. Studies of Similarity and Attraction
    1. Whyte (1956) conducted a classic study showing that proximity predicted inclusion in social events in a neighborhood, but so did similarity.
    2. Studies like that of Burgess and Wallin (1953) have found that people who intend to marry one another are similar on a variety of dimensions.
      a. Members of engaged couples were significantly more similar than members of random couples.
      b. Similarity was strongest for demographic and physical characteristics and present but weaker for personality variables.
    3. Other studies on the link between similarity and attraction have examined strangers who were thrown together for an extended period of time.
      a. Newcomb (1956, 1961) offered transfer students free rent for one year if they lived in a house with strangers and filled out weekly questionnaires.
      b. Finding: liking was predicted by similarity, particularly similarity in attitudes about other housemates.
    4. Some experimental studies supporting the theory that people are more attracted to those whom they believe to be similar use the "bogus stranger" paradigm, in which participants are given responses to attitude or personality

questionnaires supposedly filled out by another participant.

   a. Independent variable: the extent to which the questionnaire depicts this (bogus) other person as similar to the participant.

   b. Dependent variable: how much the participant reports liking the other person.

   c. Finding: people report more liking for those who are more similar.

C. But Don't "Opposites Attract"?

  1. Complementarity can be defined as the tendency for people to seek out others with characteristics that are different from and that complement their own.

  2. Logically, we would only expect complementarity when the differences between the two people fulfill one another's needs (rather than creating conflict).

  3. Studies do not support complementarity, even in the above-mentioned cases.

D. Why Does Similarity Promote Attraction?

  1. Similar others validate our beliefs and orientations.

   a. Similar others reinforce rather than challenge our beliefs, outlooks, ideologies, and personal strivings.

   b. Clore and Gormly (1974) found that participants liked the experimental assistant who agreed with their views more than the one who disagreed, and that this attraction (and dislike) was predicted by physiological arousal—more arousal meant more like or dislike.

  2. Similarity facilitates smooth interactions.

   a. Those who share similar views and beliefs and orientations with us enable us to interact without conflict over our views.

   b. Davis (1981) found that similarity fostered liking, especially for those who held similar attitudes about topics thought to be important to everyday interaction.

  3. We expect similar others to like us.

   a. People who are similar to us may also share our self-views (i.e., see us the way we see ourselves).

   b. We like people who like us.

  4. Similar others have qualities we like.

   a. People who are similar to us hold beliefs and values that are, from our perspective, "correct."

   b. We tend to think that our personality characteristics are the appropriate ones to have, and so we value others who have similar qualities.

IV. Physical Attractiveness

A. Physical attractiveness is one of the most powerful determinants of interpersonal attraction.

B. There are some important caveats to remember when reading the research on attractiveness:

  1. There is considerable individual variability in what people judge to be attractive.

  2. We like those who are attractive, but we also find those we like to be attractive.

  3. Happy couples idealize one another's physical attractiveness.

  4. A person's physical attractiveness varies across the life span.

C. Impact of Physical Attractiveness

  1. Many studies have found evidence that being judged physically attractive has a wide variety of positive benefits, including:

   a. Physically attractive people are more popular with the opposite sex.

   b. Essays are judged more favorably.

   c. Salary is higher.

   d. Men are more likely to come to the aid of a good-looking woman.

   e. Attractive defendants are more likely to be given lighter sentences.

  2. The Halo Effect

   a. The halo effect can be defined as the common belief—accurate or not—that attractive individuals possess a host of positive qualities beyond their physical appearance.

   b. Studies have found that good-looking people are consistently thought to be happier, more intelligent, more popular, and to have better personalities and higher salaries.

   c. Culturally valued characteristics are believed to be held by attractive people.

    (1) Individualistic cultures find attractive people to be dominant and assertive.

    (2) Collectivistic cultures find attractive people to be generous, sensitive, and empathetic.

   d. Validity of these beliefs

    (1) Attractive people are not more intelligent than unattractive people but are (to a small extent) happier, less stressed, more satisfied, and perceive themselves to have more control over their outcomes.

    (2) Goldman and Lewis (1977) found that participants rated unseen conversation partners as more socially skilled when experimenters had rated those partners as attractive (rather than less attractive).

e. Creating the truth
   (1) A self-fulfilling prophecy can be defined as the tendency for people to act in ways that elicit confirmation of a belief that they hold.
   (2) Snyder, Tanke, and Berscheid (1977) conducted a study in which they asked undergraduate men to have a phone conversation with undergraduate women. The men were given a photograph that they believed was a picture of the woman they were talking to (it wasn't; the men were actually randomly assigned photographs).
       (a) Independent variable: the attractiveness of the woman in the photograph (attractive or unattractive as rated by other participants in a previous pilot study).
       (b) Dependent variable: ratings of the woman's side of the conversation by raters who had not seen the photographs.
       (c) Finding: the objective ("blind") raters judged the woman who had been in the "attractive photo" condition as more sociable and warmer than the woman in the "unattractive photo" condition.
   (3) The women in the attractive photo condition were probably more sociable because of the effects of the self-fulfilling prophecy, which would say that the men elicited these reactions from the women, presumably by their belief that the person they were talking to was attractive (and, as indicated by the halo effect, more sociable). The men created confirming evidence for their preconceptions by virtue of treating the women in the attractive condition more warmly.
3. Early Effects of Physical Attractiveness
   a. Attractive infants and children receive more positive treatment than do less attractive infants and children:
      (1) Attractive newborns receive more affection and attention from their mothers than do less attractive infants.
      (2) Attractive nursery school children are more popular with their peers than are unattractive children.
      (3) Elementary school teachers assume attractive children are more intelligent and better behaved than less attractive children.
      (4) Dion (1972) found that college students rated a transgression committed by a seven-year-old as being less serious when the child was believed to be attractive rather than unattractive.
   b. Very young children also recognize different levels of attractiveness.
      (1) Langlois and her colleagues found that infants as young as three months display a preference (as judged by length of gaze) for faces rated by adults as relatively attractive.
      (2) By the end of their first year, babies will play more contentedly with an attractive versus an unattractive adult stranger.
4. Gender and the Impact of Physical Attractiveness
   a. Attractiveness is more important in determining women's life outcomes than men's, as in these examples:
      (1) Overweight girls are less likely to be accepted to college than thin peers.
      (2) Women deemed unattractive by coworkers experience more negative outcomes than unattractive men.
   b. Fredrickson and Roberts (1997) suggest that these external factors encourage women to objectify and judge their bodies.
D. Why Does Physical Attractiveness Have Such Impact?
   1. Physical appearance is easily and immediately visible.
   2. A person may be judged more positively and have more prestige if he or she has an attractive (and, therefore, valued) partner.
      a. Sigall and Landy (1973) had participants enter a waiting room in which two other supposed participants (a man and a woman) were seated.
         (1) Independent variable #1: the attractiveness of the woman (as manipulated by clothing, hair, and makeup).
         (2) Independent variable #2: whether the woman was described as the man's girlfriend or a stranger to him.
         (3) Dependent variable: the participant's first impressions of the male "participant."

(4) Finding: participants found the confederate to be more likable, friendly, and confident when his "girlfriend" was attractive versus unattractive. The woman's attractiveness had no effect when she was thought to be a stranger.

b. This prestige effect is stronger when judging heterosexual males than females.

c. The effect impacts perceptions of intelligence, income, or occupation more than impressions of personality, popularity, or happiness.

3. Biology

a. What do people find attractive?

(1) There is considerable individual and cultural variability.

(2) There is also widespread agreement as to which features of the face and body are attractive.

(a) Within Western culture, people tend to agree as to who is or is not attractive.

(b) Across other cultures and subcultures, people agree as to which Asian, white, or black faces are attractive.

(c) Infants seem to agree with adult conceptions of attractiveness, indicating some innate sense of what features are attractive.

b. What is the basis of agreement?

(1) Evolutionary psychologists argue that we have evolved to value certain physical characteristics that indicate reproductive fitness.

(a) Reproductive fitness can be defined as the capacity to get one's genes passed on to subsequent generations.

(b) An example of reproductive fitness is inheriting a genetic predisposition to like sugar, salt, and fat because our evolutionary ancestors who liked these foods were more likely to live long enough to reproduce successfully.

(2) We are attracted to features that signify reproductive fitness in others.

(a) There is evidence that we find anomalous facial features unattractive, as they may have been caused by disease or defect.

(b) Composite faces generated by computer are judged more attractive than any individual face used in the composite, presumably because the composite face is more "average" and less anomalous.

(c) Perrett, May, and Yoshikawa (1994) studied the reactions of British and Japanese participants to three different kinds of face composites.

i. Independent variable: whether the faces shown were average composites (created by averaging all sixty faces), attractive composites (created by averaging only the fifteen most attractive faces), or attractive +50 percent composites (created by calculating the differences for each feature—e.g., jaw, eyebrows, eyes, lips—between the average and attractive composites and then exaggerating the differences by 50 percent).

ii. Dependent variable: ratings of attractiveness.

iii. Finding: participants rated the attractive +50 percent composite as most attractive, the attractive composite as the next most attractive, and the average composite as least attractive.

(d) There is evidence that we favor bilateral symmetry, which may indicate health.

i. Departures from symmetry usually result from *in utero* injuries, and bodily asymmetry correlates with infection and diseases experienced by the mother during pregnancy.

ii. In a variety of species, bilaterally symmetrical individuals have been shown to have an advantage in sexual competition.

iii. Among humans, facial attractiveness is correlated with symmetry.

E. Sex Differences in Mate Preferences and Perceived Attractiveness

1. Evolutionary psychologists argue that reproductive fitness concerns lead men and women to value different features in a mate.

2. Investment in Offspring

a. Biologically, women invest more in each child than do men.

(1) Women are more selective in choosing a mate than are men.

(2) Men must compete among themselves for access to women; thus, they experience more intrasex competition, which can be defined as direct competition among two or more males or among two or more females for access to members of the opposite sex.

(3) Typically, men work harder than women for intersex attraction, which can be defined as the interest in and attraction toward a member of one sex on the part of a member of the opposite sex.

(4) Research has shown that in virtually every society studied, men are ready to have sex more quickly and are less discriminating about their partners than are women.

(5) Schmitt (2003) found that, across cultures all over the world, men expressed a desire for a greater number of sexual partners than did women.

b. Men are attracted to mates who are fertile.

(1) Men must find fertile women so that they can reproduce successfully.

(2) Youth (smooth skin, lustrous hair, full lips, and a narrower waist than hips) indirectly signals fertility.

c. Women need to find mates who can support their hefty investment in the child.

(1) There is no evolutionary pressure for women to mate with men with youthful characteristics.

(2) Women seek mates with material resources, strength, industriousness, and/or social status.

d. Various studies of personal ads in the U.S., Canada, and India support the hypothesis that men will seek youth and beauty in their mates, and women will seek resources and accomplishment in their mates.

e. Buss's research has supported this hypothesis cross-culturally.

(1) Kindness and intelligence were rated as most valued in a mate.

(2) Buss found that men in every culture rated physical attractiveness as being more important than did women and wanted younger partners.

(3) Buss found that women in nearly every culture rated good financial prospects and social status as being more important than did men and wanted older partners.

3. Critique of Evolutionary Theorizing on Sex Differences in Attraction

a. Eagly and her colleagues propose an explanation for women's attraction to men with status and material resources that does not involve evolutionary reasoning:

(1) Men may obtain and control material resources because they have greater physical size and do not suffer the "handicaps" imposed by pregnancy and nursing, whereas women do and may be economically vulnerable and hence in need of the resources men provide.

(2) Wood and Eagly (2002) reexamined Buss's data and found that the more equality there was between the sexes in a society, the less concerned women were about a mate's earning capacity, but that equality did not influence a man's preference for attractive mates.

b. Evolutionary reasoning is supported by studies of different species, but within the human species, uniformity can be explained by Eagly's explanation or by Buss's explanation.

c. Unambiguous support for evolutionary reasoning would come from any finding that can *only* be explained or predicted by invoking evolutionary theory.

(1) Gangestad and colleagues found that ovulating women demonstrated a greater preference for the scent of attractive men (without seeing the men). This was not the case among nonovulating women.

(2) Women who are ovulating prefer more masculine faces and recognize male faces as being male more quickly than nonovulating women.

V. Theoretical Integration

A. The Reward Perspective on Interpersonal Attraction

1. People tend to like those who provide rewards.

2. Rewards can be intangible, and they do not need to be immediate or direct.
3. This perspective can explain the variables featured in this chapter.
   a. Attractive partners are rewarding because of the direct aesthetic pleasure and the prestige gained.
   b. For heterosexual relationships, evolutionary theory suggests that a particular type of attractive partner offers the ultimate reward of the survival of one's genes.
   c. Similar others are rewarding because they validate our views, they like us, and they help interactions go smoothly.
   d. Proximal others are rewarding indirectly— proximity encourages good behavior, which leads to rewarding and smooth interactions.
4. This perspective suggests that if you want people to like you, provide them with rewarding interactions.
5. Some research disputes a strict reward perspective.
   a. Someone who consistently offers praise is sometimes less liked than someone who is initially less positive but later offers more enthusiastic praise.
   b. This contradicts the reward perspective since the person who was always positive gave us more rewards.
6. The broad perspective is well supported by research.

B. The Social Exchange Perspective on Interpersonal Attraction
   1. The social exchange perspective encompasses the reward perspective since people seek to maximize their rewards in a relationship.
      a. Social exchange theory can be defined as a theory based on the fact that there are costs and rewards in all relationships, and that how people feel about a relationship depends on their assessments of its costs and rewards, and the costs and rewards available to them in other relationships.
      b. People will seek out rewards in their relationships and pay costs to obtain them, but want the rewards to exceed the costs.
   2. Research suggests that, in addition to maximizing one's own satisfaction, people are also concerned about equity.
      a. Equity theory can be defined as a theory that maintains that people are motivated to pursue fairness, or equity, in their relationships.
      b. People see relationships as equitable when rewards and costs are shared roughly equally among individuals.

Testing Your Basic Knowledge

ANSWERS TO MULTIPLE-CHOICE QUESTIONS

1.	d	14.	a
2.	a	15.	b
3.	b	16.	a
4.	d	17.	a
5.	a	18.	b
6.	b	19.	c
7.	a	20.	b
8.	b	21.	a
9.	c	22.	a
10.	a	23.	c
11.	c	24.	a
12.	b	25.	a
13.	c		

Testing Your In-Depth Understanding

EXAMPLE ANSWERS TO THE GUIDED QUESTIONS FOR CRITICAL THINKING EXERCISE #2

1. First review the major processes you learned about in the chapter, and consider why the yard signs may have succeeded in their goal of influencing undecided voters.
   a. Similar others validate our beliefs—if a person whom I knew to be similar to me put up an anti-Bush yard sign and I was undecided, I might be swayed to also be anti-Bush to maintain our similarity.
   b. Similarity facilitates smooth interactions—I might also be swayed to be anti-Bush to maintain smooth interactions with this person.
   c. Similar others have qualities we like—I also might be swayed to be anti-Bush because this similar person has so many other qualities I like, and my liking for the person might encourage a liking for his or her views of Bush.
   d. The halo effect and physically attractive people may influence decisions—if the person putting up the yard sign is physically attractive, I might think that he or she is smart and knowledgeable about Bush (this is the reasoning behind many celebrity endorsements).
   e. Self-fulfilling prophecies can affect decisions— imagine that the person putting up the sign starts talking to me and assumes (as people tend to do) that I agree with his or her view of Bush. This person may encourage me to share ways in which I don't like Bush and might solicit critical views of Bush. After generating such arguments all by myself, I might come to believe (even temporarily) that I really don't like Bush or want to elect him.

2. Review the research and major findings on mere exposure. All of the studies on mere exposure suggest that the more frequently I come in contact with a stimulus, the more I will like that stimulus—from Turkish words to Chinese pictographs to photographs of people's faces. Frequency of contact breeds liking.

3. How might mere exposure predict the failure of the yard sign tactic? Even though the yard signs are against Bush, seeing his name frequently may make me like his name more, and that liking may bleed over into general favorable feelings toward the candidate himself. Just like in the "taste-test" study, where it didn't matter if they were tasting positive or negative flavors, whether the Bush signs are positive or negative won't matter.

4. Pretend you are a social psychologist and design a study with two independent variables to test your hypothesis about mere exposure: (1) positive versus negative messages about Bush; and (2) frequency of exposure to those messages. I could design a lab study in which participants are shown a series of slides. I could expose them to either the positive or negative Bush slides 1, 2, 5, 10 or 25 times—mixed in with other slides. The dependent variable could be their favorability ratings toward Bush. A problem with the study is that the participants probably had feelings about Bush before the study even started. While randomly assigning them to one of the conditions (positive or negative by frequency) should average out those different preconceptions, a better way would be to avoid that messiness in the data altogether. Thus, I might want to choose a neutral stimulus (e.g., a fake candidate) instead of Bush. According to my answer in #3, I would predict that the people who had the most exposure to the candidate's name (regardless of whether it was in a positive or negative context) would have the most favorable ratings of the candidate.

CHAPTER 4 | Relationships

The goal of this chapter is to explain why relationships are essential to psychological well-being, and how relationships influence our thoughts and feelings. The information in the chapter will also describe some of the basic ways researchers have characterized different kinds of relationships and different attitudes toward relationships. Finally, the chapter includes social psychological research investigating factors that seem to make some romantic relationships more satisfying than others.

ANNOTATED CHAPTER OUTLINE

After first reading through the chapter quickly, create a comprehensive framework for the information in the chapter by reading the outline below and filling in the missing information. Instead of simply re-copying information from the textbook, try to use your own words wherever possible; you can check your answers against the completed outline in the Answer Key section at the end of the chapter.

I. Characterizing Relationships
   A. Interpersonal relationships are attachments in which bonds of family or friendship or love or respect or hierarchy tie together two or more individuals over an extended period of time.
   B. Many social psychological studies of relationships are not true experiments, but rather look at the dynamics of existing relationships.
      1. Since many of the studies are not experiments, the methodological problem of self-selection occurs.
         a. When participants (in some manner of speaking) select their own condition, there is not random assignment.
         b. Self-selection leaves open a causality

problem in that the participants may possess multiple characteristics that led them to be in their condition.
      2. A study of feral children exemplified the self-selection problem and showed two possible causes of the children's abnormal development:
         a. _____
         _____
         _____

         b. _____
         _____
         _____
         _____
   C. Harlow (1959) conducted experimental research with baby rhesus monkeys.
      1. Harlow found that monkeys raised alone preferred to spend time with a terry-cloth covered "mother" figure that more closely resembled a real monkey mother rather than a "wire mother," even though the wire mother provided food.
      2. The monkeys raised in isolation behaved
         _____
         _____
         _____

   D. A natural experiment with elephants found that young elephants also need social interaction to function normally.
      1. A natural experiment may be defined as
         _____
         _____
         _____
         _____

2. Elephants who have lost their parents and
grown up alone

_____

_____

_____

_____

II. The Importance of Relationships
A. The Need to Belong
   1. Baumeister and Leary (1995) proposed that
   humans have an innate need to be part of
   healthy relationships.
   2. Baumeister and Leary suggested five criteria
   for judging the legitimacy of this claim. These
   criteria and research evidence supporting them
   are:
   a. _____

   _____

   _____

   _____

   b. _____

   _____

   _____

   _____

   c. _____

   _____

   _____

   _____

   d. Satiable: if this is a true need, it should
   diminish as it is satisfied.
      (1) In Western European cultures, college-
      age students seem to limit their most
      intimate relationships to about six
      people, suggesting that we stop seeking
      relationships when we have enough to
      satisfy our need to belong.
      (2.) Observational studies in prisons
      suggest that prisoners form family-like
      bonds with other inmates to replace the
      familial bonds lost through separation.
   e. _____

   _____

   _____

   _____

B. Relationships and the Sense of Self
   1. Andersen and Chen's relational self theory
   suggests that the relational self is an important
   part of one's self-concept.
   a. The relational self can be defined as

   _____

   _____

   _____

   b. We have different relational selves for
   different relationships (e.g., one may feel a

certain way about the self and believe
certain things about the self around one's
mother, and a different way around a best
friend).
   c. Andersen and Chen's relational self theory
   argues that meeting people who remind us
   of significant others (past or present) will
   activate the associated relational self.
   d. Andersen and her colleagues developed an
   experimental paradigm to assess how past
   relationships affect our current beliefs,
   thoughts, and interactions.
      (1) Pre-test:

      _____

      _____

      _____

      (2) Experimental session:

      _____

      _____

      _____

      (3) Findings from studies using this
      general setup:
         (a) Participants were asked to describe
         their own personality when they
         were with their significant other;
         results confirmed that they gave
         similar descriptions of how they
         anticipated they would act with a
         new person who was similar to
         their significant other.
         (b) Participants who read about
         someone who resembled a positive
         significant other displayed more
         positive facial expression than
         those reading about someone
         resembling a negative significant
         other.
         (c) Berk and Andersen (2000) found
         that

         _____

         _____

         _____

         _____

C. Relationships and Social Cognition
   1. Relationships as Organizing Categories
   a. In typical cognitive functioning, people
   organize information in their physical and
   social worlds into categories (e.g., physical,
   cultural, or moral categories).
   b. Sedikides et al. (1993) tested the claim that
   relationships can also serve as a kind of
   category.

(1) Participants read five pieces of information about each of four women and four men who were described as being members of married couples.

(2) Independent variable:

_____

_____

_____

(3) Dependent variables: various aspects of how participants remembered information about the people.

(4) Findings:

_____

_____

_____

_____

2. Construing Close Others as We Construe Ourselves
   a. We tend to have the same processing strategies and biases toward close others as we do toward ourselves (e.g., for ourselves and close others we accept credit for success and blame failure on external forces).
   b. The self-expansion account of relationships holds that

   _____

   _____

   _____

   _____

   c. Aron et al. (1991) tested this theory.
      (1) Married couples rated ninety traits on how accurately the trait described the self and the spouse.
      (2) Participants saw the traits on a computer screen and were asked to make decisions about their own self-concept, pressing a "like me" or "not like me" button as quickly as possible.
      (3) Findings:

      _____

      _____

      _____

      (4) Faster responses indicate that the trait is more woven into one's self-concept; thus, traits possessed by a partner are more part of the self-concept.
3. Sharing Social Construals with Close Others
   a. Transactive memory can be defined as

   _____

   _____

   _____

b. Having such knowledge allows a person to attend to different information, leading to a greater awareness of the situation as a whole once the two sets of information are combined.
c. Wegner and his colleagues (1991) conducted a study on transactive memory.
   (1) Setup:

   _____

   _____

   _____

   _____

   (2) Findings:

   _____

   _____

   _____

   _____

D. Relationships and Affective Life
   1. Relationships can intensify emotions.
   2. Relationships affect our moods and emotional well-being.
      a. Experience-sampling studies can be defined as

      _____

      _____

      _____

      b. Such studies find that people experience more positive emotions around other people (especially when they are having intimate interactions) compared to when they are alone.
      c. Research on loneliness suggests that anxiety and depression are higher in people who also report being lonely. But self-selection into the "lonely" category may create a causality problem because

      _____

      _____

      _____

      _____

      d. Experimental research also suggests that relationships powerfully influence how we feel, as demonstrated in a classic study by Baldwin and his colleagues (1990) that examined the effect of important authority figures' approval or disapproval on participants' self-evaluations.
         (1) Setup: University of Michigan psychology graduate students were asked to write down three of their latest research study ideas and then were subliminally presented with one of two photos.

(2) Independent variable:

_____

_____

_____

_____

(3) Dependent variable:

_____

_____

_____

_____

(4) Finding: students evaluated their research ideas more harshly when primed with the photo of the stern authority figure compared with when they were primed with the photo of the friendly face.

III. The Origins of How We Relate to Others

A. Attachment Theory

1. Bowlby's attachment theory argues that early attachments with parents shape our relationships for the remainder of our lives.

a. Human infants, having few innate survival skills at birth, survive by forming strong bonds with caregivers.

(1) Infants smile, coo, have large eyes and other features that evoke filial love.

(2) Parents love and have strong protective feelings toward their offspring.

b. A child's confidence in the security a parent provides is influenced by how responsive the parent is to the child's needs.

c. The attachments children develop become their first working models of relationships, which can be defined as

_____

_____

_____

_____

2. Mary Ainsworth classified attachment patterns of infants according to how the children responded to separations and reunions with their caregivers.

a. Ainsworth developed an experimental paradigm known as the strange situation, which can be defined as

_____

_____

_____

_____

b. Secure patterns: infants with responsive caregivers were comfortable moving away from the caregiver to explore the novel environment (checking back now and again).

c. Insecure patterns: infants with nonresponsive or inappropriately responsive caregivers cried or were angry in novel environments, despite the presence of the caregiver, and often rejected attention even when it was offered.

B. Attachment Styles

1. Adult attachment styles are assessed via self-report measures.

2. Researchers have concentrated on three specific styles: secure, avoidant, and anxious attachment.

a. Secure attachment style can be defined as

_____

_____

_____

_____

b. Avoidant attachment style can be defined as

_____

_____

_____

_____

c. Anxious attachment style can be defined as

_____

_____

_____

_____

3. A central claim of attachment theory is that attachment styles are typically stable across the life span. There is research evidence supporting this claim:

a. _____

_____

_____

_____

b. _____

_____

_____

_____

c. Anxiously attached persons were more likely to report having experienced parental divorce, death, or abuse during childhood.

d. In a forty-year longitudinal study, women who classified themselves as avoidant at age fifty-two also reported greater conflict in the home at age twenty-one.

4. Attachment styles are thought to exert an important influence on people's behavior in close relationships.

a. Fraley and Shaver (1998) found that

_____

_____

_____

_____

b. Self-report studies found that secure individuals were more likely to report friends stepping forward to offer support than did anxious or avoidant individuals.

c. Self-report studies also found that secure individuals tended to interpret their partners' negative behavior in more positive ways than did anxious or avoidant individuals.

5. Secure attachment predicts more positive life outcomes. Research findings support this conclusion:

a. _____
_____
_____
_____

b. _____
_____
_____
_____

c. _____
_____
_____
_____

d. Anxiously attached people are more likely to interpret life events in pessimistic, threatening ways, increasing the chance of depression; they also are more likely to suffer from eating disorders, maladaptive drinking, and substance abuse as attempts to escape anxiety.

e. Mikulincer and his colleagues found that security-related words presented below conscious awareness led participants to be less prejudicial toward outgroups and more altruistic toward others.

IV. Different Ways of Relating to Others
A. Relational models theory maintains that

_____
_____
_____
_____

1. The four kinds of relationships are communal sharing, authority ranking, equality matching, and market pricing.

a. A communal sharing relationship can be defined as

_____
_____
_____
_____

b. An authority ranking relationship can be defined as

_____
_____
_____
_____

c. An equality matching relationship can be defined as

_____
_____
_____
_____

d. A market pricing relationship can be defined as

_____
_____
_____
_____

2. We can relate to one person in each of the four different ways at different times.

3. Research suggests that we rely on these four relationship types to interpret and remember social events.

4. Fiske claims that almost all societies use all four relationship types, but different cultures emphasize different categories, as shown in these examples:

a. _____
_____
_____
_____

b. _____
_____
_____
_____

c. _____
_____
_____
_____

B. Exchange and Communal Relationships
1. Clark and Mills defined two fundamentally different types of relationships: exchange and communal.

a. Exchange relationships can be defined as

_____
_____
_____

b. Communal relationships can be defined as

_____
_____
_____
_____

2. Two research strategies show how exchange and communal relationships differ.
   a. One strategy compares the behavior of existing friends to the behavior of mere acquaintances toward each other.
   b. The other strategy experimentally manipulates the exchange versus communal status of a relationship by varying the motives of the participants in the study.
      (1) Communal condition: participants learn that their partner is new to the college and is hoping to meet people.
      (2) Exchange condition: participants learn that their partner is dissimilar from them and signed up for the study because it was at a convenient time.
   c. Findings from both lines of research
      (1) In communal relationships, people are more likely to keep track of each other's needs, as shown in the study in which

      _____

      _____

      _____

      _____

      (2) People in exchange relationships are more concerned with their own and their partner's respective contributions to a task than are those in communal relationships, as shown in the study in which

      _____

      _____

      _____

      _____

   d. Some cultures favor communal relationships, while others favor exchange relationships.
      (1) People in East Asian, Latin American, and Western Catholic countries favor a communal approach to many interactions.
      (2) People in European, Commonwealth, and Western Protestant countries favor an exchange approach.

C. Power and Hierarchical Relationships
   1. Power concerns are evident in most relationships, including marriage, parent-child relations, or even interactions among children as young as two years old.
   2. Power affects almost all facets of social life, including:
      a. _____

      _____

_____

b. _____

   _____

   _____

   _____

c. _____

   _____

   _____

   _____

3. What is power?
   a. Power can be defined as

   _____

   _____

   _____

   _____

   b. Power is related to, but different from status, authority, and dominance.
      (1) Status can be defined as

      _____

      _____

      _____

      _____

      (2) Authority can be defined as

      _____

      _____

      _____

      _____

      (3) Dominance can be defined as

      _____

      _____

      _____

      _____

4. Where does power come from?
   a. Certain individual characteristics lead people to be more likely to attain power:
      (1) _____

      _____

      _____

      (2) _____

      _____

      _____

      (3) _____

      _____

      _____

   b. Power can be derived from various interpersonal factors:
      (1) Authority: in formal hierarchies, power can derive from holding a position of authority.

(2) Expertise: power can derive from having specialized knowledge or experience.

(3) Coercion: use of force and aggression can result in power.

(4) Rewards: power can be derived from the ability to grant rewards to others.

(5) Reference power: people who are viewed as role models have power.

5. How does power influence behavior?

a. Approach/inhibition theory of power

(1) Elevated power will make you less concerned with the evaluations of others and thus less inhibited in your actions and more inclined to approach desired goals.

(2) Less power will make you more vigilant and attentive to social judgment and thus more inhibited in social behavior.

(3) The first hypothesis derived from this theory is that

_____

_____

_____

_____

(a) Participants given higher power positions in experiments pay less attention to individuating information about targets.

(b) Members of powerful groups tend to stereotype others more readily and are more likely to hold a social dominance orientation, which can be defined as

_____

_____

_____

_____

(c) High-power individuals tend to judge others' attitudes, interests, and needs less accurately and more simplistically, as shown by the following:

i. _____

_____

_____

_____

ii. _____

_____

_____

_____

iii. Older siblings are less accurate in construing the intentions and beliefs of others than are younger siblings.

(d) Power leads to less careful thought even with high incentives to deliberate carefully (e.g., minority Supreme Court decisions contain more complex arguments than the majority decisions).

(4) The second hypothesis derived from this theory is that

_____

_____

_____

_____

(a) High-power individuals are more likely to touch others and approach them closely physically.

(b) High-power partners in an experiment were more likely to flirt with low-power partners than vice versa, and the high-power participant was also inaccurate in judging how much the low-power participant wanted this attention.

(c) Low-power individuals often show inhibition.

i. They often constrict their posture.

ii. The often inhibit their speech and facial expressions.

iii. They often withdraw in group interactions.

(d) High power makes antisocial communication and behavior more likely.

i. High-power individuals tend to talk more, interrupt more, and speak out of turn more.

ii. Keltner et al. (1998) found that

_____

_____

_____

_____

(e) Power may also disinhibit aggression, leading to violence against low-power individuals as in the following situations:

i. _____

_____

_____

_____

ii. _____

_____

_____

_____

iii. _____

_____

_____

_____

6. What are we to do?
    a. Power allows people to express their true inclinations, so be careful who ends up in power.
    b. Chen et al. (2001) conducted a study to show how power amplifies the expression of people's true inclinations, both good and bad.
        (1) Self-selected Independent variable #1:

        _____

        _____

        _____

        _____

        (2) Independent variable #2:

        _____

        _____

        _____

        _____

        (3) Dependent variable: how much of a team task the participant completed before his or her partner arrived.
        (4) Finding: participants in the high-power condition behaved consistently with their predispositions; communal-oriented participants completed more of the task than exchange-oriented participants.

V. Romantic Relationships
    A. Sternberg's triangular theory of love states that

    _____

    _____

    _____

    _____

    1. intimacy + passion = _____

    _____

    2. intimacy + commitment = _____

    _____

    3. intimacy + passion + commitment = _____

    _____

    _____

    B. Relationships are an important part of social life; 90 percent of Americans and Canadians marry.
    C. Romantic relationships are an important component of well-being.
        1, Satisfying romantic relationships are one of the strongest predictors of life satisfaction.
        2. Married people are happier than divorced or single people.

3. Healthy romances are conducive to good physical health.
D. Marital Dissatisfaction
    1. There is a rise in problems with marriage, as shown by:
        a. _____

        _____

        _____

        b. _____

        _____

        _____

        c. _____

        _____

        _____

        d. Children of divorced parents can experience difficulty, both during childhood and adulthhood.
        e. Early divorce is associated with an anxious attachment style in the child.
    2. Demographic Predictors of Marital Dissatisfaction and Divorce
        a. Researchers typically ask romantic partners to fill out questionnaires about their relationship satisfaction and their personality and demographic backgrounds.
        b. Neurotic people have less happy relationships and are more likely to divorce, as shown by:
            (1) _____

            _____

            _____

            (2) _____

            _____

            _____

        c. People who are highly sensitive to rejection have greater difficulties in romantic relationships, as shown by:
            (1) Those who are highly sensitive to rejection respond with greater hostility than less sensitive people when feeling rejected by a romantic partner or friends.
            (2) _____

            _____

            _____

            (3) _____

            _____

            _____

            _____

d. People from lower SES backgrounds are more likely to divorce, as they

_____

_____

_____

_____

e. People who marry at a younger age are more likely to divorce because:

(1) _____

_____

_____

_____

(2) _____

_____

_____

_____

3. The Interaction Dynamics of Unhappy Partners

a. Gottman and Levenson's interaction dynamics approach can be defined as

_____

_____

_____

_____

b. The four negative behaviors most toxic to relationships are:

(1) _____

_____

_____

_____

(2) _____

_____

_____

_____

(3) _____

_____

_____

(4) _____

_____

_____

_____

c. The self-selection problem may lead to questions about causation, as people may be unhappy because of these four negative behaviors, or the four behaviors may occur because of an underlying unhappiness.

d. Gottman and Levenson have found that the four behaviors directly affect relationship stability, often leading to divorce.

(1) In an ongoing longitudinal study started in 1983, Gottman and Levenson have been able to predict with 93 percent accuracy which of seventy-nine couples would divorce based on an

assessment of the four negative behaviors during a fifteen-minute observation of a serious discussion between the relationship partners.

(2) The presence of negative emotion predicted earlier divorce, while the absence of positive emotion predicted later divorce.

4. Dangerous Attributions

a. Blame is problematic in maintaining romantic bonds.

b. Bradbury and Fincham (1990) reexamined twenty-three research studies to look at the relationship between partners' causal attributions and their relationship satisfaction.

(1) In distressed couples, positive partner behaviors are believed to be caused by

_____

_____

_____

_____

(2) In happy couples, positive partner behaviors are believed to be caused by

_____

_____

_____

_____

(3) In distressed couples, negative partner behaviors are believed to be caused by

_____

_____

_____

_____

(4) In happy couples, negative partner behaviors are believed to be caused by

_____

_____

_____

_____

E. Creating Stronger Romantic Bonds

1. The Investment Model of Relationship Commitment

a. Commitment is especially problematic in individualistic cultures because they value freedom and the pursuit of individual self-interest.

b. Rusbult's investment model of interpersonal relationships can be defined as

_____

_____

_____

_____

(1) One of the strongest determinants of relationship satisfaction is the degree of reward each partner feels he or she receives.

(2) The fewer possible alternative relationships a partner perceives, the more committed he or she will be to the existing relationship.

(3) A person is more likely to remain in a relationship if he or she has invested heavily in it in the past.

(4) Researchers testing the investment model have asked dating couples to report on their feelings about the three determinants of commitment, their level of commitment, and their satisfaction with the relationship.

    (a) Knowing how members of a couple feel about rewards, alternatives, and investment allows for more accurate prediction of whether the couple will remain together or not.

    (b) Each of the three components of the model are important in predicting the level of commitment.

(5) Commitment promotes more stable and satisfying bonds, as shown by these research findings:

    (a) _____

    _____

    _____

    (b) _____

    _____

    _____

    (c) _____

    _____

    _____

2. Illusions and Idealization in Romantic Relationships

  a. Murray and her colleagues have discovered that the idealization of one's partner is an important part of satisfying romantic bonds.

    (1) Murray et al. (1996) conducted a study on relationship satisfaction and perception of a partner's faults and virtues.

      (a) Study setup:

    _____

    _____

_____

_____

      (b) Finding:

_____

_____

_____

_____

    (2) Murray and Holmes (1999) examined how people idealized their romantic partners.

      (a) Study setup: participants were asked to write about their partner's greatest fault.

      (b) Finding:

_____

_____

_____

_____

  b. Hawkins et al. (2002) found that

_____

_____

_____

_____

3, Novel and Arousing Activities

  a. Having children has a devastating effect on marital satisfaction, as the married partners have less time to devote to each other.

  b. Aron et al. (2002) investigated the extent to which engaging in novel activities could boost relationship satisfaction.

    (1) Independent variable:

_____

_____

_____

_____

    (2) Dependent variable:

_____

_____

_____

_____

    (3) Finding: both compared to participants in the individual condition and compared to their own baseline, couples in the silly/novel condition reported higher marital satisfaction.

TESTING YOUR BASIC KNOWLEDGE

After studying the information in the chapter by filling in the outline above, test your basic knowledge with the following multiple-choice test. Answers are provided in the Answer Key section at the end of the chapter. If you find that you have gotten an answer wrong, it is important that you understand why it is wrong (as well as understanding why the correct answer is the better choice). Talk with peers, your tutor, or your professor if you need help.

Multiple-Choice Questions

1. Research on feral children (children who grew up in isolation from other people due to abandonment) suggests that relationships are necessary to prevent serious language and attachment deficits. In this case, the self-selection methodological problem supports which of the following statements?
   a. The research is not valid, and the conclusions should be ignored.
   b. The children may have been abandoned because of preexisting language and/or attachment deficits.
   c. The researchers may have chosen to examine only those children who would support their hypothesis.

2. Which of the following is NOT a criteria listed by Baumeister and Leary (1995) to judge whether the need to belong is a true innate need?
   a. The majority of respondents must indicate that they feel the need to belong.
   b. Belonging to social groups must serve some sort of evolutionary purpose.
   c. A lack of belonging must lead to severe negative outcomes.

3. Adam has a great relationship with his mother. He always feels confident, empowered, and optimistic when he is around his mother. Upon entering college, Adam meets Lisa. Without even knowing her all that well, Adam realizes that he feels great around Lisa—confident and optimistic. He really likes Lisa and seeks to spend more time with her. According to Andersen and Chen's relational self theory,
   a. Adam has developed a secure attachment style because of his good relationship with his mother.
   b. Lisa and Adam are likely to experience consummate love.
   c. Lisa is probably similar to Adam's mother.

4. Kelly and Roland are a married couple. Annette, a new friend of the couple, learns that Kelly is a big fan of the television show *Law and Order*. In a future interaction, however, Annette gets confused and thinks that Roland might be the fan of *Law and Order*. Of the following, what is the best social psychological explanation for this mistake?
   a. Annette is using relationships as organizing categories.
   b. Annette is unconsciously attracted to Roland.

   c. Annette uses gender stereotypes to guide her decision that Roland, the man, must be a bigger fan of a crime show than Kelly.

5. Karie's significant other, Chris, is a gourmet cook. They are supposed to go to a dinner party together but, at the last minute, Chris has to cancel. Karie decides to go on her own and has a great time, enjoying good food and conversation. After the party, Chris asks what was served for dinner. Karie realizes that, although she enjoyed the food tremendously, she simply can't remember what was served. A "transactive memory" explanation of this memory lapse would suggest that
   a. Karie's lack of interest in food and menus led to her inattention to that portion of the party.
   b. Karie has come to, typically, count on Chris to attend to food-related details and, thus, directs more of her attention to other features of a situation.
   c. Karie has adopted Chris's gourmet status as one of her own characteristics.

6. According to the Baldwin, Carrell, and Lopez (1990) study, the presence of stern and disapproving authority figures can
   a. lead to more negative self-evaluations.
   b. cause angry reactance.
   c. lead to insecure attachment styles.
   d. none of the above.

7. A recently hired live-in child-care provider notices that the parents of her charge often ignore their child or even reject their child's requests for attention or help. In turn, the child seems scared of new situations and is resistant to forming a relationship with this new child-care provider. It is likely that the child has developed a(an)
   a. secure attachment style.
   b. avoidant attachment style.
   c. anxious attachment style.

8. Brendan recently broke up with his college girlfriend. He reported dissatisfaction with the relationship, stating that his girlfriend just wouldn't open up and be close to him, despite his total devotion to her. Based on this information, which of the following could a social psychologist conclude with some confidence?
   a. Brendan has an anxious attachment style.
   b. Brendan was experiencing companionate love with his girlfriend.
   c. Brendan's girlfriend was the more powerful of the two in the relationship.

9. In a Chinese classroom, the teacher is the ultimate authority figure and maintains control of the students' behaviors. In a Japanese classroom, the teacher tends to allow students to police each other via peer pressure. According to Alan Fiske's relational models theory, relations in the Chinese classroom are a good example of _____ and relations in the Japanese classroom are a good example of _____.
   a. authority-ranking relationships; equality-matching relationships.
   b. market-pricing relationships; authority-ranking relationships.
   c. market-pricing relationship; communal-sharing relationships.
   d. authority-ranking relationships; communal-sharing relationships.

10. Unlike people in exchange relationships, Clark and Mills described people in communal relationships as being more concerned with
    a. reciprocating and maintaining equity.
    b. meeting one another's needs.
    c. maintaining sufficient intimacy.

11. David and Andrew are working on a group project together. They each, separately, complete one written portion of the project and ask the professor to look over their work. David has written his own name at the top of the page he gives to the professor. Andrew has written both David's and his name. This subtle difference may suggest that David perceives his relationship with Andrew as being a(an) _____ relationship, while Andrew perceives his relationship with David as being a(an) _____ relationship.
    a. exchange; communal
    b. communal; exchange
    c. not enough information is provided to answer this question

12. Which of the following is the best example of status without power?
    a. the "best employee of the month" recipient is asked to design the work schedule for her coworkers (deciding who works which shift)
    b. a factory line worker is fired from his job
    c. an internationally known celebrity is denied after-hours shopping at an expensive store

13. In 2005, Tom Cruise, a well-known and well-liked movie star, stated his opinion in several interviews that psychiatry is a pseudoscience and that psychiatric medications do more harm than good. Social psychologists would expect some members of the public to believe or at least seriously consider this position because Cruise has societal power. Which of the following best describes the source of Cruise's power?
    a. reference power
    b. coercion
    c. expert power

14. According to the approach/inhibition theory of power,
    a. people in high-power positions engage in less systematic decision making.
    b. people in high-power positions are more likely to engage in antisocial behavior.
    c. Both of the above are true.

15. Chen, Lee-Chai, and Bargh (2001) found that when participants were seated in high-power, professorial chairs, those who were selfishly oriented contributed less to a group task than those who were communally oriented. This research supports which of the following conclusions?
    a. Selfish people are more obsessed with power than communal people.
    b. Power enhances a person's tendency to behave in accord with his or her true dispositions.
    c. Communal-oriented people care less about power than selfish people.

16. Pat tends to flirt with others at work, interrupts when others are speaking, looks away while others are talking, and has been overheard making hostile comments about others based solely on stereotypes. Chris tends to behave more professionally, defers to others in conversation, looks down while speaking but makes good eye contact while listening, and seems to know relevant details about the lives of the people who work in the office. One of these people is the boss in the office and the other is the employee. Based on the social psychological research discussed in the chapter, who is more likely to be the boss?
    a. Pat
    b. Chris
    c. There is no way to tell from the information given.

17. Brad and Angie are just good friends; they are not romantically involved. According to Sternberg's triangular theory of love, which combination of components is most likely to exist for these two?
    a. intimacy and passion
    b. intimacy and commitment
    c. passion and commitment

18. According to the research discussed in the textbook, which of the following are risk factors for divorce?
    a. marrying later in life
    b. being sensitive to rejection
    c. being highly extraverted

19. You observe two couples, both of which are having a fierce argument. In one couple, each person is stubbornly insisting on the truth of his or her own position. In the other couple, each person is contemptuously criticizing the validity of the partner's view. According to the research by Gottman and Levenson, which couple is more likely to eventually divorce?
    a. the first couple, because not listening to one another is a toxic negative behavior
    b. the second couple, because criticism and contempt are toxic negative behaviors
    c. Both couples are equally like to divorce because arguing is a toxic negative behavior.

20. Research suggests that a couple will be more or less happy, depending on how each partner explains the other partner's positive and negative actions. Which pattern below best reflects the attributions of a member of a happy couple?
    a. Negative behaviors are attributed to specific and unintended causes.
    b. Positive behaviors are attributed to specific and unintended causes.
    c. Negative behaviors are attributed to global and stable causes.

21. According to Carol Rusbult, under what conditions might a person remain in a relationship that is unsatisfying?
    a. if the person has already invested a great deal of time and energy in the relationship
    b. if the person has a secure attachment style
    c. if the person has experienced companionate love

22. According to Carol Rusbult, what might cause a person to leave a satisfying relationship?
    a. being highly neurotic
    b. a lack of intimacy
    c. if there seem to be potentially more satisfying alternatives available

23. According to Sandra Murray's work on close relationships, which type of partner would lead to a more satisfying relationship?
    a. a partner who acknowledges and supports your efforts to overcome your faults
    b. a partner who sees your faults as endearing positive features
    c. a partner who works hard to ignore your undesirable qualities

24. Stacy and Richard are having relationship problems and choose to spend Saturday afternoon having another discussion about those problems. Keisha and James are also having relationship problems but decide to put those problems on hold and spend Saturday afternoon at the county fair participating in activities like a three-legged race. Which couple would Art Aron (Aron et al., 2000) predict would feel more satisfied in their relationship?
    a. Stacy and Richard, because communication is the key to a good relationship
    b. Keisha and James, because novelty and fun are important parts of a relationship
    c. Keisha and James, because overanalyzing one's problems only leads to arguments

25. Which of the following is not a toxic negative behavior as defined by the interaction dynamics approach?
    a. lack of communication
    b. denial
    c. criticism

Essay Questions

After you have mastered the multiple-choice questions, try testing your basic understanding by thoroughly answering each of the broad essay questions below. Because it is critical that you think through this information on your own, we have not provided any answers to these questions. Your learning and retention of this material will be greatly enhanced if you do one or more of the following to check your answers: carefully review the textbook information; compare your responses to your class lecture notes; talk over your answers with a peer; ask your professor to review your answers or review any information that is unclear to you.

1. Why is it important to have close relationships? Describe three ways in which close relationships influence our thoughts and feelings.

2. Explain the logic of attachment theory, describe the basic three attachment styles, and discuss the research supporting the existence and influence of attachment styles.

3. Describe each of Fiske's four relationship types and relate those to Clark and Mills's two types of relationships. Characterize exchange versus communal relationships by summarizing some of the research findings.

4. How does one obtain power in a relationship, and what are the possible detrimental effects of having power?

5. Discuss the factors leading to marital dissatisfaction, and describe features of strong, satisfying romantic relationships.

TESTING YOUR IN-DEPTH UNDERSTANDING

Test your in-depth understanding of the material by working through the Critical Thinking Exercises provided at the end of each textbook chapter. To maximize this learning opportunity, work together with a tutor, study group, or your professor. Alternatively, write down your thoughts and responses.

Guided questions for one of the exercises are provided below. While there are multiple ways to answer these questions, short answers are given in the Answer Key at the end of the chapter. Note that the valuable part of this exercise is not simply knowing the answer but working with the material to come up with the answer.

Guided Questions for Critical Thinking Exercise #3

If you were on a radio show and were asked to provide ten tips for avoiding divorce and having a satisfying marriage, what advice would you give? More specifically, what five things would you encourage people thinking about marrying to do to avoid marital problems? And what five things would you recommend to bring greater pleasure and joy to their relationship?

1. Review each of the major concepts in the chapter:

   need to belong
   relational self theory
   relationships as organizing categories
   self-expansion theory
   transactive memory
   relationships and affective life
   attachment styles
   relational models theory
   exchange versus communal relationships
   power in relationships
   triangular theory of love
   demographic predictors of dissatisfaction
   interaction dynamics approach
   attributions
   investment model
   idealization in romantic relationships
   novel and arousing activities

2. Now examine each concept and try to extract advice about what makes a relationship more satisfying, happy, or functional/beneficial from each concept.

3. The scenario asks you to provide advice to people who are already married (that is, presumably already committed and in long-term relationships). Pick the ten best pieces of advice from your list in #2.

4. Pretend you are a social psychologist, and figure out how you could assess whether simply providing "tips" is sufficient to help couples have more satisfying relationships.

Enhance your understanding of the chapter by thinking about and doing the remaining two Critical Thinking Exercises. Discuss your answers with your peers, study group, tutor, or professor.

Critical Thinking Exercise #1

In many ways, a central theme of this chapter is that our relationships influence how we construe our social worlds. Can you think of how our relationships influence: (a) our self-concept; (b) how we attend to and remember social information; and (c) the explanations we offer for our own and others' behavior?

Critical Thinking Exercise #2

Imagine you are working in a preschool near your college, and each day you are present when the parents drop off their children. One child, upon being dropped off, expresses extreme distress and anger when his parents leave. How would you classify this child's attachment style? As the child matures into adulthood, what would you expect of his relationships with others and particular difficulties he might encounter?

SOCIAL PSYCHOLOGY IN THE POPULAR MEDIA

You might be interested in the following popular media references, each of which relates in some way to information in this chapter.

Book

Shattuck, Roger (1980). *The Forbidden Experiment: The Story of the Wild Boy of Aveyron.* New York: Farrar Straus Giroux. Written by an award-winning cultural historian, this 220-page book tells the story of the boy described at the beginning of the textbook chapter (Victor). The book focuses on the story of Victor's discovery and his subsequent "relationships" with various caregivers.

Songs

Turn on the radio and choose *any* song. Odds are, it is about close, romantic relationships. Why is so much of our music about relationships? Evaluate the song lyrics against the research discussed in the chapter (you can find most song lyrics on the Internet by searching "song lyrics" and the title of the song). Is the song about an unrealistic depiction of what love should be? What type of love is discussed according to Sternberg's triangular theory of love? Is the song advocating a communal or an exchange perspective? If the song is about a breakup, are any of four negative behaviors (identified by Gottman and Levenson) mentioned, however indirectly.

Films

Nell (1994; directed by Michael Apted; starring Jodie Foster, Natasha Richardson, and Liam Neeson). A fictional story about a woman who grew up in the woods with no human contact except a speech-impaired mother. The story follows a doctor and psychologist who try to learn her incomprehensible language and who take her into the modern world.

The Theory of Flight (1998; directed by Paul Greengrass; starring Helena Bonham Carter and Kenneth Branagh). A troubled artist creates an airplane from the canvasses of his paintings and ends up in court for the unauthorized flight. He is sentenced to community service and ends up serving as a companion to Jane, a young woman with advanced Lou Gehrig's disease (ALS). A surprising friendship develops in the course of an improbable series of events involving robbing a bank to pay for a gigolo so that Jane can lose her virginity. It would be interesting to examine the relationship depicted in the movie alongside the research reviewed in this chapter. An offbeat, sobering, comic, and ultimately romantic tearjerker. Rated R.

Web Sites

Personality Lab—http://www.personalitylab.org/. This Web site features questionnaires on a variety of topics, including an attachment styles questionnaire. You will receive very general feedback from filling out the questionnaire, and you will (anonymously) be participating in an actual psychology study. Find other studies to participate in (most without receiving feedback, but interesting nonetheless) at http://psych.hanover.edu/Research/exponnet.html

Sexual Orientation: Science, Policy, and Education—http://psychology.ucdavis.edu/rainbow/index.html. From the Web site: "This site features work by Dr. Gregory Herek, an internationally recognized authority on sexual prejudice (also called homophobia), hate crimes, and AIDS stigma. It provides factual information to promote the use of scientific knowledge for education and enlightened public policy related to sexual orientation and HIV/AIDS." This Web site complements the chapter's focus on heterosexual relationships.

ANSWER KEY

Annotated Chapter Outline

I. Characterizing Relationships
  A. Interpersonal relationships are attachments in which bonds of family or friendship or love or respect or hierarchy tie together two or more individuals over an extended period of time.
  B. Many social psychological studies of relationships are not true experiments, but rather look at the dynamics of existing relationships.
    1. Since many of the studies are not experiments, the methodological problem of self-selection occurs.
      a. When participants (in some manner of speaking) select their own condition, there is not random assignment.
      b. Self-selection leaves open a causality problem in that the participants may possess multiple characteristics that led them to be in their condition.
    2. A study of feral children exemplified the self-selection problem and showed two possible causes of the children's abnormal development:
      a. Isolation may have led the feral children to their interpersonal difficulties.
      b. Interpersonal difficulties may have led parents to abandon the "problem" children.
  C. Harlow (1959) conducted experimental research with baby rhesus monkeys.
    1. Harlow found that monkeys raised alone preferred to spend time with a terry-cloth covered "mother" figure that more closely resembled a real monkey mother rather than a "wire mother," even though the wire mother provided food.
    2. The monkeys raised in isolation behaved fearfully, did not interact with their peers, and displayed unusual and inappropriate behavior.
  D. A natural experiment with elephants found that young elephants also need social interaction to function normally.
    1. A natural experiment may be defined as an experiment in which the conditions naturally or "accidentally" are created.
    2. Elephants who have lost their parents and grown up alone are antisocial and aggressive, unlike elephants raised with adult elephants.

II. The Importance of Relationships
  A. The Need to Belong
    1. Baumeister and Leary (1995) proposed that humans have an innate need to be part of healthy relationships.

2. Baumeister and Leary suggested five criteria for judging the legitimacy of this claim. These criteria and research evidence supporting them are:
   a. Evolutionary basis: such an innate need should be demonstrated to have been evolutionarily advantageous.
      (1) Long-term romantic bonds aided in reproduction and raising dependent offspring.
      (2) Parent-offspring attachments ensure a connection necessary for the survival of the offspring.
      (3) Friendships encourage cooperation and discourage competition (groups fare better than individuals).
   b. Universal: if evolutionarily based, then this need should be found across cultures.
   c. Guides social cognition: if this innate need was present throughout evolution, the motivation to develop and maintain social relationships should be an important influence on our thinking.
   d. Satiable: if this is a true need, it should diminish as it is satisfied.
      (1) In Western European cultures, college-age students seem to limit their most intimate relationships to about six people, suggesting that we stop seeking relationships when we have enough to satisfy our need to belong.
      (2.) Observational studies in prisons suggest that prisoners form family-like bonds with other inmates to replace the familial bonds lost through separation.
   e. Profound negative consequences: if this is truly an innate need, then the lack of adequate relational bonds should result in profound negative consequences.
      (1) Mortality rates are higher for divorced, unmarried, and widowed individuals.
      (2) Admissions to mental hospitals are higher for divorced than married people.
      (3) Suicide rates are higher for singles and divorced individuals.
      (4) Breast cancer patients live longer when involved in weekly support groups.
      (5) Social support strengthens our cardiovascular, immune, and endocrine systems.

B. Relationships and the Sense of Self
   1. Andersen and Chen's relational self theory suggests that the relational self is an important part of one's self-concept.
      a. The relational self can be defined as the beliefs, feelings, and expectations about ourselves that we derive from relationships with significant others in our lives.
      b. We have different relational selves for different relationships (e.g., one may feel a certain way about the self and believe certain things about the self around one's mother, and a different way around a best friend).
      c. Andersen and Chen's relational self theory argues that meeting people who remind us of significant others (past or present) will activate the associated relational self.
      d. Andersen and her colleagues developed an experimental paradigm to assess how past relationships affect our current beliefs, thoughts, and interactions.
         (1) Pre-test: participants write down seven positive things and seven negative things about someone they like, and then they do the same for someone they dislike.
         (2) Experimental session: participants are given a description of another person (supposedly in another room) who resembles the participant's positive significant other, negative significant other, or another person's significant other.
         (3) Findings from studies using this general setup:
            (a) Participants were asked to describe their own personality when they were with their significant other; results confirmed that they gave similar descriptions of how they anticipated they would act with a new person who was similar to their significant other.
            (b) Participants who read about someone who resembled a positive significant other displayed more positive facial expression than those reading about someone resembling a negative significant other.
            (c) Berk and Andersen (2000) found that participants liked strangers who resembled positive significant others, and showed positive emotion toward that stranger.

C. Relationships and Social Cognition
   1. Relationships as Organizing Categories
      a. In typical cognitive functioning, people

organize information in their physical and social worlds into categories (e.g., physical, cultural, or moral categories).

b. Sedikides et al. (1993) tested the claim that relationships can also serve as a kind of category.

(1) Participants read five pieces of information about each of four women and four men who were described as being members of married couples.

(2) Independent variable: participants were told which males and females were married to each other, or participants were not told which people were married to each other.

(3) Dependent variables: various aspects of how participants remembered information about the people.

(4) Findings: compared to participants who did not know who was married to whom, participants who did know who was married to whom were more likely to cluster the recalled bits of information into groupings by couple and more often confused which trait belonged to which person in a couple.

2. Construing Close Others as We Construe Ourselves

a. We tend to have the same processing strategies and biases toward close others as we do toward ourselves (e.g., for ourselves and close others we accept credit for success and blame failure on external forces).

b. The self-expansion account of relationships holds that people enter and remain in close relationships in order to incorporate their partner's resources, perspectives, experiences, and characteristics into their own self-concept.

c. Aron et al. (1991) tested this theory.

(1) Married couples rated ninety traits on how accurately the trait described the self and the spouse.

(2) Participants saw the traits on a computer screen and were asked to make decisions about their own self-concept, pressing a "like me" or "not like me" button as quickly as possible.

(3) Findings: participants responded more quickly to traits on which they were similar to their spouse and slower to

traits on which they were not similar to their spouse.

(4) Faster responses indicate that the trait is more woven into one's self-concept; thus, traits possessed by a partner are more part of the self-concept.

3. Sharing Social Construals with Close Others

a. Transactive memory can be defined as the knowledge that people in relationships have about their partner's encoding, storage, and retrieval of information (i.e., knowing the sorts of information a partner is likely to attend to).

b. Having such knowledge allows a person to attend to different information, leading to a greater awareness of the situation as a whole once the two sets of information are combined.

c. Wegner and his colleagues conducted a study on transactive memory.

(1) Setup: dating couples and couples made up of strangers completed a memory task in which sentences had words from different domains of expertise underlined and in which they were asked to remember them with their partner.

(2) Findings: romantic partners recalled significantly more sentences than pairings of strangers.

D. Relationships and Affective Life

1. Relationships can intensify emotions.

2. Relationships affect our moods and emotional well-being.

a. Experience-sampling studies can be defined as studies in which researchers give participants beepers and randomly signal them during their normal daily routines to stop and provide information about what they are doing and how they are feeling at that precise moment.

b. Such studies find that people experience more positive emotions around other people (especially when they are having intimate interactions) compared to when they are alone.

c. Research on loneliness suggests that anxiety and depression are higher in people who also report being lonely. But self-selection into the "lonely" category may create a causality problem because lonely people may be more anxious, or anxiety may lead to fewer relationships and thus to loneliness.

d. Experimental research also suggests that relationships powerfully influence how we feel, as demonstrated in a classic study by Baldwin and his colleagues (1990) that examined the effect of important authority figures' approval or disapproval on participants' self-evaluations.

    (1) Setup: University of Michigan psychology graduate students were asked to write down three of their latest research study ideas and then were subliminally presented with one of two photos.

    (2) Independent variable: a photo of either a stern, disapproving Bob Zajonc (an authority figure) or a photo of a friendly looking person.

    (3) Dependent variable: self-evaluation of research ideas.

    (4) Finding: students evaluated their research ideas more harshly when primed with the photo of the stern authority figure compared with when they were primed with the photo of the friendly face.

III. The Origins of How We Relate to Others

  A. Attachment Theory

    1. Bowlby's attachment theory argues that early attachments with parents shape our relationships for the remainder of our lives.

      a. Human infants, having few innate survival skills at birth, survive by forming strong bonds with caregivers.

        (1) Infants smile, coo, have large eyes and other features that evoke filial love.

        (2) Parents love and have strong protective feelings toward their offspring.

      b. A child's confidence in the security a parent provides is influenced by how responsive the parent is to the child's needs.

      c. The attachments children develop become their first working models of relationships, which can be defined as conceptual models of relationships with current others based on the other person's availability, warmth, and ability to provide security as derived from children's experience with how available and how warm their parents were.

    2. Mary Ainsworth classified attachment patterns of infants according to how the children responded to separations and reunions with their caregivers.

      a. Ainsworth developed an experimental paradigm known as the strange situation, which can be defined as an experimental situation designed to assess attachment to caregivers in which an infant is observed after her caregiver has left her alone in an unfamiliar room with a stranger and then reacts to reunion with the caregiver upon her return to the room.

      b. Secure patterns: infants with responsive caregivers were comfortable moving away from the caregiver to explore the novel environment (checking back now and again).

      c. Insecure patterns: infants with nonresponsive or inappropriately responsive caregivers cried or were angry in novel environments, despite the presence of the caregiver, and often rejected attention even when it was offered.

  B. Attachment Styles

    1. Adult attachment styles are assessed via self-report measures.

    2. Researchers have concentrated on three specific styles: secure, avoidant, and anxious attachment.

      a. Secure attachment style can be defined as an attachment style characterized by feelings of security in relationships; individuals with this style are comfortable with intimacy and desire to be close to others during times of threat and uncertainty.

      b. Avoidant attachment style can be defined as an attachment style characterized by feelings of insecurity in relationships; individuals with this style are prone to exhibit compulsive self-reliance, prefer distance from others, and during conditions of threat and uncertainty are dismissive and detached.

      c. Anxious attachment style can be defined as an attachment style characterized by feelings of insecurity in relationships; individuals with this style compulsively seek closeness, express continual worries about relationships, and during situations of threat and uncertainty excessively try to get closer to others.

    3. A central claim of attachment theory is that attachment styles are typically stable across the life span. There is research evidence supporting this claim:

a. Individuals typically maintain their attachment style classification from age one through early adulthood.

b. Seventy percent of adults reported the same attachment style across all four years of a longitudinal study.

c. Anxiously attached persons were more likely to report having experienced parental divorce, death, or abuse during childhood.

d. In a forty-year longitudinal study, women who classified themselves as avoidant at age fifty-two also reported greater conflict in the home at age twenty-one.

4. Attachment styles are thought to exert an important influence on people's behavior in close relationships.

a. Fraley and Shaver (1998) found that, during airport goodbyes between couples, avoidant partners sought less physical contact and shared fewer embraces than secure or anxious partners; anxious partners expressed greater fear and sadness than secure or avoidant partners.

b. Self-report studies found that secure individuals were more likely to report friends stepping forward to offer support than did anxious or avoidant individuals.

c. Self-report studies also found that secure individuals tended to interpret their partners' negative behavior in more positive ways than did anxious or avoidant individuals.

5. Secure attachment predicts more positive life outcomes. Research findings support this conclusion:

a. Secure individuals report greater relationship satisfaction than anxious or avoidant individuals.

b. Secure individuals were less likely than anxious or avoidant individuals to experience a breakup during the four years of a longitudinal study.

c. Secure individuals were more likely to be married at age fifty-two than avoidant individuals, and they reported fewer marital tensions.

d. Anxiously attached people are more likely to interpret life events in pessimistic, threatening ways, increasing the chance of depression; they also are more likely to suffer from eating disorders, maladaptive drinking, and substance abuse as attempts to escape anxiety.

e. Mikulincer and his colleagues found that security-related words presented below conscious awareness led participants to be less prejudicial toward outgroups and more altruistic toward others.

IV. Different Ways of Relating to Others

A. Relational models theory maintains that there are four qualitatively different kinds of relationships, each characterized by highly distinct ways of defining the self and others, allocating resources and work, making moral judgments, and punishing transgressions.

1. The four kinds of relationships are communal sharing, authority ranking, equality matching, and market pricing.

a. A communal sharing relationship can be defined as a relationship based on a sense of sameness and kinship and the belief that the relationship transcends the concerns of the individual (e.g., family and close friends).

b. An authority ranking relationship can be defined as a relationship based on hierarchy, status, and a linear ordering of people within a group (e.g., the military, corporations).

c. An equality matching relationship can be defined as a relationship based on equality, reciprocity, and balance (e.g., roommates, coworkers, friends).

d. A market pricing relationship can be defined as a relationship based on a sense of proportion, trade, and equity, in which people are concerned with ensuring that their inputs to a relationship correspond with what they get out of the relationship (e.g., boss and employee, salesclerk and customer).

2. We can relate to one person in each of the four different ways at different times.

3. Research suggests that we rely on these four relationship types to interpret and remember social events.

4. Fiske claims that almost all societies use all four relationship types but different cultures emphasize different categories, as shown in these examples.

a. Modern Western society relies on market pricing to organize relationships, while traditional hunter-gatherer societies use communal sharing.

b. Chinese society is based on authority ranking to exert social control, whereas Japanese society emphasizes equality matching or peer control.

c. Sweden emphasizes equality matching in distributing social benefits, while the United States bases social benefits on market pricing principles.

B. Exchange and Communal Relationships

1. Clark and Mills defined two fundamentally different types of relationships: exchange and communal.

a. Exchange relationships can be defined as short-term relationships in which the individuals feel little responsibility toward one another and in which giving and receiving are governed by concerns about equity and reciprocity (e.g., relationships among strangers, new acquaintances; these are similar to market pricing relationships).

b. Communal relationships can be defined as long-term relationships in which the individuals feel a special responsibility for one another and give and receive according to the principle of need (e.g., relationships among family members and close friends; these are similar to communal sharing relationships).

2. Two research strategies show how exchange and communal relationships differ.

a. One strategy compares the behavior of existing friends to the behavior of mere acquaintances toward each other.

b. The other strategy experimentally manipulates the exchange versus communal status of a relationship by varying the motives of the participants in the study.

(1) Communal condition: participants learn that their partner is new to the college and is hoping to meet people.

(2) Exchange condition: participants learn that their partner is dissimilar from them and signed up for the study because it was at a convenient time.

c. Findings from both lines of research

(1) In communal relationships, people are more likely to keep track of each other's needs, as shown in the study in which participants in the communal condition turned around to check and see if a partner needed help more frequently than did participants in the exchange condition.

(2) People in exchange relationships are more concerned with their own and their partner's respective contributions to a task than are those in communal relationships, as shown in the study in which participants in the exchange condition made sure to distinguish their own work on a task (with a different colored ink) from that of their partner, so that they could get the promised reward for that work, while participants in the communal condition tended to use the same colored ink as their partner.

d. Some cultures favor communal relationships, while others favor exchange relationships.

(1) People in East Asian, Latin American, and Western Catholic countries favor a communal approach to many interactions.

(2) People in European, Commonwealth, and Western Protestant countries favor an exchange approach.

C. Power and Hierarchical Relationships

1. Power concerns are evident in most relationships, including marriage, parent-child relations, or even interactions among children as young as two years old.

2. Power affects almost all facets of social life, including:

a. How we speak: low-power individuals speak politely, make requests indirectly or vaguely, whereas high-power individuals speak forcefully and directly, asking pointed questions and issuing commands.

b. How we look at each other: low-power individuals look away when speaking but look at their partner when listening, while high-power individuals do the opposite.

c. How we dress: senior doctors wear longer white lab coats than more junior doctors.

3. What is power?

a. Power can be defined as the ability to control one's own outcomes and those of others, and the freedom to act.

b. Power is related to, but different from status, authority, and dominance.

(1) Status can be defined as the outcome of an evaluation of attributes that produces differences in respect and prominence, which in part determines an individual's power within a group.

(2) Authority can be defined as power that derives from institutionalized roles or arrangements.

(3) Dominance can be defined as behavior that has the acquisition or demonstration of power as its goal.

4. Where does power come from?
   a. Certain individual characteristics lead people to be more likely to attain power:
      (1) Extraverted people often attain power in natural social groups.
      (2) People with good social skills often attain power in social hierarchies.
      (3) Physically attractive people often attain higher positions in social hierarchies.
   b. Power can be derived from various interpersonal factors:
      (1) Authority: in formal hierarchies, power can derive from holding a position of authority.
      (2) Expertise: power can derive from having specialized knowledge or experience.
      (3) Coercion: use of force and aggression can result in power.
      (4) Rewards: power can be derived from the ability to grant rewards to others.
      (5) Reference power: people who are viewed as role models have power.
5. How does power influence behavior?
   a. Approach/inhibition theory of power
      (1) Elevated power will make you less concerned with the evaluations of others and thus less inhibited in your actions and more inclined to approach desired goals.
      (2) Less power will make you more vigilant and attentive to social judgment and thus more inhibited in social behavior.
      (3) The first hypothesis derived from this theory is that high-power individuals should be less systematic and careful in how they judge the social world and therefore more likely to stereotype others.
         (a) Participants given higher power positions in experiments pay less attention to individuating information about targets.
         (b) Members of powerful groups tend to stereotype others more readily and are more likely to hold a social dominance orientation, which can be defined as the desire to see one's own group dominate other groups.
         (c) High-power individuals tend to judge others' attitudes, interests, and needs less accurately and more simplistically, as shown by the following:
            i. Tenured professors judge the attitudes of untenured professors less accurately than did other untenured professors.
            ii. Males tend to be slightly less accurate than females in interpreting expressive behavior.
            iii. Older siblings are less accurate in construing the intentions and beliefs of others than are younger siblings.
         (d) Power leads to less careful thought even with high incentives to deliberate carefully (e.g., minority Supreme Court decisions contain more complex arguments than the majority decisions).
      (4) The second hypothesis derived from this theory is that power should make disinhibited social behavior more likely, even when it is inappropriate or unethical.
         (a) High-power individuals are more likely to touch others and approach them closely physically.
         (b) High-power partners in an experiment were more likely to flirt with low-power partners than vice versa, and the high-power participant was also inaccurate in judging how much the low-power participant wanted this attention.
         (c) Low-power individuals often show inhibition.
            i. They often constrict their posture.
            ii. The often inhibit their speech and facial expressions.
            iii. They often withdraw in group interactions.
         (d) High power makes antisocial communication and behavior more likely.
            i. High-power individuals tend to talk more, interrupt more, and speak out of turn more.
            ii. Keltner et al. (1998) found that high-power fraternity brothers gave more nasty nicknames and told more humiliating stories about their fraternity brothers than did low-power fraternity brothers.

(e) Power may also disinhibit aggression, leading to violence against low-power individuals, as in the following situations:

   i. Sexual harassment is likely to increase.

   ii. Rape rises when there is female subordination to males.

   iii. Hate crimes against minority groups increase when majority group members outnumber minority group members in a neighborhood.

6. What are we to do?

  a. Power allows people to express their true inclinations, so be careful who ends up in power.

  b. Chen et al. (2001) conducted a study to show how power amplifies the expression of people's true inclinations, both good and bad.

    (1) Self-selected Independent variable #1: exchange-oriented versus communal-oriented participants.

    (2) Independent variable #2: sitting in the powerful leather professorial chair versus sitting in the low-status, plain student chair.

    (3) Dependent variable: how much of a team task the participant completed before their partner arrived.

    (4) Finding: participants in the high-power condition behaved consistently with their predispositions; communal-oriented participants completed more of the task than exchange-oriented participants.

V. Romantic Relationships

  A. Sternberg's triangular theory of love states that there are three major components of love—intimacy, passion, and commitment—which can be combined in different ways.

   1. intimacy + passion = romantic love (sexual arousal and intimacy).

   2. intimacy + commitment = companionate love (intimacy without sexual arousal).

   3. intimacy + passion + commitment = consummate love (ideal, ultimate form of love).

  B. Relationships are an important part of social life; 90 percent of Americans and Canadians marry.

  C. Romantic relationships are an important component of well-being.

1. Satisfying romantic relationships are one of the strongest predictors of life satisfaction.

2. Married people are happier than divorced or single people.

3. Healthy romances are conducive to good physical health.

D. Marital Dissatisfaction

  1. There is a rise in problems with marriage, as shown by:

   a. Fifty percent of first marriages end in divorce.

   b. Marriages are less satisfying today than those from thirty years ago.

   c. Marital conflict stimulates unhealthy stress responses.

   d. Children of divorced parents can experience difficulty, both during childhood and adulthood.

   e. Early divorce is associated with an anxious attachment style in the child.

  2. Demographic Predictors of Marital Dissatisfaction and Divorce

   a. Researchers typically ask romantic partners to fill out questionnaires about their relationship satisfaction and their personality and demographic backgrounds.

   b. Neurotic people have less happy relationships and are more likely to divorce.

    (1) They are more likely to experience negative emotion and health problems, and they react more strongly to interpersonal conflict.

    (2) These tendencies reduce relationship satisfaction.

   c. People who are highly sensitive to rejection have greater difficulties in romantic relationships as shown by:

    (1) Those who are highly sensitive to rejection respond with greater hostility than less sensitive people when feeling rejected by a romantic partner or friends.

    (2) Middle school students who are sensitive to rejection are more lonely.

    (3) Relationships end sooner if both partners are sensitive to rejection.

   d. People from lower SES backgrounds are more likely to divorce, as they often experience financial and work-related stressors, which negatively affect their marriage.

   e. People who marry at a younger age are more likely to divorce because:

    (1) They are not as effective at being a relationship partner.

(2) They are not as effective at choosing an appropriate relationship partner.

3. The Interaction Dynamics of Unhappy Partners

   a. Gottman and Levenson's interaction dynamics approach can be defined as a methodological approach to the study of the behaviors and conversations of couples, with a focus on negative behaviors such as anger, criticism, defensiveness, contempt, sadness, and fear, and positive behaviors such as affection, enthusiasm, interest, and humor.

   b. The four negative behaviors most toxic to relationships are:

      (1) Criticism: more critical partners have less satisfying relationships.

      (2) Defensiveness: not talking openly and freely about marital problems leads to dissatisfaction.

      (3) Stonewalling: the more people (especially men) withdraw, deny, or reject their partner's issues, the greater dissatisfaction there is in a relationship; the more people disclose, the more they like each other.

      (4) Contempt: the more people (especially women) express contempt for their partner the greater the dissatisfaction and likelihood of divorce.

   c. The self-selection problem may lead to questions about causation, as people may be unhappy because of these four negative behaviors, or the four behaviors may occur because of an underlying unhappiness.

   d. Gottman and Levenson have found that the four behaviors directly affect relationship stability, often leading to divorce.

      (1) In an ongoing longitudinal study started in 1983, Gottman and Levenson have been able to predict with 93 percent accuracy which of seventy-nine couples would divorce based on an assessment of the four negative behaviors during a fifteen-minute observation of a serious discussion between the relationship partners.

      (2) The presence of negative emotion predicted earlier divorce, while the absence of positive emotion predicted later divorce.

4. Dangerous Attributions

   a. Blame is problematic in maintaining romantic bonds.

   b. Bradbury and Fincham (1990) reexamined twenty-three research studies to look at the relationship between partners' causal attributions and their relationship satisfaction.

      (1) In distressed couples, positive partner behaviors are believed to be caused by unstable, specific, unintended, and selfish factors.

      (2) In happy couples, positive partner behaviors are believed to be caused by stable, general, intended, and selfless factors.

      (3) In distressed couples, negative partner behaviors are believed to be caused by stable, global factors, and the partner is thought to be selfish and blameworthy.

      (4) In happy couples, negative partner behaviors are believed to be caused by specific and unintentional factors.

E. Creating Stronger Romantic Bonds

   1. The Investment Model of Relationship Commitment

      a. Commitment is especially problematic in individualistic cultures because they value freedom and the pursuit of individual self-interest.

      b. Rusbult's investment model of interpersonal relationships can be defined as a model of interpersonal relationships that maintains that three things make partners more committed to one another: rewards, alternatives, and investment in the relationship.

         (1) One of the strongest determinants of relationship satisfaction is the degree of reward each partner feels he or she receives.

         (2) The fewer possible alternative relationships a partner perceives, the more committed he or she will be to the existing relationship.

         (3) A person is more likely to remain in a relationship if he or she has invested heavily in it in the past.

         (4) Researchers testing the investment model have asked dating couples to report on their feelings about the three determinants of commitment, their level of commitment, and their satisfaction with the relationship.

            (a) Knowing how members of a couple feel about rewards, alternatives, and investment allows for more accurate prediction of whether the couple will remain together or not.

(b) Each of the three components of the model are important in predicting the level of commitment.

(5) Commitment promotes more stable and satisfying bonds, as shown by these research findings:

(a) More-committed partners tend to represent their lives in more interdependent, intertwined ways, suggesting overlapping identities.

(b) Highly committed partners were more likely to engage in self-sacrifice and accommodation rather than retaliation, in the face of their partner's demand.

(c) Commitment promotes forgiveness.

2. Illusions and Idealization in Romantic Relationships

a. Murray and her colleagues have discovered that the idealization of one's partner is an important part of satisfying romantic bonds.

(1) Murray et al. (1996) conducted a study on relationship satisfaction and perception of a partner's faults and virtues.

(a) Study setup: married couples and dating partners rated themselves and their partner on twenty-one positive and negative attributes, and they supplied ratings of relationship satisfaction.

(b) Finding: individuals who idealized their partner (were more generous in the ratings than the partner's own self-ratings) were more satisfied in their relationships than those who did not idealize their partner.

(2) Murray and Holmes (1999) examined how people idealized their romantic partners.

(a) Study setup: participants were asked to write about their partner's greatest fault.

(b) Finding: satisfied partners saw virtue in the fault and came up with refutations ("yes, but") for why the fault was not so bad.

b. Hawkins et al. (2002) found that more satisfied partners overestimated the amount of positive emotion their partner was

showing to them (relative to judge's ratings) during a videotaped conversation.

3, Novel and Arousing Activities

a. Having children has a devastating effect on marital satisfaction, as the married partners have less time to devote to each other.

b. Aron et al. (2002) investigated the extent to which engaging in novel activities could boost relationship satisfaction.

(1) Independent variable: the couple either participated in a silly, novel game in which they were tied together at the knees and wrists, or they did the same activity individually.

(2) Dependent variable: responses to a marital satisfaction survey.

(3) Finding: both compared to participants in the individual condition and compared to their own baseline, couples in the silly/novel condition reported higher marital satisfaction.

Testing Your Basic Knowledge

ANSWERS TO MULTIPLE-CHOICE QUESTIONS

1.	b	14.	c
2.	a	15.	b
3.	c	16.	a
4.	a	17.	b
5.	b	18.	b
6.	a	19.	b
7.	b	20.	a
8.	a	21.	a
9.	a	22.	c
10.	b	23.	b
11.	a	24.	b
12.	c	25.	a
13.	a		

Testing Your In-Depth Understanding

EXAMPLE ANSWERS TO THE GUIDED QUESTIONS FOR CRITICAL THINKING EXERCISE #2

1. Summaries of each of the concepts are provided in the outline portion of this study guide chapter.

2. Now examine each concept and try to extract advice about what makes a relationship more satisfying, happy, or functional/beneficial from each concept.

need to belong—feeling that you belong with anyone will be advantageous.

relational self theory—relationships with people who remind us of those we love and feel good around will have an early advantage.

relationships as organizing categories—can't give any advice from this.

self-expansion theory—people who have characteristics we admire will create a more positive sense of self after we incorporate their qualities into our own self-concepts.

transactive memory—getting to know your partner and what types of information he or she carefully attends to will help.

relationships and affective life—positive relationships will lead to positive moods and emotions.

attachment styles—perhaps choosing a partner who is consistently attentive to your needs could help modify or bolster your working model of relationships (toward a secure attachment style).

relational models theory—can't give any advice from this.

exchange versus communal relationships—long-term relationship partners should be more concerned with meeting each other's needs than with tit-for-tat reciprocation.

power in relationships—more powerful partners may engage in antisocial behavior.

triangular theory of love—the ultimate kind of love requires a sense of intimacy, physical passion, and commitment.

demographic predictors of dissatisfaction—don't marry too young, try to have a stable financial situation, try to avoid people who are sensitive to rejection if you are, work on neurotic tendencies.

interaction dynamics approach—watch out for and work to avoid the four toxic behaviors: criticism, defensiveness, stonewalling, and (especially) contempt.

attributions—try not to blame your partner for negative events or dismiss responsibility/intention for positive events.

investment model—invest time and energy in the relationship, try to avoid noticing or being in environments that provide viable alternative relationship partners, work hard to give each other lots of positive rewards.

idealization in romantic relationships—try to see your partner's faults as positive features or try to refute the validity or importance of his or her faults.

novel and arousing activities—avoid getting in a rut, try new things, incorporate fun activities.

3. You should be able to narrow the list down on your own. Especially look for things couples who have already gotten married can feasibly do to repair a broken relationship and/or foster a healthy one.

4. Pretend you are a social psychologist and figure out how you could assess whether simply providing "tips" is sufficient to help couples have more satisfying relationships.

There are two ways to reframe this question. One is to ask whether couples will be able to apply general advice to their specific situation and formulate a plan. A second way to reframe the question is to ask whether couples can, on their own—without outside expert intervention—enact such a plan and break old patterns of behavior. The first question could be assessed in a laboratory study in which the tips are given to couples, and then the couples are asked to write down specific ways in which they could enact the tips in their everyday lives. Researchers could then analyze what the couples write to discern whether or not the couples' plans are feasible, and whether or not they accurately stick to the spirit of the tips offered. The second question would probably have to be answered with a longitudinal study. Ideally there would be four groups. One group would consist of couples who are given the tips, make approved plans, and then try to enact those plans on their own. A second group would consist of couples who make a plan and then have a marriage counselor help them enact the plan. A third group could consist of couples who visit a marriage counselor without having received the tips. A fourth group could serve as a control group (to be sure the passage of time isn't responsible for changes). If the couples are randomly assigned to the groups, then any differences in measures of relationship satisfaction (and, certainly any breakups) could be (cautiously) attributed to the "treatment" strategy.

CHAPTER 5

The Social Self

The goal of this chapter is to review research relevant to a social psychological exploration of the self. This includes information about how the self-concept develops, the role and organization of self-knowledge, how and why we evaluate ourselves, and the varying strategies people use to manipulate the self that others perceive.

ANNOTATED CHAPTER OUTLINE

After first reading through the chapter quickly, create a comprehensive framework for the information in the chapter by reading the outline below and filling in the missing information. Instead of simply re-copying information from the textbook, try to use your own words wherever possible; you can check your answers against the completed outline in the Answer Key section at the end of the chapter.

I. Foundations of the Self-Concept
   A. The self-concept can be defined as

   _____

   _____

   _____

   _____

   1. At nine months, children differentiate self from other.
   2. By fifteen to eighteen months, they have a sense of self.
      a. They will touch a red spot on their nose when they see themselves in a mirror.
      b. They will react more strongly to photos of themselves than to photos of others.
   B. Biological Dispositions
      1. Traits can be defined as

      _____

      _____

   _____

2. The Five-Factor Model is also known as the Big Five.
   a. It can be defined as

   _____

   _____

   _____

   b. The five traits go by the acronym OCEAN, and those who are high in each trait can be described in the following ways:
      (1) **O**penness:

      _____

      _____

      _____

      (2) **C**onscientiousness:

      _____

      _____

      _____

      (3) **E**xtraversion:

      _____

      _____

      _____

      (4) **A**greeableness:

      _____

      _____

      _____

      (5) **N**euroticism:

      _____

      _____

_____
_____

3. Experimental evidence suggests that these traits are partially inherited, biologically based dispositions.
   a. They are universal: people from a wide variety of cultures use the Big Five to describe themselves and other people.
   b. They are heritable: these traits depend in part on one's genes.
      (1) Heritability can be defined as

      _____
      _____
      _____
      _____

      (2) Heritability cannot be definitively determined; it can only be estimated, and any estimate is only as good as the study and sample (e.g., of twins) that generated it.
          (a) Monozygotic (identical) twins can be defined as

          _____
          _____
          _____
          _____

          (b) Dizygotic (fraternal) twins can be defined as

          _____
          _____
          _____
          _____

          (c) Studies consistently find that identical twins have more similar personalities than do fraternal twins or ordinary siblings.
          (d) Trait similarity for identical twins raised apart is even higher than for those raised together—presumably growing up together leads to a deliberate attempt to foster distinct personalities.
   c. Researchers have found that specific physical differences can be linked to possessing different levels of certain traits such as:
      (1) _____
      _____
      _____
      (2) _____
      _____
      _____
      _____

(3) _____
    _____
    _____
    _____

C. Family Influence and Sibling Dynamics
   1. Sulloway proposed that sibling rivalry is inevitable and that, as a consequence, humans have evolved a tendency toward diversification to survive such rivalry.
      a. Diversification can be defined as

      _____
      _____
      _____

      b. Older siblings are bigger, more powerful, and more invested in the status quo, whereas younger siblings are born to rebel.
   2. In a large review, Sulloway found different traits in older and younger siblings.
      a. Older siblings were

      _____
      _____
      _____

      b. Younger siblings were

      _____
      _____
      _____

   3. In a study of over 3,000 scientists from various times in history, Sulloway found:
      a. _____
      _____
      _____
      _____
      b. _____
      _____
      _____
      _____
      c. _____
      _____
      _____
      _____

D. Context and the Sense of Self
   1. Social Context: our sense of self changes in different contexts.
      a. It changes when we interact with people who remind us of different significant others.
      b. It changes when we interact with subordinates rather than equal-status peers.
      c. It changes when we are in a bad mood, with peripheral aspects of our self-concept seeming more negative at such times.

    d. It changes when we experience momentary failures, which can increase our self-criticism and self-doubt.

2. Distinctiveness

    a. The distinctiveness hypothesis can be defined as

_____

_____

_____

_____

    b. McGuire and Padawer-Singer (1978) tested this distinctiveness hypothesis by asking sixth-grade children to describe themselves and found

_____

_____

_____

_____

3. Social Comparison

    a. Festinger's social comparison theory can be defined as

_____

_____

_____

_____

    b. For accuracy, we seek similar others to whom we can compare ourselves.

    c. For a self-esteem boost, we engage in downward social comparison and compare ourselves to someone less well off or capable than we are.

    d. To learn how to be better, we engage in upward social comparison and compare ourselves to someone better (despite potential damage to self-esteem) than we are.

E. Culture and the Self-Concept

1. Western societies' view of the self can be characterized as

_____

_____

_____

_____

2. Eastern societies' view of the self can be characterized as

_____

_____

_____

_____

3. Hall (1976) characterized interdependent societies as being "high context" and independent societies as being "low context."

    a. He called Eastern cultures "high-context," since they believe that the type of social relationship is crucial to determining proper behavior and that the attributes of the self are dependent on the relationship with the person with whom one is dealing.

       (1) There are different words for "I" in Japanese depending on whom one is talking to.

       (2) There are different words for "you" in Korean depending on whom one is talking to.

    b. He called Western cultures "low-context," since role relations matter less to them and individuals have preferences, attitudes, and beliefs that are stable across situations; self-definition is not bounded by the situation.

4. Markus, Kitayama, and Triandis have formulated theories that culture-based self-conceptions shape our emotions, motivations, and perceptions of the social world, with differences between those with independent and interdependent self-construals.

    a. The independent self can be described as follows and is characteristic of people in these cultures:

       (1) It is characteristic of Western people, especially people from North American and Northern European cultures.

       (2) _____

_____

_____

_____

       (3) _____

_____

_____

_____

    b. The interdependent self can be described as follows and is characteristic of people in these cultures:

       (1) _____

_____

_____

_____

       (2) _____

_____

_____

_____

       (3) _____

_____

_____

_____

F. Gender and the Self-Concept

1. Cross and Madson (1997) found that women tend to be more interdependent and men tend

to be more independent. The following
research evidence supports this conclusion:

a. _____

_____

_____

b. _____

_____

_____

c. _____

_____

_____

d. _____

_____

_____

2. Men and women are socialized differently in
these ways:

a. _____

_____

_____

b. _____

_____

_____

c. _____

_____

_____

d. _____

_____

_____

e. _____

_____

_____

f. _____

_____

_____

II. Self-Knowledge
A. Self-knowledge consists of our understanding of our
thoughts, feelings, preferences, and beliefs.
1. Self-knowledge includes specific beliefs,
images, networks of memories and
associations, rich narratives or stories.
2. Self-beliefs are one aspect of self-knowledge,
and they include:
a. Personal beliefs, which are

_____

_____

_____

b. Social beliefs, which are

_____

_____

_____

c. Relational self-beliefs, which are

_____

_____

_____

d. The collective self, which is

_____

_____

_____

B. The Organizational Function of Self-Knowledge
1. Greenwald (1980) called self-knowledge a
"totalitarian ego" because

_____

_____

_____

2. Memory and the Self-Reference Effect
a. The self-reference effect can be defined as

_____

_____

_____

(1) Rogers, Kupier, and Kirker (1977)
conducted the first study to explore the
self-reference effect.
(a) Independent variable:

_____

_____

_____

(b) Dependent variable: number of
words participants remembered.
(c) Finding:

_____

_____

_____

(2) Participants took longer to decide
whether or not a trait was descriptive of
the self than to answer questions about
structure, sounds, and semantics of trait
adjectives, suggesting that information
about the self is elaborate and complex.

3. Self-Schemas and Self-Understanding
   a. A self-schema can be defined as

   _____

   _____

   _____

   _____

   b. Markus argued that when a person has a self-schema for a trait or characteristic, he or she will process information in that domain more quickly, retrieve information consistent with the schema more quickly, and more strongly resist contradictory information.
   c. Markus (1977) tested these hypotheses by first identifying people who considered themselves very independent or dependent ("schematic" for the concept) and people for whom dependence/independence was not important to their self-concept ("aschematic"). The three major findings from this study were:
      (1) _____

      _____

      _____

      (2) _____

      _____

      _____

      (3) _____

      _____

      _____

   d. The self-reference effect and self-schemas contribute to the stability of the self.
      (1) We are more likely to remember information that is consistent (rather than inconsistent) with our self-beliefs (thus, confirming and reinforcing them).
      (2) We are likely to resist information that is not consistent with our self-beliefs.
4. Culture and Self-Beliefs
   a. Cousins (1989) found that

   _____

   _____

   _____

   _____

   b. Japanese students were more likely to define the self in terms of personal attributes, however, when a specific situational context was specified, suggesting that the Japanese do recognize

traits in themselves, but the traits are dependent on the situation.

C. The Motivational Function of Self-Knowledge
   1. Self-knowledge helps motivate action.
   2. Our self-knowledge includes possible selves—the kinds of people we hope to be in the future.
   3. Tory Higgins's self-discrepancy theory can be defined as

   _____

   _____

   _____

   _____

   a. Higgins argues that we have three types of selves:
      (1) The actual self can be defined as

   _____

   _____

   _____

      (2) The ideal self can be defined as

   _____

   _____

   _____

      (3) The ought self can be defined as

   _____

   _____

   _____

   b. When we are primed to think about the ideal self, we have a promotion focus, which can be defined as

   _____

   _____

   _____

   c. When we are primed to think about our ought self, we have a prevention focus.
      (1) A prevention focus can be defined as

   _____

   _____

   _____

      (2) A prevention focus triggers guilt, anxiety, terror, panic, elevated physiological arousal, avoidant behavior, and sensitivity to negative outcomes.
   d. When we are primed to think about achieving our ideal self, we show elevated positive affect, heightened sensitivity to positive feedback, and approach-related behavior.

e. When we are primed to think about failing to achieve our ideal self, we show

_____

_____

_____

D. The Self as a Standard in Social Perception
1. We use our self-knowledge to judge other people, using the vivid and accessible information about ourselves to set standards.
2. The self-image bias can be defined as

_____

_____

_____

a. Lewicki (1983) found that

_____

_____

_____

b. David Dunning and colleagues suggest we use self-information as a standard to define others' traits, abilities, and social concepts.
   (1) People have egocentric construals of social categories and attributes.
   (2) In one study, college students used their own levels of studiousness and athleticism to set the standard for how much a person has to study or engage in athletic activity in order to be favorably rated as "studious" or "athletic."
3. People from interdependent cultures are more likely to rely on others as the standard for social judgments, unlike people from independent cultures, who are more likely to rely on the self as the standard.
   a. Students in the U.S. say that other people are similar to themselves more often than they say they are similar to others, suggesting that the self is the dominant category or standard.
   b. Students in Asian countries are more likely to show the opposite pattern, suggesting that the other is the more dominant or salient standard.
   c. Cohen and Gunz (2002) found that

_____

_____

_____

_____

E. Illusions and Biases about the Self
1. Taylor and Brown suggest that illusions about the self enhance psychological well-being.

a. Well-being is correlated with unrealistically positive views about the self.
   (1) Self-serving attributions can be defined as

_____

_____

_____

_____

b. Well-being is correlated with exaggerated perceptions of control.
   (1) Langer (1975) conducted a study to examine the illusion of control of participants who were entered in a lottery.
      (a) Independent variable:

_____

_____

_____

_____

      (b) Dependent variable:

_____

_____

_____

_____

      (c) Finding:

_____

_____

_____

_____

   (2) People who are depressed do not show a false perception of control.
c. Well-being is correlated with optimism about one's future.
   (1) Westerners are prone to unrealistic optimism.
      (a) College students think positive events are more likely to happen to them than to others, and they think negative events are less likely to happen to them than to others.
      (b) People tend to focus on themselves and to ignore what happens to comparison others.
   (2) People are overly optimistic about common positive events and rare negative events and overly pessimistic about rare positive events and common negative events.
2. Taylor and Brown argue that these illusions promote health in three ways:
   a. _____

_____

_____

_____

b. _____

_____

_____

_____

c. _____

_____

_____

_____

3. Critiques of Taylor and Brown include the following:
   a. Narcissists are not psychologically healthy, but display strong positive illusions of self.
   b. Overestimating academic talents is associated (in the long run) with lower self-esteem, deteriorating academic performance, and decreased school engagement.
   c. East Asians are less likely to endorse positive illusions about the self than are Westerners.
      (1) Sastry and Ross (1998) found that Asians had less perceived control in their lives than non-Asians, but that this lack of control was associated with depression and anxiety only for the non-Asians.
      (2) Well-being may be tied to values that are important to the culture.

III. Self-Evaluation
   A. A common assumption, adopted by California's self-esteem task force, is that elevating self-esteem would help to cure society's ills.
      1. The following variables are correlated with having lower self-esteem:
         a. _____

         _____

         _____

         _____

         b. _____

         _____

         _____

         _____

         c._____

         _____

         _____

         _____

         d._____

         _____

         _____

         _____

         e. _____

         _____

         _____

         _____

2. Despite the correlational evidence, the truth about self-esteem is much more complex (and not always supportive of the assumption that higher self-esteem is always a good thing).

B. Trait and State Self-Esteem
   1. Self-esteem can be defined as

   _____

   _____

   _____

   _____

      a. People with high self-esteem feel very good about themselves.
      b. People with low self-esteem feel more ambivalent, believing themselves to have both positive and negative qualities.
      c. People who truly feel horrible about themselves are rare; such feelings are almost always associated with clinical disorders like depression.
   2. Trait self-esteem can be defined as

   _____

   _____

   _____

   _____

   3. State self-esteem can be defined as

   _____

   _____

   _____

   _____

   4. Self-esteem also fluctuates with the momentary context.
      a. Current mood influences self-esteem.
      b. A temporary failure lowers self-esteem temporarily.
      c. Children of average academic ability experience lower self-esteem when in a classroom with children of higher ability.

C. Contingencies of Self-Worth
   1. Crocker and Wolfe's contingencies of self-worth theory says that self-esteem is

   _____

   _____

   _____

   _____

      a. Contingencies of self-worth include approval, appearance, academic competence (for example, "My self-esteem gets a boost when I get a good grade on an exam or paper").
      b. People vary as to the contingencies upon which their self-esteem is based.
      c. Groups and subcultures also vary as to which contingencies of self-worth are important to them (for example,

   _____

   _____

2. People will have high self-esteem if they can create environments that provide positive feedback in those domains upon which their self-esteem is based.
3. Positive feedback in contingent domains leads to high self-esteem; negative feedback in contingent domains leads to low self-esteem.
   a. Crocker, Sommers, and Luhtanen (2002) asked college seniors who had applied to graduate school to fill out a self-esteem scale every day that they received news from a grad school.
   b. Crocker, Sommers, and Luhtanen found that

   _____
   _____
   _____
   _____

4. A contingencies perspective may suggest that having more contingencies is better than having fewer contingencies.
D. Social Acceptance and Self-Esteem
   1. Leary's sociometer hypothesis maintains that

   _____
   _____
   _____

   a. Self-esteem acts as a meter for measuring inclusion; high self-esteem means adequate group belonging, and low self-esteem means inadequate group belonging.
   b. The hypothesis is derived from evolutionary reasoning that those who sought to belong to social groups would have better chances of surviving and reproducing than those who did not.
   2. Leary et al. (1995) conducted a study to test the sociometer hypothesis.
   a. Independent variable:

   _____
   _____
   _____

   b. Dependent variable:

   _____
   _____
   _____

   c. Finding:

   _____
   _____

E. Motives for Self-Evaluation
   1. The Motive to Elevate Self-Esteem
   a. Self-enhancement is a high priority in Western cultures, and people will strive to enhance their self-worth in a number of ways.
   b. Tesser's self-evaluation maintenance model says that

   _____
   _____
   _____

   (1) Through reflection, we

   _____
   _____
   _____

      (a) We wear school colors when the team wins.
      (b) Basking in reflected glory is effective only when the close other's domain of success is NOT relevant to our own self-concept.
   (2) Through social comparison, we

   _____
   _____
   _____

   (3) We will seek out relationships with close others who are highly skilled in domains not relevant to our self-esteem and less skilled in domains that are relevant to our self-esteem.
   c. Many studies support the self-evaluation maintenance model.
   (1) Tesser and Smith (1980) had pairs of friends play a word game with each other and with strangers.
      (a) Independent variable #1:

   _____
   _____
   _____

      (b) Independent variable #2:

   _____
   _____
   _____

      (c) Dependent variable: whether the participant chose to give fellow players easy items to complete or hard items to complete.

(d) Findings:

_____

_____

_____

(2) Tesser, Campbell, and Smith (1984) conducted a study with fifth and sixth graders to test whether we choose friends whom we outperform in domains relevant to our self-concept.

    (a) They asked students to identify their closest friends, the most and least important activities relevant to their self-concept, and how well they and their friends performed at those activities.

    (b) Finding:

_____

_____

_____

(3) Tesser (1980) found that eminent scientists reported remaining closer to fathers who had pursued a career in a different area, and that siblings felt closer to one another when they outperformed the sibling in an important area.

2. The Motive to Find Out the Truth about the Self

  a. Swann's self-verification theory holds that

_____

_____

_____

  b. We gather truthful information about the self in two ways:

    (1) We selectively attend to and remember information that is consistent with our self-views.

    (2) We create self-confirmatory social environments.

      (a) We signal who we are and how we wish to be treated through identity cues, which are

_____

_____

_____

      (b) We choose to enter relationships that help us maintain consistent views of the self.

3. There is evidence for both self-enhancement and self-verification.

  a. Self-enhancement seems to be the rule regarding

_____

_____

b. Self-verification seems to be the rule regarding

_____

_____

_____

F. Culture and Self-Esteem

  1. East Asian languages have no word for "self-esteem."

  2. Westerners invented the notion of "self-esteem."

  3. Interdependent people score lower on self-esteem scales than do independent respondents.

  4. Western cultures create social contexts and interactions that boost individual self-esteem. The following evidence supports this conclusion:

    a. _____

_____

_____

    b. _____

_____

_____

    c. _____

_____

_____

  5. Non-Westerners don't have low self-esteem in general; rather, they are more concerned with other ways of being a good person (e.g., self-improvement to become a better member of the collective).

    a. East Asian cultures (especially the Japanese) engage in a form of self-criticism that results in better specific skills and social harmony.

    b. Heine et al. (2001) found that

_____

_____

_____

G. Culture Change and Self-Esteem

  1. Although Westerners are generally concerned with individual distinctiveness, this is not true for people in all sectors of the society at all times.

  2. Heine and Lehman (2003) have found that

_____

_____

_____

_____

H. Possible Dangers of "High Self-Esteem"
  1. Baumeister and his colleagues suggest that fragile, inflated egotism may be problematic.
     a. Fragile, inflated egotism is not healthy self-esteem and may lead to violent action to reassert superiority and dominate challengers.
     b. Inflated egotism consists of grossly exaggerated positive views of self coupled with a volatile sensitivity to threats, insults, and challenges.
  2. There is research evidence supporting the dangers of inflated egotism:
     a. _____
        _____
        _____
        _____
     b. _____
        _____
        _____
        _____
     c. _____
        _____
        _____
        _____
     d. _____
        _____
        _____
        _____

IV. Self-Presentation
  A. Self-presentation can be defined as
     _____
     _____
     _____
     _____
     1. Impression management is
        _____
        _____
        _____
        _____
     2. Erving Goffman argued that the social selves we construct govern much of our public behavior; people use strategic self-presentation in public life.
        a. Face refers to
           _____
           _____
           _____
           _____
        b. Social interactions are how we create our "face."
        c. People depend on one another to help maintain face claims.
  B. Ideas about the Public Self

  1. Public self-consciousness can be defined as
     _____
     _____
     _____
     _____
  2. Private self-consciousness can be defined as
     _____
     _____
     _____
     _____
  3. People high in public self-consciousness overestimate the extent to which others attend to them and define identity in terms of social attributes (e.g., popularity); people high in private self-consciousness define their identity in terms of
     _____
     _____
     _____
     _____
  4. Self-monitoring can be defined as
     _____
     _____
     _____
     _____
     a. High self-monitors are like actors in that they scrutinize the situation and modify their self-presentation and behavior to be appropriate.
     b. Low self-monitors act in accord with their internal inclinations, regardless of the situation.
     c. Students often view low self-monitoring as more adaptive because people are "being true to themselves."
     d. Goffman believed that effective social functioning requires the type of strategic self-presentation that high self-monitors engage in.
  C. Self-Handicapping: Protecting Your Own Face
     1. Sometimes we will act in self-destructive ways to protect claims about the self.
     2. Self-handicapping can be defined as
        _____
        _____
        _____
        _____
        a. Self-handicapping might be not studying enough for an exam or training enough for an athletic competition.
        b. It might be showing up late or saying inappropriate things on first dates or interviews.

c. These behaviors provide an external excuse for failure and reduce the threat to self-esteem and/or face.
   (1) Self-handicapping is defined by actually engaging in a self-defeating behavior.
   (2) Sometimes people will lie about their behaviors in order to have these types of external excuses (e.g., claiming you didn't study).
d. Berglas and Jones (1978) conducted a classic, early self-handicapping study.
   (1) Independent variable:

   _____
   _____
   _____
   _____

   (2) Dependent variable: whether participants chose to take a drug that would have a side effect (supposedly) that would improve or impair test performance.
   (3) Finding:

   _____
   _____
   _____
   _____

3. The evolutionary perspective on self-handicapping argues that self-destructive tendencies may signal that potential mates have superior genes.
   a. Many animals and birds have features that are valued by potential mates but that impair survival skills (e.g., tails that hinder flight, eye pads that hinder vision).
   b. Self-handicapping theory suggests that these traits signal value in that only individuals with superior genes can afford to have them.
D. Self-Presentation and Language
   1. On-record communication can be defined as

   _____
   _____
   _____
   _____

   2. Off-record communication can be defined as

   _____
   _____
   _____
   _____

   a. Friendly teasing can be a playful, indirect way to let others know they have behaved inappropriately.

b. Flirting can allow for an exploration of romantic interest without the self-esteem and face risks of direct communication.

TESTING YOUR BASIC KNOWLEDGE

After studying the information in the chapter by filling in the outline above, test your basic knowledge with the following multiple-choice test. Answers are provided in the Answer Key section at the end of the chapter. If you find that you have gotten an answer wrong, it is important that you understand why it is wrong (as well as understanding why the correct answer is the better choice). Talk with peers, your tutor, or your professor if you need help.

Multiple-Choice Questions

1. Hannah is a sixteen-month-old human infant. In an experiment, a dab of red color is put on Hannah's nose without her realizing that it happened. Later, when put in front of a mirror, Hannah touches the red spot on her nose. This is evidence that Hannah is now beginning to develop
   a. a public identity or "face."
   b. low self-esteem.
   c. a self-concept.

2. Which of the following is an accurate list of the "Big Five" traits?
   a. openness, extraversion, self-consciousness, agitation, neurosis
   b. openness, conscientiousness, extraversion, agreeableness, neuroticism
   c. self-esteem, self-consciousness, self-monitoring, self-verification, self-image

3. A researcher is studying a new trait called misunderestimation. The researcher conducts a twin study and finds that identical twins are very similar to one another with respect to their tendency to engage in misunderestimation. In fact, twins are much more similar to one another than are ordinary siblings. This is evidence suggesting that this new trait
   a. is heritable.
   b. is a consequence of a process of diversification.
   c. is no different than the trait, extraversion.

4. A female scientist joins an all-male faculty at a college. What attribute is almost certain to be included in the female scientist's self-definition when she is at work?
   a. that she is a scientist
   b. that she is intelligent
   c. that she is a woman

5. Raymond is playing basketball with some friends. Under what conditions is he more likely to compare his own athletic skills with those of Brad, who plays equally as well as he does, rather than Pat, who plays worse than he does?
   a. if he wants accurate information
   b. if he needs a self-esteem boost
   c. if he wants tips on how to become a better player

6. If a woman has a self-schema concerning body weight, that person would tend to
   a. be especially susceptible to attempts to change her attitudes about her weight.
   b. be a low self-monitor.
   c. answer weight-related questions more quickly than neutral questions.

7. Which of the following *best* exemplifies the process of self-handicapping?
   a. attributing poor performance on an exam to the difficulty of the test
   b. telling someone you were lucky after winning a tournament
   c. waiting until just a few hours before the due date to begin writing an important paper

8. Alicia is a *high* self-monitor, and Stacy is a *low* self-monitor. Stacy is more likely than Alicia to
   a. maintain consistency in her behavior.
   b. know the rules of appropriate behavior.
   c. adjust her behavior to fit the situation.

9. Which description best fits a person from an interdependent or "high-context" culture?
   a. Self-definition is dependent upon the particular situation the person is in.
   b. Self-definition is characterized by a person's attitudes, beliefs, and preferences.
   c. Self-definition is determined by the rights and freedoms afforded in one's culture.

10. Generally speaking, woman tend to be more _____ than men.
    a. independent
    b. interdependent
    c. distinctive

11. Research on the self-reference effect suggests that people
    a. better remember information that is integrated into the self-knowledge structure.
    b. tend to find self-relevant links to even nonpersonal information.
    c. tend to associate themselves with positive outcomes and dissociate themselves from negative outcomes.

12. Benicio has incorporated a desire to be a college graduate into his ideal self. At present, he is struggling to finish high school with good enough grades to get a much needed scholarship. When he thinks about his goal and his intention to reach it no matter what, he tends to adopt a
    a. self-image bias.
    b. prevention focus.
    c. promotion focus.

13. According to Dov Cohen and Alex Gunz (2002), _____ are likely to describe a self-relevant event from their original point of view as a participant, but _____ are likely to describe a self-relevant event from the point of view of an observer.
    a. Canadians; Asians
    b. high self-monitors; low self-monitors
    c. extraverts; introverts

14. In a study, participants entered a lottery. Half of the participants were allowed to choose their own lottery ticket, and the other half were given a lottery ticket. Later, those who were allowed to choose their tickets charged a higher price for selling their ticket back than those who were just given a ticket. This finding suggests that
    a. economic "sunk-cost" is more prevalent for those allowed to choose their tickets.
    b. people have exaggerated perceptions of control.
    c. people tend to engage in self-serving attributions.

15. Crocker, Sommers, and Luhtanen (2002) found that college seniors applying to graduate school had lower self-esteem on days they received rejection letters compared to days they received acceptance letters. This finding was much stronger for students who
    a. were more contingent on academic competency.
    b. were high self-monitors.
    c. were engaging in self-handicapping.

16. Sally has a choice between becoming close with one of two acquaintances. One shares her passion for singing and is an exceptionally talented singer. The other doesn't sing at all, but is a very talented gymnast (an area that Sally knows nothing about). According to Tesser's self-evaluation maintaince theory, which acquaintance is Sally more likely to become close friends with?
    a. the singer
    b. the gymnast
    c. It is impossible to tell from the information given.

17. Research on self-enhancement and self-verification suggests that
    a. a person with a negative view of the self will feel badly after negative feedback but will judge the feedback as diagnostic.
    b. a person with a positive view of the self will feel badly after negative feedback but will judge the feedback as diagnostic.
    c. a person with a negative view of the self will feel good after negative feedback and will accept the feedback as accurate.

18. In East Asian cultures, people have a tendency to focus on _____ rather than _____ because such a focus promotes social harmony and improves specific skills.
    a. self-esteem; self-verification
    b. self-monitoring; self-handicapping
    c. self-criticism; self-esteem

19. Brian appears to think quite highly of himself. He believes the world would be a better place if he were in charge of it, and he does not like to be challenged. He takes insults very seriously and will defend himself readily. According to Roy Baumeister, we should be concerned that Brian
    a. will become violent or antisocial.
    b. really has low self-esteem that he is hiding from others.
    c. may commit suicide.

20. Alexi Santana entered Princeton University as a member of the class of 1993, was extraordinarily popular, and told stories of his fascinating and accomplished past. In reality, Alexi was James Hogue, an ex-convict who had filed a fraudulent application to get into Princeton. Erving Goffman would consider this an extreme example of
    a. self-monitoring.
    b. self-presentation.
    c. self- handicapping.

21. People who score high on private self-consciousness scales are likely to define the self in terms of
    a. personal feelings and beliefs.
    b. social attributes like popularity.
    c. role relationships with other people.

22. Harry is attracted to Heidi (who has red hair) and would like to go out with her. During a conversation, he playfully teases her, saying that he can't envision himself dating someone with red hair because he'd be scared of her feisty temper. Harry is most likely
    a. engaging in self-handicapping.
    b. engaging in off-record communication.
    c. high in public self-consciousness.

23. Wayne chooses to wear to his college orientation the T-shirt he picked up at the Coldplay concert he attended. Social psychologists would call the T-shirt a (an)
    a. contingency of self-worth.
    b. off-record communication.
    c. identity cue.

24. According to the sociometer hypothesis, low self-esteem indicates
    a. insufficient inclusion in a social group.
    b. clinical levels of depression.
    c. membership in an Asian culture.

25. Ellen's self-knowledge includes her extraversion, her belief that friends should be there for each other no matter what, her positive sense of self-esteem whenever she is with her partner, and her awareness that she is a Democrat and a Red Sox fan. Which of those pieces of information is part of the collective self?
    a. that she is a Democrat and Red Sox fan
    b. her extraversion
    c. her high self-esteem when she is with her partner

Essay Questions

After you have mastered the multiple-choice questions, try testing your basic understanding by thoroughly answering each of the broad essay questions below. Because it is critical that you think through this information on your own, we have *not* provided any answers to these questions. Your learning and retention of this material will be greatly enhanced if you do one or more of the following to check your answers: carefully review the textbook information; compare your responses to your class lecture notes; talk over your answers with a peer; ask your professor to review your answers or review any information that is unclear to you.

1. Define the self-concept and discuss the ways in which it is shaped by biology, siblings, culture, gender, and the immediate context.

2. Explain the ways in which knowledge about the self organizes other cognitive information and motivates behavior. Discuss the ways in which the self influences our judgments of others. Describe the sorts of illusions people may have about the self, why they have them, and describe evidence supporting and refuting the utility of these illusions.

3. Define trait and state self-esteem and explain the logic of contingencies of self-worth theory and the sociometer hypothesis. Describe the ways and reasons people evaluate themselves, and explain the dangers of fragile, inflated egotism. Discuss the differences in how people in Western and Eastern cultures value self-esteem.

4. Define self-presentation and impression management. More specifically, explain the difference between public and private self-consciousness, and describe the characteristics of a high self-monitor. Define self-handicapping, and explain the purpose of such self-defeating behavior. Discuss how concerns about self-presentation can affect the way we communicate with other people.

TESTING YOUR IN-DEPTH UNDERSTANDING

Test your in-depth understanding of the material by working through the Critical Thinking Exercises provided at the end of each textbook chapter. To maximize this learning opportunity, work together with a tutor, study group, or your professor. Alternatively, write down your thoughts and responses.

Guided questions for one of the exercises are provided below. While there are multiple ways to answer these questions, short answers are given in the Answer Key at the end of the chapter. Note, however, that the valuable part of this exercise is not simply knowing the answer but working with the material to come up with the answer.

Guided Questions for Critical Thinking Exercise #1

What are some of the different ways in which the self is a product of the situation?

Rather than simply listing concepts from the chapter, first try to think of a situation or example from your own life, and then analyze how different aspects of the self would be influenced by the situation. Try to *integrate* the concepts you are learning about (i.e., explore how the concepts work with each other). See the Answer Key for a discussion of the first suggested situation as an example. Also, see the suggested concepts to consider.

Suggested ideas for situations/examples:

1. A child is placed in a classroom with children who are more academically gifted.

2. A boyfriend breaks up with his girlfriend.

3. A student feels angry with his or her professor and wants to disagree with a decision versus a student feels angry with a friend and wants to disagree with a decision.

4. A soldier is ordered to torture a prisoner-of-war.

5. An African American begins a new job at a company in which everyone else is white.

Concepts to consider:

1. Aspects of the self that may be affected

   Big Five
   face
   actual self
   ought self
   ideal self
   identity cues
   personal beliefs
   relational self-beliefs
   social beliefs
   collective self
   private self-consciousness
   public self-consciousness
   self-esteem
   trait self-esteem
   state self-esteem
   self-schemas

2. Theories/processes that may have an influence in the situation

   contingencies of self-worth
   distinctiveness hypothesis
   diversification
   impression management
   self-presentation
   prevention focus
   promotion focus
   self-discrepancy theory
   self-evaluation maintenance model
   self-monitoring
   self-reference effect
   self-schemas
   self-verification theory
   social comparison theory
   sociometer hypothesis

Enhance your understanding of the chapter by thinking about and doing the remaining three Critical Thinking Exercises. Discuss your answers with your peers, study group, tutor, or professor.

Critical Thinking Exercise #2

Consider some situation bearing both potential for success and possibilities of failure. What aspect of self-understanding would be called upon in each case?

Critical Thinking Exercise #3

Independent peoples are motivated to move their actual selves into line with their "ideal" selves. What kinds of motivations do you suppose serve a similar function for changing the self for interdependent peoples?

Critical Thinking Exercise #4

Do you think interdependent people would be more likely than independent people to be high self-monitors or low self-monitors? Why?

SOCIAL PSYCHOLOGY IN THE POPULAR MEDIA

You might be interested in the following popular media references, each of which relates in some way to information in this chapter.

Book

Maguire, Gregory (1995). *Wicked: The Life and Times of the Wicked Witch of the West.* New York: Regan Books. This is the book upon which the popular Broadway musical is based. As opposed to the play, the book is a much more complex and in-depth exploration of how the Wicked Witch of the West formed her identity (from childhood through adulthood), her sense of self-worth, and how she came to be known as "wicked." This is an interesting and engaging read.

Film

Finding Forrester (2000; directed by Gus Van Sant; starring Sean Connery and Rob Brown). Jamal is an inner-city kid who excels at both athletics and writing. Sean Connery plays a famous but reclusive writer (Forrester) who ends up mentoring Jamal. The story follows each of the characters (who are from totally different cultural worlds) as they help each other foster new identities and explore the "face" they want to present to the world.

Web Site

Self-Assessment Scales—http://www.u.arizona.edu/ %7Eschmader/self.htm. Five interactive exercises about state self-esteem, self-monitoring, optimism, gender identity, and the "Who Am I" scale (i.e., Twenty Statements Test). Take the tests, find out your scores, and learn more about different areas of research related to each topic. Be sure to read the directions carefully, and make sure that your Internet browser has the necessary "plug-in" program(s).

ANSWER KEY

Annotated Chapter Outline

I. Foundations of the Self-Concept
  A. The self-concept can be defined as an understanding of the existence and properties of a separate self and its characteristics.
    1. At nine months, children differentiate self from other.
    2. By fifteen to eighteen months, they have a sense of self.
      a. They will touch a red spot on their nose when they see themselves in a mirror.
      b. They will react more strongly to photos of themselves than to photos of others.
  B. Biological Dispositions
    1. Traits can be defined as consistent ways that people think, feel, and act across classes of situations.
    2. The Five-Factor Model is also known as the Big Five.
      a. It can be defined as five personality traits (openness, conscientiousness, extraversion, agreeableness and neuroticism) that psychologists believe lie at the core of our self-definitions.
      b. The five traits go by the acronym OCEAN, and those who are high in each trait can be described in the following ways:
        (1) **O**penness: open people are imaginative, curious, artistic.
        (2) **C**onscientiousness: conscientious people are efficient, achievement-oriented, organized.
        (3) **E**xtraversion: extraverts are talkative, energetic, enthusiastic; introverts are not anti-social; they simply need more "alone time" to recharge.
        (4) **A**greeableness: agreeable people are warm, friendly, kind.
        (5) **N**euroticism: neurotic people are anxious, tense, emotionally volatile.
    3. Experimental evidence suggests that these traits are partially inherited, biologically based dispositions.
      a. They are universal: people from a wide variety of cultures use the Big Five to describe themselves and other people.
      b. They are heritable: these traits depend in part on one's genes.
        (1) Heritability can be defined as the degree to which traits or physical characteristics are determined by

genes, and hence inherited from parents.

    (2) Heritability cannot be definitively determined; it can only be estimated, and any estimate is only as good as the study and sample (e.g., of twins) that generated it.

        (a) Monozygotic (identical) twins can be defined as twins who originate from a single fertilized egg that splits into two exact replicas that then develop into two genetically identical individuals.

        (b) Dizygotic (fraternal) twins can be defined as twins who originate from two different eggs fertilized by different sperm cells; like ordinary siblings, they share on average half of their genes.

        (c) Studies consistently find that identical twins have more similar personalities than fraternal twins or ordinary siblings.

        (d) Trait similarity for identical twins raised apart is even higher than for those raised together—presumably growing up together leads to a deliberate attempt to foster distinct personalities.

  c. Researchers have found that specific physical differences can be linked to possessing different levels of certain traits, such as:

    (1) Children identified as shy when they were babies have elevated levels of cortisol, making fear responses more likely.

    (2) Neuroticism is associated with greater sympathetic autonomic nervous system activity, which is associated with elevated stress and tension.

    (3) Extraversion is related to elevated levels of dopamine, which is associated with approach-related behavior, enthusiasm, and receptiveness to rewards.

C. Family Influence and Sibling Dynamics

  1. Sulloway proposed that sibling rivalry is inevitable and that, as a consequence, humans have evolved a tendency toward diversification to survive such rivalry.

    a. Diversification can be defined as a principle that maintains that siblings develop into quite different people so that they can peacefully occupy different niches within the family environment.

    b. Older siblings are bigger, more powerful, and more invested in the status quo, whereas younger siblings are born to rebel.

  2. In a large review, Sulloway found different traits in older and younger siblings.

    a. Older siblings were more assertive, dominant, achievement-oriented, and conscientious.

    b. Younger siblings were more agreeable (to deal with dominant older sibs) and more open to novel experiences.

  3. In a study of over 3,000 scientists from various times in history, Sulloway found:

    a. Younger siblings were more open to novel ideas (like Darwin's theory).

    b. Younger siblings were more likely to endorse radical, but misguided pseudoscientific ideas.

    c. Younger siblings were more likely to excel in science, and to travel in pursuit of new ideas.

D. Context and the Sense of Self

  1. Social Context: our sense of self changes in different contexts.

    a. It changes when we interact with people who remind us of different significant others.

    b. It changes when we interact with subordinates rather than equal-status peers.

    c. It changes when we are in a bad mood, with peripheral aspects of our self-concept seeming more negative at such times.

    d. It changes when we experience momentary failures, which can increase our self-criticism and self-doubt.

  2. Distinctiveness

    a. The distinctiveness hypothesis can be defined as identifying what makes us unique in each particular context and highlighting that uniqueness in our self-definition.

    b. McGuire and Padawer-Singer (1978) tested this distinctiveness hypothesis by asking sixth-grade children to describe themselves and found that the children were more likely to mention characteristics that made them different from their classmates (for example, their gender, nationality, age, race).

3. Social Comparison
   a. Festinger's social comparison theory can be defined as the hypothesis that we compare ourselves to other people in order to evaluate ourselves.
   b. For accuracy, we seek similar others to whom we can compare ourselves.
   c. For a self-esteem boost, we engage in downward social comparison and compare ourselves to someone less well off or capable than we are.
   d. To learn how to be better, we engage in upward social comparison and compare ourselves to someone better (despite potential damage to self-esteem) than we are.

E. Culture and the Self-Concept
   1. Western societies' view of the self can be characterized as emphasizing individuality, self-actualization, freedom, and self-expression.
   2. Eastern societies' view of the self can be characterized as emphasizing knowing one's place in society, and honoring traditions and social roles.
   3. Hall (1976) characterized interdependent societies as being "high context" and independent societies as being "low context."
      a. He called Eastern cultures "high-context," since they believe that the type of social relationship is crucial to determining proper behavior and that the attributes of the self are dependent on the relationship with the person with whom one is dealing.
         (1) There are different words for "I" in Japanese depending on whom one is talking to.
         (2) There are different words for "you" in Korean depending on whom one is talking to.
      b. He called Western cultures "low-context," since role relations matter less to them and individuals have preferences, attitudes, and beliefs that are stable across situations; self-definition is not bounded by the situation.
   4. Markus, Kitayama, and Triandis have formulated theories that culture-based self-conceptions shape our emotions, motivations, and perceptions of the social world, with differences between those with independent and interdependent self-construals.
      a. The independent self can be described as follows and is characteristic of people in these cultures:
         (1) It is characteristic of Western people, especially people from North American and Northern European cultures.
         (2) The self is autonomous, and uniqueness and independence are considered to be crucial.
         (3) The focus is on internal causes for behavior; self-definition is stable across time and situation.
      b. The interdependent self can be described as follows and is characteristic of people in these cultures:
         (1) It is characteristic of people in Asian, Mediterranean, African, and South American cultures.
         (2) The self-definition is inextricably linked to other people; finding one's status or role is crucial.
         (3) The focus is on situational causes for behavior; self can vary as a function of relationships, roles, and duties.

F. Gender and the Self-Concept
   1. Cross and Madson (1997) found that women tend to be more interdependent and men tend to be more independent. The following research evidence supports this conclusion:
      a. Women are more likely than men to define themselves in terms of social relationships.
      b. When asked to select photos that reveal what they are like, women choose photographs that show them with significant others.
      c. Women report more thoughts about their partners in social interactions than do men.
      d. Men are more attuned to their own physiological responses, whereas women are more attuned to others' reactions.
   2. Men and women are socialized differently in these ways:
      a. The media portray men more often in powerful and controlling positions.
      b. Cultural stereotypes lead teachers to have different expectations for girls and boys.
      c. Parents raise boys and girls differently.
      d. Friendships from an early age are gender segregated.
      e. Girls' games tend to focus on cooperation, whereas boys' games tend to focus on competition.
      f. Gender-specific societal roles place women in more nurturing roles (e.g., raising children) than men.

II. Self-Knowledge
   A. Self-knowledge consists of our understanding of our thoughts, feelings, preferences, and beliefs.
      1. Self-knowledge includes specific beliefs, images, networks of memories and associations, rich narratives or stories.
      2. Self-beliefs are one aspect of self-knowledge, and they include:
         a. Personal beliefs, which are our personality traits, our unique abilities and attributes, and our idiosyncratic preferences, tastes, and talents.
         b. Social beliefs, which are the roles, duties, and obligations we assume in groups.
         c. Relational self-beliefs, which are our identities in specific relationships.
         d. The collective self, which is our identity and beliefs as they relate to the social categories to which we belong.
   B. The Organizational Function of Self-Knowledge
      1. Greenwald (1980) called self-knowledge a "totalitarian ego" because, like a totalitarian regime, the self interprets current situations, tolerates little contradiction, and revises personal histories to fit preexisting beliefs about the self.
      2. Memory and the Self-Reference Effect
         a. The self-reference effect can be defined as the tendency to elaborate upon and recall information that is integrated into our self-knowledge.
            (1) Rogers, Kupier, and Kirker (1977) conducted the first study to explore the self-reference effect.
               (a) Independent variable: the type of processing participants were asked to do—structural (font size), phonemic (rhyming), semantic (meaning), or self-referent (self-descriptive).
               (b) Dependent variable: number of words participants remembered.
               (c) Finding: participants remembered significantly more words processed via self-reference compared with words processed via other categories.
            (2) Participants took longer to decide whether or not a trait was descriptive of the self than to answer questions about structure, sounds, and semantics of trait adjectives, suggesting that information about the self is elaborate and complex.

3. Self-Schemas and Self-Understanding
   a. A self-schema can be defined as a knowledge-based summary of our feelings and actions and how we understand others' views about the self.
   b. Markus argued that when a person has a self-schema for a trait or characteristic, he or she will process information in that domain more quickly, retrieve information consistent with the schema more quickly, and more strongly resist contradictory information.
   c. Markus (1977) tested these hypotheses by first identifying people who considered themselves very independent or dependent ("schematic" for the concept) and people for whom dependence/independence was not important to their self-concept ("aschematic"). The three major findings from this study were:
      (1) Schematic participants processed schema-relevant traits more quickly than did aschematic participants.
      (2) Schematic participants generated more examples of behaviors for the traits than did aschematic participants.
      (3) Schematic participants were quicker and more likely to refute (bogus) personality feedback that contradicted their self-schema than were aschematic participants.
   d. The self-reference effect and self-schemas contribute to the stability of the self.
      (1) We are more likely to remember information that is consistent (rather than inconsistent) with our self-beliefs (thus, confirming and reinforcing them).
      (2) We are likely to resist information that is not consistent with our self-beliefs.
4. Culture and Self-Beliefs
   a. Cousins (1989) found that Japanese students were more likely to complete the phrase "I am" (in the Twenty Statements Test) in terms of social roles, whereas American students were more likely to complete the test in terms of personal attributes.
   b. Japanese students were more likely to define the self in terms of personal attributes, however, when a specific situational context was specified, suggesting that the Japanese do recognize traits in themselves, but the traits are dependent on the situation.

C. The Motivational Function of Self-Knowledge
1. Self-knowledge helps motivate action.
2. Our self-knowledge includes possible selves—the kinds of people we hope to be in the future.
3. Tory Higgins's self-discrepancy theory can be defined as a theory that appropriate behavior is motivated by cultural and moral standards regarding the ought self and the ideal self, and that when these standards are violated emotions like guilt and shame are produced.
   a. Higgins argues that we have three types of selves:
      (1) The actual self can be defined as the self we truly believe ourselves to be.
      (2) The ideal self can be defined as the self that embodies the wishes and aspirations we and other people maintain about ourselves.
      (3) The ought self can be defined as the self that is concerned with the duties, obligations, and the external demands we feel we are compelled to honor.
   b. When we are primed to think about the ideal self, we have a promotion focus, which can be defined as a focus on positive outcomes, approach-related behavior, and cheerful emotions that help us live up to our ideals and aspirations.
   c. When we are primed to think about our ought self, we have a prevention focus.
      (1) A prevention focus can be defined as a sensitivity to negative outcomes motivated by a desire to live up to our ought self and to avoid the guilt or anxiety that results when we fail to live up to our sense of what we ought to do.
      (2) A prevention focus triggers guilt, anxiety, terror, panic, elevated physiological arousal, avoidant behavior, and sensitivity to negative outcomes.
   d. When we are primed to think about achieving our ideal self, we show elevated positive affect, heightened sensitivity to positive feedback, and approach-related behavior.
   e. When we are primed to think about failing to achieve our ideal self, we show depression and shame, as well as reduced physiological arousal.
D. The Self as a Standard in Social Perception
1. We use our self-knowledge to judge other people, using the vivid and accessible information about ourselves to set standards.

2. The self-image bias can be defined as the tendency to judge others' personalities according to their similarity or dissimilarity to our own personality.
   a. Lewicki (1983) found that traits that people rated themselves on positively were also the traits that they rated as more central and important in their judgments about other people.
   b. David Dunning and colleagues suggest we use self-information as a standard to define others' traits, abilities, and social concepts.
      (1) People have egocentric construals of social categories and attributes.
      (2) In one study, college students used their own levels of studiousness and athleticism to set the standard for how much a person has to study or engage in athletic activity in order to be favorably rated as "studious" or "athletic."
3. People from interdependent cultures are more likely to rely on others as the standard for judgments, unlike people from independent cultures, who are more likely to rely on the self as the standard.
   a. Students in the U.S. say that other people are similar to themselves more often than they say they are similar to others, suggesting that the self is the dominant category or standard.
   b. Students in Asian countries are more likely to show the opposite pattern, suggesting that the other is the more dominant or salient standard.
   c. Cohen and Gunz (2002) found that Canadian students were more likely to report memories of past events in which they were the center of attention from their own perspective as the actor, whereas Asian students were more likely to report such events from the perspective an observer would have.
E. Illusions and Biases about the Self
1. Taylor and Brown suggest that illusions about the self enhance psychological well-being.
   a. Well-being is correlated with unrealistically positive views about the self.
      (1) Self-serving attributions can be defined as the belief that positive personal traits are more descriptive of the self than negative traits and that everyone has the same negative traits and does the

same negative actions but that positive traits and actions are unique.

   b. Well-being is correlated with exaggerated perceptions of control.

    (1) Langer (1975) conducted a study to examine the illusion of control of participants who were entered in a lottery.

     (a) Independent variable: people were either given a lottery ticket or chose it for themselves.

     (b) Dependent variable: the amount of money people asked for in order to sell their ticket back.

     (c) Finding: on average, people asked for much more money when they chose their own ticket—suggesting that they valued the ticket more and thought it had a higher chance of winning.

    (2) People who are depressed do not show a false perception of control.

   c. Well-being is correlated with optimism about one's future.

    (1) Westerners are prone to unrealistic optimism.

     (a) College students think positive events are more likely to happen to them than to others, and they think negative events are less likely to happen to them than to others.

     (b) People tend to focus on themselves and to ignore what happens to comparison others.

    (2) People are overly optimistic about common positive events and rare negative events and overly pessimistic about rare positive events and common negative events.

2. Taylor and Brown argue that these illusions promote health in three ways:

   a. Illusions about the self elevate positive mood and reduce negative mood.

   b. Illusions about the self make people more altruistic and generous, fostering healthier social bonds.

   c. A positive outlook promotes goal-directed behavior (leading to actual better outcomes).

3. Critiques of Taylor and Brown include the following:

   a. Narcissists are not psychologically healthy, but display strong positive illusions of self.

   b. Overestimating academic talents is associated (in the long run) with lower self-esteem, deteriorating academic performance, and decreased school engagement.

   c. East Asians are less likely to endorse positive illusions about the self than are Westerners.

    (1) Sastry and Ross (1998) found that Asians had less perceived control in their lives than non-Asians, but that this lack of control was associated with depression and anxiety only for the non-Asians.

    (2) Well-being may be tied to values that are important to the culture.

III. Self-Evaluation

  A. A common assumption, adopted by California's self-esteem task force, is that elevating self-esteem would help to cure society's ills.

   1. The following variables are correlated with having lower self-esteem:

    a. Less satisfaction with life

    b. More hopelessness

    c. Higher depression

    d. More malleable attitudes

    e. Disengagement from tasks after failure

   2. Despite the correlational evidence, the truth about self-esteem is much more complex (and not always supportive of the assumption that higher self-esteem is always a good thing).

  B. Trait and State Self-Esteem

   1. Self-esteem can be defined as the positive or negative overall evaluation you have of yourself.

    a. People with high self-esteem feel very good about themselves.

    b. People with low self-esteem feel more ambivalent, believing themselves to have both positive and negative qualities.

    c. People who truly feel horrible about themselves are rare; such feelings are almost always associated with clinical disorders like depression.

   2. Trait self-esteem can be defined as the enduring level of confidence and affection that people have for their defining abilities and characteristics across time.

   3. State self-esteem can be defined as the dynamic, changeable self-evaluations that are experienced as momentary feelings about the self.

4. Self-esteem also fluctuates with the momentary context.
    a. Current mood influences self-esteem.
    b. A temporary failure lowers self-esteem temporarily.
    c. Children of average academic ability experience lower self-esteem when in a classroom with children of higher ability.

C. Contingencies of Self-Worth
   1. Crocker and Wolfe's contingencies of self-worth theory says that self-esteem is contingent on successes and failures in domains upon which a person has based his or her self-worth.
       a. Contingencies of self-worth include approval, appearance, academic competence (for example, "My self-esteem gets a boost when I get a good grade on an exam or paper").
       b. People vary as to the contingencies upon which their self-esteem is based.
       c. Groups and subcultures also vary as to which contingencies of self-worth are important to them (for example, religious identity as a contingency of worth is endorsed more strongly by African Americans than by Asian or European Americans).
   2. People will have high self-esteem if they can create environments that provide positive feedback in those domains upon which their self-esteem is based.
   3. Positive feedback in contingent domains leads to high self-esteem; negative feedback in contingent domains leads to low self-esteem.
       a. Crocker, Sommers, and Luhtanen (2002) asked college seniors who had applied to graduate school to fill out a self-esteem scale every day that they received news from a grad school.
       b. Crocker, Sommers, and Luhtanen found that students in general had higher self-esteem on days when the news was acceptance and lower self-esteem on days when the news was rejection, but that these feelings were much stronger among participants who reported basing their self-esteem on academic competence.
   4. A contingencies perspective may suggest that having more contingencies is better than having fewer contingencies.

D. Social Acceptance and Self-Esteem
   1. Leary's sociometer hypothesis maintains that self-esteem is an internal, subjective index or marker of the extent to which we are included or looked on favorably by others.
       a. Self-esteem acts as a meter for measuring inclusion; high self-esteem means adequate group belonging, and low self-esteem means inadequate group belonging.
       b. The hypothesis is derived from evolutionary reasoning that those who sought to belong to social groups would have better chances of surviving and reproducing than those who did not.
   2. Leary et al. (1995) conducted a study to test the sociometer hypothesis.
       a. Independent variable: whether participants were accepted or rejected by a group.
       b. Dependent variable: state self-esteem.
       c. Finding: participants who believed they had been rejected reported lower self-esteem than those who believed they had been accepted.

E. Motives for Self-Evaluation
   1. The Motive to Elevate Self-Esteem
       a. Self-enhancement is a high priority in Western cultures and people will strive to enhance their self-worth in a number of ways.
       b. Tesser's self-evaluation maintenance model says that we are motivated to view ourselves in a favorable light, and that we do so through two processes: reflection and social comparison.
           (1) Through reflection, we flatter ourselves by association with people who are talented or accomplished.
               (a) We wear school colors when the team wins.
               (b) Basking in reflected glory is effective only when the close other's domain of success is NOT relevant to our own self-concept.
           (2) Through social comparison, we strategically try to boost our self-esteem by noting instances where we outperform others in domains that are important to our self-concept.
           (3) We will seek out relationships with close others who are highly skilled in domains not relevant to our self-esteem and less skilled in domains that are relevant to our self-esteem.
       c. Many studies support the self-evaluation maintenance model.

(1) Tesser and Smith (1980) had pairs of friends play a word game with each other and with strangers.
   (a) Independent variable #1: whether the fellow game player was a friend or a stranger.
   (b) Independent variable #2: whether the task was described as measuring verbal skills (high relevance) or whether it was described as just a game (low relevance).
   (c) Dependent variable: whether the participant chose to give fellow players easy items to complete or hard items to complete.
   (d) Findings: when the game was not relevant, participants gave easier items to their friends than to strangers, elevating the opportunity to bask in their friend's reflected glory; when the game was relevant, participants gave equally hard items to both friends and strangers, thus thwarting a close other's ability to outshine the self in a relevant domain.

(2) Tesser, Campbell, and Smith (1984) conducted a study with fifth and sixth graders to test whether we choose friends whom we outperform in domains relevant to our self-concept.
   (a) They asked students to identify their closest friends, the most and least important activities relevant to their self-concept, and how well they and their friends performed at those activities.
   (b) Finding: students rated their own performance as better than their friends' performance in the most important activities and equal to their friends' performance in the least important activities.

(3) Tesser (1980) found that eminent scientists reported remaining closer to fathers who had pursued a career in a different area, and that siblings felt closer to one another when they outperformed the sibling in an important area.

2. The Motive to Find Out the Truth about the Self
   a. Swann's self-verification theory holds that we strive for stable, accurate beliefs about the self because such beliefs give us a sense of coherence.
   b. We gather truthful information about the self in two ways:
      (1) We selectively attend to and remember information that is consistent with our self-views.
      (2) We create self-confirmatory social environments.
         (a) We signal who we are and how we wish to be treated through identity cues, which are customary facial expressions, posture, gait, clothes, haircuts, and body decorations.
         (b) We choose to enter relationships that help us maintain consistent views of the self.

3. There is evidence for both self-enhancement and self-verification.
   a. Self-enhancement seems to be the rule regarding our emotional responses to feedback about the self (people are happier after receiving positive feedback).
   b. Self-verification seems to be the rule regarding our cognitive responses to the validity of the feedback about the self (people think self-congruent feedback is more accurate and revealing than incongruent feedback).

F. Culture and Self-Esteem
   1. East Asian languages have no word for "self-esteem."
   2. Westerners invented the notion of "self-esteem."
   3. Interdependent people score lower on self-esteem scales than do independent respondents.
   4. Western cultures create social contexts and interactions that boost individual self-esteem. The following evidence supports this conclusion:
      a. Americans make more spontaneous comments favorable to the self than do the Japanese.
      b. Americans and Canadians rate themselves as having more positive than negative traits.
      c. Both Japanese and American participants rate common Japanese situations as being less self-enhancing than common American situations.

(1) Japanese are more often encouraged to engage in self-criticism.

(2) Americans are more often praised for their accomplishments.

5. Non-Westerners don't have low self-esteem in general; rather, they are more concerned with other ways of being a good person (e.g., self-improvement to become a better member of the collective).

    a. East Asian cultures (especially the Japanese) engage in a form of self-criticism that results in better specific skills and social harmony.

    b. Heine et al. (2001) found that Japanese participants worked longer on a second task if they believed they had failed a prior, similar task; Canadian participants worked for a shorter time if they believed they had failed.

G. Culture Change and Self-Esteem

1. Although Westerners are generally concerned with individual distinctiveness, this is not true for people in all sectors of the society at all times.

2. Heine and Lehman (2003) have found that as Japanese individuals have more contact with Canadian culture, they are more likely to adopt Western ways of thinking about self-esteem.

H. Possible Dangers of "High Self-Esteem"

1. Baumeister and his colleagues suggest that fragile, inflated egotism may be problematic.

    a. Fragile, inflated egotism is not healthy self-esteem and may lead to violent action to reassert superiority and dominate challengers.

    b. Inflated egotism consists of grossly exaggerated positive views of self coupled with a volatile sensitivity to threats, insults, and challenges.

2. There is research evidence supporting the dangers of inflated egotism:

    a. Psychopaths display fragile, inflated egotism.

    b. Alcohol elevates self-esteem and increases the likelihood of aggression.

    c. Murderers, bullies, and rapists display inflated self-views.

    d. Youth gang members tend to be assertive, defiant, and narcissistic, and often resort to violence when they feel threatened or disrespected.

IV. Self-Presentation

A. Self-presentation can be defined as presenting who we actually are, or who we would like others to believe we are.

1. Impression management is the attempt to control the beliefs other people have of us.

2. Erving Goffman argued that the social selves we construct govern much of our behavior; people use strategic self-presentation in public life.

    a. Face refers to who we want others to think we are.

    b. Social interactions are how we create our "face."

    c. People depend on one another to help maintain face claims.

B. Ideas about the Public Self

1. Public self-consciousness can be defined as our awareness of what other people think about our selves—our public identity.

2. Private self-consciousness can be defined as our awareness of our interior lives—our private thoughts, feelings, and sensations.

3. People high in public self-consciousness overestimate the extent to which others attend to them and define identity in terms of social attributes (e.g., popularity); people high in private self-consciousness define their identity in terms of personal feelings.

4. Self-monitoring can be defined as the tendency for people to monitor their behavior in such a way that it fits the demands of the current situation.

    a. High self-monitors are like actors in that they scrutinize the situation and modify their self-presentation and behavior to be appropriate.

    b. Low self-monitors act in accord with their internal inclinations, regardless of the situation.

    c. Students often view low self-monitoring as more adaptive because people are "being true to themselves."

    d. Goffman believed that effective social functioning requires the type of strategic self-presentation that high self-monitors engage in.

C. Self-Handicapping: Protecting Your Own Face

1. Sometimes we will act in self-destructive ways to protect claims about the self.

2. Self-handicapping can be defined as the tendency to engage in self-defeating behaviors in order to prevent others from drawing unwanted attributions about the self as a result of poor performance.

a. Self-handicapping might be not studying enough for an exam or training enough for an athletic competition.

b. It might be showing up late or saying inappropriate things on first dates or interviews.

c. These behaviors provide an external excuse for failure and reduce the threat to self-esteem and/or face.

   (1) Self-handicapping is defined by actually engaging in a self-defeating behavior.

   (2) Sometimes people will lie about their behaviors in order to have these types of external excuses (e.g., claiming you didn't study).

d. Berglas and Jones (1978) conducted a classic, early self-handicapping study.

   (1) Independent variable: participants were led to believe that they would either succeed or fail on an upcoming test.

   (2) Dependent variable: whether participants chose to take a drug that would have a side effect (supposedly) that would improve or impair test performance.

   (3) Finding: participants who anticipated failure on the test chose the drug that would impair performance more than did those who anticipated success.

3. The evolutionary perspective on self-handicapping argues that self-destructive tendencies may signal that potential mates have superior genes.

a. Many animals and birds have features that are valued by potential mates but that impair survival skills (e.g., tails that hinder flight, eye pads that hinder vision).

b. Self-handicapping theory suggests that these traits signal value in that only individuals with superior genes can afford to have them.

D. Self-Presentation and Language

1. On-record communication can be defined as the statements we make that we intend to be taken literally.

2. Off-record communication can be defined as indirect and ambiguous communication that allows us to hint at ideas and meanings that are not explicit in the words we utter.

a. Friendly teasing can be a playful, indirect way to let others know they have behaved inappropriately.

b. Flirting can allow for an exploration of romantic interest without the self-esteem and face risks of direct communication.

Testing Your Basic Knowledge

ANSWERS TO MULTIPLE-CHOICE QUESTIONS

1. c	14. b
2. b	15. a
3. a	16. b
4. c	17. a
5. a	18. c
6. c	19. a
7. c	20. b
8. a	21. a
9. a	22. b
10. b	23. c
11. a	24. a
12. c	25. a
13. a	

Testing Your In-Depth Understanding

EXAMPLE ANSWER TO THE GUIDED QUESTIONS FOR CRITICAL THINKING EXERCISE #1

Think about the **distinctiveness hypothesis** and different facets of the self. If we tend to emphasize in our self-definition aspects of ourselves that distinguish us from those around us, then our situations will have a powerful influence on many aspects of the self, including self-esteem, the actual self, and self-schemas. For example, imagine a child who is not good at English winding up in a classroom dominated by students who are good at the subject. (Maybe you can remember a time when you wound up in a class with other people who all seemed to be good at a subject at which you felt inadequate.) First let's assume that this child has academic competency as a **contingency of self-worth;** because of the emphasis placed on doing well in academics, many children of middle school age may, at least for a time, base their worth on how well or poorly they are doing in school. Given that assumption, this child's **state self-esteem** will probably take a beating with every exam or paper on which he or she receives a less-than-stellar grade. These constant blows to state self-esteem, if not offset by other accomplishments, may result in overall lower **trait self-esteem** over time. Additionally, this child will be incorporating the information that he or she is not good at English into the **actual self,** possibly setting up a greater discrepancy with the **ideal** or the **ought** self—assuming that performance in English is part of either. Last, people tend to develop **self-schemas** around important and self-defining domains. If the child has academics as a contingency of self-worth, then it makes sense that there would be an academic self-schema. This self-schema would, thus, contain information about being a "poor" English student. This type of self-schema could possibly inhibit future performance in English (perhaps via **self-handicapping**), thus reinforcing both the perception and the actuality. **Self-verification theory** suggests that the child would find negative feedback to be more accurate and diagnostic than positive feedback.

A child doesn't necessarily have to actually be in such a classroom to develop a construal that his or her skills are inadequate. People who are high in **public self-consciousness** have a tendency to overestimate the extent to which others are evaluating them and tend to define the self via social attributions. A child high in public self-consciousness may feel that his or her skill at English exercises is especially scrutinized, and the child may be drawn to defining the self via how "accepted" he or she feels in the classroom. If the child chooses a peer who "stands out" as an **upward social comparison** standard, then that child will feel inadequate and suffer all the same consequences mentioned above.

On the other hand, the chapter mentioned that people use the self as a standard in judging others. Recall the study in which college students used their own levels of studiousness and athleticism to judge that of others. This finding suggests that any given student may very well use themselves as the anchor upon which to judge how good or bad other students are at English. As noted by Taylor and Brown, people with high self-esteem are more likely to have illusions about the self. Perhaps, then, if this child had preexisting high self-esteem, he or she would judge others in accord with his or her own skills and then choose a **downward social comparison** or a comparison to a similar other to protect self-esteem. Such a comparison may, in fact boost the child's self-views of his or her English abilities (e.g., "At least I know what a predicate is . . .").

CHAPTER 6 | Social Influence

The goal of this chapter is to introduce you to some of the classic studies in social psychology that explore how and why people change their attitudes, beliefs, or behaviors as a result of the influence of other people. Different types of social influence, including conformity, compliance, and obedience, are discussed.

ANNOTATED CHAPTER OUTLINE

After first reading through the chapter quickly, create a comprehensive framework for the information in the chapter by reading the outline below and filling in the missing information. Instead of simply re-copying information from the textbook, try to use your own words wherever possible; you can check your answers against the completed outline in the Answer Key section at the end of the chapter.

I. What Is Social Influence?
   A. Social influence can be defined as

      _____

      _____

      _____

     1. We can be targets or agents of social influence.
     2. To do well in the world, we need to know when to yield to others' influence and when and how to resist social influence.
   B. Conformity can be defined as

      _____

      _____

      _____

   C. Compliance can be defined as

      _____

      _____

      _____

   D. Obedience can be defined as

      _____

      _____

      _____

   E. Conformity can be bad, good, or neither, but many instances of conformity are beneficial.
     1. Paying taxes, inhibiting anger, waiting in line facilitate human interaction.
     2. Evolutionary psychologists suggest that conformity was beneficial to reproduction and survival.

II. Conformity
   A. Automatic Mimicry and the Chameleon Effect
     1. Ideomotor action can be defined as

       _____

       _____

       _____

       a. When we see others behave in a certain way the idea of the behavior is brought to mind consciously or unconsciously.
       b. We may unconsciously mimic others' posture, facial expressions, or their behaviors.
     2. The chameleon effect can be defined as

       _____

       _____

       _____

a. Chartrand and Bargh (1999) asked participants to describe photographs to another participant.

   (1) Independent variable:

_____

_____

_____

   (2) Dependent variable:

_____

_____

_____

   (3) Finding:

_____

_____

_____

_____

b. Follow-up studies found that the chameleon effect has several conditions and advantages.

   (1) People with the traits of empathy and/or higher need for affiliation are more likely to exhibit the chameleon effect.

   (2) People tend to like those who

_____

_____

_____

   (3) People who have been mimicked are more likely to

_____

_____

_____

B. Informational Social Influence and Sherif's Conformity Experiment

  1. Sherif designed an experiment that used the autokinetic illusion to test the idea that other people can create a social frame of reference for even visual perception tasks.

  2. The autokinetic illusion can be defined as the apparent motion of a stationary point of light in a completely darkened environment.

  3. Sherif (1936) used the autokinetic effect in his study by putting participants in a completely dark room and asking them to estimate how far a dot of light was moving.

   a. Independent variable: whether participants were in a group or alone.

   b. Dependent variable:

_____

_____

c. Finding:

_____

_____

_____

_____

d. One-year follow-up finding:

_____

_____

_____

  4. Informational social influence can be defined as

_____

_____

_____

_____

C. Normative Social Influence and Asch's Conformity Experiment

  1. Asch thought Sherif's findings would not apply when there was a clearly correct (morally or otherwise) answer—that is, when the individual disagreed with the group.

  2. Asch (1956) did the famous "line study" in which he asked people to complete a series of trials in which they were asked which of three lines was the same length as a target line.

   a. Seven confederates gave the wrong answer on various trials, right before the participant (who always went last) was asked to give his answer.

   b. Asch found that 75% of all participants conformed to the majority at least once.

   c. He found that, overall,

_____

_____

_____

  3. Normative social influence can be defined as

_____

_____

_____

_____

D. Factors Affecting Conformity Pressures

  1. The distinction between normative and informational social influence is critical to a discussion of conformity.

  2. Group Size

   a. Conformity increases as group size increases.

   (1) Larger groups exert more normative social influence because

_____

_____

_____

(2) Larger groups exert more informational social influence because

_____

_____

_____

b. Increasing group size stops having an effect when there are

_____

_____

_____

   (1) Informational social influence: after 4 or 5 people, the opinions are no longer likely to be independent of one another.

   (2) Normative social influence: having 4 versus 2 people think you are stupid is a psychologically meaningful difference, but once you get up to 4 or 5, it is a "group," and the difference between 5 and 7 people is less psychologically meaningful.

3. Group Unanimity

a. In the Asch study, conformity dramatically decreased when the unanimity of the confederates was broken.

   (1) When an ally was present, participants conformed

_____

_____

_____

   (2) The ally did not have to agree with the participant, just break unanimity by disagreeing with the majority.

   (3) An ally weakens normative social influence by

_____

_____

_____

   (4) An ally weakens informational social influence by

_____

_____

_____

b. Research on group size suggests that a jury of twelve is better than a smaller jury.

   (1) Informational social influence is likely to be reduced with a jury of twelve because

_____

_____

   (2) Normative social influence is likely to be reduced with a jury of twelve because

_____

_____

_____

4. Expertise and Status

a. Expertise and status are often correlated (expertise brings status and status, sometimes incorrectly, brings an assumption of expertise).

b. Expertise affects informational social influence, and status affects normative social influence.

   (1) Expertise affects informational social influence because

_____

_____

_____

   (2) Status affects normative social influence because

_____

_____

_____

   (3) Torrance (1955) found that

_____

_____

_____

5. Culture

a. People reared in interdependent cultures are likely to be more susceptible to both forms of social influence than people in independent cultures.

b. Research supports this assumption, as shown by these studies:

   (1) Milgram (1961) found that

_____

_____

_____

   (2) Bond and Smith (1996) analyzed 133 studies and found

_____

_____

_____

_____

(3) Some studies have found that, in recent years among independent peoples,

_____

_____

_____

_____

6. Gender
   a. Women are only slightly more likely to conform than are men.
   b. Conformity is affected by socialization toward interdependence (more likely in women) or toward independence (more likely in men), but also by whether or not there is uncertainty or confusion about issues or events.
      (1) Lack of knowledge, leading to uncertainty, may lead women to be more likely to conform about

_____

_____

_____

_____

and men to be more likely to conform about

_____

_____

_____

_____

      (2) Women have greater comfort with relationships, which can give them greater knowledge and more certainty in social situations (thus offsetting their interdependent tendency to conform more).
7. Difficulty (or Ambiguity) of the Task
   a. An easy, certain, or unambiguous task or judgment is less likely to be affected by

_____

_____

_____

   b. A difficult or ambiguous task can be affected by

_____

_____

_____

_____

8. Anonymity
   a. Being anonymous eliminates normative social influence because

_____

_____

_____

   b. Informational social influence creates internalization, which can be defined as

_____

_____

_____

_____

   c. Normative social influence creates only public compliance, which can be defined as

_____

_____

_____

_____

9. The Interpretative Context of Disagreement
   a. Social influence of both types is more powerful when a person is generally uncertain how to explain or interpret a given situation.
      (1) Knowing why something is happening can reduce normative social influence because

_____

_____

_____

      (2) Knowing why something is happening can reduce informational social influence because

_____

_____

_____

_____

   b. Ross et al. (1976) replicated Asch's experiment except they offered rewards (points) for correct answers, and they asked participants to choose which of two tones matched a target tone.
      (1) Independent variable: whether any correct answer received 10 points, or whether a correct answer of "1" received 10 points while a correct answer of "2" received 100 points.
      (2) Dependent variable:

_____

_____

_____

      (3) Finding:

_____

_____

_____

E. The Influence of Minority Opinion on the Majority
   1. Moscovici et al. (1969) investigated the role of consistency in how effectively a minority could influence the answers of the majority in fairly

clear judgments of whether a color was green or blue (and the answer was almost always blue).

   a. Independent variable: whether minority group members (really confederates) consistently insisted green was the right answer, or whether the confederates randomly varied their answers between green and blue.

   b. Dependent variable:

_____

_____

_____

   c. Finding:

_____

_____

_____

   d. Follow-up results:

_____

_____

_____

2. Minorities have their influence mostly through informational social influence because people in the majority don't have normative social influence concerns.

   a. People in the majority may often make decisions quickly and automatically.

   b. Consistent pressure, even from a minority, seems to create doubt about the correctness of the majority's position, causing a more thoughtful reconsideration.

   c. Minority influence tends to create private acceptance rather than merely public compliance.

III. Obedience to Authority

  A. The Setup of the Milgram Experiments

    1. Milgram was interested in re-creating an Asch-like paradigm, except he wanted to know what would happen when people were asked to conform to something that had more profound consequences.

    2. Milgram's original experiment was meant to be the "control" condition of his study, which was going to ask participants to conform to group pressure to give shocks in response to incorrect answers.

    3. In the basic paradigm of the experiment, there would be a teacher and a learner in what was supposed to be a learning experiment, and the experimenter would ask the teacher to deliver the shocks; there would not be group conformity pressure.

     a. Participants were bogusly "assigned" to be the teacher and

_____

_____

_____

_____

     b. Shocks started at

_____

_____

_____

     c. Participants were given a test shock of

_____

_____

_____

     d. Any reservations expressed by the participant were met by

_____

_____

_____

    4. In the remote (a.k.a. distant) feedback condition, participants could not see the learner, but they could

_____

_____

_____

_____;

_____ percent of the participants continued the experiment up to 450 volts.

    5. In the voice feedback condition, participants could not see the learner, but they could

_____

_____

_____

_____;

_____ percent of participants continued with the experiment up to 450 volts.

  B. Opposing Forces

    1. Milgram's participants were caught in a battle between forces pushing them to complete the experiment and forces pushing them to stop.

     a. Forces pushing for completion of the experiment:

      (1) _____

_____

_____

      (2) _____

_____

_____

_____

(3) _____

_____

_____

_____

b. Forces pushing for halting the experiment:

(1) _____

_____

_____

_____

(2) _____

_____

_____

_____

(3) _____

_____

_____

_____

2. "Tuning in" the Learner

a. Milgram conducted a series of experimental variations exploring the role of awareness of the learner's suffering.

(1) The distant feedback condition

(a) The participants could not see or hear the learner (except for one episode of pounding).

(b) Percentage of obedience:

_____

_____

_____

_____

(2) The voice feedback condition

(a) The participants could not see the learner, but they could clearly hear his protests.

(b) Percentage of obedience:

_____

_____

_____

_____

(3) The proximity condition

(a) The participants could hear and see the learner.

(b) Percentage of obedience:

_____

_____

_____

_____

(4) The touch proximity condition

(a) The participants had to

_____

_____

_____

_____

(b) Percentage of obedience:

_____

_____

_____

_____

b. The remoteness of a victim makes the harm done to him more abstract, creating less of an effect on the perpetrator.

3. "Tuning out" the Experimenter

a. Milgram conducted a series of experimental variations exploring the role of the experimenter's presence.

(1) Experimenter present

(a) The experimenter was in the same room as the participant.

(b) Percentage of obedience:

_____

_____

_____

_____

(2) Experimenter absent

(a) The experimenter

_____

_____

_____

_____

(b) Percentage of obedience:

_____

_____

_____

_____

(3) Ordinary person experimenter

(a) An "ordinary person" (ostensibly another participant) gave instructions to shock the learner for wrong answers and then left the room.

(b) Percentage of obedience:

_____

_____

_____

_____

(4) Two experimenters condition

(a) When the learner started seriously protesting, the two experimenters

_____

_____

_____

_____

(b) Percentage of obedience:

_____

_____

_____

_____

4. Obedience dropped more when it was situationally easier to disobey than when the participants' desire to disobey was increased.

C. Most Important Factors Leading to Obedience (Would You Have Obeyed?)

1. Psychiatrists predicted that less than 1 percent of participants would obey.

2. The experimental variation didn't lead most people to feel empathy for the participants or to believe that they themselves would obey to the end.

3. Milgram's work can help explain how large portions of a population can participate in horrible acts like genocide.

   a. Exceptionalist explanations suggest that

   _____
   _____
   _____
   _____

   b. Normalist explanations suggest that

   _____
   _____
   _____
   _____

   (1) This view is supported by Milgram's work; scholars have noted that there were simply too many people involved in the "machine" of the Holocaust for every single one of those people to have been malevolent advocates of genocide.

   (2) Milgram's research offers several suggestions as to what elements of a situation may lead an otherwise normal person to end up as a participant in something horrible.

4. They Tried but Failed

   a. Milgram's participants did not participate mindlessly or without protest, as shown by the following:

   (1) _____
   _____
   _____

   (2) _____
   _____
   _____

   (3) _____
   _____

   _____
   _____

   b. Despite these protests and their strong misgivings, the participants continued to obey.

   c. Parallels in real life

   (1) Wanting to speak out against prejudice but being unable to respond quickly enough.

   (2) Wanting to reach out to someone who is being ostracized but being unable to overcome our own social concerns.

   d. Parallels in Holocaust, as shown by a group of German men who had joined a police force to avoid military service during World War II but ended up as military police in Poland.

   (1) They were ordered to round up Polish Jews in a town and to send able-bodied young men to a concentration camp and to shoot the rest.

   (2) Their resistance was present, but feeble, as shown by the following:

   (a) _____
   _____
   _____
   _____

   (b) _____
   _____
   _____

   (c) _____
   _____
   _____

   (d) _____
   _____
   _____

   e. In any situation in which people aren't playing by normal or familiar social rules, confusion and ambiguity result, and people are unlikely to act decisively.

5. Release from Responsibility

   a. Milgram thought that when the experimenter took responsibility an "agentic shift" took place in which people in a real psychological sense believed that their own actions were being caused by an external agent (e.g., "I was following orders. I had no choice.").

b. During Milgram's experiment, the experimenter provided participants with

_____

_____

_____

c. Being released from responsibility only works if the person assuming responsibility is viewed as a legitimate authority figure.

d. In all cases of genocide, someone who had authority of some sort instigated the actions.

6. Step-by-Step Involvement

a. The fact that participants started with a very low voltage (15 volts) and increased in such small increments (15 to 30 to 45 to 60, etc.) made obedience more likely because

_____

_____

_____

b. The experiment created its own momentum, which was hard to break, and the behavior became almost a normal procedure.

c. Parallels to the Holocaust

(1) The greatest atrocities in Germany happened only after a long (eight years) step-by-step buildup in which Jewish citizens first had business restrictions, then their citizenship was taken away, then they were prohibited from obtaining passports or from traveling abroad, then they had to wear Jewish badges, and then they were sent to concentration camps.

(2) Perpetrators of the Holocaust carried out duties that gradually built from everyday tasks to tasks of increasing moral weight.

(3) The strongest defiance of Nazi plans happened in countries in which the implementation of the "final solution" (concentration camps and extermination) was put in place more quickly.

IV. Compliance

A. We may comply with another person's request either because of a sense that there are good reasons to do so or because of our feelings.

B. Reason-Based Approaches

1. The norm of reciprocity can be defined as

_____

_____

_____

a. When someone does us a favor, it creates a sense of obligation that we need to reciprocate or risk social sanction (e.g., being called a "moocher").

b. A study demonstrating this asked participants to engage in a task rating paintings together.

(1) Independent variable: after a break in the procedure, one of the participants (a confederate of the experimenter) returned to the room with either nothing or with two sodas, one to share with the real participant.

(2) Dependent variable

_____

_____

_____

(3) Finding:

_____

_____

_____

c. Applications in real life include the "free gifts" given out by companies that want something from you.

2. The Reciprocal Concessions Technique (a.k.a. Door-in-the-Face)

a. This is a novel application of the norm of reciprocity.

b. The door-in-the-face can be defined as

_____

_____

_____

c. Cialdini et al. (1975) conducted a study in which they examined the effect of making a large request on compliance with a second, but smaller request.

(1) Independent variable:

_____

_____

_____

(2) Dependent variable: the number of participants agreeing to chaperone juveniles on a one-day trip to the zoo.

(3) Finding:

_____

_____

_____

(4) Follow-up finding: the technique only
works if the same person makes both
requests.

d. The That's-Not-All Technique
(1) The that's-not-all technique can be
defined as

_____
_____
_____

(2) Burger et al. (1999) conducted a study
that examined the effectiveness of the
that's-not-all technique.
(a) Independent variable:

_____
_____
_____

(b) Dependent variable: whether
participants bought the baked
goods or not.
(c) Finding:

_____
_____
_____

e. The Foot-in-the-Door Technique
(1) The foot-in-the-door technique can be
defined as

_____
_____
_____

(a) The initial request leads to a subtle
change in a person's self-image,
such that she feels that she is the
type of person who participates in
such causes or likes such products.
(b) Given that change in self-image, a
larger request in the same general
vein will be more likely to elicit
compliance.
(2) Freedman and Fraser (1966) examined
the foot-in-the-door technique by
making a small request followed by a
larger request asking residents in
California to put a big, ugly "Drive
Safely" sign on their lawn as a public
service.

(a) Independent variable:

_____
_____
_____
_____

(b) Dependent variable:

_____
_____
_____

(c) Finding:

_____
_____
_____

(3) Milgram Studies Application
(a) The step-by-step nature of the
increasing shock voltage in the
Milgram study can be understood
as an example of the foot-in-the-
door effect.
(b) The foot-in-the-door technique
relates to the Milgram study in that

_____
_____
_____

(c) Every step up the shock generator
created

_____
_____
_____

(d) When the learner's trouble
becomes more obvious, the teacher
is faced with a cognitively
complex situation of not just
justifying stopping, but justifying
his commitment to the previous
shock levels.
(4) Other Applications
(a) Many charities will use this
general logic and indicate that
"even a penny" will help.
(b) Most people would have a hard
time justifying why a penny is too
much to give, thus creating a sense
of psychological commitment to
the idea of giving something and
often leading them to make a
larger contribution.

C. Emotion-Based Approaches
  1. Positive Mood
    a. When people are in a good mood, they are more likely to comply with requests because

_____

_____

_____

_____

    b. Isen et al. (1976) had experimenters call participants and claim that they had just used their last dime on this "misdialed" call and ask if the participant would call the correct number and relay a message.
      (1) Independent variable:

_____

_____

_____

_____

      (2) Dependent variable:

_____

_____

_____

_____

      (3) Finding:

_____

_____

_____

_____

    c. Positive mood increases compliance for two reasons:
      (1) _____

_____

_____

_____

      (2) _____

_____

_____

_____

    d. Isen and Levin (1972) tested the hypothesis that the desire to maintain a good mood increases compliance.
      (1) Independent variable #1:

_____

_____

_____

      (2) Independent variable #2: participants were asked to serve as confederates who would either help or hinder another person.
      (3) Dependent variable:

_____

_____

_____

_____

      (4) Finding:

_____

_____

_____

_____

  2. Negative Mood
    a. Certain types of negative moods can also increase compliance.
    b. Guilt can increase compliance in an effort to get rid of the bad feeling.
      (1) Harris et al. (1975) found that

_____

_____

_____

      (2) Regan (1971) conducted a study to examine whether guilt would lead participants to contribute more to a charitable cause.
        (a) Setup: Regan asked participants to monitor a shock meter hooked up to a rat's cage to be sure the voltage didn't go too high.
        (b) Independent variable: whether or not and how much participants donated to a charity.
        (c) Initial finding: participants were more likely to donate to a charitable cause if, upon a momentary lapse in their attention, the voltage shot way up and the rat jumped in pain.
    c. The negative state relief hypothesis can be defined as

_____

_____

_____

      (1) When the experimenter said the rat's pain was not the fault of the participant, Regan (1971) found that

_____

_____

_____

      (2) Cialdini et al. (1973) also conducted a study to test the hypothesis that a participant in a negative mood would be more likely to agree to a request that would help another person.
        (a) Independent variable #1: participants either inadvertently caused an important stack of cards to be knocked over and hopelessly disorganized (negative state mood induction), or they did not.

(b) Independent variable #2: after knocking over the stack of cards but before the request for help, participants were either given money or verbal praise (positive mood inductions) for their performance on another task.

(c) Dependent variable:

_____

_____

_____

_____

(d) Finding:

_____

_____

_____

_____

d. Some types of guilt and sadness can lead to withdrawal, reducing the likelihood of compliance.

e. A bad mood produced by anger may have a different effect on compliance:

_____

_____

_____

V. Resisting Social Influence
A. Although people often give in to social pressure, this is not always the case.
B. Reactance theory can be defined as

_____

_____

_____

_____

C. Factors that can increase your ability to resist social influence:
1. Practicing resisting social influence.
   a. Good practice may involve

_____

_____

_____

   b. Christians who helped Jews during the Holocaust were more likely to have been

_____

_____

_____

_____

2. Having an ally: the Asch studies convincingly demonstrated the way in which having a single ally could substantially reduce normative social influence pressures.
3. Being wary of slippery slopes (trying to look ahead to likely future scenarios): it is much

easier to resist at the start of something rather than backing out once you've already begun.
4. Delaying a decision: it is easier to resist social influence if you are about to make an emotional decision because

_____

_____

_____

_____

TESTING YOUR BASIC KNOWLEDGE

After studying the information in the chapter by filling in the outline above, test your basic knowledge with the following multiple-choice test. Answers are provided in the Answer Key section at the end of the chapter. If you find that you have gotten an answer wrong, it is important that you understand why it is wrong (as well as understanding why the correct answer is the better choice). Talk with peers, your tutor, or your professor if you need help.

Multiple-Choice Questions

1. During a conversation with John, Tanya unconsciously leans forward in her seat. Also unconsciously, John then leans forward in his seat. This is an example of
   a. normative social influence.
   b. informational social influence.
   c. the chameleon effect.

2. According to Sherif's experiment with the autokinetic effect,
   a. people are likely to use one another's judgments as guides when asked to make ambiguous decisions.
   b. visual illusions have less of an impact on the perceptions of people who are alone than on those in a group.
   c. the pressure to avoid disapproval by fellow group members leads people to conform to the behavior of others.

3. In *Pretty Woman,* Julia Roberts's character is given snails to eat at a fancy restaurant. She does not know which utensil to use to eat the snails or how to use the utensil, so she watches the other people at the table and modifies her behavior to be consistent with their actions. This is best thought of as an example of
   a. the chameleon effect.
   b. informational social influence.
   c. ideomotor action.

4. Unlike Asch's line study, the task in Sherif's autokinetic effect study involved
   a. conformity.
   b. ambiguity.
   c. Both A and B are correct answers.

5. People conform under the pressure of normative social influence in order to
   a. engage in correct behavior.
   b. reassert their prerogative in response to unpleasant arousal.
   c. avoid painful social sanctions like rejection.

6. On their first night at college, Oliver and some of the guys from his dorm decide to go to a movie. They all want to see the latest Hollywood drama, but Oliver wants to see the comedy that just started playing. Oliver is most likely to go along with the group and see the drama if
   a. there are more than eight dorm mates present.
   b. there are more than five dorm mates present.
   c. Choices A and B create an equivalent likelihood for conformity.

7. In the scenario presented in question #6, under what condition is Oliver *less* likely to go along with the group?
   a. if one of the dorm mates wants to see an action thriller instead of the comedy or the drama
   b. if the comedy received better ratings than the drama
   c. neither of the above

8. While working on her final paper for her psychology class, Tiffany realizes that she is probably going to go over the stated page limit in the assignment. She asks several of her classmates what to do and receives differing advice. A group of upperclassmen who are psychology majors tell Tiffany to go ahead and go over the page limit if it means she will be more fully explaining her analysis. A group of close friends tell Tiffany to stick with the assigned page limit, even if it means abbreviating her analysis. If we assume that Tiffany is being swayed by informational social influence pressures, which group is she more likely to listen to?
   a. the psychology majors
   b. her friends
   c. there is no way of telling from the information given

9. Members of various fraternities are asked to participate in a group problem-solving task. The researchers find that solutions proposed by officers of the fraternity generate more agreement among other group members than do solutions generated by younger members who are not officers. One reason for this may be that
   a. the younger members are attempting to maintain a positive mood by being compliant.
   b. the researchers created a foot-in-the-door situation.
   c. the officers are perceived as having higher status and, thus, they are more able to exert normative social influence.

10. Fiona is from Norway. She and JoAnne, who is from the United States, are both experiencing the pressures of informational social influence. Who is more likely to be swayed by such influence and why?
    a. Fiona, because Norway is a more interdependent culture than the United States.
    b. JoAnne, because U.S. women are less likely to experience reactance.
    c. Fiona, because Norwegians are more likely to engage in the chameleon effect.

11. Research suggests that
    a. women are more susceptible to social influence attempts than men because they are less certain of their social environments.
    b. men are slightly more susceptible to social influence than women because of their more independent natures.
    c. women are slightly more susceptible to social influence than men because they are more interdependent, but this is offset by women generally having more certainty in social interactions.

12. Ross and his colleagues replicated Asch's famous line experiment, except they gave participants rewards for getting the correct answers. In one condition, they offered 10 points for *any* correct answer the participants gave. In another condition, they offered 10 points if participants chose option A and it was the correct answer, and 100 points if participants chose option B and it was the correct answer. On trials in which the correct answer was *obviously* option A, a group of confederates would often publicly choose option B. Results indicated that the real participants in the study conformed and chose option B about 25 percent of the time _____.
    a. in both conditions.
    b. only in the condition in which 10 points were offered for any correct answer.
    c. only in the condition in which 10 points were offered for option A and 100 points were offered for option B.

13. At the beginning of *Twelve Angry Men,* eleven members of a jury are ready to vote "guilty" and just one member of the jury wants to vote "not guilty." By the time the movie ends, everyone on the jury ends up voting "not guilty." According to the research reviewed in this chapter, what is the most likely strategy used by the lone man who voted "not guilty" from the beginning to persuade his fellow jurors?
    a. He probably listened carefully to everyone else's arguments and agreed with them, at least temporarily, in order to create trust with fellow jury members.

b. He probably consistently stuck by his opinion and consistently argued against points brought up by other jury members.

c. He probably argued for his point so stridently and angered the other jurors so much that they agreed to vote "not guilty" just to end their negative moods.

14. The decision to stop the experiment was difficult for participants in Milgram's obedience studies because
a. they were dealing with a conflict between a desire to fulfill their obligation to the study and a desire to avoid inflicting harm on another person.
b. the step-by-step increase in voltage made knowing exactly when to stop more ambiguous.
c. both of the above.

15. In which condition did participants in the Milgram obedience studies exhibit the most obedience?
a. distant feedback condition
b. two experimenters condition
c. experimenter absent condition

16. Your textbook relates a story about a group of German soldiers who had volunteered for police duty to avoid the violence of war. When those soldiers ended up in Poland and were ordered to execute a group of Polish Jews, the soldiers—like most of Milgram's participants—
a. did as they were ordered without question.
b. made feeble attempts to disobey.
c. refused to perpetrate such a horrible act.

17. Participants in Milgram's obedience study often asked who would be responsible if something went wrong with the learner. The experimenter was trained to reply that he would take responsibility. This response seemed to have the effect of increasing obedience because
a. the participants felt less confusion and stress because their actions seemed justified.
b. the participants then felt less concerned about the learner's distress.
c. Both A and B are correct.

18. According to the analysis in your textbook, what is the most likely outcome if Milgram had started his obedience study at 300 volts—the point at which the learner screamed and/or pounded on the wall?
a. Very few participants would have agreed to obey because stopping the study would be the clear and obviously correct action.
b. Obedience levels would have remained the same.
c. Obedience would have increased because the social influence pressures would have been immediate and, thus, stronger.

19. If Dave does Mark a favor, then Mark is more likely to later agree to help Dave out. This reflects
a. public compliance.

b. the norm of reciprocity.
c. the negative state relief hypothesis.

20. Jordan first asks his friends to participate in a psychological experiment that runs from 7:00 A.M. to 7:00 P.M. on a Saturday. They all say no. Then Jordan asks if they could maybe just come for the most important part of the study, which is from 10:00 A.M. until 11:00 A.M. on Saturday. Most actually agree, despite the fact that it is usually extremely difficult to get Jordan's friends up and awake earlier than noon on Saturdays. Jordan has implemented what compliance technique?
a. foot-in-the-door
b. door-in-the-face
c. that's-not-all

21. Isen and Levin (1972) first gave their participants cookies to put them in a good mood. Then they asked the participants to help out with the next study by serving as confederates who would either help the "true" experimental participant or hinder the "true" participant. The results of this study were interpreted to suggest that
a. being in a good mood increases the chances of agreeing to any type of request.
b. people in good moods are less susceptible to social influence.
c. people are more likely to comply with a request if the action will maintain their good mood.

22. Research suggests that feeling guilty
a. makes people more likely to comply with a request.
b. makes people less likely to comply with a request.
c. has no impact on likelihood to comply with a request.

23. According to the negative state relief hypothesis, under what conditions are participants who are made to feel upset or guilty in a study most likely to donate money to a charity?
a. if they are given positive feedback before the request for a donation
b. if they are still in a negative mood at the time of the request for a donation
c. if their guilt is accompanied by anger

24. Seth's parents tell him he cannot have a cell phone under any circumstances, even if he pays for it himself. Suddenly, Seth's originally moderate desire for a cell phone becomes an urgent, burning sense of need for the cell phone. Which concept best explains this increased desire?
a. ideomotor action
b. reactance theory
c. foot-in-the-door

25. According to the textbook, which of the following is the best strategy to avoid succumbing to normative social influence attempts?
    a. have an ally
    b. delay making a decision
    c. research the decision before making a choice

Essay Questions

After you have mastered the multiple-choice questions, try testing your basic understanding by thoroughly answering each of the broad essay questions below. Because it is critical that you think through this information on your own, we have not provided any answers to these questions. Your learning and retention of this material will be greatly enhanced if you do one or more of the following to check your answers: carefully review the textbook information; compare your responses to your class lecture notes; talk over your answers with a peer; ask your professor to review your answers or review any information that is unclear to you.

1. List each of the three different kinds of social influence discussed in this chapter, and provide an example of each.

2. Distinguish between normative social influence and informational social influence, and discuss the factors that increase both types of conformity pressures. Can a minority member of a group ever successfully influence the views of the majority?

3. Describe in detail the basic setup of the Milgram obedience experiment. Then discuss each of the variations described in the textbook, indicating what effect the variation had on obedience levels and why. According to the textbook, what were the most important and convincing explanations for the high level of obedience in these studies?

4. List and explain three reason-based approaches to eliciting compliance. Describe the ways in which a positive and negative mood can influence compliance.

5. What advice can you offer to resist social influence?

TESTING YOUR IN-DEPTH UNDERSTANDING

Test your in-depth understanding of the material by working through the Critical Thinking Exercises provided at the end of each textbook chapter. To maximize this learning opportunity, work together with a tutor, study group, or your professor. Alternatively, write down your thoughts and responses.

Guided questions for one of the exercises are provided below. While there are multiple ways to answer these questions, short answers are given in the Answer Key at the end of the chapter. Note, however, that the valuable part of this exercise is not simply knowing the answer but working with the material to come up with the answer.

Guided Questions for Critical Thinking Exercise #2

Your mother (bless her heart) does not believe that you would flip the higher voltage switches if you participated in one of Milgram's experimenters and were commanded to do so. What could you tell your mother about the Milgram situation that could get her to believe—really, truly believe—that maybe her child would act like the other participants after all?

1. List all of the major social influence pressures discussed in the chapter, including ones discussed in sections other than the Obedience portion of the chapter.

2. Next, do some brainstorming and try to come up with a way in which every social influence concept could have been related to the Milgram study—in this step, don't be picky or critical, take any crazy idea that comes into your head.

3. Last, choose the strongest and most sensible of your ideas from step 2 and try to craft the most compelling account of the situation Milgram's participants found themselves in. Don't just give a dry listing of concepts. Use the concepts to try to craft a story that you could read to your mother—perhaps an internal dialogue of one of the participants.

Enhance your understanding of the chapter by thinking about and doing the remaining two Critical Thinking Exercises. Discuss your answers with your peers, study group, tutor, or professor.

Critical Thinking Exercise #1

The "foot-in-the-door" and the "door-in-the-face" compliance techniques sound similar, but they can be better understood by comparing and contrasting them. What psychological processes are responsible for each? What conditions need to be met (that is, who must make the request, what must the nature of the request be) for each to be effective?

Critical Thinking Exercise #3

It has been reported that Milgram became interested in studying the power of various politeness norms after witnessing the extent to which participants in his obedience experiments went along with the experimenter's commands out of a sense of propriety. This led Milgram to instruct his graduate students to, for example, get on an uncrowded bus and ask someone, with plenty of empty seats for all to see, to give up his or her seat. Everyone given this task reported that it was difficult to do; some simply couldn't do it. To get a first-hand look at how powerfully such norms affect our behavior, try doing what Milgram asked his graduate students to do. Can you?

SOCIAL PSYCHOLOGY IN THE POPULAR MEDIA

You might be interested in the following popular media references, each of which relates in some way to information in this chapter.

Book

Milgram, Stanley (1974). *Obedience to Authority.* New York: Harper & Row. This is Milgram's own detailed account and reflection on his famous set of obedience experiments. Every variation of the study is discussed, as are Milgram's own reflections on the meaning of his research in understanding real-world events. Though this is a "psychology book" reporting the results of research, it was written for a general audience and is an interesting and easy read.

Song

The Milgram Obedience Song. A sampling of actual audio clips from the real Milgram obedience studies blended with music and the voice of Phillip Zimbardo commenting on the experiment (and yes, this *is* just the sort of thing a social psychologist might do in his or her spare time). This is a 40 MB streaming download, so be sure to be at a fast connection. This is more fun if you have seen the Milgram video footage in class. Available on Dan Wegner's Web site at: http://www.wjh.harvard.edu/%7Ewegner/music.htm.

Film

Twelve Angry Men (1957; directed by Sidney Lumet; starring Lee J. Cobb, Henry Fonda, Jack Klugman, Martin Balsam, E. G. Marshall, among others). This movie was remade in 1997 by HBO films and starred George C. Scott, Jack Lemmon, Tony Danza, Ossie Davis, Edward James Olmos, among others, but you really need to see the original. Captured in the film are many social psychological concepts, most notably the way in which a single member of a jury convinces the majority to rethink their positions.

Web Sites

Fads across the Decades—http://www.crazyfads.com. A fun Web site to explore what was popular (and, thus, socially normative) over time. For example, in the 1980s, you were a real "loser" or "downer" if you didn't want to go to the video game arcade.

Stanley Milgram—http://www.stanleymilgram.com/main. html. From the Web site: "The purpose of this Web site is to be a source of accurate information about the life and work of one of the most outstanding social scientists of our time, the social psychologist Stanley Milgram. His untimely death at the age of 51 on December 20, 1984, ended a life of scientific inventiveness and controversy."

The Urinal Game—http://www.crazyhill.com/hung/ other_game/urinal.swf. An amusing look at a uniquely male set of implicit social norms. Take the quiz and see how clear you are about appropriate urinal etiquette.

ANSWER KEY

Annotated Chapter Outline

I. What Is Social Influence?
   A. Social influence can be defined as the myriad ways that people impact one another, including changes in attitudes, beliefs, feelings, and behavior, that result from the comments, actions, or even the mere presence of others.
      1. We can be targets or agents of social influence.
      2. To do well in the world, we need to know when to yield to others' influence and when and how to resist social influence.
   B. Conformity can be defined as changing one's behavior or beliefs in response to explicit or implicit (whether real or imagined) pressure from others.
   C. Compliance can be defined as responding favorably to an explicit request by another person, be it someone with more power or equal power.
   D. Obedience can be defined as social influence in which a power relationship is unequal, and the more powerful person issues a command rather than a request.
   E. Conformity can be bad, good, or neither, but many instances of conformity are beneficial.
      1. Paying taxes, inhibiting anger, waiting in line facilitate human interaction.
      2. Evolutionary psychologists suggest that conformity was beneficial to reproduction and survival.

II. Conformity
  A. Automatic Mimicry and the Chameleon Effect
    1. Ideomotor action can be defined as the phenomenon whereby merely thinking about a behavior makes its actual performance more likely.
      a. When we see others behave in a certain way the idea of the behavior is brought to mind consciously or unconsciously.
      b. We may unconsciously mimic others' posture, facial expressions, or their behaviors.
    2. The chameleon effect can be defined as the nonconscious mimicry of the expressions, mannerisms, movements, and other behaviors of those with whom one is interacting
      a. Chartrand and Bargh (1999) asked participants to describe photographs to another participant.
        (1) Independent variable: the second participant (actually a confederate) either rubbed his or her face or shook his or her foot.
        (2) Dependent variable: coding by "blind" observers of videotapes for how often the real participant shook his or her foot or rubbed his or her face.
        (3) Finding: participants reliably mimicked the behavior of the confederates.
      b. Follow-up studies found that the chameleon effect has several conditions and advantages.
        (1) People with the traits of empathy and/or higher need for affiliation are more likely to exhibit the chameleon effect.
        (2) People tend to like those who mimic them more than those who do not.
        (3) People who have been mimicked are more likely to engage in pro-social behavior afterwards.
  B. Informational Social Influence and Sherif's Conformity Experiment
    1. Sherif designed an experiment that used the autokinetic illusion to test the idea that other people can create a social frame of reference for even visual perception tasks.
    2. The autokinetic illusion can be defined as the apparent motion of a stationary point of light in a completely darkened environment.
    3. Sherif (1936) used the autokinetic effect in his study by putting participants in a completely dark room and asking them to estimate how far a dot of light was moving.
      a. Independent variable: whether participants were in a group or alone.
      b. Dependent variable: the extent to which participants' estimates were similar to one another.
      c. Finding: when alone, participants gave very different estimates, but when together, participants' estimates quickly converged and fused into a group norm.
      d. One-year follow-up finding: one year later, participants tested individually still showed the influence of the group norm on their estimates.
    4. Informational social influence can be defined as the influence of other people that results from taking their comments or actions as a source of information as to what is correct, proper, or efficacious, especially in situations where the right answer is ambiguous.
  C. Normative Social Influence and Asch's Conformity Experiment
    1. Asch thought Sherif's findings would not apply when there was a clearly correct (morally or otherwise) answer—that is, when the individual disagreed with the group.
    2. Asch (1956) did the famous "line study" in which he asked people to complete a series of trials in which they were asked which of three lines was the same length as a target line.
      a. Seven confederates gave the wrong answer on various trials, right before the participant (who always went last) was asked to give his answer.
      b. Asch found that 75 percent of all participants conformed to the majority at least once.
      c. He found that, overall, participants conformed on one-third of the trials, despite the correct answer being unambiguous.
    3. Normative social influence can be defined as the influence of other people that comes from the desire to avoid their disapproval, harsh judgments, and other social sanctions (for example, barbs, ostracism).
  D. Factors Affecting Conformity Pressures
    1. The distinction between normative and informational social influence is critical to a discussion of conformity.
    2. Group Size
      a. Conformity increases as group size increases.
        (1) Larger groups exert more normative social influence because people believe it is worse to be shunned by many people.
        (2) Larger groups exert more informational social influence because a large

number of people is more likely to have the right answer than a small number of people.

    b. The size of the group leads to greater conformity until about 4 or 5 people; after that, no more conformity is elicited by more people.

        (1) Informational social influence: after 4 or 5 people, the opinions are no longer likely to be independent of one another.

        (2) Normative social influence: having 4 versus 2 people think you are stupid is a psychologically meaningful difference, but once you get up to 4 or 5, it is a "group," and the difference between 5 and 7 people is less psychologically meaningful.

3. Group Unanimity

    a. In the Asch study, conformity dramatically decreased when the unanimity of the confederates was broken.

        (1) When an ally was present, participants conformed 5 percent of the time (instead of 32 percent of the time when there was no ally).

        (2) The ally did not have to agree with the participant, just break unanimity by disagreeing with the majority.

        (3) An ally weakens normative social influence by providing the participant with someone else on his side to stand up against the majority.

        (4) An ally weakens informational social influence by providing the participant with support that different answers may be justified.

    b. Research on group size suggests that a jury of twelve is better than a smaller jury.

        (1) Informational social influence is likely to be reduced with a jury of twelve because the more people there are, the more likely it is that there will be different opinions and people voicing those opinions.

        (2) Normative social influence is likely to be reduced with a jury of twelve because someone who dissents from the majority is more likely to have an ally.

4. Expertise and Status

    a. Expertise and status are often correlated (expertise brings status and status, sometimes incorrectly, brings an assumption of expertise).

    b. Expertise affects informational social influence, and status affects normative social influence.

        (1) Expertise affects informational social influence because experts are more likely to know what they are talking about and so people are likely to trust their judgment.

        (2) Status affects normative social influence because the disapproval of a higher-status person can hurt more than that of a lower-status person.

        (3) Torrance (1955) found that, among a group of Navy crews, the suggestions of a higher-status crewmate influenced people's judgments on a problem-solving task more than the suggestions of a lower-status crewmate.

5. Culture

    a. People reared in interdependent cultures are likely to be more susceptible to both forms of social influence than people in independent cultures.

    b. Research supports this assumption, as shown by these studies:

        (1) Milgram (1961) found that the interdependent Norwegians were more likely to conform in an Asch-like paradigm than the independent French.

        (2) Bond and Smith (1996) analyzed 133 studies and found a consistent pattern that people in more interdependent cultures were more likely to conform than people in independent cultures.

        (3) Some studies have found that, in recent years among independent peoples, the willingness to resist the majority and not conform may be increasing.

6. Gender

    a. Women are only slightly more likely to conform than are men.

    b. Conformity is affected by socialization toward interdependence (more likely in women) or toward independence (more likely in men), but also by whether or not there is uncertainty or confusion about issues or events.

        (1) Lack of knowledge, leading to uncertainty, may lead women to be more likely to conform about "male" domain issues, and men to be more likely to conform about "female" domain issues.

(2) Women have greater comfort with relationships, which can give them greater knowledge and more certainty in social situations (thus offsetting their interdependent tendency to conform more).

7. Difficulty (or Ambiguity) of the Task
   a. An easy, certain, or unambiguous task or judgment is less likely to be affected by informational social influence than a difficult or ambiguous one but can still be affected by normative social influence.
   b. A difficult or ambiguous task can be affected by both informational and normative social influence.

8. Anonymity
   a. Being anonymous eliminates normative social influence because people can't be disapproving of a person's judgment when they don't know what it is.
   b. Informational social influence creates internalization, which can be defined as private acceptance of a proposition, orientation, or ideology.
   c. Normative social influence creates only public compliance, which can be defined as agreeing with someone or advancing a position in public to avoid disapproval but continuing to believe something else in private.

9. The Interpretative Context of Disagreement
   a. Social influence of both types is more powerful when a person is generally uncertain how to explain or interpret a given situation.
      (1) Knowing why something is happening can reduce normative social influence because we can assume that others also understand the situation and thus can understand why we would deviate from the majority.
      (2) Knowing why something is happening can reduce informational social influence because we have a justification for holding ground on our own decisions or judgments, assuming we understand why others might give the incorrect response.
   b. Ross et al. (1976) replicated Asch's experiment except they offered rewards (points) for correct answers, and they asked participants to choose which of two tones matched a target tone.

(1) Independent variable: whether any correct answer received 10 points, or whether a correct answer of "1" received 10 points while a correct answer of "2" received 100 points.
(2) Dependent variable: how frequently participants conformed to people giving the wrong answer.
(3) Finding: in the equal payoff condition, people conformed at about the same rate as those in the original Asch experiment, but in the differential payoff condition people conformed much less often because they understood that the other people in the study were choosing option "2" incorrectly just on the off-chance of getting that super-high reward.

E. The Influence of Minority Opinion on the Majority
   1. Moscovici et al. (1969) investigated the role of consistency in how effectively a minority could influence the answers of the majority in fairly clear judgments of whether a color was green or blue (and the answer was almost always blue).
      a. Independent variable: whether minority group members (really confederates) consistently insisted green was the right answer, or whether the confederates randomly varied their answers between green and blue.
      b. Dependent variable: how frequently majority group members agreed with "green" as the answer.
      c. Finding: when minority members were consistent, the majority agreed 8 percent of the time; when they were inconsistent, the majority agreed only 1 percent of the time.
      d. Follow-up results: a second experimenter showed participants color slides and asked them to make the blue-green judgment again; those exposed to a consistent majority identified more of the slides as green, suggesting that their actual opinions of the colors had changed.
   2. Minorities have their influence mostly through informational social influence because people in the majority don't have normative social influence concerns.
      a. People in the majority may often make decisions quickly and automatically.
      b. Consistent pressure, even from a minority, seems to create doubt about the correctness

of the majority's position, causing a more thoughtful reconsideration.

   c. Minority influence tends to create private acceptance rather than merely public compliance.

III. Obedience to Authority

  A. The Setup of the Milgram Experiments

    1. Milgram was interested in re-creating an Asch-like paradigm, except he wanted to know what would happen when people were asked to conform to something that had more profound consequences.

    2. Milgram's original experiment was meant to be the "control" condition of his study, which was going to ask participants to conform to group pressure to give shocks in response to incorrect answers.

    3. In the basic paradigm of the experiment, there would be a teacher and a learner in what was supposed to be a learning experiment, and the experimenter would ask the teacher to deliver the shocks; there would not be group conformity pressure.

      a. Participants were bogusly "assigned" to be the teacher and to deliver shocks in response to incorrect answers (the wrong word in a previously learned word pair) from a confederate who'd been assigned to be the "learner."

      b. Shocks started at 15 volts and increased in increments of 15 volts up to 450 volts.

      c. Participants were given a test shock of 45 volts.

      d. Any reservations expressed by the participant were met by scripted experimenter responses, such as "the experiment requires you to continue" or "you must continue."

    4. In the remote (a.k.a. distant) feedback condition, participants could not see the learner, but they could hear the learner when he vigorously pounded a protest on the wall at 300 volts; 66 percent of the participants continued the experiment up to 450 volts.

    5. In the voice feedback condition, participants could not see the learner, but they could hear the learner's increasingly desperate pleas and screams, ending in ominous silence; 62.5 percent of participants continued with the experiment up to 450 volts.

  B. Opposing Forces

    1. Milgram's participants were caught in a battle between forces pushing them to complete the experiment and forces pushing them to stop.

      a. Forces pushing for completion of the experiment:

        (1) Adhering to an agreement to do the study

        (2) Helping advance science

        (3) Normative social influence—a wish to avoid the disapproval of the experimenter

      b. Forces pushing for halting the experiment:

        (1) Moral desire to avoid causing pain or discomfort

        (2) Concerns about longer-term consequences (e.g., death of learner)

        (3) Fear of embarrassment or retaliation by the learner or having to take the learner's place

    2. "Tuning in" the Learner

      a. Milgram conducted a series of experimental variations exploring the role of awareness of the learner's suffering.

        (1) The distant feedback condition

          (a) The participants could not see or hear the learner (except for one episode of pounding).

          (b) 66 percent obedience

        (2) The voice feedback condition

          (a) The participants could not see the learner, but they could clearly hear his protests.

          (b) 62.5 percent obedience

        (3) The proximity condition

          (a) The participants could hear and see the learner.

          (b) 40 percent obedience

        (4) The touch proximity condition

          (a) The participant had to hold the learner's hand on the shock plate.

          (b) 30 percent obedience

      b. The remoteness of a victim makes the harm done to him more abstract, creating less of an effect on the perpetrator.

    3. "Tuning out" the Experimenter

      a. Milgram conducted a series of experimental variations exploring the role of the experimenter's presence.

        (1) Experimenter present

          (a) The experimenter was in same room as the participant.

          (b) 66.5 percent obedience

        (2) Experimenter absent

          (a) The experimenter left the room after the initial instructions, giving the remaining instructions over a telephone.

(b) 20 percent obedience
(3) Ordinary person experimenter
    (a) An "ordinary person" (ostensibly another participant) gave instructions to shock the learner for wrong answers and then left the room.
    (b) 20 percent obedience
(4) Two experimenters condition
    (a) When the learner started seriously protesting, the two experimenters gave contradictory instructions: one of the two experimenters said the study should be stopped, the other said it should continue.
    (b) No obedience
4. Obedience dropped more when it was situationally easier to disobey than when the participants' desire to disobey was increased.

C. Most Important Factors Leading to Obedience (Would You Have Obeyed?)
1. Psychiatrists predicted that less than 1 percent of participants would obey.
2. The experimental variation didn't lead most people to feel empathy for the participants or to believe that they themselves would obey to the end.
3. Milgram's work can help explain how large portions of a population can participate in horrible acts like genocide.
  a. Exceptionalist explanations suggest that only sadistic, desperate, or ethnocentric individuals would participate in crimes against humanity like the Holocaust.
  b. Normalist explanations suggest that, given the right circumstances, any given person may be led to participate in horrific acts of destruction.
    (1) This view is supported by Milgram's work; scholars have noted that there were simply too many people involved in the "machine" of the Holocaust for every single one of those people to have been malevolent advocates of genocide.
    (2) Milgram's research offers several suggestions as to what elements of a situation may lead an otherwise normal person to end up as a participant in something horrible.
4. They Tried but Failed
  a. Milgram's participants did not participate mindlessly or without protest, as shown by the following:

(1) Nearly all the participants called the experimenter's attention to the learner's suffering.
(2) Many participants explicitly refused to continue.
(3) Some participants stood up to leave.
  b. Despite these protests and their strong misgivings, the participants continued to obey.
  c. Parallels in real life
    (1) Wanting to speak out against prejudice but being unable to respond quickly enough.
    (2) Wanting to reach out to someone who is being ostracized but being unable to overcome our own social concerns.
  d. Parallels in Holocaust, as shown by a group of German men who had joined a police force to avoid military service during World War II but ended up as military police in Poland.
    (1) They were ordered to round up Polish Jews in a town and to send able-bodied young men to a concentration camp and to shoot the rest.
    (2) Their resistance was present, but feeble, as shown by the following:
      (a) They busied themselves with petty errands.
      (b) They hid in back of group.
      (c) They didn't shoot their guns if no one was watching.
      (d) They intentionally missed their targets.
  e. In any situation in which people aren't playing by normal or familiar social rules, confusion and ambiguity result, and people are unlikely to act decisively.
5. Release from Responsibility
  a. Milgram thought that when the experimenter took responsibility an "agentic shift" took place in which people in a real psychological sense believed that their own actions were being caused by an external agent (e.g., "I was following orders. I had no choice.").
  b. During Milgram's experiment, the experimenter provided participants with a justification for their actions (thus reducing the stress of dealing with opposing forces) when he said that he would take responsibility for the situation.
    (1) Many participants asked who would be responsible for what was happening

and/or said they didn't want to be responsible for hurting the learner.

    (2) The experimenter said "I will be responsible."

  c. Being released from responsibility only works if the person assuming responsibility is viewed as a legitimate authority figure.

  d. In all cases of genocide, someone who had authority of some sort instigated the actions.

6. Step-by-Step Involvement

  a. The fact that participants started with a very low voltage (15 volts) and increased in such small increments (15 to 30 to 45 to 60, etc.) made obedience more likely because it was harder to know where to draw the line for stopping (when a certain level seemed like "too much" then why wasn't the previous shock also too much?).

  b. The experiment created its own momentum, which was hard to break, and the behavior became almost a normal procedure.

  c. Parallels to the Holocaust

    (1) The greatest atrocities in Germany happened only after a long (eight years) step-by-step buildup in which Jewish citizens first had business restrictions, then their citizenship was taken away, then they were prohibited from obtaining passports or from traveling abroad, then they had to wear Jewish badges, and then they were sent to concentration camps.

    (2) Perpetrators of the Holocaust carried out duties that gradually built from everyday tasks to tasks of increasing moral weight.

    (3) The strongest defiance of Nazi plans happened in countries in which the implementation of the "final solution" (concentration camps and extermination) was put in place more quickly.

IV. Compliance

A. We may comply with another person's request either because of a sense that there are good reasons to do so or because of our feelings.

B. Reason-Based Approaches

1. The norm of reciprocity can be defined as a norm dictating that people should provide benefits to those who benefit them.

  a. When someone does us a favor, it creates a sense of obligation that we need to reciprocate or risk social sanction (e.g., being called a "moocher").

  b. A study demonstrating this asked participants to engage in a task rating paintings together.

    (1) Independent variable: after a break in the procedure, one of the participants (a confederate of the experimenter) returned to the room with either nothing or with two sodas, one to share with the real participant.

    (2) Dependent variable: the number of raffle tickets the real participant purchased from the confederate.

    (3) Finding: participants given the soda bought twice as many raffle tickets.

  c. Applications in real life include the "free gifts" given out by companies that want something from you.

2. The Reciprocal Concessions Technique (a.k.a. Door-in-the-Face)

  a. This is a novel application of the norm of reciprocity.

  b. The door-in-the-face can be defined as asking someone for a very large favor that he or she will certainly refuse, and then following that request with one for a more modest favor (that tends to be seen as a concession that the target will feel compelled to honor) and that you are really interested in obtaining.

  c. Cialdini et al. (1975) conducted a study in which they examined the effect of making a large request on compliance with a second, but smaller request.

    (1) Independent variable: half of the participants were first asked to counsel juvenile delinquents for two years; half were not asked to do so.

    (2) Dependent variable: the number of participants agreeing to chaperone juveniles on a one-day trip to the zoo.

    (3) Finding: participants who had first been asked to counsel the juveniles had only a 50 percent refusal rate, while 83 percent of the participants who had not been asked to counsel the juvenile delinquents refused to chaperone the zoo trip.

    (4) Follow-up finding: the technique only works if the same person makes both requests.

  d. The That's-Not-All Technique

    (1) The that's-not-all technique can be defined as adding something to an original offer, which is likely to create some pressure to reciprocate.

(2) Burger et al. (1999) conducted a study that examined the effectiveness of the that's-not-all technique.

   (a) Independent variable: half of the participants were offered cupcakes for 75 cents each; the other half were offered the cupcake for 75 cents and then quickly told that two cookies were also included.

   (b) Dependent variable: whether participants bought the baked goods or not.

   (c) Finding: 40 percent made the purchase in the first condition, 73 percent made the purchase in the "that's not all" condition.

e. The Foot-in-the-Door Technique

  (1) The foot-in-the-door technique can be defined as a compliance technique in which one makes an initial small request to which nearly everyone complies, followed by a larger request involving the real behavior of interest.

   (a) The initial request leads to a subtle change in a person's self-image, such that she feels that she is the type of person who participates in such causes or likes such products.

   (b) Given that change in self-image, a larger request in the same general vein will be more likely to elicit compliance.

  (2) Freedman and Fraser (1966) examined the foot-in-the-door technique by making a small request followed by a larger request asking residents in California to put a big, ugly "Drive Safely" sign on their lawn as a public service.

   (a) Independent variable: participants were either not contacted prior to the ugly sign request, were contacted and asked to put a small, three-inch "Be a safe driver" sign in their window (all agreed), or were contacted and asked to sign a petition favoring another civic issue (keeping California beautiful).

   (b) Dependent variable: the number of participants who agreed to put the big, ugly sign on their yard.

   (c) Finding: without any prior request, 17 percent agreed; with the small

"Be a safe driver" prior request, 76 percent agreed; with the less related request nearly 50 percent agreed.

  (3) Milgram Studies Application

   (a) The step-by-step nature of the increasing shock voltage in the Milgram study can be understood as an example of the foot-in-the-door effect.

   (b) The foot-in-the-door technique relates to the Milgram study in that, like agreeing to the initial small request, almost anyone asked would agree to start with the 15 volts (substantially less than the 45-volt test shock experienced by the teacher).

   (c) Every step up the shock generator created more of a sense of commitment to the procedure of the experiment.

   (d) When the learner's trouble becomes more obvious, the teacher is faced with a cognitively complex situation of not just justifying stopping, but justifying his commitment to the previous shock levels.

  (4) Other Applications

   (a) Many charities will use this general logic and indicate that "even a penny" will help.

   (b) Most people would have a hard time justifying why a penny is too much to give, thus creating a sense of psychological commitment to the idea of giving something and often leading them to make a larger contribution.

C. Emotion-Based Approaches

  1. Positive Mood

   a. When people are in a good mood, they are more likely to comply with requests because they feel expansive, charitable, and affirmative.

   b. Isen et al. (1976) had experimenters call participants and claim that they had just used their last dime on this "misdialed" call and ask if the participant would call the correct number and relay a message.

    (1) Independent variable: whether participants had been previously given

a free gift of stationery (a positive mood induction) or not.
   (2) Dependent variable: how many participants agreed to make the call.
   (3) Finding: more participants who were in the positive mood condition than in the control condition agreed to make the call; compliance decreased as the time between the free gift and the subsequent phone request increased.
c. Positive mood increases compliance for two reasons:
   (1) Requests are less likely to be seen as intrusive or threatening if a person is in a good mood.
   (2) Agreeing to do something nice for someone else can help sustain a good mood.
d. Isen and Levin (1972) tested the hypothesis that the desire to maintain a good mood increases compliance.
   (1) Independent variable #1: participants were given cookies (positive mood induction) or not.
   (2) Independent variable #2: participants were asked to serve as confederates who would either help or hinder another person.
   (3) Dependent variable: number of participants agreeing to serve as a confederate.
   (4) Finding: the good mood created by having been given the cookie increased compliance only in the helping condition, suggesting that people wanted to sustain their good mood.
2. Negative Mood
   a. Certain types of negative moods can also increase compliance.
   b. Guilt can increase compliance in an effort to get rid of the bad feeling.
      (1) Harris et al. (1975) found that Catholics were more likely to donate to a charity before entering a church (when they were feeling guilty) for confession compared to after confession.
      (2) Regan (1971) conducted a study to examine whether guilt would lead participants to contribute more to a charitable cause.
         (a) Setup: Regan asked participants to monitor a shock meter hooked up to a rat's cage to be sure the voltage didn't go too high.

      (b) Independent variable: whether or not and how much participants donated to a charity.
      (c) Initial finding: participants were more likely to donate to a charitable cause if, upon a momentary lapse in their attention, the voltage shot way up and the rat jumped in pain.
c. The negative state relief hypothesis can be defined as the idea that people engage in certain actions, such as agreeing to a request, in order to relieve negative feelings and to feel better about themselves.
   (1) When the experimenter said the rat's pain was not the fault of the participant, Regan (1971) found that participants still donated more to a charity, implying that witnessing such pain created a negative emotion and that doing the good of donating to a charity was an effort to relieve it.
   (2) Cialdini et al. (1973) also conducted a study to test the hypothesis that a participant in a negative mood would be more likely to agree to a request that would help another person.
      (a) Independent variable #1: participants either inadvertently caused an important stack of cards to be knocked over and hopelessly disorganized (negative state mood induction), or they did not.
      (b) Independent variable #2: after knocking over the stack of cards but before the request for help, participants were either given money or verbal praise (positive mood inductions) for their performance on another task.
      (c) Dependent variable: how many participants agreed to help a different experimenter make phone calls for her study.
      (d) Finding: participants who were made to feel bad by upsetting the stack of cards and who did NOT receive any sort of positive mood induction were more likely to help than the participants who either never felt the negative mood or who "recovered" from the negative mood because of the money or positive feedback.

    d. Some types of guilt and sadness can lead to withdrawal, reducing the likelihood of compliance.

    e. A bad mood produced by anger may have a different effect on compliance: often people want to stew in their anger, and so anger may have little effect on compliance rates.

V. Resisting Social Influence

  A. Although people often give in to social pressure, this is not always the case.

  B. Reactance theory can be defined as reasserting prerogatives in response to the unpleasant state of arousal experienced by people when they believe their freedoms are threatened.

  C. Factors that can increase your ability to resist social influence:

    1. Practicing resisting social influence.

      a. Good practice may involve questioning authority.

      b. Christians who helped Jews during the Holocaust were more likely to have been people who had had a previous history of helping others.

    2. Having an ally: the Asch studies convincingly demonstrated the way in which having a single ally could substantially reduce normative social influence pressures.

    3. Being wary of slippery slopes (trying to look ahead to likely future scenarios): it is much easier to resist at the start of something rather than backing out once you've already begun.

    4. Delaying a decision: it is easier to resist social influence if you are about to make an emotional decision because emotions will fade and delay will enable you to think through the decision more carefully.

Testing Your Basic Knowledge

ANSWERS TO MULTIPLE-CHOICE QUESTIONS

1. c	14. c
2. a	15. a
3. b	16. b
4. b	17. a
5. c	18. a
6. c	19. b
7. a	20. b
8. a	21. c
9. c	22. a
10. a	23. b
11. c	24. b
12. b	25. a
13. b	

Testing Your In-Depth Understanding

EXAMPLE ANSWERS TO THE GUIDED QUESTIONS FOR CRITICAL THINKING EXERCISES #1 AND #2

1. and 2. Use the list of key concepts at the end of the chapter, the chapter headings, and your chapter outline to create a list of concepts, and then brainstorm how each of those concepts might have played a role in the Milgram study.

3. You might consider writing a narrative in which YOU are the participant and, thus, reveal what is going on in your head. See the excerpt below to get you started.

When I got to the study, I was a little bit nervous. I'd never been part of a psychology experiment before. The other subject looked calm though and seemed nice. The experimenter came in and had on a white lab coat and spoke very authoritatively. I began to relax a bit because both the other subject and the experimenter seemed to be calm and to know what was going on (**informational social influence**). The experimenter explained the purpose of the study, and it sounded so official that I knew right then I wanted to do a good job and not mess up the experiment (**fair play, wanting to advance science**). We randomly got assigned to be either the learner or the teacher, and I got to be the teacher. I was given a test shock of 45 volts, which felt unpleasant but didn't hurt as much as I thought it would. The experimenter showed me how to use the shock generator, and I relaxed a bit when I realized that it wasn't technically complicated, I could imagine doing it (**ideomotor action**). At first, everything went fine. The other subject got a bunch of answers right, but when he got one wrong, I said the right answer and then flipped the shock lever for the appropriate shock. 15 volts, 30, 45, 60, 75 . . . I sort of settled into a rhythm after a while (**step-by-step involvement**). I actually found myself feeling good because I was doing this right, and I somehow wanted to please the experimenter (**normative social influence**). At one point, I heard the other subject sort of grunt when I gave the shock—that caught me off guard. I looked at the experimenter, but he didn't say anything or have any kind of unpleasant reaction, so I figured everything was okay (**informational social influence**). But then on the next shock, the other guy grunted even louder. It was obvious he had felt some pain. I looked again at the experimenter, and he said "please continue" as if everything was okay. I figured he was in charge and knew best, so I kept going (**compliance with a legitimate authority figure with expertise**). I was in such a good mood about being in an important study and all, I think that I thought doing what he asked would help me keep that good mood (**positive mood increasing compliance**). But then things started getting really crazy. The other subject started yelling that he was in pain and that his heart was bothering him. I kept looking at the experimenter, but he just kept saying the experiment required that I continue. I was so confused. I didn't want to mess up the study (**advancing science, fair play**) or make the experimenter angry at me (**normative social influence**), but I just couldn't understand why he wasn't more concerned about the other subject (**ambiguous task, confusing context of disagreement**). I tried to stop a bunch of times, once I even got up from my chair, but the experimenter just kept telling me to continue (**ineffective attempts to resist authority**), and I wasn't sure what else to do to get the situation under control. I kept telling myself that I would go up just one more shock and then stop if the guy kept yelling (**step-by-step**). But when I tried to stop, I just got all confused and didn't have time to think. I didn't want to hurt him, but I didn't want to do the wrong thing and not finish the study (**conflict of opposing forces**). I was feeling so guilty at one point that I did what the experimenter said, hoping I would feel better by knowing that I was doing the study correctly (**compliance to alleviate a negative mood**). It didn't work, because after giving the shock I just felt worse. How had I gotten into this mess? It was so easy at first. No one would have questioned anything. Now I just felt a weird sense of obligation to keep going (**foot-in-the-door**). At one point, I'd had it and knew that what was going on was wrong. The thought of causing that guy pain and how he might be seriously hurt just got to me—and I'd be the one who had caused it all. I told the experimenter I didn't want responsibility for hurting that guy. The experimenter then said something that totally knocked the wind out of my righteousness. He said, "I am responsible for what happens here." Well, when I heard that, I felt somehow a little bit relieved but then also compelled to go on, I had no choice—he was the one who was in charge of this and who was making everything happen (**release of responsibility**). . . .

You can continue the story!

The goal of this chapter is to present some of the basic social psychological knowledge concerning attitudes and, in particular, the manipulation of attitudes via persuasion. Topics include the function of attitudes, theories and studies about how attitudes are changed, individual factors that make a person more or less susceptible to persuasion attempts, and a discussion of the ways in which the ever-present media affect the attitudes of Americans.

ANNOTATED CHAPTER OUTLINE

After first reading through the chapter quickly, create a comprehensive framework for the information in the chapter by reading the outline below and filling in the missing information. Instead of simply re-copying information from the textbook, try to use your own words wherever possible; you can check your answers against the completed outline in the Answer Key section at the end of the chapter.

I. The Basics of Attitudes
   A. An attitude can be defined as

      ——————————————————
      ——————————————————
      ——————————————————
      ——————————————————

   B. The Three Components of Attitudes
     1. Affect:

       ——————————————————
       ——————————————————
       ——————————————————
       ——————————————————

     2. Cognitions:
       ——————————————————
       ——————————————————

       ——————————————————
   3. Behaviors: when attitudes are brought to mind, we tend to behave in ways that reflect those attitudes; neuroscience studies suggest that thinking about attitudes activates portions of the motor cortex reflective of those attitudes.
   C. Measuring Attitudes
     1. Attitude questionnaires are the most widely used methodology in social psychology.
     2. The Likert scale can be defined as

       ——————————————————
       ——————————————————
       ——————————————————
       ——————————————————

     3. To differentiate subtle differences in attitude strength, researchers may measure accessibility, the degree to which an attitude is ready to come to mind.
      a. Response latency can be defined as

        ——————————————————
        ——————————————————
        ——————————————————
        ——————————————————

      b. Fazio and Williams (1986) measured participants' response latencies in answering questions about presidential candidates Ronald Reagan and Walter Mondale and found that

        ——————————————————
        ——————————————————
        ——————————————————

     4. The centrality of an attitude to an individual's belief system can be determined by measuring

a variety of attitudes in a single domain and then calculating the relationship between one attitude and all the others.

5. Another way to measure attitudes is by using scenarios, wherein participants read stories and indicate how they would respond if they were in that situation.

6. Another method to measure attitudes is to code content analysis, scrutinizing and categorizing spontaneous speech to look for patterns reflecting attitudes.

II. Functions of Attitudes
  A. The Utilitarian Function of Attitudes
    1. The utilitarian function can be defined as

_____

_____

_____

    2. Attitudes toward initially neutral objects can be modified by pairing that object with other stimuli that produce a positive or negative reaction (e.g., pairing a consumer product with a pleasant picture).

    3. Food preferences/attitudes lead us to prefer to eat foods that were evolutionarily beneficial and to stay away from foods that were toxic. Two examples are:

      a. _____

_____

_____

_____

      b. _____

_____

_____

_____

  B. The Ego-Defensive Function of Attitudes
    1. An ego-defensive function can be defined as

_____

_____

_____

    2. Terror management theory can be defined as an ego-defensive theory that says that to ward off the anxiety we feel when contemplating our own demise, we cling to cultural worldviews and strongly held values out of a belief that by doing so part of us will survive death. Three examples of ways we ward off anxiety about death are:

      a. _____

_____

_____

_____

      b. _____

_____

_____

_____

      c. _____

_____

_____

_____

    3. In over seventy-five experiments, Pyszczynski (peh-ZIN-ski), Greenberg, Solomon, and colleagues have found that making people's mortality salient can have the following results:

      a. _____

_____

_____

_____

      b. _____

_____

_____

_____

      c. _____

_____

_____

_____

      d. _____

_____

_____

_____

      e. _____

_____

_____

_____

  C. The Value-Expressive Function of Attitudes
    1. A value-expressive function can be defined as

_____

_____

_____

    2. Reference groups can be defined as

_____

_____

_____

    3. Children in the United States often express a preference for Democrats or Republicans as a way to express their family's values.

    4. People low in prejudice feel shame and guilt when their actions contradict their attitudes toward minority groups.

    5. Conservative political groups tend to attract those who value economic freedom and social constraint; liberal political groups tend to attract people who value economic equality and social freedom.

6. Newcomb (1958) conducted a study at Bennington College, a liberal arts college that had liberal professors and highly conservative incoming freshmen.
   a. His study found that over the four years in college, most students' political views

   _____

   _____

   _____

   b. Liberal students tended to be

   _____

   _____

   _____

   c. Twenty-five years later, the Bennington graduates' political views

   _____

   _____

   _____

D. The Knowledge Function of Attitudes
   1. The knowledge function can be defined as

   _____

   _____

   _____

   2. Lepper, Ross, Vallone, and Keavney found that, after watching the same videotape of a presidential debate, Carter supporters thought Carter had won, Reagan supporters thought Reagan had won, and undecided voters were intermediate.

III. Persuasion and Attitude Change
   A. A Two-Process Approach to Persuasion
      1. The heuristic-systematic model can be defined as

      _____

      _____

      _____

      2. The Elaboration Likelihood Model (ELM) can be defined as

      _____

      _____

      _____

      3. The ELM assumes that there are two different ways in which people might process a persuasive message:
         a. The central route of persuasion, wherein people

         _____

         _____

   _____

      b. The peripheral route to persuasion, wherein people

   _____

   _____

   _____

   4. In general, motivation and ability determine which route people will use to process a persuasive communication.
   5. Specific factors leading to central route processing:
      a. Personal relevance:

      _____

      _____

      _____

      b. Knowledge:

      _____

      _____

      _____

      c. Responsibility:

      _____

      _____

      _____

   6. Factors leading to peripheral route processing:
      a. Anything that reduces our motivation to attend carefully to the message (e.g., low relevance).
      b. Anything that reduces our ability to attend carefully to the message (e.g., distraction).
   7. Tests of the ELM involve manipulating the strength of the arguments presented, the relevance of the issue to participants, and a peripheral cue.
      a. Petty et al. (1981) asked participants to read arguments favoring the implementation of comprehensive exams at their school.
         (1) Independent variable #1:

         _____

         _____

         _____

         (2) Independent variable #2:

         _____

         _____

         _____

         (3) Independent variable #3: whether the arguments were generated by students or by the supposed "Carnegie

Commission" and a Princeton University professor.

    (4) Dependent variable: extent to which participants said they liked the idea.

    (5) Finding:

_____

_____

_____

_____

8. The central route to persuasion leads to longer-lasting attitude change.

B. The Who, What, and Whom of Persuasion

  1. Source Characteristics (the "Who")

    a. Source characteristics can be defined as

_____

_____

_____

_____

    (1) Attractiveness: attractive communicators appear to be more persuasive than less attractive communicators, especially if people are engaging in peripheral route processing.

    (2) Credibility: communicators who appear to be high in credibility are more persuasive (especially via peripheral route processing) through their use of eye contact, expression of emotion, lack of nervousness, use of dramatic gestures, and few hesitations in speech.

    b. Hovland and Weiss (1951) conducted a classic study in which people gave their opinions about the likelihood of a nuclear submarine being built in the near (1950s) future and then read essays about its likelihood written by either a highly credible physicist or a less credible Soviet journalist.

    (1) Immediate findings:

_____

_____

_____

    (2) Four-week follow-up findings:

_____

_____

_____

    (3) The Hovland and Weiss results illustrated the sleeper effect, which is

_____

_____

    (4) Researchers explain the sleeper effect by noting that we tend to store a message and its source separately, and over time we dissociate the source of the message from its content, unless cues discrediting the noncredible source precede the message.

2. Message Characteristics (the "What")

  a. Message characteristics can be defined as

_____

_____

_____

  b. High-quality messages are more persuasive, especially when people are engaging in central route processing.

    (1) Higher-quality messages appeal to core values of the audience and promise desirable yet novel consequences if the action advocated in the message is taken.

    (2) Higher-quality messages are clear, logical, and have explicit conclusions (although implicit arguments may work better for persuading highly knowledgeable people who prefer to reach their own conclusions).

    (3) Higher-quality messages explicitly refute the opposition, giving the receiver of the message material with which to counterargue against opposing messages.

    (4) Arguing against your own self-interest creates a good argument, as seen in a study by Walster et al. (1966), which found that

_____

_____

_____

  c. Vivid information, such as a personal narrative with emotional appeal, is typically more persuasive than statistics or facts.

    (1) Hamill et al. (1980) asked participants to discuss their attitudes toward welfare.

      (a) Independent variable:

_____

_____

_____

_____

(b) Dependent variable: change in attitudes toward welfare.

(c) Finding:

_____

_____

_____

_____

(2) The identifiable victim effect can be defined as the tendency to be more moved by the plight of a single, vivid individual than by a more abstract aggregate of individuals.

d. Fear-arousing messages

(1) Fear-arousing messages are generally effective as long as the fear isn't too great and as long as a clear recommendation on how to combat the threat is also offered.

(2) Leventhal et al. (1967) tried to change the smoking habits of participants.

(a) Independent variable:

_____

_____

_____

_____

(b) Dependent variable: self-reports of smoking habits a month later.

(c) Finding:

_____

_____

_____

_____

e. Culture: Han and Shavitt (1994) found that

_____

_____

_____

_____

3. Receiver Characteristics (the "Whom")

a. Receiver characteristics can be defined as

_____

_____

_____

_____

b. The need for cognition refers to

_____

_____

_____

_____

(1) People with a high need for cognition are more likely to be persuaded by high-quality arguments and to be relatively unaffected by peripheral route cues.

(2) People with a low need for cognition are less likely to be persuaded by high-quality arguments because they don't enjoy engaging in in-depth analysis.

c. Mood: counter-attitudinal, pessimistic messages are more persuasive to people who are sad or depressed, and happier pro-attitudinal messages are more persuasive to people who are in good moods.

d. Age: younger people are more susceptible to persuasive attempts, raising the following questions:

(1) _____

_____

_____

_____

(2) _____

_____

_____

_____

(3) _____

_____

_____

_____

IV. The Media and Persuasion

A. Average Americans spend half of their waking hours with the media.

B. The third-person effect can be defined as

_____

_____

_____

_____

1. People assume others do not share their powers of rational analysis and restraint.

2. Innes and Zeitz (1988) found that

_____

_____

_____

3. In all the correlational research on media's persuasive powers, we need to be cautious in our interpretations because of

a. Self-selection bias (i.e., causality problems)

b. Errors based on retrospective self-report

C. The Surprisingly Weak Effects of the Media

1. William McGuire found remarkably small and/or nonexistent effects of media persuasion attempts.

2. Consumer Advertising

a. The correlation between the advertising budget of a product and its market share is typically

_____

_____

_____

b. Advertising seems to have indirect effects on what consumers purchase, including:

(1) _____

_____

_____

(2) _____

_____

_____

(3) _____

_____

_____

_____

3. Political Advertising
   a. Most studies find no correlation between advertising budgets and success in an election.
   b. Sometimes advertising can be helpful in the early stages of the campaign, but other factors (like the candidate's past success) are stronger predictors.
   c. Political ads mainly affect late-deciding voters.
   d. Negative political ads may lead people to vote for the other candidate or not to vote at all.
      (1) There has been an increase in negative ads, along with a decrease in voter turnout in presidential elections.
      (2) Ansolabehere and Iyengar (1995) found that

_____

_____

_____

_____

4. Public Service Announcements
   a. Public service announcements and programs promote beneficial health and social practices and warn against the dangers of behaviors such as taking drugs, smoking, and unsafe sex.
   b. Drug-prevention media campaigns seem to have little effect on knowledge of dangers of drug use and/or drug-taking behavior.
      (1) D.A.R.E. is an expensive and widely used middle school or junior high school program that aims to discourage drug use.

(2) Ten years after participating in D.A.R.E. in sixth grade, students were likely to

_____

_____

_____

_____

c. Other types of persuasion attempts, such as using scenarios to teach kids how to react to peer pressure situations, have been shown to be effective.

D. The Media and Conceptions of Social Reality
   1. It may be unrealistic to expect any one specific ad to affect any one specific behavior.
   2. The media, as a whole, may have a profound effect on our views of reality.
   3. Agenda control can be defined as

_____

_____

_____

_____

4. Iyengar and Kinder (1987) showed participants a series of newscasts.
   a. Independent variable:

_____

_____

_____

   b. Dependent variable:

_____

_____

_____

_____

   c. Finding:

_____

_____

_____

_____

5. A 1986 analysis showed that the world depicted on television is very dissimilar to the real world, as shown by these depictions on television:
   a. _____

_____

_____

_____

   b. _____

_____

_____

_____

   c. _____

_____

_____

_____

_____

6. Gerbner et al. (1986) found that heavy television viewers (those who watched five or more hours per day) misconstrued reality based on what they had seen on television:
   a. They were more racially prejudiced.
   b. _____
   _____
   _____
   _____
   c. _____
   _____
   _____
   _____
   d. _____
   _____
   _____

7. Gerbner et al.'s results may have been due to the self-selection problem: maybe people who think like this enjoy watching television more.

V. Resistance to Persuasion
   A. Attentional Biases and Resistance
      1. Selective attention is
      _____
      _____
      _____
      _____

         a. Kleinhesselink and Edwards (1975) asked students to listen to messages about the legalization of marijuana while hearing an electronic buzzing in their headphones.
            (1) Independent variable #1: students either supported or were opposed to the legalization of marijuana.
            (2) Independent variable #2: the message's seven strong and seven weak arguments (this is still a variable, even though all participants heard both the strong and the weak messages).
            (3) Dependent variable:
            _____
            _____
            _____
            _____
            (4) Finding:
            _____
            _____
            _____
            _____

         b. McPherson (1983) found that students asked to write essays about federal funding or abortion or the use of nuclear energy

used as reference material articles that supported their preexisting attitudes.

2. Selective evaluation is
   _____
   _____
   _____
   _____

   a. Ziva Kunda (1990) asked participants to read a *New York Times* (highly credible) article that provided evidence that high-caffeine consumption is related to fibrocystic disease in females.
      (1) Independent variable #1: whether participants were male or female.
      (2) Independent variable #2: whether participants were high or low in their caffeine consumption.
      (3) Dependent variable: evaluation of the article.
      (4) Finding:
      _____
      _____
      _____
      _____

   b. The belief polarization hypothesis argues that a message that is mixed (has arguments both in favor of and against something) will not result in more moderate views on both sides; rather, those in favor will only hear and believe the "pro-" parts of the message, and those opposed will only hear and believe the "anti-" parts of the message.
      (1) Lord, Ross, and Lepper (1979) had participants read two research studies about the effectiveness of the death penalty as a deterrent to later crime.
         (a) Independent variable #1: one research study suggested that the death penalty was a good deterrent and the other that it was not a good deterrent (this is still an independent variable even though all participants saw both articles).
         (b) Independent variable #2: participants were either initially in favor of or opposed to the death penalty.
         (c) Dependent variable:
         _____
         _____
         _____
         _____

(d) Finding:

_____

_____

_____

(2) Ditto and Lopez (1992) gave participants a saliva test for a fictitious medical condition.
    (a) Independent variable

_____

_____

_____

    (b) Dependent variable: how long the participants looked at the paper before accepting its conclusion.
    (c) Finding:

_____

_____

_____

_____

C. Previous Commitments and Resistance
  1. Having a previous commitment to a particular position makes attitude change less likely, as in:
    a. Political allegiance
    b. Drug-taking (consider the habit and community of friends)
  2. Public statements of one's position result in more resistance to counter-attitudinal messages.
  3. Thought polarization can be defined as

_____

_____

_____

    a. Tesser and Conlee (1975) found that

_____

_____

_____

    b. The caution here is that if someone has never really thought about the view before at all, increased thought can lead to more moderate attitudes.
D. Knowledge and Resistance
  1. Being more knowledgeable about a topic makes a person less susceptible to counter-attitudinal messages.
  2. Wood (1982) found that

_____

_____

_____

_____

E. Attitude Inoculation
  1. Attitude inoculation can be defined as

_____

_____

_____

  2. McGuire and Papageorgis (1961) asked participants the extent to which they agreed with certain truisms like "it is important to brush your teeth" and "penicillin has been good for mankind."
    a. Independent variable: participants were exposed to a counterargument or not; those exposed to a counterargument were asked to generate arguments either refuting it or supporting it.
    b. Dependent variable:

_____

_____

_____

_____

    c. Findings:

_____

_____

_____

_____

TESTING YOUR BASIC KNOWLEDGE

After studying the information in the chapter by filling in the outline above, test your basic knowledge with the following multiple-choice test. Answers are provided in the Answer Key section at the end of the chapter. If you find that you have gotten an answer wrong, it is important that you understand why it is wrong (as well as understanding why the correct answer is the better choice). Talk with peers, your tutor, or your professor if you need help.

Multiple-Choice Questions

1. Imagine that you were trying to listen to a political candidate's speech detailing why you should vote for her. During her speech, your friend keeps talking to you and, as if that weren't enough, there is construction noise in the room next door. Both of these factors make it very difficult for you to pay attention to the candidate's speech. According to the Elaboration Likelihood Model (let's assume it is working in isolation from other social factors), under which of these conditions would you be most likely to end up voting for the candidate?
    a. when the candidate is attractive, regardless of the quality of her arguments

b. when the candidate is attractive, but only if her arguments are of high quality

c. when her arguments are of high quality, regardless of her attractiveness

2. When Tamara thinks about cars, the first thing that comes to mind are warm feelings of interest, passion, and fondness. This reflects which part of her attitude toward cars?
   a. affective component
   b. cognitive component
   c. behavioral component

3. A survey asked participants to indicate how much they liked cats on a scale from 1 (hate cats) to 5 (love cats). This type of measurement is known as a
   a. response latency.
   b. Likert scale.
   c. centrality measure.

4. Women who are pregnant often experience an aversion to bitter foods. This may illustrate
   a. an ego-defensive function of attitudes.
   b. a value-expression function of attitudes.
   c. a utilitarian function of attitudes.

5. According to terror management theory, people who are primed to think about their own mortality are likely to
   a. more strongly endorse the value of cultural rules and guidelines.
   b. become depressed.
   c. develop pessimistic attitudes.

6. In 1958 Theodore Newcomb studied the highly conservative incoming class at Bennington College, a school that was known for its liberal professors. Newcomb's results revealed that
   a. as students became more integrated into college life, their attitudes became more liberal.
   b. students maintained their conservative attitudes as a means of expressing their allegiance to their families.
   c. students initially became more liberal, but after leaving the college returned to their conservative roots.

7. A referee at an American football game issues a decision against the Red team and in favor of the Blue team. A controversy ensues. Keeping in mind that all the fans saw the same event, the knowledge function of attitudes would predict that
   a. fans of the Blue and the Red teams would accept the referee's decision because he is the authority.
   b. fans of the Blue and the Red teams would reject the referee's decision because if there is controversy, the referee must be wrong.

c. fans of the Blue team would think the referee was right, but fans of the Red team would think the referee was wrong.

8. Petty and his colleagues conducted a study testing the Elaboration Likelihood Model. They had college sophomores read arguments in favor of increasing tuition. This tuition increase was either slated to happen the next academic year or ten years later. This independent variable was designed to manipulate
   a. the mood of the participants.
   b. the likelihood that participants would engage in central route processing.
   c. the potency of a peripheral cue.

9. People tend to evaluate counter-attitudinal arguments more _____ than attitude-consistent arguments.
   a. quickly
   b. favorably
   c. harshly

10. Attractive or credible speakers are more likely to be persuasive if the audience is
    a. in a good mood.
    b. engaging in central route processing.
    c. engaging in peripheral route processing.

11. Juanita heard an argument in favor of increasing taxes in her local municipality. At the end of the presentation, she learned that the argument was generated by a high school dropout who didn't even live in the same city as she did. At that time, she disregarded the message and was not persuaded. According to the sleeper effect, how is Juanita likely to feel about the proposal one month later?
    a. She will feel more favorably toward the argument than she did at first.
    b. She will be even less in favor of raising taxes.
    c. Her attitudes will have remained the same.

12. Timothy hears a vivid story about a woman who abuses the welfare system for twenty-five years. Dick hears that story, but then also reads a short article with statistics that prove the vast majority of people don't abuse welfare. Who is more likely to be in favor of ending the welfare program?
    a. Timothy, because he only knows the vivid story, not the facts
    b. Dick, because he is better educated about the truth of the welfare system
    c. They will both be equally likely to want to end welfare because vivid information has more of an impact than statistical facts.

13. Using fear in persuasive messages can be effective if
    a. the fear is moderate and a clear recommendation on how to avoid the fear-arousing situation is included.

b. the fear is strong enough to frighten people and capture their attention.

c. the intended audience is from an individualistic, as opposed to a collectivistic culture.

14. Which of the following people would be most susceptible to a persuasive message that contains high-quality arguments?
    a. an elderly woman
    b. a man who is high in need for cognition
    c. a woman who is low in need for cognition

15. Research on the effects of media advertisements suggests that
    a. media have surprisingly little direct effect on our attitudes.
    b. media do have significant indirect effects on our attitudes.
    c. Both A and B are accurate.

16. People who are heavy TV watchers (more than five hours per day) are more likely to overestimate the extent to which society is violent and the probability that they themselves will be victims of crime. This is due to
    a. the identifiable victim effect.
    b. the third-person effect.
    c. agenda control.

17. When listening to a careful discussion and debate covering the pros and cons of a given issue, research suggests that people who are on the "pro" side of the issue will
    a. selectively attend to only the "pro" arguments and not attend to the "con" arguments.
    b. become more moderate in their views after listening to the debate.
    c. Neither of the above is accurate.

18. According to the research discussed in the textbook, why does making a public statement in favor of a proposal make a person more resistant to counter-attitudinal persuasive attempts?
    a. because such public commitment usually comes as a result of more careful thought and elaboration on an issue
    b. because refuting your own public statement would be embarrassing
    c. because resisting subsequent persuasive attempts is less cognitively difficult than publicly endorsing a position

19. Wendy Wood exposed two groups of pro-environment students to messages advocating less environmental protection. What were her findings?
    a. The counter-attitudinal message led all the students to adopt more moderate views on the environment.

b. The pro-environment students who were also very knowledgeable about environmental issues were more resistant to the anti-environment messages.

c. All the students reacted negatively to the counter-attitudinal message.

20. Presenting people with weak versions of the opposition's message, and helping them develop strong arguments refuting the opposition is called
    a. the third-person effect.
    b. the thought polarization hypothesis.
    c. attitude inoculation.

21. Kevin had no interest in or knowledge of the AIDS crisis in Africa. It seemed like an issue that had very little relevance to his own life. For his political science class, however, he was required to go hear a visiting campus speaker whose talk was all about why we needed to increase U.S. financial support to Africa to combat AIDS. According to the Elaboration Likelihood Model, which of the following aspects of the talk would be most likely to persuade Kevin to sign a petition advocating increasing financial support to Africa?
    a. the careful and detailed economic argument laid out by the speaker which demonstrated that an extremely small, almost unnoticeable increase in monies from the U.S. would result in dramatic improvements in Africa
    b. a glitzy videotaped message in which a popular rock star, movie actor, and religious leader all voice support for giving more money to Africa
    c. Both features of the talk would be equally persuasive to Kevin.

22. To create a high-quality persuasive message, you should
    a. explicitly refute opposition arguments as long as your audience is well-informed.
    b. make arguments that support your own self-interest and well-being.
    c. let less knowledgeable audiences reach their own conclusions rather than having you explicitly state conclusions.

23. A major company produces two commercials, one for their audiences in Japan and the other for their audiences in the United States. The first ad stresses the way in which the product will improve the lives of an entire family, while the second ad stresses the advantages the product offers for a single individual. Which commercial should they air in Japan?
    a. the first ad
    b. the second ad
    c. Either ad would do just as well in either country.

24. If you want to persuade your girlfriend of something that is unpleasant and very much counter to her typical attitudes, you should wait until she is in what kind of mood?
    a. sad or depressed
    b. happy or optimistic
    c. neutral

25. Research suggests that negative political advertisements (i.e., those that aggressively critique the opponent) have which of the following effects?
    a. They make people angry and, thus, more likely to vote.
    b. They make people less likely to vote for the candidate who is featured in the message.
    c. They make people less likely to participate in the election at all.

Essay Questions

After you have mastered the multiple-choice questions, try testing your basic understanding by thoroughly answering each of the broad essay questions below. Because it is critical that you think through this information on your own, we have not provided any answers to these questions. Your learning and retention of this material will be greatly enhanced if you do one or more of the following to check your answers: carefully review the textbook information; compare your responses to your class lecture notes; talk over your answers with a peer; ask your professor to review your answers or review any information that is unclear to you.

1. Define an attitude, including the three basic components of an attitude. Briefly describe a few of the ways in which a social psychologist measures attitudes.

2. Explain each of the four different functions of attitudes, providing empirical support for each function.

3. Explain the Elaboration Likelihood Model, and discuss how features of the message, the source, and the audience influence the effectiveness of a persuasive attempt.

4. To what extent do media messages result directly in attitude change? How do the media's persuasive messages indirectly affect our attitudes?

5. How do attention, previous commitment, and knowledge lead to resistance to persuasion? How does attitude inoculation take advantage of those natural aspects of resistance to create resistance to attitude change?

TESTING YOUR IN-DEPTH UNDERSTANDING

Test your in-depth understanding of the material by working through the Critical Thinking Exercises provided at the end of each textbook chapter. To maximize this learning opportunity, work together with a tutor, study group, or your professor. Alternatively, write down your thoughts and responses.

Guided questions for one of the exercises are provided below. While there are multiple ways to answer these questions, short answers are given in the Answer Key at the end of the chapter. Note, however, that the valuable part of this exercise is not simply knowing the answer but working with the material to come up with the answer.

Guided Questions for Critical Thinking Exercise #2

Imagine that you had been put in charge of a political ad campaign for a young candidate running for office. She has given you the charge of appealing to two sectors of the population who have been showing low rates of voter turnout—young voters aged eighteen to twenty and busy women who have children and full-time careers. What sort of audience-specific campaigns would you propose, based on what you have learned from the dual-process approach to persuasion?

1. The dual-process approach to persuasion was discussed primarily through the lens of the Elaboration Likelihood Model. Review the basic definition of that model.

2. Do you think your audience is more likely to engage in central or peripheral route processing and why?

3. Review the individual features of the message you are going to construct, keeping in mind the audiences you are trying to reach. What would you recommend about the content of the message (and why)? What would you recommend about the source characteristics of the message (and why)?

4. Just to be thorough, review other concepts in the chapter and see if there are any tips that would help you put the finishing touches on your presentations. In particular, review the role of culture in persuasion, the value-expressive function of attitudes (and reference groups), the identifiable victim effect and the role of vividness in persuasive messages, the thought polarization hypothesis and attitude inoculation effects.

Enhance your understanding of the chapter by thinking about and doing the remaining two Critical Thinking Exercises. Discuss your answers with your peers, study group, tutor, or professor.

Critical Thinking Exercise #1

Gordon Allport, one of the founders of social psychology, argued that the notion of attitudes is the central construct in our discipline. The four important functions that attitudes serve bolster this claim. For each of the four functions of attitudes that we have covered in this chapter, discuss a finding from another chapter you have read so far that illustrates the function.

Critical Thinking Exercise #3

Imagine you were designing an anti-drug campaign for children aged nine to twelve, who are particularly vulnerable to persuasive attempts to take drugs. What sort of techniques would you use to encourage them to resist this kind of persuasion?

SOCIAL PSYCHOLOGY IN THE POPULAR MEDIA

You might be interested in the following popular media references, each of which relates in some way to information in this chapter.

Film

Network (1976; directed by Sidney Lumet; starring Peter Finch, William Holden, Faye Dunaway, Beatrice Straight, Robert Duvall). Written by Paddy Chayefsky, this is a satire about the effects of the media on public opinion, as well as the effects of ratings and consumerism on what is deemed newsworthy and covered in the television news.

Online Video

The Persuaders (Frontline Documentary, 2004, 90 minutes)—http://www.pbs.org/wgbh/pages/frontline/ shows/persuaders. You can watch the entire video online for free or purchase the DVD or VHS. From the ShopPBS Web site: "Frontline examines the "persuasion industries"—advertising and public relations. To cut through consumers' growing resistance to their pitches, marketers have developed new ways of integrating their messages into the fabric of our lives, using sophisticated market research techniques to better understand consumers and turning to the little-understood techniques of public relations to make sure their messages come from sources we trust."

Web Sites

Advertising Council Historic Campaigns— http://www.adcouncil.org/campaigns/ historic_campaigns. This Web site includes a collection of historic public service announcements that appeared on television.

Implicit Association Test—https://implicit.harvard.edu/ implicit/demo. Research suggests that all of our attitudes are not explicit (consciously known). Rather, some of our attitudes have unconscious, implicit elements. This Web site explains more and includes some tests of common attitudes like prejudice and self-esteem. Compare your consciously held beliefs with your implicit attitudes. Do they match?

Visual Cultural and Public Health Posters—http://www.nlm. nih.gov/exhibition/visualculture/vchome.html. This Web site includes a collection of public health posters from the twentieth century that are designed to persuade viewers to adopt various positive health practices.

ANSWER KEY

Annotated Chapter Outline

I. The Basics of Attitudes
A. An attitude can be defined as an evaluation of an object in a positive or negative fashion that includes the three elements of affect, cognitions, and behavior.
B. The Three Components of Attitudes
1. Affect: emotional reactions to an object.
2. Cognitions: knowledge, beliefs, ideas, memories, and images about the object.
3. Behaviors: when attitudes are brought to mind, we tend to behave in ways that reflect those attitudes; neuroscience studies suggest that thinking about attitudes activates portions of the motor cortex reflective of those attitudes.
C. Measuring Attitudes
1. Attitude questionnaires are the most widely used methodology in social psychology.
2. The Likert scale can be defined as a scale used to assess people's attitudes that includes a set of possible answers and anchors on each extreme.
3. To differentiate subtle differences in attitude strength, researchers may measure accessibility, the degree to which an attitude is ready to come to mind.
a. Response latency can be defined as the time it takes an individual to respond to a stimulus such as an attitude question.

b. Fazio and Williams (1986) measured participants' response latencies in answering questions about presidential candidates Ronald Reagan and Walter Mondale and found that the time it took them to respond predicted their perceptions of who had won the presidential debate and who they voted for six months later.

4. The centrality of an attitude to an individual's belief system can be determined by measuring a variety of attitudes in a single domain and then calculating the relationship between one attitude and all the others.

5. Another way to measure attitudes is using scenarios, wherein participants read stories and indicate how they would respond if they were in that situation.

6. Another method to measure attitudes is to code content analysis, scrutinizing and categorizing spontaneous speech to look for patterns reflecting attitudes.

II. Functions of Attitudes
   A. The Utilitarian Function of Attitudes
      1. The utilitarian function can be defined as an attitudinal function that serves to alert us to rewarding objects and situations we should approach, and costly or punishing objects or situations we should avoid.
      2. Attitudes toward initially neutral objects can be modified by pairing that object with other stimuli that produce a positive or negative reaction (e.g., pairing a consumer product with a pleasant picture).
      3. Food preferences/attitudes lead us to prefer to eat foods that were evolutionarily beneficial and to stay away from foods that were toxic. Two examples are:
         a. The preference for sweet foods helped us identify foods that provide Vitamin C.
         b. Pregnant women's aversion to bitter foods helped them to avoid toxins that would harm the fetus.
   B. The Ego-Defensive Function of Attitudes
      1. An ego-defensive function can be defined as an attitudinal function that enables us to maintain cherished beliefs about ourselves by protecting us from awareness of our negative attributes and impulses or from facts that contradict our cherished beliefs or desires.
      2. Terror management theory can be defined as an ego-defensive theory that says that to ward off the anxiety we feel when contemplating our own demise, we cling to cultural worldviews

and strongly held values out of a belief that by doing so part of us will survive death. Three examples of ways we ward off anxiety about death are:
      a. Developing religious systems which promise an afterlife.
      b. Participating in cultural traditions that make us feel part of something larger than ourselves.
      c. Creating literature and art that will allow part of us to live on

3. In over seventy-five experiments, Pyszczynski (peh-ZIN-ski), Greenberg, Solomon, and colleagues have found that making people's mortality salient can have the following results:
      a. More positive attitudes toward their group.
      b. Greater conformity to cultural guidelines.
      c. Greater patriotism.
      d. Increased religious conviction.
      e. Greater inclination to punish moral transgressions (against established society/culture).

   C. The Value-Expressive Function of Attitudes
      1. A value-expressive function can be defined as an attitudinal function whereby attitudes help us express our most cherished values—usually in groups in which they can be supported and reinforced.
      2. Reference groups can be defined as groups whose opinions matter to us and that affect our opinions and beliefs.
      3. Children in the United States often express a preference for Democrats or Republicans as a way to express their family's values.
      4. People low in prejudice feel shame and guilt when their actions contradict their attitudes toward minority groups.
      5. Conservative political groups tend to attract those who value economic freedom and social constraint; liberal political groups tend to attract people who value economic equality and social freedom.
      6. Newcomb (1958) conducted a study at Bennington College, a liberal arts college that had liberal professors and highly conservative incoming freshmen.
         a. His study found that over the four years in college, most students' political views changed; their conservatism dropped dramatically; they adopted more liberal voting preferences.
         b. Liberal students tended to be more respected and better integrated into the

Bennington community than more conservative students.

    c. Twenty-five years later, the Bennington graduates' political views still tended to be liberal, and they were still more likely to vote for liberal than for conservative candidates.

D. The Knowledge Function of Attitudes

    1. The knowledge function can be defined as an attitudinal function whereby attitudes help organize our understanding of the world, guiding how we attend to, store, and retrieve information.

    2. Lepper, Ross, Vallone, and Keavney found that, after watching the same videotape of a presidential debate, Carter supporters thought Carter had won, Reagan supporters thought Reagan had won, and undecided voters were intermediate.

III. Persuasion and Attitude Change

A. A Two-Process Approach to Persuasion

    1. The heuristic-systematic model can be defined as a model of persuasion that says there are two different routes of persuasion: the systematic route and the heuristic route.

    2. Elaboration Likelihood Model (ELM) can be defined as a model of persuasion that says there are two different routes of persuasion: the central route and the peripheral route.

    3. The ELM assumes that there are two different ways in which people might process a persuasive message:

        a. The central route of persuasion, wherein people think carefully and deliberately about the content of a message, attending to its logic, cogency, and arguments, as well as to related evidence and principles.

        b. The peripheral route to persuasion, wherein people attend to relatively simple, superficial cues related to the message, such as the length of the message or expertise or attractiveness of the communicator.

    4. In general, motivation and ability determine which route people will use to process a persuasive communication.

    5. Specific factors leading to central route processing:

        a. Personal relevance: we are more likely to engage in central processing of issues if the message bears upon our goals, concerns, or well-being.

        b. Knowledge: we are more likely to engage in central processing of issues we are more knowledgeable about.

        c. Responsibility: we are more likely to engage in central processing of issues if we feel responsible in some way for some action or outcome related to an issue (e.g., having to explain the message to someone else).

    6. Factors leading to peripheral route processing:

        a. Anything that reduces our motivation to attend carefully to the message (e.g., low relevance).

        b. Anything that reduces our ability to attend carefully to the message (e.g., distraction).

    7. Tests of the ELM involve manipulating the strength of the arguments presented, the relevance of the issue to participants, and a peripheral cue.

        a. Petty et al. (1981) asked participants to read arguments favoring the implementation of comprehensive exams at their school.

            (1) Independent variable #1: strong or weak arguments.

            (2) Independent variable #2: whether the exams would start next year or in ten years.

            (3) Independent variable #3: whether the arguments were generated by students or by the supposed "Carnegie Commission" and a Princeton University professor.

            (4) Dependent variable: extent to which participants said they liked the idea.

            (5) Finding: when the message was not relevant (ten years later condition), the more "expert" sounding source was persuasive, but the strength of the argument didn't matter; when the message was relevant, the peripheral cue didn't matter, but the strength of the argument did. Thus, those in the relevant condition were processing centrally, and those in the nonrelevant condition were processing peripherally.

    8. The central route to persuasion leads to longer-lasting attitude change.

B. The Who, What, and Whom of Persuasion

    1. Source Characteristics (the "Who")

        a. Source characteristics can be defined as characteristics of the person who delivers the message, including the person's attractiveness, credibility, and expertise.

            (1) Attractiveness: attractive communicators appear to be more persuasive than less attractive communicators, especially if people are engaging in peripheral route processing.

(2) Credibility: communicators who appear to be high in credibility are more persuasive (especially via peripheral route processing) through their use of eye contact, expression of emotion, lack of nervousness, use of dramatic gestures, and few hesitations in speech.

b. Hovland and Weiss (1951) conducted a classic study in which people gave their opinions about the likelihood of a nuclear submarine being built in the near (1950s) future and then read essays about its likelihood written by either a highly credible physicist or a less credible Soviet journalist.

(1) Immediate findings: there was greater attitude change among the participants who had read the essay attributed to a famous physicist rather than among participants who had read the essay attributed to a Soviet journalist.

(2) Four-week follow-up findings: people who read the essay attributed to a Soviet journalist now indicated greater persuasion than they had initially.

(3) The Hovland and Weiss results illustrated the sleeper effect, which is an effect that occurs when messages from unreliable sources initially exert little influence but later cause individuals' attitudes to shift.

(4) Researchers explain the sleeper effect by noting that we tend to store a message and its source separately, and over time we dissociate the source of the message from its content, unless cues discrediting the noncredible source precede the message.

2. Message Characteristics (the "What")

a. Message characteristics can be defined as aspects of the message itself, including the quality of the evidence and the explicitness of its conclusions.

b. High-quality messages are more persuasive, especially when people are engaging in central route processing.

(1) Higher-quality messages appeal to core values of the audience and promise desirable yet novel consequences if the action advocated in the message is taken.

(2) Higher-quality messages are clear, logical, and have explicit conclusions

(although implicit arguments may work better for persuading highly knowledgeable people who prefer to reach their own conclusions).

(3) Higher-quality messages explicitly refute the opposition, giving the receiver of the message material with which to counterargue against opposing messages.

(4) Arguing against your own self-interest creates a good argument, as seen in a study by Walster et al. (1966), which found that a prisoner arguing for longer prison sentences was more persuasive than a prisoner arguing for shorter prison sentences.

c. Vivid information, such as a personal narrative with emotional appeal, is typically more persuasive than statistics or facts.

(1) Hamill et al. (1980) asked participants to discuss their attitudes toward welfare.

(a) Independent variable: participants heard a vivid story about a lifetime welfare recipient who exploited the system, or they heard facts indicating that most recipients of welfare are only on it temporarily, or they both heard the story and got the facts.

(b) Dependent variable: change in attitudes toward welfare.

(c) Finding: participants were more likely to change their attitudes (negatively) after the story, even if they also heard the facts refuting the story.

(2) The identifiable victim effect can be defined as the tendency to be more moved by the plight of a single, vivid individual than by a more abstract aggregate of individuals.

d. Fear-arousing messages

(1) Fear-arousing messages are generally effective as long as the fear isn't too great and as long as a clear recommendation on how to combat the threat is also offered.

(2) Leventhal et al. (1967) tried to change the smoking habits of participants.

(a) Independent variable: participants saw a graphic film of lung cancer and lung cancer surgery, or they were given a pamphlet with tips on how to stop smoking, or they both saw the film and were given the pamphlet.

   (b) Dependent variable: self-reports of smoking habits a month later.

   (c) Finding: participants who had both seen the film and received the pamphlet reduced their smoking to a greater extent than those in any other condition.

  e. Culture: Han and Shavitt (1994) found that American ads are more likely to emphasize benefits to the individual, while Korean ads are more likely to focus on benefits to the collective, and that individual-oriented ads are more effective with American participants and collectivistic-ads are more effective with Korean participants.

3. Receiver Characteristics (the "Whom")

  a. Receiver characteristics can be defined as characteristics of the person who receives the message, including his or her age, mood, and motivation to attend to the message.

  b. The need for cognition refers to the degree to which people like to think deeply about issues.

   (1) People with a high need for cognition are more likely to be persuaded by high-quality arguments and to be relatively unaffected by peripheral route cues.

   (2) People with a low need for cognition are less likely to be persuaded by high-quality arguments because they don't enjoy engaging in in-depth analysis.

  c. Mood: counter-attitudinal, pessimistic messages are more persuasive to people who are sad or depressed, and happier pro-attitudinal messages are more persuasive to people who are in good moods.

  d. Age: younger people are more susceptible to persuasive attempts, raising the following questions:

   (1) Are children reliable witnesses in court cases?

   (2) Should advertisers be allowed to target children?

   (3) Does this attitude research (conducted on young adults) generalize to older participants?

IV. The Media and Persuasion

  A. Average Americans spend half of their waking hours with the media.

B. The third-person effect can be defined as the assumption by most people that "other people" are more prone to being influenced by persuasive messages (such as those in media campaigns) than they themselves are.

  1. People assume others do not share their powers of rational analysis and restraint.

  2. Innes and Zeitz (1988) found that participants rated others as more likely to be influenced by a political ad, a depiction of media violence, and a campaign to reduce drunk driving than they themselves would be.

  3. In all the correlational research on media's persuasive powers, we need to be cautious in our interpretations because of

   a. Self-selection bias (i.e., causality problems)

   b. Errors based on retrospective self-report

C. The Surprisingly Weak Effects of the Media

  1. William McGuire found remarkably small and/or nonexistent effects of media persuasion attempts.

  2. Consumer Advertising

   a. The correlation between the advertising budget of a product and its market share is typically nonexistent or short-lived (e.g., less than one year).

   b. Advertising seems to have indirect effects on what consumers purchase, including:

    (1) An increase in product loyalty

    (2) An increase in product awareness

    (3) An increase in warm or excited feelings about the product

  3. Political Advertising

   a. Most studies find no correlation between advertising budgets and success in an election.

   b. Sometimes advertising can be helpful in the early stages of the campaign, but other factors (like the candidate's past success) are stronger predictors.

   c. Political ads mainly affect late-deciding voters.

   d. Negative political ads may lead people to vote for the other candidate or not to vote at all.

    (1) There has been an increase in negative ads, along with a decrease in voter turnout in presidential elections.

    (2) Ansolabehere and Iyengar (1995) found that, during the 1992 Senate campaigns, areas with negative campaigns had lower voter turnout (49.7 percent) than areas with positive campaigns (57 percent).

4. Public Service Announcements
   a. Public service announcements and programs promote beneficial health and social practices and warn against the dangers of behaviors such as taking drugs, smoking, and unsafe sex.
   b. Drug-prevention media campaigns seem to have little effect on knowledge of dangers of drug use and/or drug-taking behavior.
      (1) D.A.R.E. is an expensive and widely used middle school or junior high school program that aims to discourage drug use.
      (2) Ten years after participating in D.A.R.E. in sixth grade students were likely to be no different than students who had not participated in the program.
   c. Other types of persuasion attempts, such as using scenarios to teach kids how to react to peer pressure situations, have been shown to be effective.
D. The Media and Conceptions of Social Reality
   1. It may be unrealistic to expect any one specific ad to affect any one specific behavior.
   2. The media, as a whole, may have a profound effect on our views of reality.
   3. Agenda control can be defined as efforts of the media to select certain events and topics to emphasize, and thereby shape what issues and events we think of as important.
   4. Iyengar and Kinder (1987) showed participants a series of newscasts.
      a. Independent variable: participants saw no, three, or six stories about U.S. dependence on foreign energy sources.
      b. Dependent variable: how many participants reported energy use as an important problem facing the country.
      c. Finding: 65 percent of participants seeing six stories rated energy as being one of the top three problems facing the country, 50 percent of those seeing three stories did so, and 24 percent of those seeing no stories (a control condition) did so.
   5. A 1986 analysis showed that the world depicted on television is very dissimilar to the real world, as shown by these depictions on television:
      a. Women, ethnic minorities, young children, and the elderly were substantially underrepresented.
      b. Service industry jobs and blue-collar jobs were underrepresented.
      c. Crime was heavily overrepresented.

6. Gerbner et al. (1986) found that heavy television viewers (those who watched five or more hours per day) misconstrued reality based on what they had seen on television:
   a. They were more racially prejudiced.
   b. They assumed women were less capable than men.
   c. They overestimated the prevalence of violent crime.
   d. They overestimated the number of doctors and lawyers in the population.
7. Gerbner et al.'s findings may have been due to the self-selection problem: maybe people who think like this enjoy watching television more.

V. Resistance to Persuasion
   A. Attentional Biases and Resistance
      1. Selective attention is paying more attention to information that confirms our preexisting attitudes and less attention to information that challenges our attitudes.
         a. Kleinhesselink and Edwards (1975) asked students to listen to messages about the legalization of marijuana while hearing an electronic buzzing in their headphones.
            (1) Independent variable #1: students either supported or were opposed to the legalization of marijuana.
            (2) Independent variable #2: the message's seven strong and seven weak arguments (this is still a variable, even though all participants heard both the strong and the weak messages).
            (3) Dependent variable: when participants pressed a button to temporarily turn off the buzzing so as to better hear an argument.
            (4) Finding: participants in favor of legalizing marijuana pressed the button more often when strong arguments about legalizing marijuana were being stated; participants opposed to legalizing marijuana pressed the button more often when weak (easy-to-refute) arguments were being stated.
         b. McPherson (1983) found that students asked to write essays about federal funding or abortion or the use of nuclear energy used as reference material articles that supported their preexisting attitudes.
      2. Selective evaluation is favorably evaluating information that supports our preexisting attitudes and negatively evaluating information that refutes our attitudes.

a. Ziva Kunda (1990) asked participants to read a *New York Times* (highly credible) article that provided evidence that high-caffeine consumption is related to fibrocystic disease in females.
   (1) Independent variable #1: whether participants were male or female.
   (2) Independent variable #2: whether participants were high or low in their caffeine consumption.
   (3) Dependent variable: evaluation of the article.
   (4) Finding: all men and the women who were low in caffeine consumption found the article convincing; high-caffeine-use women, however, found the article less convincing and were more critical of it.

b. The belief polarization hypothesis argues that a message that is mixed (has arguments both in favor of and against something) will not result in more moderate views on both sides; rather, those in favor will only hear and believe the "pro-" parts of the message, and those opposed will only hear and believe the "anti-" parts of the message.
   (1) Lord, Ross, and Lepper (1979) had participants read two research studies about the effectiveness of the death penalty as a deterrent to later crime.
      (a) Independent variable #1: one research study suggested that the death penalty was a good deterrent and the other that it was not a good deterrent (this is still an independent variable even though all participants saw both articles).
      (b) Independent variable #2: participants were either initially in favor of or opposed to the death penalty.
      (c) Dependent variable: participants' critiques of the studies.
      (d) Finding: death penalty advocates harshly criticized the design and details of the article suggesting that the death penalty was not a deterrent; those against the death penalty harshly criticized the other article; in the end, all participants endorsed their original attitudes more strongly than at the start of the study.

   (2) Ditto and Lopez (1992) gave participants a saliva test for a fictitious medical condition.
      (a) Independent variable: half of the participants were told that they had the condition if the saliva test paper remained yellow; the other half were told that they had the condition if the paper turned dark green.
      (b) Dependent variable: how long the participants looked at the paper before accepting its conclusion.
      (c) Finding: participants told that no color change meant they had the disorder looked longer at the paper than those told no color change meant they did not have the disorder; it was more difficult to accept the evidence when it was undesirable news.

C. Previous Commitments and Resistance
   1. Having a previous commitment to a particular position makes attitude change less likely, as in:
      a. Political allegiance
      b. Drug-taking (consider the habit and community of friends)
   2. Public statements of one's position result in more resistance to counter-attitudinal messages.
   3. Thought polarization can be defined as the hypothesis that more extended thought about a particular issue tends to produce more extreme, entrenched attitudes.
      a. Tesser and Conlee (1975) found that, after first stating an opinion, participants gave a stronger endorsement of that view after being asked to think about it for a few minutes and then state their opinion a second time.
      b. The caution here is that if someone has never really thought about the view before at all, increased thought can lead to more moderate attitudes.

D. Knowledge and Resistance
   1. Being more knowledgeable about a topic makes a person less susceptible to counter-attitudinal messages.
   2. Wood (1982) found that pro-preservation students who were also very knowledgeable about the subject were less persuaded by counter-attitudinal messages than were pro-preservation students who were not especially knowledgeable about the topic.

E. Attitude Inoculation
   1. Attitude inoculation can be defined as small attacks upon our beliefs that engage our attitudes, prior commitments, and knowledge structures, enabling us to counteract a subsequent stronger attack and be resistant to persuasion.
   2. McGuire and Papageorgis (1961) asked participants the extent to which they agreed with certain truisms like "it is important to brush your teeth" and "penicillin has been good for mankind."
      a. Independent variable: participants were exposed to a counterargument or not; those exposed to a counterargument were asked to generate arguments either refuting it or supporting it.
      b. Dependent variable: the extent to which participants continued to believe in the truisms they had earlier endorsed after being hit with a very strong message against the truism.
      c. Findings: participants who were exposed to the counterargument and asked to refute it were least resistant to attitude change.

Testing Your Basic Knowledge

ANSWERS TO MULTIPLE-CHOICE QUESTIONS

1. a	14. b
2. a	15. c
3. b	16. c
4. c	17. a
5. a	18. a
6. a	19. b
7. c	20. c
8. b	21. b
9. c	22. a
10. c	23. a
11. a	24. a
12. c	25. c
13. a	

Testing Your In-Depth Understanding

EXAMPLE ANSWERS TO THE GUIDED QUESTIONS FOR CRITICAL THINKING EXERCISE #2

1. The Elaboration Likelihood Model argues that people process persuasive messages via one of two routes: a central route or a peripheral route. If people are engaged in central route processing, they will be very attentive to the actual arguments that are being presented and will be listening for facts, evidence, and information to support or refute those arguments. People are likely to engage in central route processing when the message is very relevant to them and when they have the time and cognitive ability to listen carefully. Some people have a personality characteristic of being high in need for cognition and, thus, they will typically engage in central route processing. If people are engaged in peripheral route processing, they are paying less attention to the central aspects of the message and are engaging in more superficial processing. As a result, they are likely to be more swayed by peripheral cues like the attractiveness of the speaker and/or the extent to which the speaker appears to have credibility or expertise. People are more likely to engage in peripheral route processing when the message is not relevant to their own lives, and/or when they do not have sufficient time or cognitive ability to process the message carefully.

2. The young adults may be more likely to engage in peripheral route processing for several reasons, but primarily because of the issue of personal relevance. It is commonly said that today's youth are disengaged from the political process (some argue it is the fault of the political process; others argue it is the fault of the youth). As such, many young people simply may not believe that their vote counts (consider the 2000 presidential election) or that, even if it does count, that the politicians in office can't or won't do anything to make their lives better. Also, generally speaking, issues relevant to voters in this age group are not typically focal points in the campaigns of politicians. For all of these reasons, young voters may not engage in central route processing because the entire campaign process seems irrelevant to them. Moms who also have jobs outside the home may also be likely to engage in peripheral route processing, but probably for different reasons. Many issues highly relevant to their lives are often discussed during campaigns (education, childcare, retirement age, taxes, etc.). But anyone who is a Mom knows how unimaginably busy that job is alone, much less also being a full-time member of the workforce. These woman may simply lack the time or energy to pay close attention to campaign issues, especially given the difficulty of finding clear, unbiased, compact sources of information.

3. Given the analysis above, I would most certainly want to address the peripheral route to communication for both groups of voters. I would want to find spokespeople for the campaign who would be viewed as attractive and/or credible by the voters. Generally, that means finding people who meet American beauty ideals/stereotypes

and finding people who speak without hesitation, are enthusiastic, make eye contact, and use bold gestures. More specifically, I could find people who are attractive and credible to each group. For example, a popular movie star, singer/songwriter, or political activist might be especially appealing to a younger voter. A fellow "working Mom" might be especially appealing to the working Moms. In addition to having sources that engage the peripheral route, however, I would also want to give these voters a reason or a way to engage in central route processing, especially if my candidate genuinely wanted to reach out to these voters. For the young adults, that would mean talking about issues that are relevant to them, and demonstrating the relevance. For the women, it would mean staging my speeches and rallies at convenient times and locations, and thinking carefully about how and where to put informative advertisements. Certainly providing support for something like a compact "voters guide" would be a good idea.

4. Review other concepts in the chapter and see if there are any tips that would help you put the finishing touches on your presentation:

- The role of culture in persuasion: while Americans in general tend to be individualistic, women in American culture are more collectivistic and, thus, they may respond to appeals oriented toward making a stronger family or more harmonious society.

- The value-expressive function of attitudes (and reference groups): to the extent that a candidate can associate him or herself with reference groups that are valued by these two groups of voters, the more support the candidate may get. Consider the successful way in which George W. Bush during the 2004 presidential election managed to associate himself with patriotism and support for the military. To be against Bush was to be against the United States and the troops in Iraq.

- The identifiable victim effect and the role of vividness in persuasive messages: remembering that vivid individual accounts are usually more persuasive than facts and figures, even those messages targeting people engaged in central route processing should include vivid stories.

- The thought polarization hypothesis and attitude inoculation effects: assuming a certain level of knowledge on a given subject, thinking more about one's attitudes will strengthen those attitudes. The candidate could engage such thought with either real or rhetorical questions during appearances. In a similar vein, the candidate could also inoculate those present at speeches against the appeals of his or her opponents by offering weak versions of their messages and suggesting lots of ways to refute those messages. Moreover, asking audience members to state a public commitment at the end of the rally would really cement their support.

CHAPTER 8 | Attitudes and Behavior

The goal of this chapter is to discuss instances in which our attitudes do not predict our behavior, the ways in which our behaviors can influence our attitudes, and the importance of consistency among our thoughts, feelings, and behaviors. Festinger's cognitive dissonance theory is featured in the chapter. The conditions that lead to dissonance and the ways in which people resolve dissonance are discussed. In addition, challenges to dissonance theory, as well as a resolution to that challenge, are described.

ANNOTATED CHAPTER OUTLINE

After first reading through the chapter quickly, create a comprehensive framework for the information in the chapter by reading the outline below and filling in the missing information. Instead of simply re-copying information from the textbook, try to use your own words wherever possible; you can check your answers against the completed outline in the Answer Key section at the end of the chapter.

I. Predicting Behavior from Attitudes
    A. LaPiere (1934) conducted a famous social psychological study in which he traveled around the country with a young Chinese couple, visiting numerous hotels and restaurants; prejudice toward the Chinese was high at this time. He found that:
        1. _____
        _____
        _____
        _____
        2. _____
        _____
        _____
        _____

    B. Numerous studies found the same general trend: people's attitudes often do not predict their behavior; this was surprising to social psychologists who had spent their lives studying attitudes (with the assumption that attitudes predicted behavior).
    C. We think attitudes should predict behavior because we see so many easily viewed (salient) examples.
        1. Correlation does not necessarily mean causation: are the attitudes predicting the behavior, or is the behavior affecting the attitudes?
        2. There are many nonsalient examples of people NOT engaging in behavior that would be consistent with their attitudes.
    D. Attitudes Sometimes Conflict with Other Powerful Determinants of Behavior
        1. Attitudes toward a behavior have to compete with lots of other determinants of behavior, and attitudes don't always win.
        2. Social norms about the behavior can weaken the relationship between attitudes and behavior.
        4. The theory of reasoned action can be defined as
        _____
        _____
        _____
        _____

        a. Manstead et al. (1983) tested the theory of reasoned action by studying the attitudes of expectant mothers toward breast feeding.
            (1) Predictor variable #1: the mother's own attitude toward breast-feeding.
            (2) Predictor variable #2: how the mother thought close others thought about

breast-feeding and whether she cared about their views.
(3) Outcome variable: whether or not the mother breast-fed her baby.
(4) Finding:

_____

_____

_____

_____

b. The intention to perform certain simple behaviors usually leads to the behavior.
4. The theory of planned behavior can be defined as

_____

_____

_____

_____

a. Perceived control has a direct effect on the action of the behavior and an indirect effect via a person's intention.
b. Using all three components of the theory, behaviors (e.g., academic performance, exercising, success at dieting, condom use) can be predicted quite well.

E. Attitudes are Sometimes Inconsistent
1. Inconsistency between Affective and Cognitive Components of Attitudes
a. When the affective and cognitive components of an attitude are inconsistent, the attitude is a poor predictor of behavior.
b. Norman (1975) found that

_____

_____

_____

_____

2. Introspecting about the Reasons for Our Attitudes
a. Wilson et al. (1984) found that asking participants to list why they felt the way they did about their romantic partner could undermine the correlation between their overall attitude toward their partner and later relationship status.
b. Wilson's research also found that introspecting before making an affective choice can lead to greater regret about that choice.
c. Introspection may lead us to focus on

_____

_____

_____

_____

d. Introspection is likely to be harmful in situations in which we try to cognitively analyze affectively based attitudes, since this is a mismatch.

F. Attitudes are Sometimes Based on Secondhand Information
1. Attitudes based on direct experience predict subsequent behavior much better than attitudes based on indirect hearsay.
2. Regan and Fazio (1977) asked students to give their attitudes about a housing shortage at Cornell University.
a. Independent variable:

_____

_____

_____

_____

b. Dependent variable:

_____

_____

_____

_____

c. Finding: the correlation was much higher among the students who were directly affected (those who thought it was a problem were more likely to sign the petition than those who didn't), but the attitudes of the students who were not directly affected did not predict whether or not they would sign the petition.

G. Mismatched Attitudes and Actual Attitude Targets
1. Attitude-behavior consistency is higher when the assessed attitude is at the same level of specificity as the behavior one is trying to predict.
2. Davidson and Jaccard (1979) found that

_____

_____

_____

_____

3. Attitude-behavior consistency can also explain LaPiere's findings:

_____

_____

_____

_____

4. Lord et al. (1984) asked male college students about their views toward gay males and about their idea of a typical gay man.
a. Independent variable:

_____

_____

_____

_____

b. Dependent variable:

_____

_____

_____

c. Finding:

_____

_____

_____

H. "Automatic" Behavior That Bypasses Conscious Attitudes

1. Sometimes our behavior is reflexive and happens in response to situational stimuli.
    a. One of the purposes of attitudes is to allow for quick behavioral responses.
    b. Some behavior bypasses attitudes entirely.
2. A prime can be defined as

_____

_____

_____

3. Bargh, Chen, and Burrows (1996) examined the effect of priming by having participants perform a sentence-completion task and seeing if stereotypical words associated with the elderly affected their subsequent behavior.
    a. Independent variable: half the participants, in this study were unwittingly primed with words related to stereotypes about the elderly during the sentence-completion task; the rest of the participants were not primed with these words.
    b. Dependent variable:

_____

_____

_____

c. Finding:

_____

_____

_____

4. Activation of many concepts—for example, traits, stereotypes, goals—can lead to this sort of automatic behavior (bypassing attitudes).
5. Dijksterhuis et al. (1998) conducted a study to examine the effect of priming general categories or specific instances of the categories on behavior.
    a. Independent variable: participants were primed to think about the general categories of professors or supermodels or about

specific instances of those categories (Albert Einstein for professors or Claudia Schiffer for supermodels).

b. Dependent variable:

_____

_____

_____

c. Finding:

_____

_____

_____

_____

II. Predicting Attitudes from Behavior

A. When there is a mismatch, people will tend to bring their attitudes in line with their actions, illustrating a strong urge to justify behavior and minimize inconsistencies.

B. Cognitive Consistency Theories

1. Heider's balance theory can be defined as

_____

_____

_____

a. If you have an enemy who dislikes Person X, then balance theory would predict you would like Person X since you don't like your enemy and s/he doesn't like Person X.
b. Any imbalance will motivate you to exert psychological energy to achieve or restore balance.
c. Research findings support balance theory:
    (1) _____

_____

_____

    (2) _____

_____

_____

2. Cognitive Dissonance Theory
    a. Festinger's cognitive dissonance theory can be defined as

_____

_____

_____

b. People are troubled by inconsistencies between their thoughts, sentiments, and behaviors, and they will try to eliminate this inconsistency by changing one or more of the discrepant cognitions (usually the attitude in attitude-behavior inconsistencies).

C. Experiencing and Reducing Dissonance
   1. Decisions and Dissonance
      a. Deciding between two close alternatives can raise dissonance, and people will rationalize their decisions by inflating their opinion of the chosen alternative and derogating the unchosen alternative.
      b. Knox and Inkster (1968) found that

      _____

      _____

      _____

      _____

      c. Voters express greater confidence in their chosen candidate if polled after voting than before voting.
      d. More recent evidence suggests that, once one alternative is favored but before an irrevocable choice is made, people may subconsciously distort subsequent information in favor of the chosen alternative.
   2. Effort Justification
      a. Effort justification can be defined as

      _____

      _____

      _____

      _____

      b. Aronson and Mills (1959) conducted an early study on effort justification by recruiting female participants who thought they were going to join an ongoing discussion of sexuality.
         (1) Independent variable:

         _____

         _____

         _____

         _____

         (2) Dependent variable:

         _____

         _____

         _____

         _____

         (3) Finding:

         _____

         _____

         _____

         _____

         (4) Logic:
            (a) Two dissonant cognitions were held only by those in the severe initiation condition:
               i. _____

               _____

               _____

      _____

      _____

         ii. _____

      _____

      _____

      _____

      _____

            (b) Resolution to dissonance:

      _____

      _____

      _____

      c. Cooper (1980) recruited participants who suffered from an inability to be assertive.
         (1) Independent variable: 1/3 of the participants were in a control condition and received no treatment; 1/3 received a standard "behavioral rehearsal" treatment; 1/3 received a bogus physical exercise treatment.
         (2) Dependent variable:

         _____

         _____

         _____

         _____

         (3) Finding:

         _____

         _____

         _____

         _____

         (4) Logic: engaging in any sort of effortful behavior will produce a need to justify that behavior; in this instance, participants needed to feel that their ability to be assertive was improved by the treatment.
   3. Induced Compliance and Attitude Change
      a. Induced (forced) compliance can be defined as

      _____

      _____

      _____

      _____

      b. Festinger and Carlsmith (1959) conducted the first study examining this effect by having participants engage in an incredibly boring and repetitive peg-turning task.
         (1) Independent variable: 1/3 of the participants were in a control condition; 1/3 were asked to lie to the next participant and say the task was interesting in exchange for $1; 1/3 were asked to lie in exchange for $20.

(2) Dependent variable:

_____
_____
_____
_____

(3) Finding:

_____
_____
_____
_____

(4) Logic:

    (a) Two dissonant cognitions held by those in the $1 condition:

       i. _____

_____
_____
_____
_____

       ii. _____

_____
_____
_____
_____

    (b) Resolution to dissonance: the behavior couldn't be undone, so ratings of the task become more favorable in order to create more consistency with the act of saying the task was interesting.

c. If inducements to engaging in a behavior are too substantial, people will use the inducements to justify their actions, and true attitude change will be less likely to occur.

d. Forbidden toy paradigm: children are told they can play with any of five toys except their second favorite, and they are told that the experimenter will either be "annoyed" (mild threat condition) or "very angry" (severe threat condition) if they do play with their second-favorite toy.

    (1) Finding:

_____
_____
_____
_____

    (2) Logic:

       (a) Two dissonant cognitions held by the children in the mild threat condition:

         i. I really want to play with that toy.

         ii. I'm not playing with it, and the threat of the experimenter being a little annoyed with me hardly

seems to justify inhibiting my strong desire.

    (b) Resolution to dissonance:

_____
_____
_____
_____

    (3) Further research found that children were still derogating the toy six weeks later.

    (4) Other research found that children who had been in the mild threat condition were also less likely to cheat on a test when given the opportunity; this may have been because they resolved their prior dissonance by also making a self-image adjustment and concluding "I'm a good kid, and I do what I'm told, and I don't cheat."

D. When Does Inconsistency Produce Dissonance?

  1. Elliot Aronson's research suggests that cognitions and behaviors that are inconsistent with one's core sense of self will produce dissonance.

  2. Free Choice

    a. Linder et al. (1967) offered college students money to write a counter-attitudinal essay.

      (1) Independent variable #1:

_____
_____
_____
_____

      (2) Independent variable #2:

_____
_____
_____
_____

      (3) Dependent variable: attitude change in favor of the position advocated in the essay.

      (4) Finding:

_____
_____
_____
_____

      (5) Logic: I will only feel dissonance about engaging in a behavior that is against my attitudes when I feel like I freely and voluntarily chose to do it.

  3. Insufficient Justification

    a. If a person's behavior is justified by external incentives, then there will not be any dissonance.

b. Dissonance-reducing attitude change in the previously reviewed studies was only observed in conditions in which

_____

_____

_____

_____

4. Negative Consequences
   a. Nel et al. (1969) asked participants to write a counter-attitudinal essay in favor of legalizing marijuana.
      (1) Independent variable #1:

_____

_____

_____

      (2) Independent variable #2:

_____

_____

_____

_____

      (3) Dependent variable: the extent to which participants changed their attitudes to be in favor of legalizing marijuana.
      (4) Finding:

_____

_____

_____

      (5) Logic: I can dismiss inconsistencies that are about inconsequential issues, but when my actions have negative consequences, the dissonance is greater.
   b. Adding another condition to the paradigm devised by Festinger and Carlsmith (1959), Cooper and Worchel (1970) studied the effect of perceived negative consequences and found that participants in the $1 condition only altered their attitudes if they were led to believe that their lie had been convincing.

5. Foreseeability
   a. When a negative consequence can be foreseen, more dissonance will result, as this will threaten our self-image as a moral and decent person.
   b. The importance of foresight was demonstrated in experiments in which

_____

_____

_____

_____

E. Self-Affirmation and Dissonance
   1. Self-affirmation can be defined as

_____

_____

_____

_____

   2. To demonstrate the effects of self-affirmation, Steele (1988) asked participants to rate music CDs and then choose one to take home with them.
      a. Independent variable #1: participants were either business majors or science majors.
      b. Independent variable #2:

_____

_____

_____

_____

      c. Dependent variable: the extent to which participants inflated their opinions of the chosen music CD and deflated their opinions of the unchosen CDs after making their choice.
      d. Finding:

_____

_____

_____

      e. Logic: science students who wore the lab coat were reminded of their core identity, which minimized the self-esteem threat of the CD choice ("Why did I choose A instead of B? Did I make a rational, good decision?").

F. Is Dissonance Universal?
   1. Research suggests that those with independent and interdependent self-concepts both experience dissonance, but under different circumstances.
      a. Heine and Lehman (1997) found that

_____

_____

_____

_____

      b. Sakai (1981) found that Japanese participants who were induced to do something they didn't want to do did exhibit dissonance-reducing attitude change when they thought others were observing their behavior.
      c. Kitayama et al. (2004) found that

_____

_____

_____

_____

d. Hoshino-Browne et al. (2004) showed that Asian-identified students were much more likely to experience dissonance when making a choice for a friend as opposed to making a choice for themselves.

2. Those with independent self-concepts may be more likely to experience dissonance in situations

_____

_____

_____ ;

those with interdependent self-concepts may be more likely to experience dissonance in situations

_____

_____

_____

_____

III. Self-Perception Theory
  A. Inferring Attitudes
    1. Self-perception theory can be defined as

_____

_____

_____

    2. Bem believed that people often come to understand their attitudes in the exact same way (via inference) that they come to understand others' attitudes.
    3. Bem argued that making self-inferences as if we were an outside observer would only be necessary for weakly held and/or ambiguous attitudes.
    4. Bem claimed that the participants in the dissonance studies were not experiencing aversive arousal due to inconsistency; rather, their attitudes reflected their behaviors because of a rational inference process.
  B. Evidence of Self-Directed Inference
    1. Bem offered two main types of evidence for self-directed inference.
      a. If participants could infer their attitudes from observing their own behavior and its context, anyone else making these observations should also be able to infer the participants' true attitudes.
        (1) Interpersonal simulations can be defined as

_____

_____

_____

_____

(2) Bem found that

_____

_____

_____

_____

(3) Given that others can come to the same conclusion rationally, Bem assumed that the original subject developed his or her opinion rationally.
  b. Bem also argued that often there is no stored attitude to recall, and so people formulate their attitudes in the moment, based on currently available evidence, as shown by a standard dissonance study with a twist.
    (1) Independent variable #1:

_____

_____

_____

_____

(2) Independent variable #2: after writing the counter-attitudinal essay, participants were either asked to give their current attitude toward the issue or to recall their previous attitude toward the issue.
(3) Dependent variable: the extent to which the reported attitudes were favorable toward the issue.
(4) Finding:

_____

_____

_____

_____

C. Testing for Arousal
  1. Self-perception and dissonance theory make virtually identical predictions in almost all circumstances.
  2. The one difference between the two theories is physiological arousal.
    a. Dissonance theory argues that inconsistent cognitions lead to arousal, which motivates attitude change.
    b. Self-perception theory argues that no arousal is present or necessary.
  3. Researchers sought to determine whether participants were aroused or not in the classic dissonance situations.
    a. Waterman (1969) found that

_____

_____

_____

_____

b. Zanna and Cooper (1974) attempted to influence the impact of the arousal by altering how it is interpreted.
   (1) Independent variable #1:

   _____

   _____

   _____

   (2) Independent variable #2:

   _____

   _____

   _____

   (3) Dependent variable: how favorably participants felt toward the issue after writing the essay.
   (4) Finding: in the control condition, participants who wrote the essay under free choice rated the issue more favorably than those under no choice; in the unpleasant side effects condition, participants' attitudes did not differ as a function of choice; in the relaxing side effect condition, participants in the free-choice condition rated the issue much more favorably than in the no choice condition.
   (5) Logic:

   _____

   _____

   _____

   _____

D. Reconciling the Dissonance and Self-Perception Accounts
   1. There is evidence for both dissonance-reduction and self-perception-generated attitude change.
   2. Empirical research indicates that dissonance-reduction processes occur when

   _____

   _____

   _____

   _____,

   but that self-perception effects occur when

   _____

   _____

   _____

   _____

   3. This explanation is consistent with Bem's explanation of self-perception theory as applying to weak and ambiguous attitudes, empirical evidence, and intuitive observations of rationalization.

4. What is surprising is the frequency with which our attitudes are weak and ambiguous, as shown by these examples:
   a. _____

   _____

   _____

   _____

   b. _____

   _____

   _____

   _____

   c. _____

   _____

   _____

   _____

   d. _____

   _____

   _____

5. Evidence from neuroscience provides more support for the prevalence of self-perception processes.
   a. The brain is organized into function-specific modules, including a module that interprets and makes sense of all other inputs.
   b. "Split-brain" patients have

   _____

   _____

   _____

   c. When their left hemisphere "sees" a snowy scene and their right hemisphere "sees" a bird's claw
      (1) Split-brain patients will then use their right hand to point to a picture of a snow shovel and their left hand to point to a picture of hens.
      (2) When asked to explain their choices, split-brain patients

   _____

   _____

   _____

   _____

E. A Final Caution
   1. Research evidence suggests that people will often believe that others will be irrational, but that they themselves will be rational.
   2. There is plenty of evidence to support the view that everyone experiences the effects of dissonance and self-perception.

TESTING YOUR BASIC KNOWLEDGE

After studying the information in the chapter by filling in the outline above, test your basic knowledge with the following multiple-choice test. Answers are provided in the Answer Key section at the end of the chapter. If you find that you have gotten an answer wrong, it is important that you understand why it is wrong (as well as understanding why the correct answer is the better choice). Talk with peers, your tutor, or your professor if you need help.

Multiple-Choice Questions

1. In 1934, Richard LaPiere published a study reporting how he had toured the country with a Chinese couple and later asked the restaurants they had visited about their general policy toward serving "Orientals." His work revealed
   a. prejudiced attitudes toward "Orientals."
   b. a lack of correspondence between attitudes and behavior.
   c. Both A and B are correct.

2. Susan is pregnant with her first child. She has mixed feelings about breast-feeding, but she reluctantly is willing to give it a try. Her family and friends, however, feel very strongly that breast-feeding is the right thing to do. According to the theory of reasoned action, Susan is likely to
   a. breast-feed because of the strong subjective norms and her willingness to at least think about trying.
   b. not breast-feed because her attitude does not match that of her family and friends.
   c. breast-feed because what her family and friends think is more important than what she thinks.

3. Pauly is certain that if he studies hard, he can get an "A" in his psychology course. According to the theory of planned behavior, this sense of perceived control
   a. may lead him to study hard even without an explicit intention to get an "A."
   b. won't cause him to study unless he really cares about the class.
   c. is not relevant to his studying.

4. Nyla has a strongly held cognition that donating blood is a good and worthy activity. Her feelings about donating blood, however, are more mixed. In this instance, Nyla's attitude about donating blood will probably
   a. lead her to donate blood.
   b. lead her to avoid donating blood.
   c. not be a good predictor of whether or not she will donate blood.

5. Tim participates in a psychology experiment about the aesthetics of various impressionist painters. At the end of the study, he is given a "thank you gift" and is allowed to choose between a poster of a cute kitten barely hanging onto a tree and a Monet landscape. Prior to making his final choice, Tim is asked to list reasons in favor of each picture. He is able to list several reasons for choosing the kitten picture (e.g., "it is cute," "reminds me of my cat at home," "my girlfriend will like it"). Although he knows he likes the Monet poster better, Tim can't articulate any reason for choosing the Monet landscape other than "I just like it." According to research done by Wilson and his colleagues, which of the following scenarios is most likely to result from Tim's introspection?
   a. Tim will choose the landscape poster and regret the choice later.
   b. Tim will choose the kitten poster and regret the choice later.
   c. Time will choose the kitten poster and remain happy with his choice.

6. Given the recent talk about a worldwide flu epidemic, Quita develops a strong attitude in favor of getting a flu shot, even though she has never had one before. Darrell shares her opinion and has regularly received flu shots each year. Which person's attitude will be a more reliable predictor of their behavior?
   a. Darrell's attitude will predict his behavior; Quita's attitude will not predict her behavior.
   b. Quita's attitude will predict her behavior; Darrell's attitude will not predict his behavior.
   c. It is impossible to judge whether either person's attitude will predict his or her behavior.

7. Which of the following attitudes would be the best indicator of whether or not a person would buy an environmentally friendly Toyota Prius hybrid (gasoline and electric) automobile in the next six months?
   a. attitude toward hybrid car technology
   b. attitude toward buying a Toyota brand car
   c. attitude toward buying a Prius in the near future

8. Participants in a study are asked to unscramble sentences. Although not aware of it, the sentences include several words that prime the concept of "rudeness" for half the participants and "politeness" for the other half. Participants had been instructed to tell the experimenter in the next room when they were finished in order to get participation credit and be allowed to leave. When each participant (individually) enters the next room, he or she finds the experimenter in a conversation with another researcher. Neither person makes any effort to acknowledge the participant, although it is obvious he or she is in the room and

waiting for them to finish. Still, they continue a seemingly unimportant conversation about the college sports team's latest game. Time passes. Research by Bargh, Chen, and Burrows suggests which of the following results?

a. Participants in the rudeness condition will be quicker to interrupt the conversation than participants in the politeness condition.

b. Participants in the politeness condition will be quicker to interrupt the conversation than participants in the rudeness condition.

c. Participants who have more assertive personalities will be more likely to interrupt the experimenter.

9. For reasons only they understand, Peter and Kara absolutely hate one another. Peter and Chris are best friends. Balance theory suggests that Chris will feel psychologically balanced only if

a. he finds a way to resolve the conflict between Peter and Kara.

b. he also dislikes Kara.

c. he learns to hate Peter.

10. Although Ellen loves animals and cares very much about their well-being, she drives right by a dog who has obviously been abandoned on the side of the road. Ellen is very likely to

a. feel cognitive dissonance.

b. feel physiologically aroused.

c. Both A and B are accurate.

11. Malena is asked to choose between two music CDs she likes equally well. After she finally makes her choice, her attitude toward the CD she didn't choose is likely to

a. remain the same.

b. change such that she reports liking the CD less than she initially did.

c. change such that she reports liking the CD more than she initially did.

12. Jim spends three years in graduate school training to become a clinical social worker. His first job out of graduate school is, in actuality, horrible. Briefly, Jim worries that he has made the wrong choice for his career. But he quickly changes his mind and decides that, although it isn't his dream job, the position is not so bad after all. The most likely social psychological explanation for this attitude change is that

a. Jim has engaged in a rational reanalysis of his situation.

b. needing to justify the effort he put into his training, Jim altered his attitude to be more favorable toward the job.

c. Jim's colleagues must have persuaded him that the job was satisfactory.

13. Maria wants to teach her daughter, Lisa, to value and enjoy reading. According to the logic of cognitive dissonance theory, which of the following strategies would be the best way to cultivate such an attitude?

a. Reward Lisa when she chooses to read books with small rewards, preferably simple verbal praise.

b. Encourage Lisa to read as many books as possible by entering her in a program that offers bigger prizes (e.g., a bicycle) the more books the child reads.

c. Forbid Lisa to play her favorite computer game each afternoon until after she reads at least one chapter.

14. Elliot Aronson found that cognitive dissonance was more likely in cases where inconsistency

a. was unavoidable.

b. reflected poorly on a person's self-image.

c. resulted in positive outcomes.

15. Participants are asked to write a counter-attitudinal essay. Dissonance is most likely to occur when

a. the essay is written rather than spoken.

b. participants write an essay with high-quality arguments.

c. participants write the essay of their own free will.

16. Natalie participates in a study in which she writes an essay in favor of legalizing marijuana, although she is actually opposed to such legalization. Nate participates in the same study and is also opposed to legalizing marijuana. In Natalie's condition of the study, she learns that high school students will read her essay. In Nate's condition of the study, he learns that the researchers in charge of the study will read his essay. Which of the following is most likely?

a. Natalie will experience more dissonance than Nate because there is a chance that impressionable high school students might be convinced by her essay.

b. Nate will experience more dissonance than Natalie because his essay will be read by people who have high status and expertise.

c. Natalie and Nate will experience equal amounts of dissonance.

17. After writing a counter-attitudinal essay, a group of participants is asked to reflect on their best qualities and core values. These participants, unlike those in a control condition, do not show any dissonance-reducing attitude change. What can explain this seeming resilience to the effects of dissonance?

a. Participants were able to self-affirm, and thus restored their sense of being rational, competent people.

b. Participants were distracted from the original topic of the essay.

c. Neither of the above are accurate explanations.

18. People from independent cultures are most likely to experience dissonance in situations when they are making decisions for _____, while people from interdependent cultures are likely to experience dissonance when making decisions for _____.
    a. their friends; themselves.
    b. themselves; their friends.
    c. the future; the present.

19. Self-perception theory is most applicable in cases where
    a. cognitive dissonance is strong.
    b. attitudes are strong and well-defined.
    c. attitudes are weak and ambiguous.

20. Bem used interpersonal simulations to demonstrate that
    a. other people can accurately infer the attitudes of those who participate in dissonance studies.
    b. only people who have personally participated in a dissonance study can predict the outcomes of such studies.
    c. people from interdependent cultures are more likely to experience dissonance than people from independent cultures.

21. Self-perception studies suggest that, in certain instances,
    a. people may not remember their initial attitudes.
    b. people make inferences about their attitudes based on their own behavior.
    c. Both A and B are accurate.

22. The main difference between self-perception theory and cognitive dissonance theory is
    a. the amount of evidence supporting each theory.
    b. the way in which people change their attitudes after engaging in a counter-attitudinal behavior.
    c. the role of arousal.

23. Neuroscience and "split-brain" patient studies suggest that there is a portion of our brain (a module) that is responsible for interpreting and making sense of information input from other parts of the brain. This information supports
    a. self-perception theory.
    b. self-affirmation.
    c. the theory of planned behavior.

24. According to the logic of cognitive dissonance theory, which of the following would be the best strategy to help Dale adopt a lifelong new diet in which he eats less junk food and loses weight?
    a. Restrict Dale's access to the junk food so he can't give in to temptation.
    b. Give Dale small rewards each day for eating a healthy, moderate amount of food.
    c. Promise Dale he can have the vacation of his dreams if he stays away from junk food for one month.

25. Marla is told by her professor that she is required to write an essay in favor of increasing tuition. Marla is opposed to increasing tuition. She is unlikely to experience dissonance because
    a. she has sufficient external justification for her counter-attitudinal behavior.
    b. her counter-attitudinal behavior was not freely chosen.
    c. Both A and B are accurate.

Essay Questions

After you have mastered the multiple-choice questions, try testing your basic understanding by thoroughly answering each of the broad essay questions below. Because it is critical that you think through this information on your own, we have not provided any answers to these questions. Your learning and retention of this material will be greatly enhanced if you do one or more of the following to check your answers: carefully review the textbook information; compare your responses to your class lecture notes; talk over your answers with a peer; ask your professor to review your answers or review any information that is unclear to you.

1. Discuss and provide research evidence for five reasons why attitudes sometimes fail to predict behavior.

2. Define cognitive dissonance theory, and provide a detailed description of an experiment that illustrates the theory. Discuss the types of situations that might lead to dissonance-induced attitude change, and discuss the conditions that increase the probability of experiencing dissonance.

3. In what way does self-affirmation change our understanding of dissonance?

4. Do people from non-Western cultures experience cognitive dissonance?

5. Define self-perception theory, and explain how this theory challenged cognitive dissonance theory. How did researchers resolve the controversy, and what is the resolution?

TESTING YOUR IN-DEPTH UNDERSTANDING

Test your in-depth understanding of the material by working through the Critical Thinking Exercises provided at the end of each textbook chapter. To maximize this learning opportunity, work together with a tutor, study group, or your professor. Alternatively, write down your thoughts and responses.

Guided questions for one of the exercises are provided below. While there are multiple ways to answer these questions, short answers are given in the Answer Key at the end of the chapter. Note that the valuable part of this exercise is not simply knowing the answer but working with the material to come up with the answer.

Guided Questions for Critical Thinking Exercise #2

Benjamin Franklin was apparently fond of quoting an adage to the effect that, "He that has once done you a kindness will be more ready to do you another than he whom you yourself have obliged." How would a dissonance theorist make sense of this adage? A self-perception theorist?

1. Rephrase the adage and make sure you understand what Ben was trying to say.

2. Review the basic definition of cognitive dissonance theory, and try to determine what two dissonant cognitions are set up by the situation Ben Franklin describes, and how doing you a second favor would resolve that dissonance.

3. Review the basic definition of self-perception theory, and try to work through the rational inference process that would end with a person doing multiple favors for you.

4. Pretend you are a social psychologist. How could you create an experiment to test whether cognitive dissonance theory or self-perception theory was more relevant to this situation?

Enhance your understanding of the chapter by thinking about and doing the remaining two Critical Thinking Exercises. Discuss your answers with your peers, study group, tutor, or professor.

Critical Thinking Exercise #1

The effects of body movements on cognition that we discussed in Box 8.3 strike many people as implausible. But you can try it yourself and see. First, try nodding your head up and down while saying to yourself "human beings will land on Mars sometime during my lifetime." Does that proposition sound plausible? Now try shaking your head back and forth while saying "eating an apple a day helps to ward off cancer." Does that sound plausible? The key question: Does the first proposition seem more plausible to you than the second? (It will help our case if you nod your head up and down while considering this last question!)

Critical Thinking Exercise #3

In the induced-compliance experiments such as Festinger and Carlsmith's $1/$20 experiment, all participants agree to say or write something that is at variance with their true, initial beliefs. The typical result is an inverse relationship between what they are paid and their subsequent belief in what they were induced to say or write: those who were paid more believe what they said less. But what do you think the relationship between the amount paid and the final attitude would be if the incentives were not sufficient to get participants to say or write something they didn't believe? If everyone turned down payment to express a belief that is counter to their true attitudes, with some turning down more money than others, what do you think the relationship would be between the amount offered and final attitudes?

SOCIAL PSYCHOLOGY IN THE POPULAR MEDIA

You might be interested in the following popular media references, each of which relates in some way to information in this chapter.

Film

The Big Chill (1983; directed by Lawrence Kasdan; starring Tom Berenger, Glenn Close, Jeff Goldblum, William Hurt, Kevin Kline, Mary Kay Place, Meg Tilly, JoBeth Williams, Don Galloway). A classic 1980s film featuring a group of 40-something friends who met in college and reunite years later to attend a funeral of a fellow friend. They were radicals and hippies in college, but their current lives look very different. Claude Steele refers briefly to this movie in his discussion of the role of rationalization in self-affirmation and cognitive dissonance. One famous conversation from the movie: *Michael: "I don't know anyone who could get through the day without two or three juicy rationalizations. They're more important than sex." Sam: "Ah, come on. Nothing's more important than sex." Michael: "Oh yeah? Ever gone a week without a rationalization?"*

Book

Stone, Jon R. (Ed.). (2000). *Expecting Armageddon: Essential Readings in Failed Prophecy*. New York: Routledge. From the back cover of the paperback edition: "This volume gathers together classic essays addressing the intriguing question first raised by Leon Festinger in his 1956 work *When Prophecy Fails*. Assembling both sociological and psychological perspectives on a striking theme in religious history, *Expecting Armageddon* brings together forty years of work on how belief in prophecy survives even when prophecy fails."

Web Site

Olde English Sketch Comedy—http://www.oldeenglish.org/puppy.html. A comic, offbeat, and inarguably off-color look at people's publicly stated attitudes about how much money they would have to receive in order to voluntarily kill a puppy, and then their actual behavior when confronted with a live puppy and a blank check. The end of this comedy sketch assures us that no puppies were harmed in the making of the sketch. Some foul language.

ANSWER KEY INFORMATION

Annotated Chapter Outline

I. Predicting Behavior from Attitudes
    A. LaPiere (1934) conducted a famous social psychological study in which he traveled around the country with a young Chinese couple, visiting numerous hotels and restaurants; prejudice toward the Chinese was high at this time. He found that:
        1. Only 1 out of 250 establishments refused to serve the Chinese couple.
        2. In a subsequent questionnaire, 90 percent of those same establishments said that it was their policy to turn away Chinese patrons.
    B. Numerous studies found the same general trend: people's attitudes often do not predict their behavior; this was surprising to social psychologists who had spent their lives studying attitudes (with the assumption that attitudes predicted behavior).
    C. We think attitudes should predict behavior because we see so many easily viewed (salient) examples.
        1. Correlation does not necessarily mean causation: are the attitudes predicting the behavior, or is the behavior affecting the attitudes?
        2. There are many nonsalient examples of people NOT engaging in behavior that would be consistent with their attitudes.
    D. Attitudes Sometimes Conflict with Other Powerful Determinants of Behavior
        1. Attitudes toward a behavior have to compete with lots of other determinants of behavior, and attitudes don't always win.
        2. Social norms about the behavior can weaken the relationship between attitudes and behavior.
        3. The theory of reasoned action can be defined as the theory that maintains that people's deliberate behavior can be accurately predicted by knowing their attitudes toward specific behaviors and their subjective norms.
            a. Manstead et al. (1983) tested the theory of reasoned action by studying the attitudes of expectant mothers toward breast-feeding.
                (1) Predictor variable #1: the mother's own attitude toward breast-feeding.
                (2) Predictor variable #2: how the mother thought close others thought about breast-feeding and whether she cared about their views.
                (3) Outcome variable: whether or not the mother breast-fed her baby.
                (4) Finding: the mother's subsequent decision to breast-feed or not was best predicted when both her own attitude and her views of subjective norms were taken into account.
            b. The intention to perform certain simple behaviors usually leads to the behavior.
        4. The theory of planned behavior can be defined as the successor to the theory of reasoned action; it maintains that the best predictors of deliberate behavior are people's attitudes toward specific behaviors, their subjective norms, and their beliefs about whether they can successfully perform the behavior in question.
            a. Perceived control has a direct effect on the action of the behavior and an indirect effect via a person's intention.
            b. Using all three components of the theory, behaviors (e.g., academic performance, exercising, success at dieting, condom use) can be predicted quite well.
    E. Attitudes are Sometimes Inconsistent
        1. Inconsistency between Affective and Cognitive Components of Attitudes
            a. When the affective and cognitive components of an attitude are inconsistent, the attitude is a poor predictor of behavior.
            b. Norman (1975) found that students who had consistent feelings and thoughts about participating in psychology experiments were likely to agree to participate in another psychology experiment, and thus their behavior was predictable; the behavior of those who had inconsistent thoughts and feelings about psychology experiments was unpredictable.
        2. Introspecting about the Reasons for Our Attitudes
            a. Wilson et al. (1984) found that asking participants to list why they felt the way they did about their romantic partner could

undermine the correlation between their overall attitude toward their partner and later relationship status.

  b. Wilson's research also found that introspecting before making an affective choice can lead to greater regret about that choice.

  c. Introspection may lead us to focus on reasons that are easy to identify, but not on the true reasons.

  d. Introspection is likely to be harmful in situations in which we try to cognitively analyze affectively based attitudes, since this is a mismatch.

F. Attitudes are Sometimes Based on Secondhand Information

  1. Attitudes based on direct experience predict subsequent behavior much better than attitudes based on indirect hearsay.

  2. Regan and Fazio (1977) asked students to give their attitudes about a housing shortage at Cornell University.

    a. Independent variable: some of the students were directly affected by the shortage (had no rooms), and some only read about it in the newspaper.

    b. Dependent variable: the relationship between a student's stated attitude about the shortage and his or her tendency to sign a petition encouraging action.

    c. Finding: the correlation was much higher among the students who were directly affected (those who thought it was a problem were more likely to sign the petition than those who didn't), but the attitudes of the students who were not directly affected did not predict whether or not they would sign the petition.

G. Mismatched Attitudes and Actual Attitude Targets

  1. Attitude-behavior consistency is higher when the assessed attitude is at the same level of specificity as the behavior one is trying to predict.

  2. Davidson and Jaccard (1979) found that women's general attitudes toward birth control was not a good predictor of whether the women used birth control pills during the period of the study; the women's specific attitudes toward the use of birth control pills in the near future was a much stronger predictor.

  3. Attitude-behavior consistency can also explain LaPiere's findings: general attitudes toward "the Chinese" failed to predict how restaurant owners would act toward a specific, nicely dressed Chinese couple.

  4. Lord et al. (1984) asked male college students about their views toward gay males and about their idea of a typical gay man.

    a. Independent variable: the description of the gay male campus visitor was either fit to the participant's stereotypical gay male or not.

    b. Dependent variable: participants' willingness to give this visitor a tour.

    c. Finding: attitudes toward gay men (positive or negative) predicted the participant's willingness to show the gay visitor around campus only in the condition in which the gay visitor matched their stereotype of gay men.

H. "Automatic" Behavior That Bypasses Conscious Attitudes

  1. Sometimes our behavior is reflexive and happens in response to situational stimuli.

    a. One of the purposes of attitudes is to allow for quick behavioral responses.

    b. Some behavior bypasses attitudes entirely.

  2. A prime can be defined as a stimulus (typically a word or image) presented to mentally activate a concept, and hence make it accessible.

  3. Bargh, Chen, and Burrows (1996) examined the effect of priming by having participants perform a sentence-completion task and seeing if stereotypical words associated with the elderly affected their subsequent behavior.

    a. Independent variable: half the participants, in this study were unwittingly primed with words related to stereotypes about the elderly during the sentence-completion task; the rest of the participants were not primed with these words.

    b. Dependent variable: the length of time it took to walk down a hallway after the sentence-completion task.

    c. Finding: those primed with the elderly stereotype took longer to walk down the hallway, thus illustrating an automatic behavior.

  3. Activation of many concepts—for example, traits, stereotypes, goals—can lead to this sort of automatic behavior (bypassing attitudes).

  4. Dijksterhuis et al. (1998) conducted a study to examine the effect of priming general categories or specific instances of the categories on behavior.

    a. Independent variable: participants were primed to think about the general categories of professors or supermodels or about specific instances of those categories (Albert Einstein for professors or Claudia Schiffer for supermodels).

   b. Dependent variable: how participants performed on a general-knowledge test.

   c. Finding: participants primed with the general category of professors performed better than those primed with the general category of supermodels, presumably because the general category unconsciously shifted their self-construals; however, participants primed with Albert Einstein performed worse than participants primed with Claudia Schiffer, presumably because comparison to a specific instance of the category led to a poorer self-image.

II. Predicting Attitudes from Behavior

  A. When there is a mismatch, people will tend to bring their attitudes in line with their actions, illustrating a strong urge to justify behavior and minimize inconsistencies.

  B. Cognitive Consistency Theories

    1. Heider's balance theory can be defined as a theory that says that people try to maintain balance among their beliefs, cognitions, and sentiments.

      a. If you have an enemy who dislikes Person X, then balance theory would predict you would like Person X since you don't like your enemy and s/he doesn't like Person X.

      b. Any imbalance will motivate you to exert psychological energy to achieve or restore balance.

      c. Research evidence supports balance theory:

        (1) Studies have shown that people make assumptions about relationships based on balance theory.

        (2) Studies have shown that people remember balanced relationships better and rate them more favorably.

    2. Cognitive Dissonance Theory

      a. Festinger's cognitive dissonance theory can be defined as the theory that inconsistencies among a person's thoughts, sentiments, and actions create an aversive emotional state (dissonance) that leads to efforts to restore consistency.

      b. People are troubled by inconsistencies between their thoughts, sentiments, and behaviors, and they will try to eliminate the inconsistency by changing one or more of the discrepant cognitions (usually the attitude in attitude-behavior inconsistencies).

  C. Experiencing and Reducing Dissonance

    1. Decisions and Dissonance

      a. Deciding between two close alternatives can raise dissonance, and people will rationalize their decisions by inflating their opinion of the chosen alternative and derogating the unchosen alternative.

      b. Knox and Inkster (1968) found that participants who were placing bets at the racetrack gave the horse they were going to bet on an "average" chance of winning when asked before making the bet, while participants who had already finished making the bet gave their chosen horse an "excellent" chance of winning.

      c. Voters express greater confidence in their chosen candidate if polled after voting than before voting.

      d. More recent evidence suggests that, once one alternative is favored but before an irrevocable choice is made, people may subconsciously distort subsequent information in favor of the chosen alternative.

    2. Effort Justification

      a. Effort justification can be defined as the tendency to reduce dissonance by finding reasons for why a person has devoted time, effort, or money for something that turned out to be unpleasant or disappointing to the person.

      b. Aronson and Mills (1959) conducted an early study on effort justification by recruiting female participants who thought they were going to join an ongoing discussion of sexuality.

        (1) Independent variable: 1/3 of the participants were in a control condition and only had to read a list of innocuous words out loud; 1/3 were in a mild initiation condition and had to read a list of somewhat embarrassing words out loud; 1/3 were in a severe initiation condition and had to read "dirty" words and a highly explicit passage.

        (2) Dependent variable: how favorably the participants rated the incredibly boring discussion they listened in on.

        (3) Finding: participants in the severe initiation condition rated the discussion most favorably.

(4) Logic:
    (a) Two dissonant cognitions were held only by those in the severe initiation condition:
        i. I went through something horribly effortful and costly to get into this group.
        ii. This group is really really boring and not worth that effort.
    (b) Resolution to dissonance: the behavior can't be undone, so ratings of the boring group become more favorable, thus providing psychological justification for going through the severe initiation.

c. Cooper (1980) recruited participants who suffered from an inability to be assertive.
    (1) Independent variable: 1/3 of the participants were in a control condition and received no treatment; 1/3 received a standard "behavioral rehearsal" treatment; 1/3 received a bogus physical exercise treatment.
    (2) Dependent variable: percentage of participants who asked for the full payment when given only half of the amount of money promised for participation in the study.
    (3) Finding: participants in both treatment conditions requested full payment more often than participants in the control condition.
    (4) Logic: engaging in any sort of effortful behavior will produce a need to justify that behavior; in this instance, participants needed to feel that their ability to be assertive was improved by the treatment.

3. Induced Compliance and Attitude Change
    a. Induced (forced) compliance can be defined as situations in which individuals are subtly induced (or forced) to behave in a manner that is inconsistent with their beliefs, attitudes, or values, which typically leads to dissonance and often to a change in the original attitudes or values in order to reduce their dissonance.
    b. Festinger and Carlsmith (1959) conducted the first study examining this effect by having participants engage in an incredibly boring and repetitive peg-turning task.
        (1) Independent variable: 1/3 of the participants were in a control condition; 1/3 were asked to lie to the next participant and say the task was interesting in exchange for $1; 1/3 were asked to lie in exchange for $20.
        (2) Dependent variable: participant ratings of the task.
        (3) Finding: participants in the $1 condition rated the task more favorably than participants in the control or $20 condition.
        (4) Logic:
            (a) Two dissonant cognitions held by those in the $1 condition:
                i. The task was incredibly boring.
                ii. I told the other participant it was interesting, and $1 is hardly enough money to justify why I told that lie.
            (b) Resolution to dissonance: the behavior couldn't be undone, so ratings of the task become more favorable in order to create more consistency with the act of saying the task was interesting.

c. If inducements to engaging in a behavior are too substantial, people will use the inducements to justify their actions, and true attitude change will be less likely to occur.
d. Forbidden toy paradigm: children are told they can play with any of five toys except their second favorite, and they are told that the experimenter will either be "annoyed" (mild threat condition) or "very angry" (severe threat condition) if they do play with their second-favorite toy.
    (1) Finding: children in the mild threat condition came to view the forbidden toy less favorably.
    (2) Logic:
        (a) Two dissonant cognitions held by the children in the mild threat condition:
            i. I really want to play with that toy.
            ii. I'm not playing with it, and the threat of the experimenter being a little annoyed with me hardly seems to justify inhibiting my strong desire.
        (b) Resolution to dissonance: since I didn't play with the toy and don't have external justification for my inhibition, I must not like the toy

as much as I originally thought I did (or an internal justification like "I always follow the rules no matter what").

   (3) Further research found that children were still derogating the toy six weeks later.

   (4) Other research found that children who had been in the mild threat condition were also less likely to cheat on a test when given the opportunity; this may have been because they resolved their prior dissonance by also making a self-image adjustment and concluding "I'm a good kid, and I do what I'm told, and I don't cheat."

D. When Does Inconsistency Produce Dissonance?

  1. Elliot Aronson's research suggests that cognitions and behaviors that are inconsistent with one's core sense of self will produce dissonance.

  2. Free Choice

    a. Linder et al. (1967) offered college students money to write a counter-attitudinal essay.

      (1) Independent variable #1: students were offered 50¢ or $2.50 to write the essay.

      (2) Independent variable #2: the freedom to decline the request entirely was emphasized for half the participants.

      (3) Dependent variable: attitude change in favor of the position advocated in the essay.

      (4) Finding: participants in the 50¢ condition experienced more dissonance-reducing attitude change, but only when free choice was emphasized.

      (5) Logic: I will only feel dissonance about engaging in a behavior that is against my attitudes when I feel like I freely and voluntarily chose to do it.

  3. Insufficient Justification

    a. If a person's behavior is justified by external incentives, then there will not be any dissonance.

    b. Dissonance-reducing attitude change in the previously reviewed studies was only observed in conditions in which external justification was minimal (e.g., 50¢ or $1).

  4. Negative Consequences

    a. Nel et al. (1969) asked participants to write a counter-attitudinal essay in favor of legalizing marijuana.

      (1) Independent variable #1: participants were offered either 50¢ or $5.00 to write the essay.

      (2) Independent variable #2: participants were told their essays would be shared with people who already had made up their mind on the issue, or with people who were undecided.

      (3) Dependent variable: the extent to which participants changed their attitudes to be in favor of legalizing marijuana.

      (4) Finding: participants in the 50¢ condition were more likely to change their attitudes if they believed their essays would be read to people who were undecided.

      (5) Logic: I can dismiss inconsistencies that are about inconsequential issues, but when my actions have negative consequences, the dissonance is greater.

    b. Adding another condition to the paradigm devised by Festinger and Carlsmith (1959), Cooper and Worchel (1970) studied the effect of perceived negative consequences and found that participants in the $1 condition only altered their attitudes if they were led to believe that their lie had been convincing.

  5. Foreseeability

    a. When a negative consequence can be foreseen, more dissonance will result, as this will threaten our self-image as a moral and decent person.

    b. The importance of foresight was demonstrated in experiments in which research participants who knew their counter-attitudinal essays would or could be heard by an influential audience were more likely to experience dissonance.

E. Self-Affirmation and Dissonance

  1. Self-affirmation can be defined as taking stock of one's good qualities and core values, which can help one cope with threats to self-esteem.

  2. To demonstrate the effects of self-affirmation, Steele (1988) asked participants to rate music CDs and then choose one to take home with them.

    a. Independent variable #1: participants were either business majors or science majors.

    b. Independent variable #2: participants either wore an official-looking lab coat or did not.

    c. Dependent variable: the extent to which participants inflated their opinions of the chosen music CD and deflated their opinions of the unchosen CDs after making their choice.

d. Finding: participants engaged in dissonance-reducing attitude change unless they were science majors and wore the lab coat.

e. Logic: science students who wore the lab coat were reminded of their core identity, which minimized the self-esteem threat of the CD choice ("Why did I choose A instead of B? Did I make a rational, good decision?").

F. Is Dissonance Universal?

1. Research suggests that those with independent and interdependent self-concepts both experience dissonance, but under different circumstances.

   a. Heine and Lehman (1997) found that Canadians exhibited more dissonance-reducing attitude change than Japanese participants in a free-choice, self-afirmation paradigm.

   b. Sakai (1981) found that Japanese participants who were induced to do something they didn't want to do did exhibit dissonance-reducing attitude change when they thought others were observing their behavior.

   c. Kitayama et al. (2004) found that Japanese participants were more likely to exhibit dissonance-reducing attitude change in the free-choice paradigm when researchers primed the notion of a meaningful social other, a manipulation that did not affect Canadian students.

   d. Hoshino-Browne et al. (2004) showed that Asian-identified students were much more likely to experience dissonance when making a choice for a friend as opposed to making a choice for themselves.

2. Those with independent self-concepts may be more likely to experience dissonance in situations that reflect back on them as individuals; those with interdependent self-concepts may be more likely to experience dissonance in situations that reflect back on their ability to make socially acceptable decisions.

III. Self-Perception Theory

A. Inferring Attitudes

1. Self-perception theory can be defined as a theory that people come to know their own attitudes by looking at their behavior and the context in which it occurred and inferring what their attitudes must be.

2. Bem believed that people often come to understand their attitudes in the exact same way (via inference) that they come to understand others' attitudes.

3. Bem argued that making self-inferences as if we were an outside observer would only be necessary for weakly held and/or ambiguous attitudes.

4. Bem claimed that the participants in the dissonance studies were not experiencing aversive arousal due to inconsistency; rather, their attitudes reflected their behaviors because of a rational inference process.

B. Evidence of Self-Directed Inference

1. Bem offered two main types of evidence for self-directed inference.

   a. If participants could infer their attitudes from observing their own behavior and its context, anyone else making these observations should also be able to infer the participants' true attitudes.

      (1) Interpersonal simulations can be defined as experiments in which an "observer-participant" is given a detailed description of one condition of a dissonance experiment, is told how a participant behaved in that situation, and is asked to predict the attitude of that participant.

      (2) Bem found that the predictions of the observer-participants do mirror the attitudes expressed by the dissonance-study participants.

      (3) Given that others can come to the same conclusion rationally, Bem assumed that the original subject developed his or her opinion rationally.

   b. Bem also argued that often there is no stored attitude to recall, so people formulate their attitudes in the moment, based on currently available evidence, as shown by a standard dissonance study with a twist.

      (1) Independent variable #1: participants were given a choice or no choice to write a counter-attitudinal essay.

      (2) Independent variable #2: after writing the counter-attitudinal essay, participants were either asked to give their current attitude toward the issue or to recall their previous attitude toward the issue.

      (3) Dependent variable: the extent to which the reported attitudes were favorable toward the issue.

(4) Finding: participants in the free-choice condition both reported current attitudes that were more in favor of the issue and misremembered their past attitudes as having been favorable toward the issue.

C. Testing for Arousal

1. Self-perception and dissonance theory make virtually identical predictions in almost all circumstances.

2. The one difference between the two theories is physiological arousal.

   a. Dissonance theory argues that inconsistent cognitions lead to arousal, which motivates attitude change.

   b. Self-perception theory argues that no arousal is present or necessary.

3. Researchers sought to determine whether participants were aroused or not in the classic dissonance situations.

   a. Waterman (1969) found that participants who were asked to write a counter-attitudinal essay performed worse than baseline on a difficult task and better than baseline on an easy task (results consistent with the presence of arousal).

   b. Zanna and Cooper (1974) attempted to influence the impact of the arousal by altering how it is interpreted.

      (1) Independent variable #1: a placebo pill was said to have no side effects, unpleasantly arousing side effects, or relaxing side effects.

      (2) Independent variable #2: participants were asked to write a counter-attitudinal essay under free-choice or no choice conditions.

      (3) Dependent variable: how favorably participants felt toward the issue after writing the essay.

      (4) Finding: in the control condition, participants who wrote the essay under free choice rated the issue more favorably than those under no choice; in the unpleasant side effects condition, participants' attitudes did not differ as a function of choice; in the relaxing side effect condition, participants in the free-choice condition rated the issue much more favorably than in the no choice condition.

      (5) Logic: when there was unpleasant arousal and the participant thought it was due to the drug, no attitude change occurred; when there was unpleasant arousal and the participant believed he or she was supposed to be relaxed, attitude change was even stronger.

D. Reconciling the Dissonance and Self-Perception Accounts

1. There is evidence for both dissonance-reduction and self-perception-generated attitude change.

2. Empirical research indicates that dissonance-reduction processes occur when people act contrary to preexisting, important attitudes, but that self-perception effects occur when people act contrary to weaker or more ambiguous attitudes.

3. This explanation is consistent with Bem's explanation of self-perception theory as applying to weak and ambiguous attitudes, empirical evidence, and intuitive observations of rationalization.

4. What is surprising is the frequency with which our attitudes are weak and ambiguous, as shown by these examples:

   a. Likelihood of contributing to the public good

   b. Likelihood of cheating to reach a goal

   c. Current emotion and strength of emotion

   d. One's assessment of one's own personality traits

5. Evidence from neuroscience provides more support for the prevalence of self-perception processes.

   a. The brain is organized into function-specific modules, including a module that interprets and makes sense of all other inputs.

   b. "Split-brain" patients have had the communication pathway between their two hemispheres severed to control epileptic seizures.

   c. When their left hemisphere "sees" a snowy scene and their right hemisphere "sees" a bird's claw

      (1) Split-brain patients will then use their right hand to point to a picture of a snow shovel and their left hand to point to a picture of hens.

      (2) When asked to explain their choices, split-brain patients generate a single plausible explanation that encompasses both choices (e.g., "I pointed to the hens because of the picture of the bird's claw, and you need a shovel to clean out a hen's cage"); this supports the idea of a "sense-making" module that observes our behaviors and generates consistent explanations.

E. A Final Caution
  1. Research evidence suggests that people will often believe that others will be irrational, but that they themselves will be rational.
  2. There is plenty of evidence to support the view that everyone experiences the effects of dissonance and self-perception.

Testing Your Basic Knowledge

ANSWERS TO MULTIPLE-CHOICE QUESTIONS

1. c	14. b
2. a	15. c
3. a	16. a
4. c	17. a
5. b	18. b
6. a	19. c
7. c	20. a
8. a	21. c
9. b	22. c
10. c	23. a
11. b	24. b
12. b	25. c
13. a	

Testing Your In-Depth Understanding

EXAMPLE ANSWER TO THE GUIDED QUESTIONS FOR CRITICAL THINKING EXERCISE #2

1. "He that has once done you a kindness will be more ready to do you another than he whom you yourself have obliged." If you want someone to do you a favor, ask a person who has already helped you out in the past, rather than someone you have helped.

2. Cognitive dissonance theory generally argues that we want our thoughts, feelings, and behaviors to be consistent with one another. If there is an inconsistency, we will feel an unpleasant arousal as a result, and we will try to resolve the inconsistency by changing one of the cognitions. In this circumstance, there are several possibilities. First, the person who did us a favor may have been uncertain why he or she was so nice to us. This situation would raise the two dissonant cognitions: (1) "I just went out of my way to help this person," and (2) "I don't know him all that well and didn't get anything in return. Why did I bother"? The way to resolve this dissonance would be to change the second cognition to something more like "I really like this person" or "Helping out others provides its own rewards; it is my personality to be helpful." Either resolution would make this person likely to help you again in the future. A second scenario could be that the dissonance arises when you make your second request for help. Assuming the person would rather not help you initially, the two dissonant cognitions would be: (1) "I don't want to say yes and help this person," and (2) "I helped him in the past, what justification do I have to say no and act differently this time?" Assuming no sufficient external justification can be found, the person would resolve his dissonance by changing the cognition of not wanting to help. In short, Ben Franklin was smart enough to realize that, after someone helps you out once, a sense of commitment or obligation is formed, and later refusing to help creates dissonance by conflicting with that obligation or relationship.

3. Self-perception theory suggests that when people's attitudes are weak or ambiguous, they may form those attitudes right on the spot, taking into account their recent behaviors as evidence about what their attitudes must be. So, in this scenario, a person who has done you a favor in the past would be more likely to do you a favor again in the future simply by making a rational inference that he or she either likes you or is a helpful person by nature.

4. A social psychologist could see whether self-perception theory or cognitive dissonance theory was operating in this scenario by taking physiological arousal into account. Remember that arousal is the key difference between the two theories: dissonance theory says we change our attitudes because of arousal; self-perception theory says it is a cold, rational process with no arousal. So, one possible experiment would be to set up the situation and actually measure people's physiological arousal with psychophysiological measurement equipment. Another possible experiment would be to use the misattribution of arousal paradigm described on pp. 327–328 of the text. Go ahead and design the specific study yourself for practice.

CHAPTER 9 | Causal Attribution

The goal of this chapter is to discuss the types of explanations people give when trying to understand their own and, particularly, other people's behavior. The bulk of the chapter discusses the circumstances that lead to dispositional (internal) versus situational (external) explanations. Errors and biases in our attributions are also discussed, as are the reasons for such errors. Finally, the chapter also details the way in which cultures differ in the types of attributions they are most likely to make.

ANNOTATED CHAPTER OUTLINE

After first reading through the chapter quickly, create a comprehensive framework for the information in the chapter by reading the outline below and filling in the missing information. Instead of simply re-copying information from the textbook, try to use your own words wherever possible; you can check your answers against the completed outline in the Answer Key section at the end of the chapter.

I. Attribution theory can be defined as

_____

_____

_____

_____

II. Why Social Psychologists Study Causal Attribution
   A. Attribution can be defined as

_____

_____

_____

   B. The Pervasiveness and Importance of Attribution
      1. We all make attributions.

2. The attributions we choose have tremendous significance, including effects on:
   a. Health outcomes
   b. Educational outcomes
C. Explanatory Style and Attribution
   1. Explanatory style can be defined as

_____

_____

_____

_____

   2. Typically explanatory style is assessed along three dimensions: internality/externality, stability/instability, and globality/specificity.
      a. Internal/external dimension: is the cause due to something about you or something about the other people or circumstances?
      b. Stable/unstable dimension:

_____

_____

_____

_____

      c. Global/specific dimension: does the cause influence other aspects of your life or just this specific situation?
   3. A tendency to use stable, global, and internal attributions is considered a

_____

explanatory style, which is associated with lower grades compared to a(n)

_____

style.

4. Peterson et al. (1988) did an archival study examining the explanatory styles and health outcomes for a group of 1940s Harvard graduates.

    a. Variable #1:

    _____

    _____

    _____

    b. Variable #2:

    _____

    _____

    _____

    c. Finding: explanatory style in younger years predicted health outcomes in later years.

5. Weiner and Anderson looked at the extent to which a cause is perceived as controllable.

    a. Controllable causes encourage perseverance, while uncontrollable causes lead to giving up.

    b. In judging others' behavior, controllable "stigmas" and excuses are viewed more negatively than uncontrollable "stigmas" and excuses, as in the following examples:

    (1) _____

    _____

    _____

    (2) _____

    _____

    _____

6. More adaptive attributional styles can be taught.

7. Girls and boys may be socialized into certain attributional styles in elementary school, as studied by Dweck et al. (1978), who examined the effects of attributional style of giving negative and positive feedback to boys and to girls in fourth- and fifth-grade classrooms. Dweck found that

    a. Negative feedback to girls was

    _____

    _____

    _____

    b. Negative feedback to boys was

    _____

    _____

    _____

    c. Positive feedback to girls was

    _____

    d. Positive feedback to boys was

    _____

    _____

    _____

    e. Girls may learn that poor performance means lack of ability while boys may learn that poor performance means lack of effort or other nonintellectual aspects of their work.

III. The Processes of Causal Attribution

    A. When making attributions, people ask whether the cause of the behavior was dispositional or situational.

    1. Dispositional causes:

    _____

    _____

    _____

    2. Situational causes:

    _____

    _____

    _____

    B. Attribution and Single-Instance Observation

    1. The discounting principle can be defined as

    _____

    _____

    _____

    2. The augmentation principle can be defined as

    _____

    _____

    _____

    3. Jones et al. (1961) demonstrated that these principles mean it is easier to make a certain attribution about a person if he or she is doing something out of character or against his or her own self-interest.

    a. Independent variable #1:

    _____

    _____

    _____

    b. Independent variable #2:

    _____

    _____

    _____

c. Dependent variable: how extreme the participants' personality ratings of the job candidate were.

d. Findings:

_____

_____

_____

_____

4. People made different causal attributions about Muhammad Ali's behavior.

a. Those attending to the dangers of being a soldier in Vietnam used the

_____

_____

_____

_____

to argue that he was lying about being a conscientious objector.

b. Those attending to the damage done to his career used the

_____

_____

_____

_____

to argue that he must believe strongly in his conscientious objector principles.

C. Attribution and Covariation

1. Sometimes we can make attributions about a particular behavior based on our knowledge of other instances of the same or similar behavior by the same or other people.

2. The covariation principle can be defined as

_____

_____

_____

_____

a. We can examine if the effect occurs when the supposed cause is present, and if it fails to occur when the supposed cause is absent.

b. If this happens, it increases our confidence that we have identified the true cause.

3. Three types of covariation information:

a. Consensus:

_____

_____

_____

_____

b. Distinctiveness:

_____

_____

_____

_____

c. Consistency:

_____

_____

_____

_____

4. Situational attributions arise from judgments of high consensus, high consistency, and high distinctiveness.

5. Dispositional attributions arise from judgments of high consistency, low consensus, and low distinctiveness.

6. McArthur (1972) studied whether people use covariation information.

a. Setup: she gave participants statements to read about a behavior and statements indicating high or low consensus, consistency, and distinctiveness.

b. Finding:

_____

_____

_____

_____

D. Attribution and Imagining an Alternate Chain of Events

1. We sometimes make causal attributions on the basis of imagined outcomes under different situations.

2. The Influence of What Almost Happened

a. Wells and Gavanski (1989) had participants read about a situation in which a boss ordered dinner containing a wine sauce for his employee, without knowing that she was allergic to wine; she became ill and died.

(1) Independent variable:

_____

_____

_____

_____

(2) Dependent variable: how much blame people assigned to the boss.

(3) Finding:

_____

_____

_____

_____

b. Counterfactual thoughts can be defined as

_____

_____

_____

_____

c. Emotional amplification can be defined as

_____

_____

_____

_____

(1) The pain or joy people derive from any event may be influenced by counter-factual thoughts.

(2) A father blamed himself when his child died in an airplane crash because, just prior to boarding the plane, she had cried and said she didn't want to go, and the father insisted.

d. Time and distance influence the extent to which people have counterfactual thinking, as found by Medvec et al. (1995), who analyzed the facial expressions of medalists in the 1992 Summer Olympics and found that

_____

_____

_____

_____

3. The Influence of Exceptions versus Routines

a. Behavior that deviates from the normal routine is more likely to lead to counterfactual thinking.

b. Miller and McFarland (1986) studied counterfactual thinking by having participants read a story about a man who had been severely injured during a store robbery.

(1) Independent variable:

_____

_____

_____

_____

(2) Dependent variable: the amount of money participants thought he should get to compensate him for his injuries.

(3) Finding:

_____

_____

_____

_____

_____

IV. Errors and Biases in Attribution

A. The Self-Serving Bias

1. Self-serving bias is the tendency to

_____

_____

_____

_____

_____

a. An example is when students take credit for doing well in a class but blame failure on the professor.

b. Lau and Russell (1980) found that

_____

_____

_____

_____

2. Self-serving bias is most commonly thought of as caused by a desire for high self-esteem, and hence is a motivational bias that is particularly strong when the motivation for self-esteem is very high.

3. Self-serving bias can also be rational, because success is more closely associated with intention and effort than failure.

a. Beckman (1970) used an experimental paradigm to demonstrate this in which participants were asked to tutor a child; the child did poorly on the first test and then received a second round of tutoring.

(1) Independent variable:

_____

_____

_____

_____

(2) Dependent variable: attributions for the child's second test performance.

(3) Finding:

_____

_____

_____

_____

(4) Logic: when the child fails both the first and the second test, there is no correlation between the child's performance and the teacher's tutoring; when the child first fails and then (after more tutoring) succeeds, there is a correlation with the tutoring.

b. Findings: people in happy marriages make external attributions for their partner's negative behavior and internal attributions for their partner's positive behavior; people in unhappy marriages

_____

_____

_____

_____

B. The Fundamental Attribution Error

1. The correspondence bias can be defined as

_____

_____

_____

_____

2. The fundamental attribution error can be defined as

_____

_____

_____

_____

3. A more classic definition of the fundamental attribution error is a tendency to overestimate dispositional causes and underestimate situational causes when making an attribution for another person's behavior.

4. Experimental Demonstrations of the Fundamental Attribution Error
   a. Jones and Harris (1967) in their "Castro essay study" asked participants to read essays either supporting or opposing Fidel Castro's government in Cuba.
      (1) Independent variable #1:

      _____

      _____

      _____

      _____

      (2) Independent variable #2: half the participants were told the essay writer was assigned to the stance take (pro or anti) and half were told the essay writer was free to choose his or her stance.
      (3) Dependent variable: the extent to which participants believed the essay writer was in favor of or against Fidel Castro.
      (4) Findings:

      _____

      _____

      _____

      _____

      (5) Logic: despite knowing that the essay writers were assigned to support the attitude portrayed in the essay, participants still believed the content of the essay revealed something about the participant—that is, they underestimated the role that the situation (being assigned to the position) had in the writers' behavior (writing the pro-Castro or anti-Castro essay).
   b. In the perceiver-induced constraint paradigm, participants are randomly assigned to be either the questioner or the responder.
      (1) Independent variable: whether the questioner tells the responder to read

an altruistic or a selfish response from a script.
      (2) Dependent variable:

      _____

      _____

      _____

      _____

      (3) Finding:

      _____

      _____

      _____

      _____

5. The Fundamental Attribution Error and Perceptions of the Disadvantaged
   a. Ross, Amabile, and Steinmetz (1977) in their "quiz-show study" assigned participants to be questioners or contestants in a mock quiz show; questioners were asked (in front of everyone) to draw on their own idiosyncratic areas of knowledge to develop challenging trivia questions; most contestants did poorly.
   b. The questioners had a role-conferred advantage, and the contestants had a built-in role-conferred disadvantage.
   c. Dependent variable:

   _____

   _____

   _____

   _____

   d. Findings for contestants:

   _____

   _____

   _____

   _____

   e. Findings for observers:

   _____

   _____

   _____

   _____

   f. Findings for questioners:

   _____

   _____

   _____

   _____

   g. Observers committed the fundamental attribution error—they did not account for the role-conferred advantage held by the questioners when making their intelligence judgments.

6. Causes of the Fundamental Attribution Error
   a. Motivated anxiety reduction: dispositional inferences allow us to "blame the victim"

for bad outcomes, thus assuring ourselves that it couldn't happen to us.

(1) The just world hypothesis can be defined as

_____

_____

_____

_____

(2) Victims of rape and domestic abuse are often viewed as responsible for their fates.

(3) People tend to generally derogate (rate unfavorably) the character of the victim.

b. Perceptual salience: we tend to give responsibility to the elements that stand out, and since people are typically more salient than elements of the situation, we make dispositional attributions.

(1) Taylor and Fiske (1975) conducted a study on the effect of perceptual salience by asking participants to watch a videotape of an interaction.

(a) Independent variable:

_____

_____

_____

_____

(b) Dependent variable: participants judged who was most responsible for or in charge of the course of the interaction.

(c) Finding:

_____

_____

_____

_____

(d) Similar findings: participants make more dispositional attributions about people who have been made more salient with lighting or brightly colored clothing (compared to less salient people).

(2) Perceptual salience explains cases in which the situation is relatively "invisible."

c. Gilbert (2002) examined cases in which the situation was highly visible (e.g., the perceiver-induced constraint paradigm).

(1) When observing a behavior, we first make an automatic dispositional attribution.

(2) After the initial attribution,

_____

_____

(3) We only make these adjustments if we have the time, energy, and motivation to do so, and even when we do make the adjustments, we typically fail to adjust far enough in favor of the situation.

(4) Gilbert (1989) demonstrated that we make automatic dispositional attributions and will only adjust if we have the cognitive resources to do so by having participants watch a videotape with no audio in which a young woman was showing a great deal of anxiety during an interview.

(a) Independent variable #1:

_____

_____

_____

(b) Independent variable #2: half of the participants were asked to memorize a list of words while watching the videotape (creating an extra demand on their attention), and half were not.

(c) Dependent variable:

_____

_____

_____

_____

(d) Finding:

_____

_____

_____

_____

C. The Actor-Observer Difference in Causal Attributions

1. The actor-observer difference can be defined as

_____

_____

_____

2. Participants will more often refer to characteristics of the person when making attributions for someone else's behavior, but will refer to aspects of the situation when making attributions for their own behavior.

3. Explanations for actor-observer differences:

a. _____

_____

_____

_____

b. _____

_____

_____

c. _____

_____

_____

d. False consensus: observers may judge their own behaviors as being relatively common and, thus, be predisposed to judge behaviors that are different from their own as being due to the actor's unique disposition.

(1) The false consensus effect can be defined as

_____

_____

_____

(2) Ross et al. (1977) asked participants to choose to either wear a large sandwich-board sign around campus with the word "Repent" in bold letters or to do a more standard experimental task.

(a) Independent variable: whether the participant agreed to wear the sign or refused to wear the sign but agreed to do a standard task.

(b) Dependent variable: estimating the percentage of students who would be willing to wear the sign.

(c) Finding:

_____

_____

_____

(3) Causes of the false consensus effect:

(a) _____

_____

_____

(b) _____

_____

_____

(c) _____

_____

_____

_____

V. Culture and the Fundamental Attribution Error

A. Cultural Differences in Attending to Context

1. Collectivistic cultures (i.e., interdependent peoples) attend more to contextual factors, which are seen as "background" to individualistic cultures (i.e., independent peoples).

2. Masuda et al. (2004) studied the effects of context on Japanese and American participants by showing them a picture of a cartoon face (the target) with a particular facial expression (e.g., happy or sad) in the foreground surrounded by other cartoon people with contrary facial expressions.

a. Independent variable #1: a happy target face surrounded by sad faces or a sad target face surrounded by happy faces.

b. Independent variable #2: whether the participant was Japanese or American.

c. Dependent variable: judgments about the facial expression of the target.

d. Finding:

_____

_____

_____

3. Masuda and Nisbett (2001) showed Japanese and American students animated cartoons of underwater scenes with background information (e.g., rocks, plants) and foreground information (e.g., particular fish) and found that:

a. _____

_____

_____

b. _____

_____

_____

c. Japanese participants noticed more context information, and the focal information was "bound" to the environment in their perceptions and memories.

4. The Rod and Frame test is used to judge the effect of context on perception of inanimate, static objects.

a. Participants are asked to look at a frame and rod inside a long box; the rod and frame can both be tilted to various angles independently of one another, creating various optical illusions with respect to the length of the rod and angle of tilt of the rod.

b. Ji et al. (2000) found that

_____
_____
_____

5. Kitayama et al. (2002) asked American and Japanese participants to examine a square with a line drawn at the bottom and then draw a line on a square of a different size.
a. Independent variable #1:

_____
_____
_____

b. Independent variable #2: whether the participant was American or Japanese.
c. Dependent variable: how accurately the line was drawn.
d. Finding:

_____
_____
_____

B. Causal Attributions for Independent and Interdependent Peoples
1. Because Asians are more likely to be interdependent and, since they see themselves and others as embedded in a context, they are more likely to make situational attributions; Westerners see themselves as more independent entities and, since they also see others in that way, make more dispositional attributions.
2. Miller (1984) found that

_____
_____
_____

a. These cultural differences did not emerge until

_____
_____
_____

b. East Indians who grew up in Westernized environments

_____
_____
_____

3. Morris and Peng (1994) found that

_____
_____
_____
_____

4. Al-Zahrani and Kaplowitz (1993) found that

_____
_____
_____

5. Within the Americas, Puerto Rican children, Mexicans, and Mexican Americans were less likely to make dispositional inferences than Anglos.

C. Priming Culture
1. Research suggests that people who are exposed to both independent and interdependent types of cultures (e.g., Asian Americans, people in Hong Kong) will make attributions consistent with the culture that is salient to them.
2. Hong et al. (1997) studied the effect of priming by first presenting participants with cultural images and then showing them an animation of a lone fish swimming in front of a group of fish and asking them why this was happening.
a. Independent variable:

_____
_____
_____

b. Dependent variable: how dispositional or situational their explanations were.
c. Finding:

_____
_____
_____

3. Peng and Knowles (2003) studied the effect of priming by asking Asian-American participants to recall experiences that either primed their American or Asian identity and then showing them abstract drawings of physical objects and asking them the extent to which they thought the action of the object was due to the internal properties of the object (e.g., its weight) or contextual factors (e.g., friction).
a. Independent variable:

_____
_____
_____

b. Dependent variable: how they rated the importance of internal versus external causes.
c. Finding:

_____
_____
_____

D. Dispositions: Fixed or Flexible?
  1. Asians use both situations and dispositions to judge people's personalities.
     a. Norenzayan et al. (1999) found that Koreans and Americans rated the importance of personality

     _____
     _____
     _____
     _____,

        but Koreans rated situations

     _____
     _____
     _____

     b. Norenzayan found that although Koreans believe personality is an important dimension, they rate personality as being more changeable than do Americans.
  2. Interdependent people believe that abilities are malleable through the environment and effort (more so than do independent peoples) and that effort can overcome inadequacy.
  3. Heine et al. (2001) studied the belief in the value of effort by asking participants to do a creativity task.
     a. Independent variable #1: participants were either Canadian or Japanese.
     b. Independent variable #2:

     _____
     _____
     _____

     c. Dependent variable:

     _____
     _____
     _____

     d. Finding:

     _____
     _____
     _____
     _____

VI. Beyond the Internal/External Dimension
  A. Questions beyond the internal/external dimension are asked to gain more nuanced understanding.
  B. People want to understand various aspects of events in order to make their worlds more predictable and seek information about:
     1. _____
        _____

     _____
  2. _____
     _____
     _____
     _____

  3. A person's intentions
     a. Their desires
     b. Their beliefs

TESTING YOUR BASIC KNOWLEDGE

After studying the information in the chapter by filling in the outline above, test your basic knowledge with the following multiple-choice test. Answers are provided in the Answer Key section at the end of the chapter. If you find that you have gotten an answer wrong, it is important that you understand why it is wrong (as well as understanding why the correct answer is the better choice). Talk with peers, your tutor, or your professor if you need help.

Multiple-Choice Questions

1. Social psychologists would call the explanations people gave for why Muhammad Ali was refusing to fight in Vietnam
   a. implicit theories.
   b. attributions.
   c. biases.

2. According to the textbook, people _____ make attributions.
   a. never
   b. occasionally
   c. constantly

3. Bob tends to explain his grades in school as being due to his own lack of ability; he predicts that he will always have this lack of ability, and he feels that his lack of ability extends across all academic subjects in general. Bob's explanatory style is
   a. pessimistic.
   b. discounting.
   c. augmenting.

4. Weiner and his colleagues found that attributions for behavior that imply controllability are more likely to lead to _____ than attributions that imply a lack of controllability.
   a. forgiveness
   b. perseverance
   c. anger

5. Dweck's research found that elementary school girls are more likely than elementary school boys to be led to believe their failures are due to intellectual inadequacies. This type of socialization may lead
   a. girls to attribute failure to uncontrollable causes.
   b. boys to attribute failure to uncontrollable causes.
   c. Both of the above are correct.

6. While riding up a ski lift, you see a skier falling down the mountain. You decide that the skier must not have been very skilled and should have been on an easier slope. Your friend, however, thinks the skier fell because conditions on the mountain were dangerous. You are making a _____ attribution and your friend is making a _____ attribution.
   a. dispositional (internal); situational (external)
   b. situational (external); dispositional (internal)
   c. Neither of the above is correct.

7. Muhammad Ali claimed he was a conscientious objector and that he should be legally allowed to avoid Army duty during the Vietnam War. Some people saw his behavior and immediately applied the discounting principle. This means that they
   a. realized Ali was standing up for his true beliefs.
   b. thought there was a high likelihood that Ali just wanted to avoid getting hurt or killed in the war and thus was lying about being a conscientious objector.
   c. discounted the role that Ali's history as a boxer played in his behavior.

8. In judging Muhammad Ali's refusal to fight in Vietnam, other people used the augmentation principle and considered the negative backlash (including jail time) against the once popular Ali. This means that they
   a. took into account how much Ali lost in terms of his freedom, career, and reputation by taking this stand, and decided that he was telling the truth about being a conscientious objector.
   b. believed that his profession as a boxer detracted from the legitimacy of his claim.
   c. decided that Ali must be telling the truth because of an implicit association between religious conviction and attitudes against war.

9. In an office, the boss yells at Hannah. No one else yells at Hannah. The boss yells at all the employees, not just Hannah. The boss always yells at Hannah. Which pattern of covariation information accurately depicts this situation?
   a. high consensus, high distinctiveness, high consistency
   b. low consensus, high distinctiveness, high consistency
   c. low consensus, low distinctiveness, high consistency

10. John laughed at a comedian. His behavior has high consensus, high distinctiveness, and high consistency. If asked to explain John's behavior, what type of attribution does this pattern of covariation information call for?
    a. dispositional (internal)
    b. situational (external)
    c. An accurate attribution cannot be determined from the information given.

11. To celebrate his promotion, a boss and employee go out for dinner. The boss orders a dish for his employee that contains wine. The employee, unaware of the ingredients, eats the meal but is highly allergic to wine and ends up dying after having a reaction. Researchers suggest that the boss would experience more counterfactual thoughts under which of the following conditions:
    a. He did not know about the employee's allergy to wine.
    b. He almost ordered another dish that did not contain wine.
    c. The wine was not listed as an ingredient on the menu.

12. A jury hears a case in which a man is severely injured during a robbery at a grocery store. In which situation is the jury likely to award the most money to compensate the man for his injuries?
    a. when they learn that the man was a friend of the person who owned the store
    b. when they learn that the man was visiting a store he often went to as a loyal customer
    c. when they learn that the man was visiting a store he rarely went to just for a "change of pace"

13. According to the self-serving bias, which of the following is the most likely explanation a student would give for doing poorly on a psychology test?
    a. The professor made an unfairly difficult test.
    b. I should have studied harder.
    c. Either explanation is equally likely.

14. People make self-serving attributions
    a. to make themselves feel better.
    b. because good outcomes are more consistent with one's intentions than bad outcomes.
    c. Both of the above are correct.

15. Carl attributes the positive behaviors his wife, Rose, does to internal causes, and her negative behaviors to external causes. Is Carl's marriage likely to be a happy or unhappy one?
    a. happy
    b. unhappy
    c. It is impossible to tell from the information given.

16. The new cashier at the cafeteria angrily tells Tony he'd "better get his act together" when Tony reveals he forgot his meal card and needs to fill out a form to pay for his lunch. According to the fundamental attribution error, Tony is likely to
    a. not eat lunch and leave the cafeteria.
    b. decide the cashier is a mean, angry person.
    c. erroneously conclude that the cashier needed more training before starting work.

17. In the famous "Quiz Show study" by Ross, Amabile, and Steinmetz (1977), what finding best demonstrated the fundamental attribution error?
    a. the fact that the observers rated the intelligence of the questioners higher than that of the contestants, even though they knew the details of how the experiment was set up
    b. the correspondence participants drew between the type of essay the author wrote about Castro and his or her true attitudes about Castro
    c. the fact that the questioners rated the respondents as more altruistic even though the questioners assigned those answers to the respondents

18. People want to believe that good things happen to good people and bad things happen only to bad people. This is called the
    a. correspondence bias.
    b. just world hypothesis.
    c. attribution theory.

19. Dan Lassiter and his colleagues have conducted numerous studies using the following paradigm: The confession of a prisoner is recorded on videotape. The defense is claiming the confession was coerced by a manipulative interrogator who carefully guided the conversation and tricked the prisoner into confessing. The prosecution is arguing that the prisoner confessed of his own free will and was entirely responsible for his words on the videotape. According to research done by Taylor and Fiske (1975) which of the following video angles would most likely lead viewers to believe the defense?
    a. an angle that only shows the prisoner's face
    b. an angle that only shows the interrogator's face
    c. an angle that shows both the prisoner and the interrogator

20. According to Gilbert (2002), why do people tend to commit the fundamental attribution error?
    a. because they automatically make dispositional attributions and it is only with time and effort that they may adjust those attributions to more accurately take the situation into account

    b. because, after first making a situational attribution, they tend to adjust their explanations to take into account vivid, dispositional behaviors
    c. because they overestimate the extent to which people have the same thoughts, feelings, and behaviors that they do

21. Angelina very abruptly ends a conversation with Jennifer and hangs up the phone. Jennifer explains this behavior by assuming that Angelina is a rude person. Angelina explains this behavior by noting that Jennifer had just insulted her. What social psychological principle explains the difference between these two attributions?
    a. the augmenting hypothesis
    b. the actor-observer difference
    c. the fundamental attribution error

22. According to a great deal of research, why are people in independent cultures more likely to commit the fundamental attribution error than people in interdependent cultures?
    a. because people who have independent self-concepts are more likely to understand the powerful effects a situation can have on an individual's behavior
    b. because people in interdependent cultures have been shown to rate personality and individual differences as far less important than environment and situational context
    c. because those with interdependent self-concepts see the self as being embedded in and influenced by a situation and so also see others as being influenced by situations

23. Peng and Knowles (2003) found that Asian-American participants were more likely to make internal attributions
    a. when their American identities were primed.
    b. when they were told to ignore the situational context.
    c. never; they were far more likely to make external attributions.

24. After failure, _____ students are more likely to seek self-improvement and work more on the failed skill.
    a. American
    b. Canadian
    c. Japanese

25. Miller's (1984) work with American and East Indian children suggests that cultural differences in attribution styles are
    a. taught by the culture.
    b. present at birth.
    c. responsible for prejudice among young children.

Essay Questions

After you have mastered the multiple-choice questions, try testing your basic understanding by thoroughly answering each of the broad essay questions below. Because it is critical that you think through this information on your own, we have not provided any answers to these questions. Your learning and retention of this material will be greatly enhanced if you do one or more of the following to check your answers: carefully review the textbook information; compare your responses to your class lecture notes; talk over your answers with a peer; ask your professor to review your answers or review any information that is unclear to you.

1. Define the term "attribution" and explain why social psychologists view attributions as so important.

2. How do people generally make an attribution when they have only one instance of a behavior? How do they make attributions when they have multiple examples of behavior? What is counterfactual thinking and how does it influence attributions?

3. Describe the self-serving bias, the fundamental attribution error, and actor-observer differences and for each explain why they occur. Provide empirical studies to support those explanations where possible.

4. In what ways do the typical attributions of people from collectivistic cultures differ from those of people from individualistic cultures? Why do these differences exist? Provide empirical evidence supporting your explanations.

5. Besides determining whether an action is caused by a person's disposition or the situation, what other types of information might people seek when they engage in causal attribution?

TESTING YOUR IN-DEPTH UNDERSTANDING

Test your in-depth understanding of the material by working through the Critical Thinking Exercises provided at the end of each textbook chapter. To maximize this learning opportunity, work together with a tutor, study group, or your professor. Alternatively, write down your thoughts and responses.

Guided questions for one of the exercises are provided below. While there are multiple ways to answer these questions, short answers are given in the Answer Key at the end of the chapter. Note that the valuable part of this exercise is not simply knowing the answer but working with the material to come up with the answer.

Guided Questions for Critical Thinking Exercise #4

In what ways do the "role-conferred self-presentational advantages" explored in the quiz-game study help to boost the impressions made by the professors in your university? What specific self-presentational advantages do they enjoy?

1. Review the basic design and findings of the Ross, Amabile, and Steinmetz (1977) quiz-show study.

2. What role-conferred advantages were present in that study, and whom did they benefit and how?

3. Many American college students will be familiar with the television game show *Jeopardy* in which contestants are asked extremely challenging general-knowledge questions. The host of that program, Alex Trebek, is known for offering additional nuggets of specialized knowledge after a contestant answers the question. Contrast this to another television game show that is also popular in America: *Wheel of Fortune.* In this game, contestants see place holders for the letters composing a word or phrase and try to be the first to fill in enough correct letters (one at a time) to guess the phrase the letters spell. The host of this show, Pat Sajak, has the primary job of letting contestants know if they guessed a letter of the alphabet that is or isn't in the phrase. Alex Trebek is commonly thought to be much more intelligent than Pat Sajak. Explain this attribution via the notion of role-conferred advantage and the fundamental attribution error.

4. Now consider your favorite professor. What kinds of positive, dispositional attributions might students be likely to make about the professor? Can you think of any situational causes for those characteristics? In other words, in what ways might your professor be able to shape the situation that leads students to reach those positive conclusions?

Enhance your understanding of the chapter by thinking about and doing the remaining three Critical Thinking Exercises. Discuss your answers with your peers, study group, tutor, or professor.

Critical Thinking Exercise #1

Can you think of any current events that seem to illustrate the actor-observer difference in attribution? That is, are there any events, controversies, or conflicts being covered in the news in which one "side" is offering situational explanations of its behavior and the other side is offering a dispositional account of that very same behavior?

Critical Thinking Exercise #2

Tell yourself a dispositional tale of your life—that is, how you got to where and who you are right now by virtue of your personal characteristics, traits, and decisions. Try to describe, in other words, the ways in which, if you weren't just the kind of person you are, you would not be where you are today, doing the kinds of things you are doing. After telling yourself that tale and letting it sink in, now tell a situational tale of your life—that is, how you got to where and who you are by virtue of the intervention of others, external circumstances, or simple chance. Which tale is more compelling or are they equally compelling? What does this tell you about the causes of human behavior?

Critical Thinking Exercise #3

From what you've read, either in the newspapers, for one of your classes, or from your general reading, who would you say were the most and least liked U.S. presidents in recent times? What would you say were their "attributional styles"? Does there appear to be any relationship between attributional style and popularity?

SOCIAL PSYCHOLOGY IN THE POPULAR MEDIA

You might be interested in the following popular media references, each of which relates in some way to information in this chapter.

Books

Ali, Muhammad, and Ali, Hana Yasmeen (2004). *The Soul of a Butterfly: Reflections on Life's Journey.* New York: Simon & Schuster. From an Audiophile book review on Amazon.com: "Muhammad Ali's memoir focuses largely on his spiritual evolution from his childhood to his years as a boxing star, through fatherhood and into his role as a Parkinson's disease advocate and peace activist."

Roese, Neal (2005). *If Only: How to Turn Regret Into Opportunity.* New York: Broadway. Neil Roese, a leading researcher on counterfactual thinking, wrote this book on counterfactual thinking for a general audience. From the front flap of the hardcover edition: ". . . The surprising message of *If Only* is that we can manage our regret style to maximize the gain and minimize the pain. In an entertaining and upbeat book that weds lively science writing to practical self-help, Dr. Roese mines the research and shares simple strategies for managing your life to make the most of regret. . . ."

Web Site

Michotte Demonstration of Causal Attributions— http://cogweb.ucla.edu/Discourse/Narrative/ michotte-demo.swf. Examining this Web site may help you to better understand the attribution studies discussed in the culture section of the chapter. The Web site provides the explanations that a typical Western viewer would have (i.e., a Western viewer would judge the larger red ball as being more salient). How might Eastern viewers respond differently? *Note: requires Macromedia Flash (SWF) browser "plug-in" available at http://www.macromedia.com/software/flashplayer/.

ANSWER KEY INFORMATION

Annotated Chapter Outline

I. Attribution theory can be defined as an umbrella term used to describe the set of theoretical accounts of how people assign causes to the events around them and the effects that people's causal assessments have.

II. Why Social Psychologists Study Causal Attribution
   A. Attribution can be defined as linking a cause to an instance of behavior, one's own or that of other people.
   B. The Pervasiveness and Importance of Attribution
      1. We all make attributions.
      2. The attributions we choose have tremendous significance, including effects on:
         a. Health outcomes
         b. Educational outcomes
   C. Explanatory Style and Attribution
      1. Explanatory style can be defined as a person's habitual way of explaining events.
      2. Typically explanatory style is assessed along three dimensions: internality/externality, stability/instability, and globality/specificity.
         a. Internal/external dimension: is the cause due to something about you or something about the other people or circumstances?
         b. Stable/unstable dimension: will the cause be present again in the future or not?
         c. Global/specific dimension: does the cause influence other aspects of your life or just this specific situation?
      3. A tendency to use stable, global, and internal attributions is considered a pessimistic explanatory style, which is associated with lower grades compared to an optimistic style.
      4. Peterson et al. (1988) did an archival study examining the explanatory styles and health outcomes for a group of 1940s Harvard graduates.

a. Variable #1: medical records of the Harvard graduates were scored by doctors along a scale of 1 (good health) to 5 (deceased).

b. Variable #2: judges rated explanatory style by content coding essays written by the Harvard graduates about their most difficult experience during World War II.

c. Finding: explanatory style in younger years predicted health outcomes in later years.

5. Weiner and Anderson looked at the extent to which a cause is perceived as controllable.

a. Controllable causes encourage perseverance, while uncontrollable causes lead to giving up.

b. In judging others' behavior, controllable "stigmas" and excuses are viewed more negatively than uncontrollable "stigmas" and excuses, as in the following examples:

(1) Those against a gay lifestyle have more sympathy for gays if they believe homosexuality is caused by biology rather than by choice.

(2) Excuses for poor performance that refer to uncontrollable events lead to more forgiveness than excuses that refer to controllable events.

6. More adaptive attributional styles can be taught.

7. Girls and boys may be socialized into certain attributional styles in elementary school, as studied by Dweck et al. (1978), who examined the effects of attributional style of giving negative and positive feedback to boys and to girls in fourth- and fifth-grade classrooms. Dweck found that

a. Negative feedback to girls was almost entirely related to intellectual ability.

b. Negative feedback to boys was related to effort 45 percent of the time.

c. Positive feedback to girls was related to intellectual ability less than 80 percent of the time.

d. Positive feedback to boys was related to intellectual ability 94 percent of the time.

e. Girls may learn that poor performance means lack of ability while boys may learn that poor performance means lack of effort or other nonintellectual aspects of their work.

III. The Processes of Causal Attribution

A. In making attributions, people ask whether the cause of the behavior was dispositional or situational.

1. Dispositional causes: something that is internal to the actor.

2. Situational causes: something that is external to the actor, such as the surrounding circumstance or context.

B. Attribution and Single-Instance Observation

1. The discounting principle can be defined as the idea that we should assign reduced weight to a particular cause of behavior if there are other plausible causes that might have produced it.

2. The augmentation principle can be defined as the idea that we should assign greater weight to a particular cause of behavior if there are other causes present that normally would produce the opposite outcome.

3. Jones et al. (1961) demonstrated that these principles mean it is easier to make a certain attribution about a person if he or she is doing something out of character or against his or her own self-interest.

a. Independent variable #1: participants were led to believe a job candidate was being interviewed for either a submariner job (close contact with lots of people) or an astronaut job (long periods alone).

b. Independent variable #2: the job candidate behaved in an introverted or extraverted way.

c. Dependent variable: how extreme the participants' personality ratings of the job candidate were.

d. Findings: participants made only mild personality inferences about the introverted candidate for the astronaut position and the extraverted candidate for the submariner position; they made extreme inferences about the introverted candidate for the submariner position and the extraverted candidate for the astronaut position, as these were both instances of the behavior going against the role.

4. People made different causal attributions about Muhammad Ali's behavior.

a. Those attending to the dangers of being a soldier in Vietnam used the discounting principle to argue that he was lying about being a conscientious objector.

b. Those attending to the damage done to his career used the augmenting principle to argue that he must believe strongly in his conscientious objector principles.

C. Attribution and Covariation

1. Sometimes we can make attributions about a particular behavior based on our knowledge of other instances of the same or similar behavior by the same or other people.

2. The covariation principle can be defined as the idea that we should attribute behavior to potential causes that co-occur with the behavior.
   a. We can examine if the effect occurs when the supposed cause is present, and if it fails to occur when the supposed cause is absent.
   b. If this happens, it increases our confidence that we have identified the true cause.
3. Three types of covariation information:
   a. Consensus: what most people would do in a given situation—that is, whether most people would behave the same way or few or no other people would behave that way in that situation.
   b. Distinctiveness: what an individual does in different situations—that is, whether the behavior is unique to a particular situation or occurs in all situations.
   c. Consistency: what an individual does in a given situation on different occasions—that is, whether the next time the behavior under the same circumstances would be the same or would differ.
4. Situational attributions arise from judgments of high consensus, high consistency, and high distinctiveness.
5. Dispositional attributions arise from judgments of high consistency, low consensus, and low distinctiveness.
6. McArthur (1972) studied whether people use covariation information.
   a. Setup: she gave participants statements to read about a behavior and statements indicating high or low consensus, consistency, and distinctiveness.
   b. Findings: people tend to make attributions as outlined above, but consensus information is less important than consistency or distinctiveness information.
D. Attribution and Imagining an Alternate Chain of Events
   1. We sometimes make causal attributions on the basis of imagined outcomes under different situations.
   2. The Influence of What Almost Happened
      a. Wells and Gavanski (1989) had participants read about a situation in which a boss ordered dinner containing a wine sauce for his employee without knowing that she was allergic to wine; she became ill and died.
         (1) Independent variable: participants learned that the boss almost ordered another dish instead, and it did or did not contain wine.
         (2) Dependent variable: how much blame people assigned to the boss.
         (3) Finding: people assigned more blame to the boss when told that the other dish he almost ordered did not contain wine.
      b. Counterfactual thoughts can be defined as thoughts of what might have, could have, or should have happened "if only" something had been done differently.
      c. Emotional amplification can be defined as a ratcheting up of an emotional reaction to an event that is proportional to how easy it is to imagine the event not happening.
         (1) The pain or joy people derive from any event may be influenced by counterfactual thoughts.
         (2) A father blamed himself when his child died in an airplane crash because, just prior to boarding the plane, she had cried and said she didn't want to go, and the father insisted.
      d. Time and distance influence the extent to which people have counterfactual thinking, as found by Medvec et al. (1995), who analyzed the facial expressions of medalists in the 1992 Summer Olympics and found that silver medal winners seemed more upset than the bronze medal winners, presumably because the silver medalists could more easily see how close they had come to winning the gold.
   3. The Influence of Exceptions versus Routines
      a. Behavior that deviates from the normal routine is more likely to lead to counterfactual thinking.
      b. Miller and McFarland (1986) studied counterfactual thinking by having participants read a story about a man who had been severely injured during a store robbery.
         (1) Independent variable: the man was either visiting a store he went to often or visiting a store he rarely went to.
         (2) Dependent variable: the amount of money participants thought he should get to compensate him for his injuries.
         (3) Finding: participants awarded the man $100,000 more in the condition in which he was injured in a store he rarely visited, presumably because it was easier for participants to imagine how the injuries could have been prevented.

IV. Errors and Biases in Attribution
   A. The Self-Serving Bias
      1. Self-serving bias is the tendency to attribute failure and other bad events to external circumstances, but to attribute success and other good events to oneself.
         a. An example is when students take credit for doing well in a class but blame failure on the professor.
         b. Lau and Russell (1980) found that 80 percent of explanations for sports victories were attributed to something about one's team, while only 53 percent of defeats were attributed to something about one's team; only 20 percent of the explanations for victories were attributed to external events, but 47 percent of the explanations for defeats were attributed to external events.
      2. Self-serving bias is most commonly thought of as caused by a desire for high self-esteem, and hence is a motivational bias that is particularly strong when the motivation for self-esteem is very high.
      3. Self-serving bias can also be rational, because success is more closely associated with intention and effort than failure.
         a. Beckman (1970) used an experimental paradigm to demonstrate this in which participants were asked to tutor a child; the child did poorly on the first test and then received a second round of tutoring.
            (1) Independent variable: the child either does well or poorly on the second test.
            (2) Dependent variable: attributions for the child's second test performance.
            (3) Finding: teachers take credit if the child succeeds, but they blame the child if he or she fails.
            (4) Logic: when the child fails both the first and the second test, there is no correlation between the child's performance and the teacher's tutoring; when the child first fails and then (after more tutoring) succeeds, there is a correlation with the tutoring.
         b. Findings: people in happy marriages make external attributions for their partner's negative behavior and internal attributions for their partner's positive behavior; people in unhappy marriages do the opposite.
   B. The Fundamental Attribution Error
      1. The correspondence bias can be defined as the tendency to draw an inference about a person that "corresponds" to the behavior observed;

also referred to as the fundamental attribution error.
      2. The fundamental attribution error can be defined as a tendency to believe mistakenly that a behavior is due to a person's disposition rather than the situation in which the person finds himself.
      3. A more classic definition of the fundamental attribution error is a tendency to overestimate dispositional causes and underestimate situational causes when making an attribution for another person's behavior.
      4. Experimental Demonstrations of the Fundamental Attribution Error
         a. Jones and Harris (1967) in their "Castro essay study" asked participants to read essays either supporting or opposing Fidel Castro's government in Cuba.
            (1) Independent variable #1: half the participants read a pro-Castro essay and half read an anti-Castro essay.
            (2) Independent variable #2: half the participants were told the essay writer was assigned to the stance take (pro or anti) and half were told the essay writer was free to choose his or her stance.
            (3) Dependent variable: the extent to which participants believed the essay writer was in favor of or against Fidel Castro.
            (4) Findings: in the free-choice condition, participants rated pro-Castro essay writers as being strongly pro-Castro and anti-Castro essay writers as being strongly anti-Castro; in the assigned condition, participants made the same attributions (just less strongly).
            (5) Logic: despite knowing that the essay writers were assigned to support the attitude portrayed in the essay, participants still believed the content of the essay revealed something about the participant—that is, they underestimated the role that the situation (being assigned to the position) had in the writers' behavior (writing the pro-Castro or anti-Castro essay).
         b. In the perceiver-induced constraint paradigm, participants are randomly assigned to be either the questioner or the responder.
            (1) Independent variable: whether the questioner tells the responder to read an altruistic or a selfish response from a script.

(2) Dependent variable: the questioner's rating of the responder's personality traits.

(3) Finding: despite the highly salient situational constraint, questioners still rated the responders who were told to give more altruistic responses more favorably than the responders who were told to give more selfish responses.

5. The Fundamental Attribution Error and Perceptions of the Disadvantaged

   a. Ross, Amabile, and Steinmetz (1977) in their "quiz-show study" assigned participants to be questioners or contestants in a mock quiz show; questioners were asked (in front of everyone) to draw on their own idiosyncratic areas of knowledge to develop challenging trivia questions; most contestants did poorly.

   b. The questioners had a role-conferred advantage, and the contestants had a built-in role-conferred disadvantage.

   c. Dependent variable: ratings of general knowledge and intelligence.

   d. Findings for contestants: rated questioners more highly than themselves.

   e. Findings for observers: rated questioners more highly than contestants.

   f. Findings for questioners: rated themselves equal to average student.

   g. Observers committed the fundamental attribution error—they did not account for the role-conferred advantage held by the questioners when making their intelligence judgments.

6. Causes of the Fundamental Attribution Error

   a. Motivated anxiety reduction: dispositional inferences allow us to "blame the victim" for bad outcomes, thus assuring ourselves that it couldn't happen to us.

     (1) The just world hypothesis can be defined as the belief that people get what they deserve and deserve what they get.

     (2) Victims of rape and domestic abuse are often viewed as responsible for their fates.

     (3) People tend to generally derogate (rate unfavorably) the character of the victim.

   b. Perceptual salience: we tend to give responsibility to the elements that stand out, and since people are typically more salient than elements of the situation, we make dispositional attributions.

     (1) Taylor and Fiske (1975) conducted a study on the effect of perceptual salience by asking participants to watch a videotape of an interaction.

       (a) Independent variable: half the participants saw just one individual, and the other half saw both individuals.

       (b) Dependent variable: participants judged who was most responsible for or in charge of the course of the interaction.

       (c) Finding: participants who saw just one individual rated that person as more responsible than the other, but participants who saw both people rated both people as equally responsible.

       (d) Similar findings: participants make more dispositional attributions about people who have been made more salient with lighting or brightly colored clothing (compared to less salient people).

     (2) Perceptual salience explains cases in which the situation is relatively "invisible."

   c. Gilbert (2002) examined cases in which the situation was highly visible (e.g., the perceiver-induced constraint paradigm).

     (1) When observing a behavior, we first make an automatic dispositional attribution.

     (2) After the initial attribution, we make effortful and deliberate adjustments to that attribution to account for elements of the situation.

     (3) We only make these adjustments if we have the time, energy, and motivation to do so, and even when we do make the adjustments, we typically fail to adjust far enough in favor of the situation.

     (4) Gilbert (1989) demonstrated that we make automatic dispositional attributions and will only adjust if we have the cognitive resources to do so by having participants watch a videotape with no audio in which a young woman was showing a great deal of anxiety during an interview.

       (a) Independent variable #1: half of the participants were told the woman was being asked anxiety provoking questions; the other half were told she was being asked harmless questions.

   (b) Independent variable #2: half of the participants were asked to memorize a list of words while watching the videotape (creating an extra demand on their attention), and half were not.

   (c) Dependent variable: the extent to which participants judged the woman to be dispositionally anxious.

   (d) Finding: those who were not cognitively busy (who did not have to memorize the list of words), rated the woman as more dispositionally anxious when told she was being asked harmless questions; those who were cognitively busy rated her as dispositionally anxious no matter what kind of questions they were told she was answering.

C. The Actor-Observer Difference in Causal Attributions

  1. The actor-observer difference can be defined as differences in attribution based on who is making the causal assessment: the actor (who is relatively disposed to make situational attributions) or the observer (who is relatively disposed to make dispositional attributions).

  2. Participants will more often refer to characteristics of the person when making attributions for someone else's behavior, but will refer to aspects of the situation when making attributions for their own behavior.

  3. Explanations for actor-observer differences

    a. Assumptions about person: when explaining one's own behavior, the personality, character, and preferences of the person may be taken as a "given," thus leaving situational forces as the central unknown to be explained.

    b. Perceptual salience: when explaining one's own behavior, the situation is perceptually salient (actors' attention is directed outward); when explaining someone else's behavior, the person doing the behavior is perceptually salient.

    c. Access to information: actors have access to their own intentions and know whether a behavior is typical, so they can better judge whether a given behavior is distinctive or not.

    d. False consensus: observers may judge their own behaviors as being relatively common

and, thus, be predisposed to judge behaviors different from their own as being due to the actor's unique disposition.

   (1) The false consensus effect can be defined as the tendency for people to think that their behavior (as well as their attitudes, preferences, or responses more generally) is relatively common.

   (2) Ross et al. (1977) asked participants to choose to either wear a large sandwich-board sign around campus with the word "Repent" in bold letters or to do a more standard experimental task.

    (a) Independent variable: whether the participant agreed to wear the sign or refused to wear the sign but agreed to do a standard task.

    (b) Dependent variable: estimating the percentage of students who would be willing to wear the sign.

    (c) Finding: participants who agreed to wear the sign thought that 64 percent would do the same, but participants who refused to wear the sign thought that only 23 percent would wear the sign. In reality, 50 percent agreed to wear the sign.

   (3) Causes of the false consensus effect

    (a) Self-serving desire to know our views are shared by others.

    (b) Association with others who are, in fact, similar to us.

    (c) Failure to realize that other people could construe a choice in a different way than we do.

V. Culture and the Fundamental Attribution Error

A. Cultural Differences in Attending to Context

  1. Collectivistic cultures (i.e., interdependent peoples) attend more to contextual factors, which are seen as "background" to individualistic cultures (i.e., independent peoples).

  2. Masuda et al. (2004) studied the effects of context on Japanese and American participants by showing them a picture of a cartoon face (the target) with a particular facial expression (e.g., happy or sad) in the foreground surrounded by other cartoon people with contrary facial expressions.

    a. Independent variable #1: a happy target face surrounded by sad faces or a sad target face surrounded by happy faces.

b. Independent variable #2: whether the participant was Japanese or American.

c. Dependent variable: judgments about the facial expression of the target.

d. Finding: Japanese judgments about the target figure's facial expression were more influenced by the background faces than the American judgments.

3. Masuda and Nisbett (2001) showed Japanese and American students animated cartoons of underwater scenes with background information (e.g., rocks, plants) and foreground information (e.g., particular fish) and found that:

a. Japanese and American participants reported the same amount of information about foreground objects, but Japanese participants reported 60 percent more information about the context/environment.

b. When asked if they had seen objects from the scene, Japanese participants were less certain of their judgments when the objects were presented in novel versus familiar background contexts; it didn't matter to the Americans whether the focal object was presented in the familiar context or a new scene.

c. Japanese participants noticed more context information, and the focal information was "bound" to the environment in their perceptions and memories.

4. The Rod and Frame test is used to judge the effect of context on perception of inanimate, static objects.

a. Participants are asked to look at a frame and rod inside a long box; the rod and frame can both be tilted to various angles independently of one another, creating various optical illusions with respect to the length of the rod and angle of tilt of the rod.

b. Ji et al. (2000) found that, when asked to ignore the frame and make judgments about the degree to which the rod was vertical, Chinese participants' judgments were more influenced by the angle of the frame than American judgments, suggesting that the Chinese participants had a harder time ignoring the context of the frame.

5. Kitayama et al. (2002) asked American and Japanese participants to examine a square with a line drawn at the bottom and then draw a line on a square of a different size.

a. Independent variable #1: whether participants were asked to draw a line the exact same length as the original or to draw a line that was the same relative length as the original (relative to the size of the square).

b. Independent variable #2: whether the participant was American or Japanese.

c. Dependent variable: how accurately the line was drawn.

d. Finding: Japanese participants more accurately drew the line when asked to make the relative judgment (requiring attention to context); American participants were better when asked to make the absolute judgment (requiring them to ignore the context).

B. Causal Attributions for Independent and Interdependent Peoples

1. Because Asians are more likely to be interdependent and, since they see themselves and others as embedded in a context, they are more likely to make situational attributions; Westerners see themselves as more independent entities and, since they also see others in that way, make more dispositional attributions.

2. Miller (1984) found that American adults gave more dispositional attributions for an acquaintance's behavior, and Hindu East Indian adults gave more situational attributions.

a. These cultural differences did not emerge until the age of adolescence (implying that these ways of thinking are culturally taught).

b. East Indians who grew up in Westernized environments gave attributions that were midway between American and East Indian attributions.

3. Morris and Peng (1994) found that Americans rated even the behavior of an animated fish as being more dispositional than Chinese participants.

4. Al-Zahrani and Kaplowitz (1993) found that American participants made more internal attributions than Saudi Arabian participants.

5. Within the Americas, Puerto Rican children, Mexicans, and Mexican Americans were less likely to make dispositional inferences than Anglos.

C. Priming Culture

1. Research suggests that people who are exposed to both independent and interdependent types of cultures (e.g., Asian Americans, people in Hong Kong) will make attributions consistent with the culture that is salient to them.

2. Hong et al. (1997) studied the effect of priming by first presenting participants with cultural images and then showing them an animation of a lone fish swimming in front of a group of fish and asking them why this was happening.
   a. Independent variable: participants were primed with Western cultural icons, Chinese cultural cues, or neutral stimuli.
   b. Dependent variable: how dispositional or situational their explanations were.
   c. Finding: those primed with Western cues gave more dispositional reasons for the lone fish being in front, those primed with Chinese cues gave more situational reasons, and those with neutral priming fell in between the other two groups.

3. Peng and Knowles (2003) studied the effect of priming by asking Asian-American participants to recall experiences that either primed their American or Asian identity and then showing them abstract drawings of physical objects and asking them the extent to which they thought the action of the object was due to the internal properties of the object (e.g., its weight) or contextual factors (e.g., friction).
   a. Independent variable: participants were asked to think of an experience that either made their American or their Asian identity salient.
   b. Dependent variable: how they rated the importance of internal versus external causes.
   c. Finding: those primed with their American identity rated the internal causes as more important than did those primed with their Asian identity.

D. Dispositions: Fixed or Flexible?
   1. Asians use both situations and dispositions to judge people's personalities.
      a. Norenzayan et al. (1999) found that Koreans and Americans rated the importance of personality the same, but Koreans rated situations as being more important than did Americans.
      b. Norenzayan found that although Koreans believe personality is an important dimension, they rate personality as being more changeable than do Americans.
   2. Interdependent people believe that abilities are malleable through the environment and effort (more so than do independent peoples) and that effort can overcome inadequacy.

3. Heine et al. (2001) studied the belief in the value of effort by asking participants to do a creativity task.
   a. Independent variable #1: participants were either Canadian or Japanese.
   b. Independent variable #2: positive or negative feedback.
   c. Dependent variable: whether or not participants continued to work on the task.
   d. Finding: Canadian participants were more likely to continue the task when told they had done well; Japanese participants were more likely to continue the task when told they had done poorly.

VI. Beyond the Internal/External Dimension
   A. Questions beyond the internal/external dimension are asked to gain more nuanced understanding.
   B. People want to understand various aspects of events in order to make their worlds more predictable and seek information about:
      1. A person's traits
      2. The situation itself
      3. A person's intentions
         a. Their desires
         b. Their beliefs

Testing Your Basic Knowledge

ANSWERS TO MULTIPLE-CHOICE QUESTIONS

1. b	14. c
2. c	15. a
3. a	16. b
4. b	17. a
5. a	18. b
6. a	19. b
7. b	20. a
8. a	21. b
9. c	22. c
10. b	23. a
11. b	24. c
12. c	25. a
13. a	

Testing Your In-Depth Understanding

EXAMPLE ANSWER TO THE GUIDED QUESTIONS FOR CRITICAL THINKING EXERCISE #4

1. Ross, Amabile, and Steinmetz (1977) randomly assigned participants to be either questioners or contestants in an experimental paradigm that resembled a game show. An important thing to note is that

everyone involved in the study heard and saw all of the directions (including the random assignment to questioner or contestant role). The questioners were instructed to use any specialized, unique trivia knowledge they had to come up with challenging questions to pose to the contestant. Once the "game show" started, the contestant got most of the questions wrong. After the game show ended, all the participants were asked to rate the general intelligence and knowledge levels of everyone involved. Observers also watched these proceedings (including the instructions) and rated the questioner and contestant.

2. The questioner was given a role-conferred advantage in this scenario because he or she was allowed to come up with the questions. Everyone knows some sort of special knowledge that isn't shared by others (e.g., maybe you are a dancer, football player, Tour de France fan, avid reader of Edgar Allan Poe, biology major, gourmet cook, photographer, etc.—each one of those areas offers great trivia questions like "what is an f/stop?" or "who came in second place in this year's Tour de France?"). Thus, whoever is the questioner probably will look smarter than the contestant, even if he or she really isn't smarter. Observers of the game-show event failed to take this situational factor into account and rated the questioner as being smarter than the contestant. Contestants did the same thing. Questioners, however, had the actor's perspective and knew how hard it was to come up with the trivia questions, how many topics they dismissed because they didn't know enough, and so on. Thus, the questioners did not commit the fundamental attribution error; they rated their own level of knowledge as equal to that of the average college student.

3. Alex Trebek has a role-conferred advantage over Pat Sajak. In his role as host of *Jeopardy,* Trebek has the opportunity to show his knowledge of geography, history, literature, etc. Pat Sajak may very well have the exact same knowledge (or more), but his role as host of *Wheel of Fortune* does not give him the opportunity to display that knowledge. In fact, if anything, Sajak has a role-conferred disadvantage because he has to act excited over letters of the alphabet! According to the fundamental attribution error, however, people will tend to overlook these aspects of Sajak and Trebek's situations and instead just assume that Trebek's knowledge comes from his dispositional intelligence.

4. One attribution I made about my favorite professor in college was that she was very smart. She explained the concepts so clearly and could answer unexpected questions with ease. She gave so many good examples that were not in the textbook and seemed to devise such clever discussion questions. Now that I (your study guide author) am a professor, I have the actor's perspective on being a professor. I receive Instructor's Manuals that have helpful tips for what to include in lectures and ideas for classroom discussions. I also receive multiple copies of textbooks, each of which explains a single concept in a slightly different way and provides different examples to clarify the concept. I also have detailed (if somewhat painful) recollections of all the student questions I was unable to answer when I first started teaching and how I looked up every one of those answers. Those experiences now allow me to generally predict the most typical questions students will ask. Most of all, I have become more comfortable picking and choosing which topics to bring into the classroom. I tend to focus on the topics that are most important in psychology, but also on those topics that I find most interesting and that I have spent the most time thinking about. And I have been considerably humbled in instances where I've been forced to lecture on topics about which, prior to preparing the lecture, I knew virtually nothing. I leave it up to you, then, to translate my "actor's perspective" into a situational explanation for why your favorite professor may appear to be so (dispositionally) intelligent. And why that, sadly, may be an example of the fundamental attribution error. As an aside: Social psychology professors both love and hate this example of the fundamental attribution error. It is a great example, but the consequence of sharing it is that we look less smart! So, given that, what attribution would people make about our motives for sharing this explanation (consider the discounting and augmenting principles)?

CHAPTER 10 | Social Judgment

The goal of this chapter is to discuss the basic principles associated with social judgment. It reviews the way in which schemas can influence what information we attend to, as well as our memory and construal of that information. This chapter seeks to help us understand normal functioning by examining mistakes, a method that has been used by psychologists in many areas of psychology. In particular, the chapter focuses on situations in which we rely too much on quick, intuitive judgments called heuristics. Moreover, the chapter discusses in detail the two most studied heuristics in social psychology (availability and representativeness).

ANNOTATED CHAPTER OUTLINE

After first reading through the chapter quickly, create a comprehensive framework for the information in the chapter by reading the outline below and filling in the missing information. Instead of simply re-copying information from the textbook, try to use your own words wherever possible; you can check your answers against the completed outline in the Answer Key section at the end of the chapter.

I. Why Study Social Judgment
   A. The chapter examines social judgment in general, discussing how people come to make judgments that help them interpret the past, understand the present, and predict the future.
   B. Social stimuli indirectly influence people's behavior through the way they are interpreted and construed.
   C. Social psychologists, like other psychologists, often scrutinize mistakes as a way of understanding how everyday judgment works.

II. The Information Available for Judgment
   A. Biases in Information Presented Firsthand

1. Firsthand information is not filtered through other people, who might slant the facts in a particular direction.
2. Firsthand knowledge may not be accurate because it may be

   _____
   _____
   _____
   _____

3. Pluralistic Ignorance
   a. Pluralistic ignorance can be defined as

   _____
   _____
   _____
   _____

   b. Pluralistic ignorance can lead people to conclude that there is group consensus when there is not and, thus, that they are deviant.
     (1) Examples include gang members who disapprove of brutal initiations; prison guards who sympathize with prisoners.
     (2) Prentice and Miller (1993) found that

   _____
   _____
   _____
   _____

     (3) Schroeder and Prentice (1998) found that an accurate knowledge of peers' views on drinking led to less drinking.
4. Memory Biases
   a. Memory is not a passive recording; rather, it is an active process of construction in which inferences, attitudes, and beliefs can influence what we recall.

b. Research shows that sometimes even the most vivid memories can be inaccurate.
   (1) Flashbulb memories can be defined as

   _____

   _____

   _____

   (2) Neisser and Harsch (1992) found that

   _____

   _____

   _____

c. Beliefs about the stability or change inherent in certain characteristics can influence our memories.
   (1) Goethals and Reckman (1973) asked participants to fill out a questionnaire about busing and then to participate in a group discussion.
      (a) Participants were assigned to a group in which everyone either supported or opposed busing.
      (b) A confederate was present in the group and argued the other side.
      (c) Dependent variable:

      _____

      _____

      _____

      _____

      (d) Findings:

      _____

      _____

      _____

   (2) Conway and Ross (1984) found that

   _____

   _____

   _____

B. Biases in Information Presented Secondhand
   1. Sharpening and Leveling
      a. Sharpening can be defined as

      _____

      _____

      _____

      b. Leveling can be defined as

      _____

      _____

      _____

   2. Secondhand Impressions of Other People
      a. Secondhand accounts tend to lead to more extreme impressions of other people because

      _____

      _____

      _____

      b. Research studies using firsthand and secondhand impressions support this.
         (1) A first-generation participant rates a person on trait dimensions after watching a videotape in which a person gives a description of autobiographical events.
         (2) The first-generation participant records a description (firsthand impression) of the person.
         (3) A second-generation participant listens to the firsthand description and makes more extreme trait judgments (secondhand impression).
   3. Ideological Distortions
      a. Sharpening and leveling are accentuated when there is motivation to slant the story in a particular direction.
      b. People may innocently or deliberately sharpen and level their accounts of events to

      _____

      _____

      _____

   4. Distortion in the Media
      a. A particularly troubling type of distortion is the overrepresentation of violence and crime in the media:
         (1) As represented in the media, 80 percent of all crime is violent, but only 20 percent of crime in real life is violent.
         (2) _____

         _____

         _____

         (3) _____

         _____

         _____

      b. There is a positive correlation between the amount of television a person watches and the fear of being the victim of a crime.
      c. More specific research reveals that this correlation is particularly high in

      _____

      _____

      _____

      _____

5. Perceptual Vigilance and the Asymmetry between Positive and Negative Information
   a. We seem to be more attentive to negative information than positive information.
   b. This may arise from a need to

   _____

   _____

   _____

   _____

III. How Information Is Presented
   A. Order Effects
      1. Hyman and Sheatsley (1950) asked people the same two questions, but half of the participants were asked the questions in one order, and the other half were asked the questions in the reverse order, which changed the results even though the questions themselves did not change.
         a. 36 percent of respondents thought the U.S. should let communist Russian reporters into the country when that question was asked before a question about whether American reporters should be let into Russia.
         b. 73 percent of respondents thought the U.S. should let communist Russian reporters into the U.S. when that question was asked after a question about U.S. reporters being allowed into communist Russia.
      2. Schwarz et al. (1991) found that

         _____

         _____

         _____

      3. The primacy effect can be defined as

         _____

         _____

         _____

      4. The recency effect can be defined as

         _____

         _____

         _____

      5. In a study of order effects, Asch (1946) found that

         _____

         _____

         _____

      6. Order effects may occur for three reasons:
         a. _____

         _____

         _____

   b. _____

   _____

   _____

   _____

   c. _____

   _____

   _____

   B. Framing Effects
      1. The framing effect can be defined as

         _____

         _____

         _____

         _____

      2. Spin Framing
         a. "Spin" involves varying the content of what is presented so as to highlight favored information, as in these examples:
            (1) _____

            _____

            _____

            (2) _____

            _____

            _____

            (3) _____

            _____

            _____

         b. Because it is so easy to spin information, it is important to know who is behind it and to be alert to the exact wording of questions.
      3. Gains and Losses
         a. The Weber-Fechner laws of perception indicate that a fixed amount of something can feel like more or less than it really is, depending on the surrounding circumstances.
            (1) Five pounds can be a really noticeable amount to add to your backpack if you aren't carrying anything else, but will be almost unnoticeable if you already had thirty pounds of books in the backpack and added five more.
            (2) Consider gaining $20 if you had nothing to start with versus gaining $20 if you had $20 to start with; although you are gaining $20 in both instances, you are likely to be more happy if you end up with $20 after starting with nothing.

(3) Consider losing $100 if you had $100 to start with versus losing $100 if you had $1,100 to start with; although you are losing $100 in both instances, chances are you'll be more upset if you end up with nothing rather than $1,000.

b. People's perceptions of loss and gain have implications for risk taking in that they

_____

_____

_____

_____

(1) It is possible to frame an outcome as either a gain or loss, which will affect people's judgments and decisions.

(2) Tversky and Kahneman (1981) presented participants with a set of options regarding how to save 600 people who had contracted a rare disease.

(a) Half the participants compared one option that was framed as definitely saving 200 people to another option that was framed as having a one-third chance of saving 600 people.

(b) Half the participants compared one option that was framed as definitely ending with 400 people dying to another option that was framed as having a one-third chance of no one dying.

(c) Despite the fact that these two groups of people were faced with the exact same options (i.e., 200 people living = 400 people dying, and 600 people living = no one dying), the options were viewed differently by virtue of how they were framed.

(d) Findings:

_____

_____

_____

_____

c. Because welfare to the poor is construed as a direct handout (my money is being given away; I am losing money) and "corporate welfare" is more often distributed via tax breaks (I am not losing anything; the corporations are just paying less in taxes), people are more upset about welfare to the poor than corporate welfare, even though individual taxpayers end up paying higher

taxes to even out the federal budget in both instances.

d. Framing organ donation programs as "opt in" or "opt out" affects donation rates:

_____

_____

_____

_____

IV. Prior Knowledge and Knowledge Structures
A. New information and prior knowledge both affect perceiving and understanding the world.
1. Bottom-up processes can be defined as

_____

_____

_____

_____

2. Top-down processes can be defined as

_____

_____

_____

_____

3. Knowledge structures can be defined as coherent configurations (known as schemas, scripts, frames, prototypes, or personae) in which related information is stored together.

4. A schema can be defined as

_____

_____

_____

_____

B. How Do Schemas Influence Judgment?
1. Attention
a. Because we cannot actively notice and attend to everything in our perceptual field simultaneously, conscious attention selectively allocates cognitive resources to certain elements of our environment and ignores the rest.
b. Simons and Chabris (1999) showed how schemas

_____

_____

_____

_____

2. Inference and Construal
a. Higgins et al. (1977) conducted an experiment in which they examined the effect of priming on evaluation.
(1) Independent variable:

_____

_____

_____

_____

(2) Dependent variable: how participants judged the risk-taking "Donald."
(3) Finding:

_____
_____
_____
_____

b. Information stored in the brain can influence how we construe new information, especially when that information is ambiguous.
3. Memory
a. Because schemas influence attention, they also influence memory and consequently judgments that are made based on remembered information.
b. Cohen (1981) studied the impact of schemas on memory in a study in which participants watched a videotape of a husband and wife having dinner.
(1) Independent variable: participants were told that the woman on the video was a librarian or a waitress.
(2) Dependent variable: how accurately participants remembered various stereotype-consistent versus inconsistent aspects of the scene.
(3) Finding:

_____
_____
_____
_____

b. Information that is consistent with preexisting stereotypes and/or schemas is usually more easily remembered than stereotype-inconsistent information.
(1) Encoding can be defined as

_____
_____
_____

(2) Retrieval can be defined as

_____
_____
_____

(3) Studies show that schemas can influence both encoding and retrieval of information, but the effect on encoding is typically much stronger.
C. How Is Incoming Information Mapped onto Preexisting Schemas?
1. Similarity or Feature Matching

a. The extent to which the current stimulus shares critical features (or "fits with") an existing schema is an important predictor of whether a given schema will be activated.
b. Sometimes a schema can be misapplied because the stimulus shares certain irrelevant, superficial features with the schema.
c. Gilovich (1981) studied the effect of feature matching by presenting students with information about a conflict between two fictitious countries.
(1) Independent variable: participants were primed to either think about World War II (thus invoking a desire to stand up to Hitler-like figures) or the Vietnam War (thus invoking a desire to avoid drawn-out convoluted conflicts).
(2) Dependent variable:

_____
_____
_____
_____

(3) Finding:

_____
_____
_____
_____

2. Expectations
a. Our expectations about what is going to occur in an interaction can activate a schema consistent with that expectation.
b. If the expectation is warranted, this can save much mental energy.
3. Recent Activation
a. If a schema has been used recently, it is more easily activated in subsequent circumstances.
b. Higgins et al. (1977) found that

_____
_____
_____
_____

4. Consciousness of Activation: Necessary or Not?
a. Most research evidence suggests that participants are not aware of the activation of particular schemas and, indeed, may not even need to be aware of the stimuli that lead to such activation.
b. Bargh and Pietromonaco (1982) presented words on a computer screen so quickly that participants could not consciously report what the words were, but this "subliminal" presentation still had an impact.

(1) Independent variable:

_____

_____

_____

(2) Dependent variable:

_____

_____

_____

(3) Finding:

_____

_____

_____

   c. Subliminal can be defined as

_____

_____

_____

_____

V. Reason, Intuition, and Heuristics
  A. Responses to stimuli are guided by two systems of thought: intuition and reason.
    1. Intuition operates quickly and automatically, is based on associations, and performs many operations simultaneously.
    2. Reason (rational thought) is slower and more controlled, is based on rules and deduction, and performs its operations one at a time.
    3. The intuitive system almost always provides a response to a situation, and that response may or may not be overridden by the slower rational thought process. Three possible outcomes of the rational and intuitive systems are:
      a. _____

_____

_____

_____

      b. _____

_____

_____

_____

      c. _____

_____

_____

_____

    4. Heuristics can be defined as

_____

_____

_____

_____

  B. The Availability Heuristic
    1. The availability heuristic can be defined as

_____

_____

2. The implicit logic of the availability heuristic is compelling and sometimes accurate: if we can easily bring lots of examples to mind, there must actually be lots of examples, so a high frequency estimate is warranted.
3. Sometimes certain examples are more easily retrieved than others, making availability a fallible guide.
4. Disentangling Ease of Retrieval from the Amount of Information Retrieved
  a. Ease of recall and number of examples retrieved are not synonymous, but the two interpretations are hard to disentangle.
  b. Schwarz et al. (1991) asked participants to think back to their experiences with being assertive.
    (1) Independent variable #1: one group was asked to list six examples, another twelve examples.
    (2) Independent variable #2: participants were either asked to list examples of when they were assertive or unassertive.
    (3) Dependent variable:

_____

_____

_____

_____

    (4) Finding:

_____

_____

_____

_____

  c. Conclusion: ease of retrieval was a more important influence on judgment than number of instances retrieved.
5. Biased Assessments of Risk
  a. Overreporting of information in the press affects the availability of information.
  b. Excessive news coverage of violent or sensational events has the effect of

_____

_____

_____

_____

6. Biased Estimates of Contributions to Joint Projects
  a. Ross and Sicoly (1979) found in several studies that people overestimate their own efforts in a joint project, presumably because their own efforts are vivid and easy to recall, as in these examples:

(1) _____

_____

_____

(2) _____

_____

_____

b. These results hold true for negative as well as positive outcomes, suggesting it is availability, not simple self-enhancement, that accounts for the biased estimates.

C. The Representativeness Heuristic

1. Biased judgments can arise from false assessments of how representative an individual is of a group category or how common those in the group are in the general population.

a. The representativeness heuristic can be defined as

_____

_____

_____

_____

b. Although people often resemble the prototypical member of their group, and effects often resemble causes, leaning exclusively on similarity judgments to reach likelihood estimates can lead to errors.

c. Base-rate information can be defined as

_____

_____

_____

_____

2. The Resemblance between Members and Categories: Base-Rate Neglect

a. Kahneman and Tversky (1973) conducted a study in which participants had to decide which academic discipline best fit Tom and which discipline he chose to study in graduate school after they read a description of Tom in high school.

(1) Independent variable:

_____

_____

_____

(2) Dependent variable: participant's ratings of nine academic disciplines or ratings of Tom's similarity to students in each discipline.

(3) Finding:

_____

_____

_____

b. Base-rate information is more likely to be considered if it relates to a cause for a behavior, or if the person making the judgment is encouraged to take a broader perspective.

3. The Planning Fallacy

a. The planning fallacy can be defined as

_____

_____

_____

_____

b. Buehler et al. (1994) found that

_____

_____

_____

_____

c. Follow-up research suggests that this effect happens because people are focusing too much on the inside perspective (the project at hand) and not taking the outside perspective (looking at a broader picture, which includes other people doing similar projects and/or their own track record).

4. The Resemblance between Cause and Effect

a. People assume that big effects have big causes and little effects have little causes; in general, they assume that causes will somehow "go with" effects.

b. Examples in health and medicine of erroneous matches between causes and effects are:

(1) _____

_____

_____

(2) _____

_____

_____

(3) _____

_____

_____

(4) Nemeroff and Rozin (1989) found that college students rated the traits of fictitious tribes in line with their perceived diet (those who ate turtle were thought to be generous and good swimmers, while those who ate wild boar were thought to be aggressive and likely to have beards).

c. Astrology or graphology are other examples of conflating cause and effect.

D. The Joint Operation of Availability and Representativeness

1. Illusory correlation can be defined as

_____

_____

_____

_____

a. The representativeness heuristic can make us think two things belong to the same category.

b. This schema can make instances of co-occurrence very noticeable.

c. The availability heuristic translates the ease of coming up with examples into a belief in the frequency of occurrence.

2. Chapman and Chapman (1967) randomly paired pictures drawn by both psychotic patients and graduate students with phony descriptions of the person's supposed mental health symptoms and found that

_____

_____

_____

_____

a. They thought that larger eyes drawn on the person meant that the person was paranoid.

b. They thought that people insecure about their intelligence draw smaller heads.

E. Training in statistics, research methods, psychology, and economics, since it increases the scope and sophistication of rational and deliberate judgment tools, has been shown to reduce many of the kinds of judgment errors discussed in this chapter.

TESTING YOUR BASIC KNOWLEDGE

After studying the information in the chapter by filling in the outline above, test your basic knowledge with the following multiple-choice test. Answers are provided in the Answer Key section at the end of the chapter. If you find that you have gotten an answer wrong, it is important that you understand why it is wrong (as well as understanding why the correct answer is the better choice). Talk with peers, your tutor, or your professor if you need help.

Multiple-Choice Questions

1. Your psychology professor finishes up her lecture and asks if anyone has any questions. No one raises a hand. You were hopelessly confused by the lecture, but assume everyone else must have understood it since no one asked anything. Later, you find out that your friends in the class were also confused but each thought he or she was the only one. Social psychologists would call this confusion a consequence of
   a. availability heuristic.
   b. pluralistic ignorance.
   c. representativeness.

2. Research has verified that vivid "flashbulb memories" are
   a. always incorrect because high emotion distorts memory for past events.
   b. typically highly accurate accounts of events.
   c. sometimes inaccurate.

3. Conway and Ross (1984) asked participants in a study-skill-building program whether or not the program was successful. Most participants said it was very successful and anticipated receiving higher grades. Actual evidence suggested the program was not successful. What is the explanation for this discrepancy?
   a. The participants assumed their skills would improve, and that assumption led them to remember their initial study skills as being worse than they really were.
   b. The actual evidence cannot take into account the role of positive thinking.
   c. The study design was flawed.

4. Amanda told her friends about her first date with Max. In telling the story, she emphasized the most interesting parts, which involved Max's rude table manners (chewing with his mouth open, talking too loud, etc.), and deemphasized the parts that seemed less relevant to her (e.g., Max paid for dinner and held doors open for her). Amanda's friends decide that Max is crude and rude and make a mental note to exclude him from future dinner parties. In her account, Amanda engaged in what behaviors?
   a. sharpening and leveling
   b. generalizing and diminishing
   c. augmenting and discounting

5. Instead of asking the question "should the President of the United States be granted the line item veto," a survey written by a politician who is in favor of the line item veto asks: "should the President of the United States be granted the line item veto in order to eliminate governmental waste?" This technique of asking a leading question is called
   a. leveling.
   b. spin framing.
   c. media distortion.

6. Research reported in this chapter suggests that there is a positive correlation between the amount of television people watch and
   a. the ease with which people can be persuaded by political messages.

b. the amount of money people spend each year on new clothing fashions.

c. perceptions about the likelihood of being a victim of crime.

7. One reason negative feedback may be more salient to us than positive feedback is that
   a. negative feedback may give information about a potential threat.
   b. positive feedback is usually disingenuous.
   c. negative feedback causes a blow to our self-esteem.

8. According to Schwarz et al. (1991), there is a stronger correlation between marital satisfaction and life satisfaction when
   a. the life satisfaction question is asked first.
   b. the marital satisfaction question is asked first.
   c. people are unhappy in their marriages.

9. According to the primacy effect, which of the following people will be rated more favorably: Person A, who is described as being "intelligent, stubborn and lazy," or Person B, who is described as being "stubborn, lazy and intelligent"?
   a. Person A
   b. Person B
   c. Both people will be rated the same.

10. Dr. Doolittle is the director of an animal shelter that suffers an outbreak of a rare disease. The doctor has to choose a treatment to use and asks the staff for advice. The doctor says to Lori, "Treatment Option A will definitely save 100 of our 300 animals, but with Treatment Option B there is a 30 percent chance of saving all the animals." When talking with Teena, the doctor says, "Treatment Option A will lead to the death of 200 of our 300 animals, but Treatment Option B offers a 30 percent chance that no animal will die." According to research by Kahneman and Tversky, which options are Lori and Teena likely to recommend?
    a. Lori will recommend Option A, and Teena will recommend Option B.
    b. Teena will recommend Option A, and Lori will recommend Option B.
    c. Both will recommend Option B.
    d. Both will recommend Option A.

11. Research suggests that sometimes people can forget about even vivid and crazy things that happen in the course of an otherwise ordinary event (e.g., a man in a gorilla suit running through a game of catch). Why?
    a. It is threatening to our self-concepts to deal with unexpected and strange events.
    b. Our schema for the event selectively "tunes" our attention toward expected events and away from unexpected events.

c. The availability heuristic prevents the event from being encoded.

12. Olga just read a story about Donald, who is really confident and independent. Tiffany just read a story about Donald who is an irresponsible, stubborn guy. Both learn that Donald has taken up skydiving. What are their impressions of Donald likely to be?
    a. Tiffany will think Donald is reckless, and Olga will think Donald is adventurous.
    b. Tiffany and Olga will both think Donald is being reckless.
    c. It is impossible to judge from the information given.

13. Daniel, a recovering alcoholic, is interested in dating Stephanie, who is a librarian at an elementary school. He runs into her at a party and observes her for a while—she seems very pretty and nice. Daniel's friend asks if he is sure he wants to date Stephanie, given how she has been drinking beer all night at the party. Try as he might, Daniel can't remember Stephanie drinking beer; he is certain she has been drinking soda all night. What might explain this?
    a. Daniel has sharpened and leveled his recollection of Stephanie.
    b. Daniel's schemas about librarians led him to improperly encode what she was drinking.
    c. Daniel's friend is secretly interested in dating Stephanie himself.

14. Gilovich (1981) conducted a study in which he asked students to read an account of a fictitious conflict between two countries. He then asked the students to indicate the extent to which the United States should intervene in the conflict. Which group of students felt more strongly that the U.S. should stay out of the conflict?
    a. The students who were told the countries involved had no strategic relationship with the U.S.
    b. The students who were primed with reminders of World War II and the evils of Hitler.
    c. The students who were primed with reminders of the protracted Vietnam War.

15. Bargh and Pietromonaco (1982) showed participants words related to hostility so quickly that the words could not be consciously recognized. They found that this presentation of words
    a. did not have any significant impact on the participants' social judgments.
    b. resulted in more hostile judgments about a target person.
    c. led participants to be in a more negative mood after the study.

16. Social psychologists study the mistakes that people make in social judgment
    a. to prevent those mistakes from happening in the future.
    b. to understand how social judgments are generated.
    c. Both A and B are accurate.

17. Many people believe that dying as a consequence of homicide is much more common than dying as a consequence of suicide. One reason for this (incorrect) belief may be the
    a. representativeness heuristic.
    b. availability heuristic.
    c. order effect.

18. Research by Norbert Schwarz and his colleagues (1991) provided strong evidence that the availability heuristic inflates likelihood estimates because of the ease with which examples come to mind, not because of the number of examples that come to mind. How did the Schwarz et al. study determine this?
    a. Participants who were asked to write down six examples of unassertive behaviors judged themselves as being more likely to have a dissociative personality disorder than did those who wrote down twelve examples of unassertive behaviors.
    b. Participants who rated themselves as more assertive were able to generate more examples of assertive behaviors.
    c. Participants who wrote down twelve examples of being assertive believed there was a higher likelihood that they had problems being assertive than those who came up with six examples.

19. Participants read a story about Linda, who was described as a social activist who enjoyed reading books and biographies, frequently traveled, and had strongly held Democratic and pro-choice beliefs. Participants were then asked to indicate which of the following two options was more likely: Option A— Linda was a bank teller; or Option B—Linda was a bank teller and a feminist. Most participants usually chose Option B. Which of the following provides the best explanation?
    a. the representativeness heuristic
    b. the availability heuristic
    c. the planning fallacy

20. In choosing Option B after reading the story about Linda (in question 19), participants were also engaging in which of the following behaviors?
    a. pluralistic ignorance
    b. planning fallacy
    c. ignoring base-rate information

21. John frequently watches *The Sopranos,* a television show that portrays Italian Americans as members of a mob family. John slowly finds himself actually believing the stereotype that many Italian Americans are affiliated with the mob because he keeps noticing real-life examples of Italian-American mobsters. Assuming that an Italian American is actually relatively unlikely to be a member of the mob, which of the following best explains John's beliefs?
    a. representativeness heuristic
    b. illusory correlation
    c. availability heuristic

22. Teenagers often believe that eating greasy potato chips will give them greasy, acne-prone skin. What may account for this erroneous belief?
    a. primacy effect
    b. representativeness heuristic
    c. planning fallacy

23. Sophie confidently asserts that she can finish her final term paper on time, despite having needed extensions for all of her past papers. She may be falling prey to the
    a. planning fallacy.
    b. availability heuristic.
    c. recency effect.

24. Devon and Missy speak with their professor about their relative contributions to a group project. Both are absolutely certain of their own dedication and commitment to the project and both criticize the other for not contributing as much. According to information in this chapter, a smart professor will ask for details about what each young woman did at each stage of the project rather than count on each person's estimated amount of contribution. Why?
    a. because both Devon and Missy can easily retrieve information about their own efforts, but may have a harder time remembering what the other partner did
    b. because both Devon and Missy are trying to get the best grade they can
    c. because the professor is the authority figure

25. Katie goes to her first college party and is surprised to see a beer in everyone's hand. As she takes the beer that is offered to her, she is troubled by the thought of drinking while underage, but experiences pluralistic ignorance while looking around the room at all her underage dorm mates who are also holding beers. This is problematic because
    a. the students at the party may ignore Katie because of the concern and discomfort on her face.
    b. Katie may end up drinking more than she really wants to in an effort to "fit in."
    c. Katie may be rejected by potential friends because of her non-normative attitudes.

Essay Questions

After you have mastered the multiple-choice questions, try testing your basic understanding by thoroughly answering each of the broad essay questions below. Because it is critical that you think through this information on your own, we have not provided any answers to these questions. Your learning and retention of this material will be greatly enhanced if you do one or more of the following to check your answers: carefully review the textbook information; compare your responses to your class lecture notes; talk over your answers with a peer; ask your professor to review your answers or review any information that is unclear to you.

1. What are the ways in which we can make inaccurate social judgments based on firsthand information? What about based on secondhand information?

2. Explain how order effects and framing can change the types of social judgments we make.

3. Describe how schemas influence information processing, giving empirical evidence wherever possible.

4. Define the availability heuristic, give examples and empirical evidence supporting its existence, and discuss the effects that it has on social judgments.

5. Define the representativeness heuristic, give examples and empirical evidence supporting its existence, and discuss the effects that it has on social judgments.

6. Discuss the way in which the availability heuristic and representativeness heuristic can operate together to produce and perpetuate illusory correlations.

TESTING YOUR IN-DEPTH UNDERSTANDING

Test your in-depth understanding of the material by working through the Critical Thinking Exercises provided at the end of each textbook chapter. To maximize this learning opportunity, work together with a tutor, study group, or your professor. Alternatively, write down your thoughts and responses.

Guided questions for one of the exercises are provided below. While there are multiple ways to answer these questions, short answers are given in the Answer Key at the end of the chapter. Note, however, that the valuable part of this exercise is not simply knowing the answer but working with the material to come up with the answer.

Guided Questions for Critical Thinking Exercise #3

Suppose you've had a long run of good luck when a friend asks you, "How are things going?" As soon as you respond,

"Great; life has really been treating me well," you feel a compulsion to say "knock on wood," even though you don't believe in jinxes. Why, according to ideas discussed in this chapter, would someone feel such a compulsion?

1. Review the definitions for the following terms and concepts, all of which could apply to this question: feature-matching activation of schemas, unconscious schema activation, schema-biased retrieval of memories, availability heuristic, illusory correlation, base-rate neglect, representativeness heuristic, sharpening and leveling, asymmetry between positive and negative information, recency effect.

2. Now go back and brainstorm an application for each concept individually to answer the question.

3. Try to weave the individual concepts together, emphasizing how the occurrence of one event can lead to the occurrence of another.

Enhance your understanding of the chapter by thinking about and doing the remaining two Critical Thinking Exercises. Discuss your answers with your peers, study group, tutor, or professor.

Critical Thinking Exercise #1

How successful do you think the United States is in getting people to be organ donors? What is the waiting period, in other words, for patients who urgently need crucial organs such as kidneys or livers? Do you think the United States has an "opt in" program or an "opt out" program?

Critical Thinking Exercise #2

Perhaps the most successful government intervention to increase savings in the United States and in other countries has been the introduction of payroll deduction plans in which a portion of an employee's salary goes directly into an investment account. What ideas introduced in this chapter help to explain why people find it so easy to save through such plans and so difficult to save otherwise?

SOCIAL PSYCHOLOGY IN THE POPULAR MEDIA

You might be interested in the following popular media references, each of which relates in some way to information in this chapter.

Film

Peggy Sue Got Married (1986; directed by Francis Ford Coppola; starring Kathleen Turner and Nicolas Cage). A middle-aged woman has a heart attack and, while hanging between life and death, finds herself transported back in time as a teenaged girl again. She meets her future husband all over again and is determined to avoid making what she thinks were mistakes from the first time around. Through her journey, she discovers that her memories of events were not all accurate and that she didn't have all the information she needed to make accurate social judgments. Not an award winner, but a fun film that explores the idea of how accurate our past memories are, and whether or not we really would do things differently if we had the chance.

Books

Myers, David. (2002). *Intuition: Its Powers and Perils.* New Haven, CT: Yale University Press. Social psychologist David Meyers examines the extremes of intuitive thinking. From the front flap of the hardcover edition: "How reliable is our intuition? How much should we depend on gut-level instinct rather than rational analysis when we play the stock market, choose a mate, hire an employee, or assess our own abilities? In this engaging and accessible book, David G. Myers shows us that while intuition can provide us with useful—and often amazing—insights, it can also dangerously mislead us."

Wilson, Timothy (2002). *Strangers to Ourselves: Discovering the Adaptive Unconscious.* Cambridge, MA: Harvard University/Belknap Press. Chapter 10 briefly discusses the way in which even unconsciously held or activated schemas can influence our social judgments. Social psychologist Timothy Wilson reviews in much greater depth current theories on what the unconscious is, how it works, and how we can access it.

Web Site

Vision Cognition Lab—http://viscog.beckman.uiuc.edu/grafs/demos/11.html. These are videos created by Daniel J. Simons to demonstrate the role of schemas. According to the Web site, they are "videos and demos that reveal the limits of our ability to perceive, remember, and make sense of our visual world." Click on the second video listed on the page and see if you can identify all nine of the intentional changes in subtle features during the film. While it won't have anything as dramatic as the Simons and Chabris (1999) gorilla appear in the frame, it does note the difficulty of seeing change in an interaction for which our schemas dictate that there should not be any change. Explore the page for more examples of "blindness" to changes due to different causes. (Must have QuickTime and a fast Internet connection.)

ANSWER KEY INFORMATION

Annotated Chapter Outline

I. Why Study Social Judgment
   A. The chapter examines social judgment in general, discussing how people come to make judgments that help them interpret the past, understand the present, and predict the future.
   B. Social stimuli indirectly influence people's behavior through the way they are interpreted and construed.
   C. Social psychologists, like other psychologists, often scrutinize mistakes as a way of understanding how everyday judgment works.

II. The Information Available for Judgment
   A. Biases in Information Presented Firsthand
      1. Firsthand information is not filtered through other people, who might slant the facts in a particular direction.
      2. Firsthand knowledge may not be accurate because it may be biased by inattention, misconstrual, or unrepresentative experiences.
      3. Pluralistic Ignorance
         a. Pluralistic ignorance can be defined as misperception of a group norm that results from observing people who are acting at variance with their private beliefs out of a concern for the social consequences—behavior that reinforces the erroneous norm.
         b. Pluralistic ignorance can lead people to conclude that there is group consensus when there is not and, thus, that they are deviant.
            (1) Examples include gang members who disapprove of brutal initiations; prison guards who sympathize with prisoners.
            (2) Prentice and Miller (1993) found that Princeton college students rated themselves as being (privately) less comfortable with excessive drinking than they believed others were.
            (3) Schroeder and Prentice (1998) found that an accurate knowledge of peers' views on drinking led to less drinking.
      4. Memory Biases
         a. Memory is not a passive recording; rather, it is an active process of construction in which inferences, attitudes, and beliefs can influence what we recall.
         b. Research shows that sometimes even the most vivid memories can be inaccurate.
            (1) Flashbulb memories can be defined as vivid recollections of the moment one

learned some dramatic, emotionally charged news.

(2) Neisser and Harsch (1992) found that people's recollections of the space shuttle *Challenger* explosion the day after it happened and two and a half years later were often dramatically different accounts.

c. Beliefs about the stability or change inherent in certain characteristics can influence our memories.

(1) Goethals and Reckman (1973) asked participants to fill out a questionnaire about busing and then to participate in a group discussion.

   (a) Participants were assigned to a group in which everyone either supported or opposed busing.

   (b) A confederate was present in the group and argued the other side.

   (c) Dependent variable: participants' attitudes toward busing after the discussion.

   (d) Findings: participants' attitudes toward busing changed as a consequence of the confederate's arguments, and their recollection of their previous attitudes were now inaccurate and biased in the direction of their new attitudes.

(2) Conway and Ross (1984) found that college students who had participated in a study skills program inaccurately recalled their initial study skills as being worse than they really were and, thus, inaccurately thought the program had improved their skills.

B. Biases in Information Presented Secondhand

1. Sharpening and Leveling

   a. Sharpening can be defined as emphasizing important or more interesting elements in telling a story to someone else.

   b. Leveling can be defined as eliminating or deemphasizing seemingly less important details when telling a story to someone else.

2. Secondhand Impressions of Other People

   a. Secondhand accounts tend to lead to more extreme impressions of the people because people tend to sharpen dispositional information and level situational information, failing to mention the influence of extenuating circumstances.

   b. Research studies using firsthand and secondhand impressions support this.

      (1) A first-generation participant rates a person on trait dimensions after watching a videotape in which a person gives a description of autobiographical events.

      (2) The first-generation participant records a description (firsthand impression) of the person.

      (3) A second-generation participant listens to the firsthand description and makes more extreme trait judgments (secondhand impression).

3. Ideological Distortions

   a. Sharpening and leveling are accentuated when there is motivation to slant the story in a particular direction.

   b. People may innocently or deliberately sharpen and level their accounts of events to support their own beliefs or ideals.

4. Distortion in the Media

   a. A particularly troubling type of distortion is the overrepresentation of violence and crime in the media:

      (1) As represented in the media, 80 percent of all crime is violent, but only 20 percent of crime in real life is violent.

      (2) News coverage of crime remains steady even in the face of actual increases and decreases in the crime rate.

      (3) The murder rate in the U.S. dropped by one-third from 1990–1998 while news coverage of murders increased by over 400 percent.

   b. There is a positive correlation between the amount of television a person watches and the fear of being the victim of a crime.

   c. More specific research reveals that this correlation is particularly true in high-crime areas.

5. Perceptual Vigilance and the Asymmetry between Positive and Negative Information

   a. We seem to be more attentive to negative information than positive information.

   b. This may arise from a need to be more vigilant for potential threats than potential benefits.

III. How Information Is Presented
   A. Order Effects
      1. Hyman and Sheatsley (1950) asked people the same two questions, but half of the participants were asked the questions in one order, and the other half were asked the questions in the reverse order, which changed the results even though the questions themselves did not change.
         a. 36 percent of respondents thought the U.S. should let communist Russian reporters into the country when that question was asked before a question about whether American reporters should be let into Russia.
         b. 73 percent of respondents thought the U.S. should let communist Russian reporters into the U.S. when that question was asked after a question about U.S. reporters being allowed into communist Russia.
      2. Schwarz et al. (1991) found that marital satisfaction and life satisfaction were highly correlated when respondents answered the two questions in that order, but they were less highly correlated when respondents answered the broader question about general life satisfaction first.
      3. The primacy effect can be defined as the disproportionate influence on judgment of information presented first in a body of evidence.
      4. The recency effect can be defined as the disproportionate influence on judgment of information presented last in a body of evidence.
      5. In a study of order effects, Asch (1946) found that participants rated a person more favorably if he or she was described as intelligent, industrious, impulsive, critical, stubborn, and envious than if he or she was described with the traits in the opposite order—envious, stubborn, critical, impulsive, industrious.
      6. Order effects may occur for three reasons:
         a. We feel pressure to be consistent with previous responses.
         b. We have information-processing limitations.
            (1) We may pay more attention to information presented first and lose focus with later information, leading to the primacy effect.
            (2) The most recent information may be easier to remember, leading to the recency effect.
         c. Initial information may change our construals of later information.
   B. Framing Effects
      1. The framing effect can be defined as the influence on judgment resulting from the way information is presented, including the order of presentation.
      2. Spin Framing
         a. "Spin" involves varying the content of what is presented so as to highlight favored information, as in these examples:
            (1) Advertisers spin to support the products' greatest strengths.
            (2) Politicians spin to highlight their most popular positions.
            (3) Pollsters can spin to get the results they want (e.g., leading questions).
         b. Because it is so easy to spin information, it is important to know who is behind it and to be alert to the exact wording of questions.
      3. Gains and Losses
         a. The Weber-Fechner laws of perception indicate that a fixed amount of something can feel like more or less than it really is, depending on the surrounding circumstances.
            (1) Five pounds can be a really noticeable amount to add to your backpack if you aren't carrying anything else, but will be almost unnoticeable if you already had thirty pounds of books in the backpack and added five more.
            (2) Consider gaining $20 if you had nothing to start with versus gaining $20 if you had $20 to start with; although you are gaining $20 in both instances, you are likely to be more happy if you end up with $20 after starting with nothing.
            (3) Consider losing $100 if you had $100 to start with versus losing $100 if you had $1,100 to start with; although you are losing $100 in both instances, chances are you'll be more upset if you end up with nothing rather than $1,000.
         b. People's perceptions of loss and gain have implications for risk taking in that they tend to be scared to take a risk in order to add to what they already have, but relatively more eager to take a risk if it means avoiding the loss of something.
            (1) It is possible to frame an outcome as either a gain or loss, which will affect people's judgments and decisions.

(2) Tversky and Kahneman (1981) presented participants with a set of options regarding how to save 600 people who had contracted a rare disease.

    (a) Half the participants compared one option that was framed as definitely saving 200 people to another option that was framed as having a one-third chance of saving 600 people.

    (b) Half the participants compared one option that was framed as definitely ending with 400 people dying to another option that was framed as having a one-third chance of no one dying.

    (c) Despite the fact that these two groups of people were faced with the exact same options (i.e., 200 people living = 400 people dying, and 600 people living = no one dying), the options were viewed differently by virtue of how they were framed.

    (d) Findings: 72 percent of the first group wanted to definitely save 200 people given the dismal one-third chance of saving everyone; 78 percent of the second group wanted to take the one-third chance that no one would die, given the depressing option of definitely having 400 people die.

c. Because welfare to the poor is construed as a direct handout (my money is being given away; I am losing money) and "corporate welfare" is more often distributed via tax breaks (I am not losing anything; the corporations are just paying less in taxes), people are more upset about welfare to the poor than corporate welfare, even though individual taxpayers end up paying higher taxes to even out the federal budget in both instances.

d. Framing organ donation programs as "opt in" or "opt out" affects donation rates: countries that have an organ donation program that automatically enrolls you unless you "opt out" have a 90 percent participation rate versus programs that require you to "opt in" to be an organ donor, which have a 20 percent participation rate.

IV. Prior Knowledge and Knowledge Structures

  A. New information and prior knowledge both affect perceiving and understanding the world.

    1. Bottom-up processes can be defined as "data-driven" mental processing in which one takes in and forms conclusions on the basis of the stimuli encountered in one's experience.

    2. Top-down processes can be defined as "theory-driven" mental processing in which one filters and interprets new information in light of preexisting knowledge and expectations.

    3. Knowledge structures can be defined as coherent configurations (known as schemas, scripts, frames, prototypes, or personae) in which related information is stored together.

    4. A schema can be defined as a knowledge structure consisting of any organized body of stored information.

  B. How Do Schemas Influence Judgment?

    1. Attention

      a. Because we cannot actively notice and attend to everything in our perceptual field simultaneously, conscious attention selectively allocates cognitive resources to certain elements of our environment and ignores the rest.

      b. Simons and Chabris (1999) showed how schemas influence our attention by noting that only one-half of their participants watching a videotaped game of "catch" with a basketball remembered seeing an out-of-place feature: a person in a gorilla costume strolling through the action.

    2. Inference and Construal

      a. Higgins et al. (1977) conducted an experiment in which they examined the effect of priming on evaluation.

        (1) Independent variable: participants were either primed with words relating to self-confidence and adventurousness or with words relating to recklessness and conceit.

        (2) Dependent variable: how participants judged the risk-taking "Donald."

        (3) Finding: those primed with adventurous concepts rated Donald more favorably than those primed with reckless concepts.

      b. Information stored in the brain can influence how we construe new information, especially when that information is ambiguous.

3. Memory
   a. Because schemas influence attention, they also influence memory and consequently judgments that are made based on remembered information.
   b. Cohen (1981) studied the impact of schemas on memory in a study in which participants watched a videotape of a husband and wife having dinner.
      (1) Independent variable: participants were told that the woman on the video was a librarian or a waitress.
      (2) Dependent variable: how accurately participants remembered various stereotype-consistent versus inconsistent aspects of the scene.
      (3) Finding: people told that the woman was a librarian were more likely to remember items consistent with the stereotype of a librarian, and people told that she was a waitress were more likely to remember items consistent with that stereotype.
   b. Information that is consistent with preexisting stereotypes and/or schemas is usually more easily remembered than stereotype-inconsistent information.
      (1) Encoding can be defined as filing information away in memory based on what is attended to and the initial interpretation of the information.
      (2) Retrieval can be defined as the extraction of information from memory.
      (3) Studies show that schemas can influence both encoding and retrieval of information, but the effect on encoding is typically much stronger.

C. How Is Incoming Information Mapped onto Preexisting Schemas?
   1. Similarity or Feature Matching
      a. The extent to which the current stimulus shares critical features (or "fits with") an existing schema is an important predictor of whether a given schema will be activated.
      b. Sometimes a schema can be misapplied because the stimulus shares certain irrelevant, superficial features with the schema.
      c. Gilovich (1981) studied the effect of feature matching by presenting students with information about a conflict between two fictitious countries.
         (1) Independent variable: participants were primed to either think about World War II (thus invoking a desire to stand up to Hitler-like figures) or the Vietnam War (thus invoking a desire to avoid drawn-out convoluted conflicts).
         (2) Dependent variable: degree of U.S. military intervention that was recommended.
         (3) Finding: participants primed with World War II recommended stronger military intervention than those primed with the Vietnam War.
   2. Expectations
      a. Our expectations about what is going to occur in an interaction can activate a schema consistent with that expectation.
      b. If the expectation is warranted, this can save much mental energy.
   3. Recent Activation
      a. If a schema has been used recently, it is more easily activated in subsequent circumstances.
      b. Higgins et al. (1977) found that recent activation with appealing trait adjectives led to more favorable impressions of Donald.
   4. Consciousness of Activation: Necessary or Not?
      a. Most research evidence suggests that participants are not aware of the activation of particular schemas and, indeed, may not even need to be aware of the stimuli that lead to such activation.
      b. Bargh and Pietromonaco (1982) presented words on a computer screen so quickly that participants could not consciously report what the words were, but this "subliminal" presentation still had an impact.
         (1) Independent variable: some participants saw mainly hostile words and some saw mainly neutral words.
         (2) Dependent variable: how participants rated a person after reading a paragraph about this person's moderately hostile behavior.
         (3) Finding: participants primed with hostile words rated the person more negatively than those primed with neutral words.
      c. Subliminal can be defined as below the threshold of conscious awareness.

V. Reason, Intuition, and Heuristics
  A. Responses to stimuli are guided by two systems of thought: intuition and reason.
     1. Intuition operates quickly and automatically, is based on associations, and performs many operations simultaneously.
     2. Reason (rational thought) is slower and more controlled, is based on rules and deduction, and performs its operations one at a time.
     3. The intuitive system almost always provides a response to a situation, and that response may or may not be overridden by the slower rational thought process. Three possible outcomes of the rational and intuitive systems are:
        a. Reason and intuition can agree.
        b. Reason and intuition can disagree.
        c. The intuitive response may be accepted before the rational system develops an answer.
     4. Heuristics can be defined as intuitive mental operations that allow us to make a variety of judgments quickly and efficiently.
  B. The Availability Heuristic
     1. The availability heuristic can be defined as the process whereby judgments of frequency or probability are based on the ease with which pertinent instances are brought to mind.
     2. The implicit logic of the availability heuristic is compelling and sometimes accurate: if we can easily bring lots of examples to mind, there must actually be lots of examples, so a high frequency estimate is warranted.
     3. Sometimes certain examples are more easily retrieved than others, making availability a fallible guide.
     4. Disentangling Ease of Retrieval from the Amount of Information Retrieved
        a. Ease of recall and number of examples retrieved are not synonymous, but the two interpretations are hard to disentangle.
        b. Schwarz et al. (1991) asked participants to think back to their experiences with being assertive.
           (1) Independent variable #1: one group was asked to list six examples, another twelve examples.
           (2) Independent variable #2: participants were either asked to list examples of when they were assertive or unassertive.
           (3) Dependent variable: self-ratings of assertiveness.
           (4) Finding: despite the fact that people in the twelve-example condition had

more examples of being assertive or unassertive, it was difficult to come up with twelve examples; thus, people in the six-example condition rated themselves as more assertive than people in the twelve-example condition; the same pattern was found for ratings of low assertiveness, with people in the six-example condition rating themselves as less assertive than people in the twelve-example condition.
        c. Conclusion: ease of retrieval was a more important influence on judgment than number of instances retrieved.
     5. Biased Assessments of Risk
        a. Overreporting of information in the press affects the availability of information.
        b. Excessive news coverage of violent or sensational events has the effect of making such events come to mind with greater ease, thus leading to an overestimation of their likelihood.
     6. Biased Estimates of Contributions to Joint Projects
        a. Ross and Sicoly (1979) found in several studies that people overestimate their own efforts in a joint project, presumably because their own efforts are vivid and easy to recall, as in these examples:
           (1) Conversation partners each gave themselves more credit than their partner for contributing to the conversation.
           (2) Each partner in a married couple took over 50 percent of the credit for doing housework, maintaining the social calendar, starting arguments, and so on.
        b. These results hold true for negative as well as positive outcomes, suggesting it is availability, not simple self-enhancement, that accounts for the biased estimates.
  C. The Representativeness Heuristic
     1. Biased judgments can arise from false assessments of how representative an individual is of a group category or how common those in the group are in the general population.
        a. The representativeness heuristic can be defined as the process whereby judgments of likelihood are based on assessments of similarity between individuals and group prototypes, or between cause and effect.

b. Although people often resemble the prototypical member of their group, and effects often resemble causes, leaning exclusively on similarity judgments to reach likelihood estimates can lead to errors.

c. Base-rate information can be defined as information about the relative frequency of events or of members of different categories in the population.

2. The Resemblance between Members and Categories: Base-Rate Neglect

   a. Kahneman and Tversky (1973) conducted a study in which participants had to decide which academic discipline best fit Tom and which discipline he chose to study in graduate school after they read a description of Tom in high school.

     (1) Independent variable: participants either rated how similar Tom was to a student in each of nine academic disciplines, how likely it was that Tom chose to study in one of those disciplines, or (those not shown the description of Tom) the percentage of all graduate students studying in each of the nine areas.

     (2) Dependent variable: participant's ratings of nine academic disciplines or ratings of Tom's similarity to students in each discipline.

     (3) Finding: the ratings for which discipline Tom chose to study were almost identical to the ratings for which type of student Tom most strongly resembled; base-rate information about how many students there actually are in each discipline had relatively no influence on the ratings of Tom's similarity to prototypical students in the discipline or whether Tom chose to study in that field.

   b. Base-rate information is more likely to be considered if it relates to a cause for a behavior, or if the person making the judgment is encouraged to take a broader perspective.

3. The Planning Fallacy

   a. The planning fallacy can be defined as the tendency for people to be unrealistically optimistic about how quickly they can complete a project.

   b. Buehler et al. (1994) found that fewer than one-third of honors thesis students finished their theses by the deadline they had estimated, and fewer than one-half finished by a deadline they had estimated if "everything went as poorly as it possibly could."

   c. Follow-up research suggests that this effect happens because people are focusing too much on the inside perspective (the project at hand) and not taking the outside perspective (looking at a broader picture, which includes other people doing similar projects and/or their own track record).

4. The Resemblance between Cause and Effect

   a. People assume that big effects have big causes and little effects have little causes; in general, they assume that causes will somehow "go with" effects.

   b. Examples in health and medicine of erroneous matches between causes and effects are:

     (1) In ancient China, people with vision problems were fed ground-up bats because people believed bats had excellent vision.

     (2) Early Western physicians prescribed the lungs of a fox (known for endurance) for asthmatics.

     (3) Today people think greasy potato chips contribute to greasy skin and acne.

     (4) Nemeroff and Rozin (1989) found that college students rated the traits of fictitious tribes in line with their perceived diet (those who ate turtle were thought to be generous and good swimmers, while those who ate wild boar were thought to be aggressive and likely to have beards).

   c. Astrology or graphology are other examples of conflating cause and effect.

D. The Joint Operation of Availability and Representativeness

1. Illusory correlation can be defined as the belief that two variables are correlated when in fact they are not.

   a. The representativeness heuristic can make us think two things belong to the same category.

   b. This schema can make instances of co-occurrence very noticeable.

   c. The availability heuristic translates the ease of coming up with examples into a belief in the frequency of occurrence.

2. Chapman and Chapman (1967) randomly paired pictures drawn by both psychotic patients and graduate students with phony descriptions of the person's supposed mental health symptoms and found that untrained college undergraduates came to believe in the same relationships that trained clinical psychologists saw.
   a. They thought that larger eyes drawn on the person meant that the person was paranoid.
   b. They thought that people insecure about their intelligence draw smaller heads.
E. Training in statistics, research methods, psychology, and economics, since it increases the scope and sophistication of rational and deliberate judgment tools, has been shown to reduce many of the kinds of judgment errors discussed in this chapter.

Testing Your Basic Knowledge

ANSWERS TO MULTIPLE-CHOICE QUESTIONS

1. b	14. c
2. c	15. b
3. a	16. c
4. a	17. b
5. b	18. c
6. c	19. a
7. a	20. c
8. b	21. b
9. a	22. b
10. a	23. a
11. b	24. a
12. a	25. b
13. b	

Testing Your In-Depth Understanding

EXAMPLE ANSWER TO THE GUIDED QUESTIONS FOR CRITICAL THINKING EXERCISE #3

1. Use your textbook and other sections of this study guide chapter to review each of the concepts.

2. Feature-matching activation of schemas: even though you don't believe in jinxes, if you have an awareness of them (which most college-aged students in American culture certainly do, from horror films if from no other source), saying that "things are great" may activate that schema.

Unconscious schema activation: the rich, elaborated web of jinx-related schema information may be activated consciously or unconsciously.

Schema-biased retrieval of memories: a jinx schema may lead you to remember events that are consistent with the schema (times when you said "things are great" only to have everything fall apart a moment later).

Availability heuristic: the ease with which jinx-consistent examples come to mind will influence your estimate of the likelihood of a "jinx" happening to you.

Illusory correlation: you may come to falsely link together your saying "things are great" and having bad luck happen to you.

Base-rate neglect: you may fail to keep accurate notes on how often you say "things are great" versus "things are bad" and how often each response is followed by the opposite turn of events.

Representativeness heuristic: because saying "things are great" is highly similar to the prototypical "famous last words" category of events, you may incorrectly worry that this time will fall into that category.

Sharpening and leveling: in recalling past times you said "things are great," you may sharpen interesting and remarkable details (e.g., bad events after saying that phrase) and level out details that would soften that picture (e.g., you said "things are great" but also you predicted some problems, or the bad turn of events actually happened weeks after your pronouncement that all was well).

Asymmetry between positive and negative information: you may be more inclined to remember when events take a turn for the worse.

Recency effect: if this type of "jinx" happened to you or someone you know recently, you may be more likely to recall it in this instance and have that recollection influence your judgment.

3. Use the snippets above to craft a coherent, interlinked answer for yourself. To get you started, consider the following: Your "jinx" schema may be (even initially unconsciously) activated by the similarity that your saying "things are great" bears to the popular cultural belief in jinxes. Once this schema is activated, all sorts of memory and judgment processes are influenced by the schema. You are more likely to attend to events that are consistent with that schema and thus to remember those events. With such a schema activated, it may be easy to bring examples of jinxes to mind, thus leading to the availability heuristic. Continue, trying to interlace the concepts together (e.g., how do representativeness and availability work together to produce illusory correlation?)

CHAPTER 11 | Stereotyping, Prejudice, and Discrimination

The goal of this chapter is to present the core social psychological information relating to how and why people hold stereotypes, feel prejudice, and engage in discrimination. The chapter breaks the research into three major categories: an economic (conflict over resources) perspective, a motivational (seeking self-esteem) perspective, and a cognitive (preserving cognitive resources but accentuating faulty reasoning and information distortion) perspective. The chapter concludes with a brief discussion of two prominent areas of the stigma literature: attributional ambiguity and stereotype threat.

ANNOTATED CHAPTER OUTLINE

After first reading through the chapter quickly, create a comprehensive framework for the information in the chapter by reading the outline below and filling in the missing information. Instead of simply re-copying information from the textbook, try to use your own words wherever possible; you can check your answers against the completed outline in the Answer Key section at the end of the chapter.

I. Characterizing Intergroup Bias
  A. Stereotypes can be defined as

  _____
  _____
  _____

   1. Some stereotypes may or may not have a kernel of truth, but the biggest concern is over inaccurate stereotypical beliefs that can lead to prejudice and discrimination.
   2. Stereotypes respresent the cognitive or belief component of ingroup/outgroup relations.

  B. Prejudice can be defined as

  _____
  _____
  _____
  _____

   1. Prejudice involves prejudgment of others because they belong to a particular category.
   2. Prejudice represents the attitudinal or affective component of ingroup/outgroup relations.
  C. Discrimination can be defined as

  _____
  _____
  _____
  _____

   1. Discrimination represents the behavioral component of ingroup/outgroup relations.
   2. Discrimination involves negative behavior toward someone, not because of his own character or behavior, but simply because he is identified as being part of a group.
  D. Typically stereotypes, prejudice, and discrimination are all present together, but they can exist separately—civil rights laws in the U.S. have served to prevent discrimination, even in cases where prejudiced attitudes still exist.
  E. Modern Racism and Sexism
   1. Blatant racism has (arguably) mostly disappeared in the United States, but it has been replaced by a more subtle type of racism.
   2. Modern (symbolic) racism can be defined as

  _____
  _____
  _____
  _____

3. Modern racism reflects a conflict between rejecting blatantly racist beliefs but still holding animosity fueled by the belief, whether correct or not, that blacks (for example) are undermining American self-reliance and family values (e.g., via affirmative action, welfare, or violent activity).

4. Gaertner and Dovidio (1986) suggest that many Americans have unconscious and unacknowledged prejudice toward minority groups that will only emerge in their behavior when suitable nondiscriminatory rationalization is available.

    a. Gaertner and Dovidio (1977) conducted a study on modern racism in which they put white participants in a position to provide medical assistance to another person.

       (1) Independent variable #1:

       _____

       _____

       _____

       (2) Independent variable #2:

       _____

       _____

       _____

       (3) Dependent variable:

       _____

       _____

       _____

       (4) Finding:

       _____

       _____

       _____

    b. Hodson et al. (2002) conducted a study in which they had white participants rate differentially qualified black and white applicants to college.

       (1) Independent variable #1: whether the participant was prejudiced or unprejudiced.

       (2) Independent variable #2: whether the college applicant was strongly qualified, weakly qualified, or ambiguously qualified.

       (3) Independent variable #3: whether the college applicant was black or white.

       (4) Dependent variable: how favorably participants rated the applicant.

       (5) Finding:

       _____

       _____

_____

5. Benevolent Racism and Sexism

    a. Benevolent sexism is a subjectively favorable, chivalrous ideology that offers protection and affection to women who embrace traditional gender roles.

    b. Hostile sexism is

       _____

       _____

       _____

       _____

    c. "Ambivalent" or benevolent racism and sexism are resistant to change because:

       (1) _____

       _____

       _____

       _____

       (2) _____

       _____

       _____

       _____

6. Measures to Assess True Attitudes

    a. Self-report surveys of people's prejudiced beliefs should not be fully trusted because

       _____

       _____

       _____

    b. The Implicit Association Test (IAT)

       (1) The implicit association test (IAT) is

       _____

       _____

       _____

       (2) The test uses reaction times to assess nonconscious beliefs, comparing one's speed at associating whites (for example) with good things and blacks with bad things and vice versa.

       (3) Participants who have taken the test on the Web have shown these results:

           (a) _____

           _____

           _____

           (b) _____

           _____

           _____

           (c) _____

           _____

           _____

(4) Some researchers question whether associations indicated from reaction times to press computer keys can predict discriminatory behavior and actual prejudicial beliefs (as opposed to an awareness of the cultural stereotypes).

    (a) Phelps et al. (2000) did a brain-imaging study that

_____

_____

_____

_____

    (b) McConnell and Leibold (2001) found that

_____

_____

_____

_____

c. Priming and Implicit Prejudice

    (1) Priming can be defined as

_____

_____

_____

_____

    (2) Measures of prejudice look at how quickly a person identifies a positive versus a negative word after being primed to think about members of a minority versus majority group.

    (3) Many research studies have found that people who would deny explicit prejudice seem to have negative associations with minority group primes.

II. The Economic Perspective

  A. Realistic Group Conflict Theory

    1. Realistic group conflict theory can be defined as

_____

_____

_____

_____

    a. The theory predicts that prejudice and discrimination will increase under conditions of economic difficulty.

    b. It also predicts that prejudice and discrimination will be strongest among groups that stand to lose the most from another group's economic advance.

    c. Ethnocentrism can be defined as

_____

_____

_____

2. The Robbers Cave Experiment: Sherif et al. (1961) took twenty-two "average" and similar fifth-grade boys to a two-week summer camp.

    a. Phase One: the boys were divided into two groups, and each group was unaware of the other group's presence; the boys engaged in ordinary camp activities designed to promote group cohesion.

    b. Phase Two: the two groups were brought together to compete against one another in a five-day tournament, leading to the following behaviors:

      (1) _____

_____

_____

      (2) _____

_____

_____

      (3) _____

_____

_____

    c. Phase Three: Reducing Intergroup Conflict through Superordinate Goals

      (1) Simply having the boys in contact with one another in noncompetitive environments did nothing to reduce the intergroup hostility.

      (2) The researchers contrived crises that could only be resolved through the cooperation of the two groups:

        (a) Moving a truck that broke down by pulling it with a rope.

        (b) Inspecting a long water-pipe system after the water supply to the camp was disrupted.

      (3) Superordinate goals can be defined as

_____

_____

_____

      (4) The boys' experiences with superordinate goals rather quickly reduced intergroup hostility and eventually prompted friendships between the members of the two groups.

  B. Evaluating the Economic Perspective

    1. The economic perspective explains the success of integrating blacks with whites in the

military because of the salient superordinate goals.

2. Integration in colleges and universities has been successful, but it has not been as much of a success as integration in the military.
   a. Intergroup contact is often limited to the classroom, while students self-segregate based on race or ethnicity in dorms, dining halls, and even fields of study.
   b. There is not a salient sense of cooperation or superordinate goals.
3. A weakness in this perspective is that

   _____
   _____
   _____
   _____

III. The Motivational Perspective
   A. The Minimal Group Paradigm
      1. The minimal group paradigm can be defined as

         _____
         _____
         _____
         _____

      2. In the paradigm, participants are divided into two groups supposedly based on their responses on a meaningless task, such as estimating dots on a screen ("overestimators" versus "underestimators"), and then are asked to choose point allocations that can either maximize the absolute gain (more points) for the ingroup or maximize the relative gain for the ingroup (fewer overall points but more points than for the outgroup).
      3. Numerous studies show that people are interested in maximizing the ingroup's relative standing above the outgroup, even if it means a smaller overall payoff.
   B. Social Identity Theory
      1. Tajfel and Turner's social identity theory can be defined as

         _____
         _____
         _____
         _____

      2. Boosting the Status of One's Ingroup: people do what they can to boost the standing of an ingroup, as this potentially boosts their own self-esteem.
         a. Research suggests

            _____
            _____
            _____
            _____

   b. Other research shows

      _____
      _____
      _____
      _____

3. Basking in reflected glory can be defined as

   _____
   _____
   _____
   _____

   a. Cialdini et al. (1976) found that college students wore their school colors more often after their football team won a game than after it lost.
   b. Inclusive pronouns like "we" were used more often after a win, while pronouns like "they" were used more often after a loss.
   C. Frustration-Aggression Theory
      1. Frustration-aggression theory can be defined as

         _____
         _____
         _____
         _____

      2. From Generalized to Targeted Aggression
         a. When we cannot aggress against the actual source of our frustration, we may lash out against a weak, vulnerable, or "safe" target (like a member of a stigmatized group).
         b. Hovland and Sears (1940) found that

            _____
            _____
            _____
            _____

         c. Hepworth and West (1988) found that

            _____
            _____
            _____
            _____

      3. Bolstering Self-Esteem
         a. Fein and Spencer (1997) conducted a study that showed that people will tend to stereotype and exhibit prejudice when their self-esteem is threatened.
            (1) Independent variable #1:

               _____
               _____
               _____

            (2) Independent variable #2:

               _____
               _____
               _____
               _____

(3) Dependent variable: evaluations of the job applicant.
(4) Finding:

_____

_____

_____

_____

b. Sinclair and Kunda (1999) also conducted a study to see if derogating people in outgroups bolsters participants' self-esteem.
(1) Independent variable #1:

_____

_____

_____

(2) Independent variable #2: whether the doctor delivering the feedback was white or black.
(3) Dependent variable: speed at recognizing words associated with the black stereotype or with the medical profession.
(4) Finding:

_____

_____

_____

_____

D. Evaluating the Motivational Perspective
1. The motivational perspective does not pinpoint which groups will be the target of intergroup hostility and conflict.
2. Two strengths of the perspective are:
a. _____

_____

_____

b. _____

_____

_____

_____

IV. The Cognitive Perspective
A. A core tenet of this perspective is that stereotypes provide simplifying categories that help us organize and deal with the huge volume of social stimuli present in everyday life.
B. Stereotypes and Conservation of Mental Reserves
1. People are more likely to use stereotypes when they are overloaded, tired, or mentally taxed, and need a shortcut.
2. Bodenhausen (1990) demonstrated that people are more likely to fall back on stereotypes when they lack cognitive energy during the low point in their circadian rhythm:
a. _____

_____

_____

_____

b. _____

_____

_____

_____

3. Macrae et al. (1994) demonstrated that people using stereotypes have greater cognitive resources available for other tasks.
a. Independent variable: whether participants were given a stereotype that went along with a list of traits or just the list of traits.
b. Dependent variable: how well participants remembered both the traits and details about a secondary audio message (a lecture on Indonesia).
c. Finding:

_____

_____

_____

_____

C. Construal Processes and Distortions
1. Stereotypes can lead us to misconstrue information, thus confirming and perpetuating those stereotypes.
2. Accentuation of Ingroup Similarity and Outgroup Difference
a. Merely dividing a group of people into two categories will lead people to see less variability within each group and more variability between the two groups.
b. Research demonstrates that people will assume their attitudes are more similar to fellow ingroup members than to those of outgroup members, even when the groups are created based on minimal and meaningless criteria.
3. The Outgroup Homogeneity Effect
a. The outgroup homogeneity effect can be defined as

_____

_____

_____

_____

b. Quattrone and Jones (1980) examined the outgroup homogeneity effect by asking participants to watch a videotape of students making a decision and then asking them what percentage of students from the same group would make the same decision.
(1) Independent variable #1: whether the participant was from Rutgers or rival Princeton.

(2) Independent variable #2:

_____

_____

_____

_____

(3) Dependent variable: ratings of the percentage of students at the same university who would make the same decision as seen on tape.

(4) Finding:

_____

_____

_____

_____

c. Reasons for the outgroup homogeneity effect:

(1) _____

_____

_____

_____

(2) _____

_____

_____

_____

4. Biased Information Processing

a. Stereotype-consistent behavior is more likely to be noticed and remembered, but stereotype-inconsistent information is likely to be ignored, dismissed, or forgotten as not meaningful.

b. Duncan (1976 conducted a study demonstrating that stereotypes can change the way the exact same action is interpreted.

(1) Independent variable:

_____

_____

_____

(2) Dependent variable: ratings of the hostility intended in the shove.

(3) Finding:

_____

_____

_____

c. Stone et al. (1997) conducted a study on the effects of secondhand information on information processing.

(1) Independent variable: whether the target basketball player was portrayed as white or black.

(2) Dependent variable: how participants characterized the player's performance after listening to an audio play-by-play.

(3) Finding:

_____

_____

_____

_____

5. Self-Fulfilling Prophecies

a. A self-fulfilling prophecy can be defined as

_____

_____

_____

(1) Social psychologists define "self-fulfilling prophecy" as involving two people: a target and a perceiver.

(2) You should think of this as a three-step process:

(a) The perceiver has an expectation about the target.

(b) The perceiver's behavior reflects that expectation, thus treating the target in a certain way.

(c) The target responds to the perceiver's behavior and thus appears to provide evidence confirming the original expectation.

b. Word et al. (1974) conducted a study illustrating the role of self-fulfilling prophecies in providing (false) confirming evidence for stereotypes.

(1) First phase of experiment: independent judges monitored job interviews and found that

_____

_____

_____

(2) Second phase of the experiment:

(a) White interviewers were trained to interview white applicants using either the open and interested style or the closed and disinterested style.

(b) When the independent judges evaluated the white applicants, they rated

_____

_____

_____

_____

(3) The self-fulfilling prophecy was demonstrated, as shown by these findings:

(a) Perceivers expected black applicants to be less qualified.

(b) Perceivers behaved in a way that reflected this expectation.

(c) Targets treated in a negative manner actually did make a worse impression.

(d) The bad impression was caused by the interviewer's behavior, not by an actual lack of qualifications.

6. Distinctiveness and Illusory Correlations

a. An illusory correlation can be defined as

_____

_____

_____

_____

b. Because we attend to distinctive or unusual events, they may become overrepresented in our memories, and we may tend to always associate them with each other.

c. The occurrence of two distinctive events close in time can lead to paired distinctiveness, which is

_____

_____

_____

_____

(1) Minority members are distinctive, as are negative behaviors (being relatively less frequent than positive behaviors); thus, an illusory correlation can create or perpetuate negative stereotypes about minority group members.

(2) Hamilton and Gifford (1976) illustrated the effect of paired distinctiveness by having participants view slides describing positive or negative behaviors initiated by different members of fictitious groups, and then estimate how often such behaviors were associated with each group.

(a) More of the behaviors were done by members of Group A than Group B, making Group B the minority group and hence distinctive.

(b) More of the behaviors were positive than negative, making negative behaviors distinctive.

(c) Findings:

_____

_____

_____

(d) When the positive behaviors were made distinctive, participants rated Group B more positively and overestimated the number of positive behaviors performed by members of Group B, demonstrating that the researchers had created paired distinctiveness in the study.

D. Immunity to Disconfirmation: stereotypes persist even in the face of disconfirming evidence.

1. Anyone who behaves contrary to the stereotype is set aside as an exception.

2. Confirming evidence is accepted at face value, but disconfirming evidence is critically analyzed and discounted.

a. Confirming behavior is attributed to dispositions, while disconfirming behavior is attributed to situational factors.

b. Maass et al. (1989) found that

_____

_____

_____

_____

E. Automatic and Controlled Processing

1. Devine (1989) started a line of research that demonstrated that an important distinction between a "prejudiced" and "non-prejudiced" person is the extent to which he or she consciously resists unconsciously held stereotypes.

a. Automatic processes can be defined as

_____

_____

_____

_____

b. Controlled processes can be defined as

_____

_____

_____

_____

c. Devine's first study found that

_____

_____

_____

_____

d. Devine's second study found that

_____

_____

_____

_____

2. Subsequent research notes that it is more difficult to activate automatic, negative

stereotypes regarding stigmatized groups among non-prejudiced participants (though still possible) than among prejudiced participants.

3. Supporting the automatic/controlled distinctions, Cunningham et al. (2004) found that participants have greater amygdala activation in response to black compared to white faces when the faces are presented for 30 milliseconds, but do not show this difference when the faces are presented for 535 milliseconds (although seeing black faces does cause more activity in the prefrontal cortex, indicating efforts to control and regulate automatic responses).

4. Dovidio et al. (2002) found that

_____

_____

_____

_____

5. Payne (2001) found that

_____

_____

_____

_____

6. Judd et al. (2004) extended this study to show that African-American faces facilitated recognition of both negative stereotypical stimuli (weapons) and positive stereotypical stimuli (e.g., athletic equipment) associated with African Americans, but did not facilitate recognition of non-stereotypical stimuli.

7. Cornell et al. (2002) found that

_____

_____

_____

_____

F. Evaluating the Cognitive Perspective
   1. Some argue that since automatic stereotype activation is so brief in lab studies and so quickly dissipates, it does not have real-world implications or address causes of prejudice and discrimination.
   2. Even brief activations can have immediate, tragic consequences, or can begin processes that will have lasting effects.

V. Being a Member of a Stigmatized Group
   A. Attributional Ambiguity
      1. Members of stigmatized groups always have to weigh the possibility that the outcomes they are receiving are due to prejudicial reactions to their group membership (either discrimination

or excessive behaviors designed to prove a lack of prejudice).
   2. Crocker et al. (1991) illustrated this effect in a study often called the "blinds up/blinds down" study.
      a. Independent variable #1: whether the participant was white or black.
      b. Independent variable #2: whether the blinds over a two-way mirror were up (allowing an evaluator to see the participant and her race) or down (preventing an evaluator from identifying the participant's race).
      c. Independent variable #3: positive or negative feedback.
      d. Dependent variable:

_____

_____

_____

_____

      e. Finding:

_____

_____

_____

_____

B. Stereotype Threat
   1. Steele's stereotype threat can be defined as

_____

_____

_____

_____

   2. Steele argues that the mere existence of the stereotype puts pressure on the stigmatized group members to make sure their performance disconfirms the stereotype, and that this extra pressure can, ironically, lead to poorer performance compared to those who do not face such extra pressure.
   3. Spencer et al. (1999) examined the stereotype that women perform less well in math than do men.
      a. Independent variable #1: participants were either male or female.
      b. Independent variable #2:

_____

_____

_____

_____

      c. Dependent variable: performance on a challenging math test.
      d. Finding:

_____

_____

_____

_____

4. Inzlicht and Ben-Zeev (2000) found that

_____

_____

_____

5. Steele and Aronson (1995) looked at the stereotype that blacks are less intellectually competent than whites.
   a. Independent variable #1: participants were either white or black.
   b. Independent variable #2:

   _____

   _____

   _____

   c. Dependent variable: performance on the test.
   d. Finding:

   _____

   _____

   _____

6. Aronson et al. (1999) found that white male math performance deteriorated when participants were reminded of the stereotype of Asian superiority in math.

7. Stone et al. (1999) examined golf putting skill and accuracy in light of differing stereotypes about white and black athletes.
   a, Independent variable #1: participants were either white or black.
   b. Independent variable #2:

   _____

   _____

   _____

   c. Dependent variable: performance on the task.
   d. Finding:

   _____

   _____

   _____

8. Although any group for whom there is a stereotype may experience stereotype threat, Steele's research suggests that the global stereotype that blacks are intellectually inferior to other racial groups is particularly dangerous and has particularly far-reaching academic consequences (leading to disidentification with academic pursuits and producing negative economic consequences for them as adults).

TESTING YOUR BASIC KNOWLEDGE

After studying the information in the chapter by filling in the outline above, test your basic knowledge with the following multiple-choice test. Answers are provided in the Answer Key section at the end of the chapter. If you find that you have gotten an answer wrong, it is important that you understand why it is wrong (as well as understanding why the correct answer is the better choice). Talk with peers, your tutor, or your professor if you need help.

Multiple-Choice Questions

1. Believing that women with blonde hair are dumb is an example of _____, while refusing to hire a woman with blonde hair is an example of

   _____.
   a. prejudice; a stereotype.
   b. a stereotype; discrimination.
   c. discrimination; a stereotype.

2. Ben doesn't harbor overtly negative feelings about minorities from Group X. But he does believe that members of Group X threaten the American value of self-reliance because he thinks welfare recipients are mostly from Group X. This is an example of
   a. modern racism.
   b. old-fashioned racism.
   c. a self-fulfilling prophecy.

3. Research indicates that in today's modern world, the average person will engage in discrimination
   a. only when there is a suitable "disguise" or rationalization for such behavior.
   b. never.
   c. only if they are clinging to the beliefs of old-fashioned racism.

4. Benevolent sexism refers to
   a. the positive stereotypes associated with women (e.g., they are nurturing).
   b. the offer of protection for those women who conform to traditional gender roles.
   c. an acceptance of feminism.

5. Tests like the Implicit Association Test (IAT) are preferred to self-report measures of prejudice because
   a. modern racism is more subtle than old-fashioned racism.
   b. self-report measures may not reflect unconsciously held prejudice.
   c. Both A and B are accurate.

6. The blue group is in competition with the green group for a million-dollar prize. The group that wins gets the million dollars, but also fame and future opportunities to

make more money. As the competition unfolds, hostility between the groups grows. The blue group members come to see the green group members as mean and stupid; the green group members see members of the blue group as petty and weak. What is the *best* explanation for the emergence of these feelings?
a. stereotype threat
b. social identity theory
c. realistic group conflict theory

7. Sam is a member of a club called the Eagles, and John is a member of a rival club called the Rattlers. They end up rooming together at summer camp and initially hate each other. Which of the following is the best strategy to get them to like each other more?
a. have them work together to carry a heavy canoe from the lake to the storage shed
b. have them sit down together and talk about their reasons for not liking each other
c. pair them up at the same table at meal times so that they have as much contact as possible

8. Integrating African Americans into the United States military is regarded as a largely successful endeavor. Which of the following was most responsible for this success?
a. social identity theory
b. superordinate goals
c. the reduction of old-fashioned prejudice

9. A professor breaks a group of twenty students into two groups of ten on the basis of the color of the students' shirts ("cool" spectrum colors like blue versus "warm" spectrum colors like red). These students then engage in a class activity in which points are awarded. According to the research on minimal groups,
a. members of both groups will try to get more points for their own group compared to points earned by the opposing group.
b. members of both groups will seek to earn the most points for their own group without regard for the points earned by the opposing group.
c. members of both groups will exert minimal effort in the activity because the groups are meaningless.

10. According to social identity theory, self esteem results from evaluations of
a. personal identity.
b. other people's views of our personal identity.
c. group memberships and personal identity.

11. One Friday night, the local football team wins their game and Colin is heard to say, "we played such a great game!!" The next Friday, the team loses. If Colin's identity is boosted by basking in reflected glory, which of the following is most likely to be his response after the loss?

a. "They lost this one."
b. "We played such a bad game, but we'll do better next time."
c. "We are a good team; we just had a bad night."

12. In the old South, Hovland and Sears found that as the economy grew worse, the number of lynchings of black men increased. This is best explained by
a. social identity theory
b. stereotype threat
c. frustration-aggression theory

13. Fein and Spencer (1997) told half of their participants that they had failed an intelligence test, while they gave positive feedback to the other half. In a subsequent task,
a. participants reacted more quickly to positive words when they were primed first with African-American faces.
b. participants rated a Jewish job candidate more negatively than a candidate who was not a member of a stigmatized group.
c. participants aggressed against another participant who was made up to look like the experimenter.

14. Sinclair and Kunda (1999) found that, after being criticized by an African-American doctor, research participants seemed to
a. think of the doctor more in terms of a derogatory black stereotype.
b. think of the doctor more in terms of his medical expertise.
c. take the advice to change their poor health habits more seriously.

15. The cognitive perspective argues that, to a certain extent, stereotyping is beneficial because
a. people appreciate knowing their place in society.
b. without the order and status hierarchies created by stereotyping, society would be a mess.
c. it helps people organize and cope with the huge amount of social stimuli they face everyday.

16. Bodenhausen (1990) found that "morning people" were more likely to engage in stereotyping at night and "night people" were more likely to engage in stereotyping in the morning. Which of the following is the best explanation?
a. People rely on stereotyping when they have insufficient cognitive resources to fully process a stimulus.
b. People are more likely to engage in stereotyping when they are engaging in a social judgment task while in a grumpy mood.
c. People feel a greater sense of self-esteem threat when asked to make social judgments during non-optimal hours.

17. Julie believes that all the students at a rival college are conservative Republicans. At her own college, however, Julie knows that there is a mix of liberals, conservatives, Democrats, and Republicans. Julie may be experiencing
    a. stereotype threat.
    b. the outgroup homogeneity effect.
    c. a self-fulfilling prophecy.

18. In a classic study, Duncan (1976) had participants watch a videotape of a discussion between two men. At one point in the tape, one of the men shoved the other's shoulder. What were the findings of this study?
    a. Black participants viewed the shove as being hostile, while white participants thought it was harmless.
    b. All participants viewed the shove as being hostile when it was committed by a black versus a white actor.
    c. Participants rated the person doing the shoving more favorably than the person being shoved.

19. Nick is convinced that women are just not smart enough to work at a high-power financial firm, but he grudgingly agrees to include women in his interview process. When he interviews Maria, he perceives her behavior as awkward and nervous. When he interviews Dan, he feels a real connection and ease throughout their conversation. If the self-fulfilling prophecy was operating, what might explain the difference between Maria and Dan's interviews?
    a. Dan was more successful at believing in himself, believing that he could give a good interview.
    b. Nick treated Maria poorly because of his expectations, and Maria responded to that behavior.
    c. Maria's nervousness undermined her confidence, and she ended up giving the bad interview she feared she would.

20. Billy lives in Sameville, U.S.A., where there are very few instances of crime and very few immigrants. On the news one night, Billy hears a story about a Russian immigrant who robbed a local jewelry store. Billy now assumes that Russian immigrants are thieves. This may be a consequence of
    a. illusory correlation.
    b. self-fulfilling prophecy.
    c. social identity theory.

21. When faced with evidence that disconfirms a stereotype, people tend to
    a. change their stereotypes to fit the new information.
    b. re-consider the legitimacy of all of their stereotypes.
    c. forget or diminish the legitimacy of the disconfirming information.

22. According to Devine's work on automatic versus controlled processes, the primary difference between someone who is "high" in prejudice and someone who is "low" in prejudice is
    a. the extent to which automatically activated stereotypes are consciously controlled.
    b. how many stereotypes are activated in a reaction-time task.
    c. Both A and B are accurate.

23. Studies using brain-imaging technology have found that
    a. exposure to white faces leads to greater activation in the amygdala.
    b. different parts of the brain are activated, depending on whether the exposure to the stereotyped group happens at a conscious or unconscious level.
    c. people who are high in prejudice show more activity in their prefrontal cortex in response to black faces.

24. Attributional ambiguity refers to
    a. ambiguity experienced by modern racists as they attempt to understand the reasons for their actions toward a member of a stigmatized group.
    b. the lack of confidence members of a stereotyped group feel as they attempt to disconfirm a stereotype.
    c. the uncertainty members of a stigmatized group face in deciding whether a given outcome was due to individual achievement or due to prejudicial responses.

25. Claude Steele and his colleagues conducted a study in which black and white students took a test that was described as being diagnostic of intelligence. Half of these students indicated their race on a demographic form immediately before the test. The other half did not. According to the logic of stereotype threat theory, what is the most likely consequence of this subtle manipulation?
    a. Black students did not do as well on the test as white students, especially when race was primed.
    b. White students did more poorly on the test than black students when race was primed.
    c. Black students did more poorly on the test because it was described as being diagnostic.

Essay Questions

After you have mastered the multiple-choice questions, try testing your basic understanding by thoroughly answering each of the broad essay questions below. Because it is critical that you think through this information on your own, we have not provided any answers to these questions. Your learning and retention of this material will be greatly enhanced if you do one or more of the following to check your answers: carefully review the textbook information; compare your responses to your class lecture notes; talk over your answers with a peer; ask your professor to review your answers or review any information that is unclear to you.

1. Define and distinguish stereotyping, prejudice, and discrimination. Also, explain the way in which modern racism differs from "old-fashioned" racism and describe at least one study providing empirical support.

2. Define and distinguish benevolent sexism from hostile sexism.

3. Review the basic logic of the IAT and priming techniques to measure prejudice, and explain why these techniques are often preferable to self-report measures.

4. Define realistic conflict theory and describe the way in which the Robbers Cave experiment illustrates this theory. Be sure to describe the role of superordinate goals in reducing prejudice.

5. Describe at least two different ways in which we are motivated to show prejudice or to discriminate. Provide empirical studies illustrating each point.

6. What is the central message of the cognitive perspective on stereotyping? In what ways do stereotypes influence our construals?

7. Distinguish between automatic and controlled processing, and present research studies that illustrate the significance of this distinction for stereotyping.

8. Describe attributional ambiguity and stereotype threat, describing at least one study that illustrates each.

TESTING YOUR IN-DEPTH UNDERSTANDING

Test your in-depth understanding of the material by working through the Critical Thinking Exercises provided at the end of each textbook chapter. To maximize this learning opportunity, work together with a tutor, study group, or your professor. Alternatively, write down your thoughts and responses.

Guided questions for one of the exercises are provided below. The "answers" provided in the Answer Key section are not hard and fast "correct" responses. You are encouraged to talk over your responses with your classmates, tutor, and/or professor, keeping in mind that there may not be just one "correct" answer to each question. That being said, however, there are ways to answer these questions that indicate more or less reflective thought and more or less understanding and integration of the material from the chapter.

Guided Questions for Critical Thinking Exercise #1

Anthony Greenwald and Mazarin Banaji have made the implicit association test (IAT) available on the Web for anyone to try—and you should try it. It's illuminating. Web versions of the IAT are available to assess your implicit prejudice toward blacks and whites, young and old, men and women, and even George W. Bush versus Franklin Delano Roosevelt! Go to https://implicit.harvard.edu/implicit

1. Take one of the IAT tests. What is your opinion of the test? Do you think people could deliberately manipulate their results in the way that they deliberately manipulate answers to a self-report survey?

2. Why would black participants score as having more favorable views toward whites?

3. Are there any other explanations for why a black participant would score in a way that the IAT researchers would interpret as "prejudiced"?

4. The textbook discusses the black/white IAT at length, describing the way in which it indicates implicit prejudice toward blacks. Do you think that the young/old IAT results would indicate prejudice toward old people and the men/women IAT would indicate prejudice toward women, or do those IATs seem somehow different?

5. Why would a person's scores on the IAT matter? What "real life" outcomes might an IAT score predict?

Enhance your understanding of the chapter by thinking about and doing the remaining two Critical Thinking Exercises. Discuss your answers with your peers, study group, tutor, or professor.

Critical Thinking Exercise #2

It has been said (in this chapter, in fact) that race relations have progressed more smoothly in the U.S. military than on college campuses, and that this pattern fits with findings from the Robbers Cave experiment. In what other areas might we expect (and you have observed) race relations to progress rather smoothly? Do these examples also fit with the lessons of the Robbers Cave study? In what other areas might we expect (and you might have observed) race relations to progress less smoothly?

Critical Thinking Exercise #3

Close your eyes and try to picture in detail an aggressive act on the part of a construction worker. Briefly write down what you imagined. Now close your eyes and try to picture an aggressive act on the part of a housewife. Write down that as well. Are there any differences between the two episodes you imagined? If so, why are they different, and does this have anything to say about your stereotypes of construction workers and housewives?

SOCIAL PSYCHOLOGY IN THE POPULAR MEDIA

You might be interested in the following popular media references, each of which relates in some way to information in this chapter.

Film

Crash (2004; directed by Paul Haggis; starring Don Cheadle, Matt Dillon, Sandra Bullock, Brendan Fraser, Tony Danza, Jennifer Esposito, Terrence Howard, Thandie Newton, among others). A fascinating film that weaves together separate stories of life in Los Angeles that together paint a complex and thought-provoking picture of modern-day race relations and social identity concerns. Very highly recommended. Rated R.

Songs

Tracy Chapman. (1985). "Across the Lines." From the album *Tracy Chapman*. A moving song musing about the damage done across race lines during a riot and the sharp line that exists between blacks and whites in American towns.

They Might Be Giants. (1990). "Your Racist Friend." From the album *Flood*. They Might Be Giants was known in the 1990s for funny, offbeat music and lyrics that are sometimes hard to interpret. But this song includes very lucid lyrics in which the narrator discusses how he is leaving a party because he can't listen to "you and your racist friend."

Book

Suskind, Ron (1998). *A Hope in the Unseen: An American Odyssey from the Inner City to the Ivy League*. New York: Broadway Books. A fascinating true narrative by Pulitzer Prize–winning journalist Ron Suskind. Suskind follows Cedric Jennings, a high-achieving African-American male, as he finishes high school in a tough Washington, D.C., neighborhood and begins college in the radically different environment of Brown University. The book does a beautiful job of capturing the multiple pressures of class, race, and adolescence, as it explores Cedric's thoughts and feelings about his circumstances. Highly recommended.

Web Site

Implicit Association Test—<u>https://implicit.harvard.edu/ implicit</u>. As discussed directly in the chapter, this is the Web site for the IAT.

ANSWER KEY

Annotated Chapter Outline

I. Characterizing Intergroup Bias
   A. Stereotypes can be defined as beliefs about attributes that are thought to be characteristic of members of particular groups.
      1. Some stereotypes may or may not have a kernel of truth, but the biggest concern is over inaccurate stereotypical beliefs that can lead to prejudice and discrimination.
      2. Stereotypes respresent the cognitive or belief component of ingroup/outgroup relations.
   B. Prejudice can be defined as a negative attitude or affective response toward a certain group and its individual members.
      1. Prejudice involves prejudgment of others because they belong to a particular category.
      2. Prejudice represents the attitudinal or affective component of ingroup/outgroup relations.
   C. Discrimination can be defined as unfair treatment of members of a particular group based on their membership in that group.
      1. Discrimination represents the behavioral component of ingroup/outgroup relations.
      2. Discrimination involves negative behavior toward someone, not because of his own character or behavior, but simply because he is identified as being part of a group.
   D. Typically stereotypes, prejudice, and discrimination are all present together, but they can exist separately—civil rights laws in the U.S. have served to prevent discrimination, even in cases where prejudiced attitudes still exist.
   E. Modern Racism and Sexism
      1. Blatant racism has (arguably) mostly disappeared in the United States, but it has been replaced by a more subtle type of racism.
      2. Modern (symbolic) racism can be defined as prejudice directed at other racial groups that exists alongside a rejection of explicitly racist beliefs.
      3. Modern racism reflects a conflict between rejecting blatantly racist beliefs but still holding animosity fueled by the belief, whether correct or not, that blacks (for example) are

undermining American self-reliance and family values (e.g., via affirmative action, welfare, or violent activity).

4. Gaertner and Dovidio (1986) suggest that many Americans have unconscious and unacknowledged prejudice toward minority groups that will only emerge in their behavior when suitable nondiscriminatory rationalization is available.

   a. Gaertner and Dovidio (1977) conducted a study on modern racism in which they put white participants in a position to provide medical assistance to another person.
      (1) Independent variable #1: the person needing assistance was either white or black.
      (2) Independent variable #2: the participant thought he or she was the only one who could help or was one of several people who could help.
      (3) Dependent variable: frequency with which participants offered help.
      (4) Finding: participants were less likely to help the black victim than the white victim when they could rationalize this prejudice by suggesting that they assumed someone else would help; when they were the only one available participants were actually slightly more likely to help the black victim.

   b. Hodson et al. (2002) conducted a study in which they had white participants rate differentially qualified black and white applicants to college.
      (1) Independent variable #1: whether the participant was prejudiced or unprejudiced.
      (2) Independent variable #2: whether the college applicant was strongly qualified, weakly qualified, or ambiguously qualified.
      (3) Independent variable #3: whether the college applicant was black or white.
      (4) Dependent variable: how favorably participants rated the applicant.
      (5) Finding: prejudiced and unprejudiced participants rated highly qualified applicants the same and weakly qualified applicants the same, but prejudiced and unprejudiced participants diverged in their ratings of ambiguously qualified black applicants; the prejudiced participants rated the ambiguously qualified black applicants less favorably than did the unprejudiced participants; the prejudiced participants justified their response by saying that the areas the black applicant failed in were especially important.

5. Benevolent Racism and Sexism
   a. Benevolent sexism is a subjectively favorable, chivalrous ideology that offers protection and affection to women who embrace traditional gender roles.
   b. Hostile sexism is an antipathy toward women who are viewed as usurping men's power.
   c. "Ambivalent" or benevolent racism and sexism are resistant to change because:
      (1) People can claim it isn't prejudice since it is "positive."
      (2) People who don't fulfill the stereotypes are disparaged while people who do fulfill the stereotypes are treated positively, and such reactions inhibit efforts toward equality.

6. Measures to Assess True Attitudes
   a. Self-report surveys of people's prejudiced beliefs should not be fully trusted because people may be hesitant to reveal prejudice and/or people may not actually be aware of their prejudiced feelings.
   b. The Implicit Association Test (IAT)
      (1) The implicit association test (IAT) is a technique for revealing nonconscious prejudices toward particular groups.
      (2) The test uses reaction times to assess nonconscious beliefs, comparing one's speed at associating whites (for example) with good things and blacks with bad things and vice versa.
      (3) Participants who have taken the test on the Web have shown these results:
         (a) Both young and older respondents show a strong preference for young people over older people.
         (b) Two-thirds of all white respondents show a strong-to-moderate preference for whites over blacks.
         (c) Half of all black respondents show some preference for white faces.
      (4) Some researchers question whether associations indicated from reaction times to press computer keys can predict discriminatory behavior and actual prejudicial beliefs (as opposed to an awareness of the cultural stereotypes).

(a) Phelps et al. (2000) did a brain-imaging study that found that IAT scores, but not self-report measures of prejudice, correlated with the amount of amgydala activation (indicating emotional evaluation) when viewing white and black faces.

(b) McConnell and Leibold (2001) found that IAT scores predicted how white participants interacted with and treated white versus black experimenters.

c. Priming and Implicit Prejudice

(1) Priming can be defined as a procedure used to increase the accessibility of a concept or schema (for example, a stereotype).

(2) Measures of prejudice look at how quickly a person identifies a positive versus a negative word after being primed to think about members of a minority versus majority group.

(3) Many research studies have found that people who would deny explicit prejudice seem to have negative associations with minority group primes.

II. The Economic Perspective

A. Realistic Group Conflict Theory

1. Realistic group conflict theory can be defined as a theory that group conflict, prejudice, and discrimination are likely to arise over competition between groups for limited desired resources.

a. The theory predicts that prejudice and discrimination will increase under conditions of economic difficulty.

b. It also predicts that prejudice and discrimination will be strongest among groups that stand to lose the most from another group's economic advance.

c. Ethnocentrism can be defined as glorifying one's own group while vilifying other groups.

2. The Robbers Cave Experiment: Sherif et al. (1961) took twenty-two "average" and similar fifth-grade boys to a two-week summer camp.

a. Phase One: the boys were divided into two groups, and each group was unaware of the other group's presence; the boys engaged in ordinary camp activities designed to promote group cohesion.

b. Phase Two: the two groups were brought together to compete against one another in a five-day tournament, leading to the following behaviors:

(1) The two groups almost immediately hurled insults at one another, threatened fights, engaged in raids, stole the other group's flag, and engaged in other expressions of intergroup hostility.

(2) Within each group, leadership shifted to whichever members were athletic enough to win competitions and/or to those members who were most aggressive toward the other group.

(3) Individual boys showed ingroup favoritism—assuming good outcomes for their fellow group members.

c. Phase Three: Reducing Intergroup Conflict through Superordinate Goals

(1) Simply having the boys in contact with one another in noncompetitive environments did nothing to reduce the intergroup hostility.

(2) The researchers contrived crises that could only be resolved through the cooperation of the two groups:

(a) Moving a truck that broke down by pulling it with a rope.

(b) Inspecting a long water-pipe system after the water supply to the camp was disrupted.

(3) Superordinate goals can be defined as goals that transcend the interests of one individual group, and that can be achieved more readily by two or more groups working together.

(4) The boys' experiences with superordinate goals rather quickly reduced intergroup hostility and eventually prompted friendships between the members of the two groups.

B. Evaluating the Economic Perspective

1. The economic perspective explains the success of integrating blacks with whites in the military because of the salient superordinate goals.

2. Integration in colleges and universities has been successful, but it has not been as much of a success as integration in the military.

a. Intergroup contact is often limited to the classroom, while students self-segregate based on race or ethnicity in dorms, dining halls, and even fields of study.

    b. There is not a salient sense of cooperation or superordinate goals.

  3. A weakness in this perspective is that it fails to explain which groupings will be perceived as the source of economic competition when things are not as clear as they were in the Robbers Cave study.

III. The Motivational Perspective

  A. The Minimal Group Paradigm

    1. The minimal group paradigm can be defined as an experimental setup in which researchers create groups based on arbitrary and seemingly meaningless criteria, and then examine how the members of these "minimal groups" are inclined to behave toward one another.

    2. In the paradigm, participants are divided into two groups supposedly based on their responses on a meaningless task, such as estimating dots on a screen ("overestimators" versus "underestimators"), and then are asked to choose point allocations that can either maximize the absolute gain (more points) for the ingroup or maximize the relative gain for the ingroup (fewer overall points but more points than for the outgroup).

    3. Numerous studies show that people are interested in maximizing the ingroup's relative standing above the outgroup, even if it means a smaller overall payoff.

  B. Social Identity Theory

    1. Tajfel and Turner's social identity theory can be defined as a theory that a person's self-concept and self-esteem not only derive from personal identity and accomplishments, but from the status and accomplishments of the various groups to which the person belongs.

    2. Boosting the Status of One's Ingroup: people do what they can to boost the standing of an ingroup, as this potentially boosts their own self-esteem.

    a. Research suggests that participants given an opportunity to display ingroup favoritism report higher self-esteem than those not given the opportunity.

    b. Other research shows that people who have especially strong ingroup pride are more likely to engage in ingroup favoritism and to react to criticism of the group as if it were criticism of the self.

    3. Basking in reflected glory can be defined as the tendency to take pride in the accomplishments

of those with whom we are in some way associated (even if it is only weakly), as when fans identify with a winning team.

    a. Cialdini et al. (1976) found that college students wore their school colors more often after their football team won a game than after it lost.

    b. Inclusive pronouns like "we" were used more often to refer to wins, while pronouns like "they" were used more often for losses.

  C. Frustration-Aggression Theory

    1. Frustration-aggression theory can be defined as the theory that frustration leads to aggression.

    2. From Generalized to Targeted Aggression

    a. When we cannot aggress against the actual source of our frustration, we may lash out against a weak, vulnerable, or "safe" target (like a member of a stigmatized group).

    b. Hovland and Sears (1940) found a negative correlation between the price of cotton and the number of lynchings of black men in the South.

    c. Hepworth and West (1988) showed that all lynchings (of blacks and whites) increased with lower cotton prices, but that the relationship was stronger for lynchings of blacks.

    3. Bolstering Self-Esteem

    a. Fein and Spencer (1997) conducted a study that showed that people will tend to stereotype and exhibit prejudice when their self-esteem is threatened.

      (1) Independent variable #1: positive or negative feedback of the participant on an intelligence test.

      (2) Independent variable #2: whether the job applicant was Jewish or not.

      (3) Dependent variable: evaluations of the job applicant.

      (4) Finding: participants who received negative feedback evaluated the Jewish target more negatively than the non-Jewish target, and ended up with higher self-esteem at the end of the study.

    b. Sinclair and Kunda (1999) also conducted a study to see if derogating people in outgroups bolsters participants' self-esteem.

      (1) Independent variable #1: praise or criticism of the participant.

      (2) Independent variable #2: whether the doctor delivering the feedback was white or black.

(3) Dependent variable: speed at recognizing words associated with the black stereotype or with the medical profession.

(4) Finding: participants who received criticism from the black doctor showed an activation of words associated with black stereotypes, while participants who received praise from the black doctor showed an activation of words associated with the medical profession.

D. Evaluating the Motivational Perspective

1. The motivational perspective does not pinpoint which groups will be the target of intergroup hostility and conflict.

2. Two strengths of the perspective are:

a. It explains the pervasive "us" versus "them" tendency and the fact that our ingroups affect our self-esteem.

b. It explains the tendency to aggress when frustrated.

IV. The Cognitive Perspective

A. A core tenet of this perspective is that stereotypes provide simplifying categories that help us organize and deal with the huge volume of social stimuli present in everyday life.

B. Stereotypes and Conservation of Mental Reserves

1. People are more likely to use stereotypes when they are overloaded, tired, or mentally taxed, and need a shortcut.

2. Bodenhausen (1990) demonstrated that people are more likely to fall back on stereotypes when they lack cognitive energy during the low point in their circadian rhythm:

a. "Morning people" were more likely to use stereotypes in judgments when tested at night.

b. "Night people" were more likely to use stereotypes in judgments when tested in the morning.

3. Macrae et al. (1994) demonstrated that people using stereotypes have greater cognitive resources available for other tasks.

a. Independent variable: whether participants were given a stereotype that went along with a list of traits or just the list of traits.

b. Dependent variable: how well participants remembered both the traits and details about a secondary audio message (a lecture on Indonesia).

c. Finding: participants who were given the stereotype to guide their processing remembered both more traits and more about the secondary audio message (details about the economy and geography of Indonesia).

C. Construal Processes and Distortions

1. Stereotypes can lead us to misconstrue information, thus confirming and perpetuating those stereotypes.

2. Accentuation of Ingroup Similarity and Outgroup Difference

a. Merely dividing a group of people into two categories will lead people to see less variability within each group and more variability between the two groups.

b. Research demonstrates that people will assume their attitudes are more similar to fellow ingroup members than to those of outgroup members, even when the groups are created based on minimal and meaningless criteria.

3. The Outgroup Homogeneity Effect

a. The outgroup homogeneity effect can be defined as the tendency to assume that within-group similarity is much stronger for outgroups than for ingroups.

b. Quattrone and Jones (1980) examined the outgroup homogeneity effect by asking participants to watch a videotape of students making a decision and then asking them what percentage of students from the same group would make the same decision.

(1) Independent variable #1: whether the participant was from Rutgers or rival Princeton.

(2) Independent variable #2: whether the students in the videotape were portrayed as being from Rutgers or Princeton.

(3) Dependent variable: ratings of the percentage of students at the same university who would make the same decision as seen on tape.

(4) Finding: participants gave higher estimates of the percentage of students who would make the same decision when they believed the students on the tape were from a different university than their own.

c. Reasons for the outgroup homogeneity effect:

(1) We have more contact with ingroup members and, thus, we are more likely to see divergent views.

(2) We see ingroup members as individuals but outgroup members as representatives of the group (thus, their unique characteristics fade into the background).

4. Biased Information Processing
   a. Stereotype-consistent behavior is more likely to be noticed and remembered but stereotype-inconsistent information is likely to be ignored, dismissed, or forgotten as not meaningful.
   b. Duncan (1976 conducted a study demonstrating that stereotypes can change the way the exact same action is interpreted.
      (1) Independent variable: whether the "ambiguous shove" in the videotape was delivered by a white man or a black man.
      (2) Dependent variable: ratings of the hostility intended in the shove.
      (3) Finding: participants saw the white man's shove as benign (e.g., "just playing around"), but saw the black man's shove as a hostile, aggressive action.
   c. Stone et al. (1997) conducted a study on the effects of secondhand information on information processing.
      (1) Independent variable: whether the target basketball player was portrayed as white or black.
      (2) Dependent variable: how participants characterized the player's performance after listening to an audio play-by-play.
      (3) Finding: participants who thought he was black characterized the player as being more athletic and having played better; participants who thought he was white characterized him as having greater "hustle" and playing a smarter game (stereotypes common in the sports world).

5. Self-Fulfilling Prophecies
   a. A self-fulfilling prophecy can be defined as acting on a belief in a way that tends to support the original belief, as when we act toward members of certain groups in ways that encourage the very behavior we expect from them.
      (1) Social psychologists define "self-fulfilling prophecy" as involving two people: a target and a perceiver.

(2) You should think of this as a three-step process:
   (a) The perceiver has an expectation about the target.
   (b) The perceiver's behavior reflects that expectation, thus treating the target in a certain way.
   (c) The target responds to the perceiver's behavior and thus appears to provide evidence confirming the original expectation.
   b. Word et al. (1974) conducted a study illustrating the role of self-fulfilling prophecies in providing (false) confirming evidence for stereotypes.
      (1) First phase of experiment: independent judges monitored job interviews and found that white participants showed an open and interested style when interviewing a white job applicant, but showed a closed and disinterested style (sitting further away, hemming and hawing, terminating early) while interviewing black job applicants.
      (2) Second phase of experiment:
         (a) White interviewers were trained to interview white applicants using either the open and interested style or the closed and disinterested style.
         (b) When the independent judges evaluated the white applicants, they rated those interviewed with the closed style more negatively than those interviewed with the open style.
      (3) The self-fulfilling prophecy was demonstrated, as shown by these findings:
         (a) Perceivers expected black applicants to be less qualified.
         (b) Perceivers behaved in a way that reflected this expectation.
         (c) Targets treated in a negative manner actually did make a worse impression.
         (d) The bad impression was caused by the interviewer's behavior, not by an actual lack of qualifications.

6. Distinctiveness and Illusory Correlations
   a. An illusory correlation can be defined as an erroneous belief about a connection between events, characteristics, or categories that are not, in fact, related.

b. Because we attend to distinctive or unusual events, they may become overrepresented in our memories, and we may tend to always associate them with each other.

c. The occurrence of two distinctive events close in time can lead to paired distinctiveness, which is the pairing of two distinctive events that stand out even more because they co-occur.

    (1) Minority members are distinctive, as are negative behaviors (being relatively less frequent than positive behaviors); thus, an illusory correlation can create or perpetuate negative stereotypes about minority group members.

    (2) Hamilton and Gifford (1976) illustrated the effect of paired distinctiveness by having participants view slides describing positive or negative behaviors initiated by different members of fictitious groups, and then estimate how often such behaviors were associated with each group.

        (a) More of the behaviors were done by members of Group A than Group B, making Group B the minority group and hence distinctive.

        (b) More of the behaviors were positive than negative, making negative behaviors distinctive.

        (c) Findings: even though the proportion of negative to positive behaviors was identical between the two groups, participants rated members of Group B more negatively and overestimated the number of negative behaviors performed by members of Group B.

        (d) When the positive behaviors were made distinctive, participants rated Group B more positively and overestimated the number of positive behaviors performed by members of Group B, demonstrating that the researchers had created paired distinctiveness in the study.

D. Immunity to Disconfirmation: stereotypes persist even in the face of disconfirming evidence.

    1. Anyone who behaves contrary to the stereotype is set aside as an exception.

    2. Confirming evidence is accepted at face value, but disconfirming evidence is critically analyzed and discounted.

      a. Confirming behavior is attributed to dispositions, while disconfirming behavior is attributed to situational factors.

      b. Maass et al. (1989) found that actions consistent with one's stereotypes are likely to be described with abstract terms (thus, accepting a person's disposition as the causal explanation), while actions inconsistent with one's stereotypes are likely to be described in very concrete and specific terms (thus, invoking the situation as the causal explanation).

E. Automatic and Controlled Processing

    1. Devine (1989) started a line of research that demonstrated that an important distinction between a "prejudiced" and "non-prejudiced" person is the extent to which he or she consciously resists unconsciously held stereotypes.

      a. Automatic processes can be defined as processes that occur outside of our awareness, without conscious control.

      b. Controlled processes can be defined as processes that occur with conscious direction and deliberate thought.

      c. Devine's first study found that both explicitly prejudiced and non-prejudiced participants rated an ambiguous action as being hostile after being primed with the black stereotype outside of conscious awareness.

      d. Devine's second study found that prejudiced participants listed many more negative characteristics than non-prejudiced participants when asked to list characteristics of black Americans.

    2. Subsequent research notes that it is more difficult to activate automatic, negative stereotypes regarding stigmatized groups among non-prejudiced participants (though still possible) than among prejudiced participants.

    3. Supporting the automatic/controlled distinctions, Cunningham et al. (2004) found that participants have greater amgydala activation in response to black compared to white faces when the faces were presented for 30 milliseconds, but do not show this difference when the faces are presented for 535 milliseconds (although seeing black faces does

cause more activity in the prefrontal cortex, indicating efforts to control and regulate automatic responses).

4. Dovidio et al. (2002) found that explicit measures of prejudice predicted outward signs of friendliness (what was said) toward black interaction partners, while implicit measures of prejudice predicted subtle, nonverbal cues that were more difficult to control.

5. Payne (2001) found that white participants identified a weapon as a weapon more quickly when unconsciously primed with African-American faces, and identified a tool (e.g., pliers) as a tool more quickly when primed with white faces.

6. Judd et al. (2004) extended this study to show that African-American faces facilitated recognition of both negative stereotypical stimuli (weapons) and positive stereotypical stimuli (e.g., athletic equipment) associated with African Americans, but did not facilitate recognition of non-stereotypical stimuli.

7. Cornell et al. (2002) found that white and black video game players were more likely to make the mistake of shooting an unarmed black target than failing to shoot an armed black target, but made both mistakes equally often if the target was white.

F. Evaluating the Cognitive Perspective

1. Some argue that since automatic stereotype activation is so brief in lab studies and so quickly dissipates it does not have real-world implications or address causes of prejudice and discrimination.

2. Even brief activations can have immediate, tragic consequences, or can begin processes that will have lasting effects.

V. Being a Member of a Stigmatized Group

A. Attributional Ambiguity

1. Members of stigmatized groups always have to weigh the possibility that the outcomes they are receiving are due to prejudicial reactions to their group membership (either discrimination or excessive behaviors designed to prove a lack of prejudice).

2. Crocker et al. (1991) illustrated this effect in a study often called the "blinds up/blinds down" study.

a. Independent variable #1: whether the participant was white or black.

b. Independent variable #2: whether the blinds over a two-way mirror were up (allowing an evaluator to see the participant and her race) or down (preventing an evaluator from identifying the participant's race).

c. Independent variable #3: positive or negative feedback.

d. Dependent variable: participants' reactions to feedback.

e. Finding: black and white participants both experienced lower self-esteem following negative feedback and higher self-esteem following positive feedback when the blinds were down, but black participants' self-esteem was unaffected by positive or negative feedback when the blinds were up.

B. Stereotype Threat

1. Steele's stereotype threat can be defined as the fear that one will confirm the stereotypes that others have regarding some salient group of which one is a member.

2. Steele argues that the mere existence of the stereotype puts pressure on the stigmatized group members to make sure their performance disconfirms the stereotype, and that this extra pressure can, ironically, lead to poorer performance compared to those who do not face such extra pressure.

3. Spencer et al. (1999) examined the stereotype that women perform less well in math than do men.

a. Independent variable #1: participants were either male or female.

b. Independent variable #2: whether participants were told before taking the math test that there was no gender difference on this test or that there was (as is common) a gender difference favoring men.

c. Dependent variable: performance on a challenging math test.

d. Finding: women underperformed relative to men in the condition in which they had been told there was a gender difference, but this performance difference disappeared when they had been told there was no gender difference.

4. Inzlicht and Ben-Zeev (2000) found that women performed better on a math test when they were in the presence of other women versus in the presence of men (which activated the stereotype).

5. Steele and Aronson (1995) looked at the stereotype that blacks are less intellectually competent than whites.

a. Independent variable #1: participants were either white or black.

b. Independent variable #2: the test was described as a simple lab activity, or as a task that would measure intellectual ability.

c. Dependent variable: performance on the test.

d. Finding: the manipulation did not affect white students' performance, but blacks underperformed relative to whites when the test was said to be diagnostic of intellectual ability; when the test was not thought to be diagnostic (and, thus, not "threatening") this performance difference disappeared.

6. Aronson et al. (1999) found that white male math performance deteriorated when participants were reminded of the stereotype of Asian superiority in math.

7. Stone et al. (1999) examined golf putting skill and accuracy in light of differing stereotypes about white and black athletes.

a, Independent variable #1: participants were either white or black.

b. Independent variable #2: a golf putting task was described as measuring "natural athletic ability" or "sports intelligence," or "sports psychology."

c. Dependent variable: performance on the task.

d. Finding: white and black students performed equally well when the task was described as measuring "sports psychology"; white students performed worse when the task was described as measuring "natural athletic ability" (thus emphasizing the stereotype that whites are bad at sports compared to blacks); blacks performed worse when the task was described as measuring "sports intelligence" (thus emphasizing the stereotype that blacks aren't as "smart" as whites).

8. Although any group for whom there is a stereotype may experience stereotype threat, Steele's research suggests that the global stereotype that blacks are intellectually inferior to other racial groups is particularly dangerous and has particularly far-reaching academic consequences (leading to disidentification with academic pursuits and producing negative economic consequences for them as adults).

Testing Your Basic Knowledge

ANSWERS TO MULTIPLE-CHOICE QUESTIONS

1.	b	14.	a
2.	a	15.	c
3.	a	16.	a
4.	b	17.	b
5.	c	18.	b
6.	c	19.	b
7.	a	20.	a
8.	b	21.	c
9.	a	22.	a
10.	c	23.	b
11.	a	24.	c
12.	c	25.	a
13.	b		

Testing Your In-Depth Understanding

EXAMPLE ANSWER TO THE GUIDED QUESTIONS FOR CRITICAL THINKING EXERCISE #1

1. What *is* your opinion of the test now that you have taken it? The researchers are often asked about people "controlling" their responses. In general, when people try to control their responses, they end up with reaction times that are significantly greater than uncontrolled responses (e.g., 800 milliseconds instead of 300 milliseconds). The researchers can identify those unusually long reaction times and discount those responses and/or participants.

2. An interesting question with lots of potential answers. Those who are skeptical that the IAT really measures actual prejudice point to this result as evidence for their argument. They suggest that the IAT measures knowledge of the stereotype (i.e., an awareness of the negative associations between blacks and negative things), but not endorsement of the stereotype. Explore the Web site; ask your professor; if you are white, talk with a person of color (show them the Web site); or search the psychology literature for more perspectives on this topic.

3. Find the opposing explanation offered by researchers like Andy Karpinski and James Hilton by exploring the Web site, asking your professor, or searching the psychology literature.

4. In a way, this question is asking whether the cultural stereotypes are all held equally strongly. For example, you may have a hard time envisioning a white person raised in mainstream America who would not receive scores on the IAT indicating an attitude "favoring"

whites. But perhaps it is easier to imagine people who would not score as favoring women or young people. Search the Web site, ask your professor, or explore the psychological literature for more information. You may also want to consider talking to a woman if you are a man, or talking to an elderly person if you are a young person.

5. This information is addressed in the textbook chapter, most directly in the section on the Cognitive Perspective. The short answer is that our underlying cognitions are the starting point for many decisions ("is that a gun in that black man's hand?"), behaviors ("what questions should I ask this job candidate?") and emotions ("do I like this person?") reviewed throughout the chapter. This is particularly true in the absence of sufficient cognitive energy or motivation to "correct" for inaccurate or undesired stereotyping.

CHAPTER 12 | Emotion

The goal of this chapter is to describe the relevant and recent social psychological research on emotions. The chapter first defines and explores what an emotion is, and then presents and integrates what initially appears to be conflicting research regarding the universality versus cultural specificity of emotion. Next, the chapter explores the extent to which emotions are "located" in our physiology or in our minds, and it examines the effects of unconscious activation of emotions. The chapter then challenges the notion that emotions are "silly" or "useless" and notes the different ways in which emotions influence our thinking and judgments. Last, the chapter explores one particularly important emotion: happiness.

ANNOTATED CHAPTER OUTLINE

After first reading through the chapter quickly, create a comprehensive framework for the information in the chapter by reading the outline below and filling in the missing information. Instead of simply re-copying information from the textbook, try to use your own words wherever possible; you can check your answers against the completed outline in the Answer Key section at the end of the chapter.

I. Characterizing Emotion
  A. Defining Emotion
    1. Emotions can be defined as

    _____

    _____

    _____

    2. Emotions are brief (moods last longer).
      a. Facial expressions of emotion typically last between one and five seconds.

      b. Physical responses (for example, elevated heart rate) last only dozens of seconds.
    3. Emotions are reactions to specific people and events (moods can be a result of unspecified stimuli).
    4. Emotions motivate behavior toward certain objectives, or goals.
    5. Emotions serve a social function; for example,

    _____

    _____

    _____

    _____

  B. The Components of Emotion
    1. Physiological responses
      a. Different brain regions and neurotransmitters are involved in different emotions; for example, the amygdala plays a central role in evaluative reactions.
      b. Emotions are associated with changes in the autonomic nervous system (ANS), which consists of

      _____

      _____

      _____

        (1) The sympathetic autonomic nervous system (SANS) prepares the body for action.
        (2) The parasympathetic autonomic nervous system (PANS) restores the body's resources.
    2. Emotions involve cognitive processes; for example:
      a. _____

      _____

_____
_____
b. _____
_____
_____
_____

3. Emotions involve expressive behaviors; for example, we communicate with:

   a. _____
   _____
   _____

   b._____
   _____
   _____
   _____

   c._____
   _____
   _____
   _____

   d. _____
   _____
   _____
   _____

II. Universality and Cultural Specificity in Emotion
   A. Both the evolutionary approach and the cultural approach contribute to our understanding of emotion.
      1. The evolutionary approach contends that
      _____
      _____
      _____
      _____

      2. The cultural approach assumes that emotions are strongly influenced by values, roles, institutions, socialization, and construal, and that these vary in different cultures.
   B. Darwin and Emotional Expression
      1. Darwin linked human expressions of emotion to animal displays.
      2. Displays are
      _____
      _____
      _____
      _____

   C. Studies of the Universality of Facial Expression
      1. The encoding hypothesis can be defined as
      _____
      _____
      _____
      _____

      2. The decoding hypothesis can be defined as
      _____

3. Ekman et al. (1969) took photos of actors displaying each of six emotions (anger, disgust, fear, happiness, sadness, and surprise), and then showed the photos to participants in Japan, Brazil, Argentina, Chile, and the U.S. to see which emotion they identified with which emotion.

   a. Findings:
   _____
   _____
   _____
   _____

   b. Critique: all the cultures chosen had high exposure to Western media, and participants may have learned about the expressions instead of innately knowing them.

4. Ekman and Friesen (1971) studied the remote Fore tribe in Papua, New Guinea, where there was no Western or outside influence at all.

   a. Findings for the Fore participants in matching facial expressions with stories for each emotion:
   _____
   _____
   _____
   _____

   b. Findings for the U.S. participants in interpreting facial expressions of Fore for each emotion:
   _____
   _____
   _____
   _____

5. Because of these studies and many others, facial expressions of emotion are considered to be universal in all people.

D. Critiques of the Universality Studies
   1. The free-response critique can be defined as
   _____
   _____
   _____
   _____

   a. Participants might have chosen "happiness" when another, more specific, positive emotion (such as "gratitude" or "pride") was more true for them.

   b. Studies have subsequently asked participants to use their own words, and the results have indicated that participants across cultures do choose similar words to describe the six different facial expressions.

2. The forced-choice critique can be defined as

_____

_____

_____

  a. Subsequent research has added "none of the above" as a response option.

  b. Such research indicates that accuracy rates are still very high.

3. Ekman and Friesen only studied six different emotions.

  a. It would be wrong to conclude that only these six emotions have universally recognizable facial expressions.

  b. Embarrassment, shame, and sympathy have all also been shown to have facial expressions that are recognizable across cultures.

E. Cultural Specificity of Emotion

  1. Cultural Variation in Emotional Expression

    a. Researchers have found great cultural variation in the expression of emotion.

    b. Cultures may have different display rules, which are

_____

_____

_____,

    and may include these ways of altering emotional expression:

    (1) _____

_____

_____

    (2) _____

_____

_____

    (3) _____

_____

_____

_____

    (4) _____

_____

_____

_____

  c. Ekman (1992) and Friesen (1972) found support for this hypothesis by videotaping students while they were watching a disturbing videotape that typically evoked disgust.

    (1) Independent variable #1:

_____

_____

_____

    (2) Independent variable #2:

_____

_____

_____

_____

    (3) Independent variable #3:

_____

_____

_____

_____

    (4) Dependent variable: how coders rated the facial expressions the participants displayed.

    (5) Findings:

_____

_____

_____

_____

  d. Matsumoto and Ekman (1989) found that Japanese college students attribute more intense emotion to the same facial expressions than do American college students.

  e. Ritualized displays can be defined as

_____

_____

_____

_____

  2. Culture and the Language of Emotion

    a. Based on reading hundreds of ethnographies written by anthropologists, Russell (1991) found that almost all languages have words for anger, fear, happiness, sadness, and disgust.

    b. Cultures vary in the number of words they have to represent emotions; for example:

    (1) _____

_____

_____

    (2) _____

_____

_____

_____

    (3) _____

_____

_____

_____

    c. Cultures vary in which emotions they have words for; for example:

    (1) _____

_____

_____

_____

   (2) _____

_____

_____

_____

   (3) _____

_____

_____

_____

  d. Cultures vary according to whether they hypercognize a given emotion.
     (1) Hypercognize can be defined as

_____

_____

_____

     (2) Tahitians have forty-six different words that refer to anger.

3. Cultural Similarities and Differences in the Elicitors of Emotion
  a. Boucher and Brandt (1981) found that

_____

_____

_____

_____

  b. Kitayama and colleagues showed that cultures can differ in terms of which emotions are triggered by which events, particularly along the dimension of engagement or disengagement with other people.
     (1) People in interdependent cultures tend to have positive emotions triggered

_____

_____

_____

     (2) People in independent cultures tend to have positive emotions triggered

_____

_____

_____

4. Cultural Differences in the Construal of Events
  a. Cultures vary in how they construe the same particular event and, thus, in what emotions are elicited by the event.
  b. Mesquita and Ellsworth (2001) found that

_____

_____

_____

_____

  c. In a nomadic tribe from Egypt, being dependent on others triggers shame because

being in the presence of a more powerful person is construed as a reminder of weakness; in contrast, in Japan, there is a positive feeling associated with dependence because it is construed as a manifestation of social harmony.

5. Cultural Differences in the Attentiveness to Emotional Cues: Ishii et al. (2003) presented spoken words to participants and asked them to make judgments about the meaning of the words and also the tone with which the words were spoken.
  a. Independent variable #1:

_____

_____

_____

  b. Independent variable #2: word meanings were either pleasant or unpleasant.
  c. Independent variable #3: tone of voice saying the words was either pleasant or unpleasant.
  d. Dependent variable: how quickly participants identified the meaning and tone.
  e. Finding:

_____

_____

_____

_____

  f. Japanese participants were attending more closely to tone, and American participants were attending more closely to meaning.

III. Emotion in the Mind and Body
  A. William James and Emotion-Specific Physiology
    1. In seeking to understand the experience of emotion, James theorized that

_____

_____

_____

    2. James's thesis raised two questions:
      a. To what extent does emotion reside in the body (ANS), and to what extent does emotion reside in the mind (cognitive interpretation)?
      b. Are there distinct ANS patterns for the different emotions?
  B. Schachter and Singer's Two-Factor Theory of Emotion
    1. The two-factor theory of emotion can be defined as

_____

_____

_____

_____

2. Emotion is experienced when a person in a state of general physiological arousal attributes that arousal to a specific emotional stimulus.

3. To test this theory, Schachter and Singer (1962) conducted a study in which they led participants to believe that they were testing a vitamin compound's effects on vision.

   a. Independent variable #1: participants were given an injection of epinephrine or a placebo.

   b. Independent variable #2 (only for those in the epinephrine-informed condition): half of the participants were informed that the shot would make them jittery and physiologically aroused; half were not told this information.

   c. Independent variable #3:

   _____

   _____

   _____

   _____

   d. Dependent variables: self-reported feelings of anger and happiness, and angry or happy behaviors.

   e. Findings:

   _____

   _____

   _____

   _____

4. Misattribution of arousal can be defined as

   _____

   _____

   _____

   _____

   a. People find cartoons funnier and erotica sexier when they view it after engaging in physiologically arousing exercise.

   b. Some people fall asleep faster when given a placebo they think will make them jittery because they can attribute anxiety about life to the pill and feel more relieved and able to sleep.

C. Emotion in the Body: Evidence for ANS Specificity in Emotion

   1. Schachter and Singer's research suggests that there are no emotion-specific ANS responses.

   2. Levenson et al. (1990) believe that these are emotion-specific ANS responses and had participants deliberately manipulate their facial muscles according to very specific guidelines created after thousands of hours of observing real facial expressions of emotion.

      a. They asked participants to move their facial muscles to conform to the expressions of the six basic emotions, and measured their ANS activity as they held the expressions for ten seconds.

      b. Findings: there were different patterns of ANS activity for each emotion, including these patterns:

      (1) _____

      _____

      _____

      (2) _____

      _____

      _____

      (3) _____

      _____

      _____

   3. Research suggests that blushing (increased blood flow to the face) is unique to situations involving negative, self-focused attention.

IV. Unconscious and Conscious Elicitation of Emotion

A. Appraisal Processes

   1. Appraisal processes can be defined as

   _____

   _____

   _____

   _____

   2. There are three questions that arise in relation to processing emotions:

      a. How can we study automatic, unconscious emotional responses to stimuli?

      b. How do we appraise the environment in ways that give rise to specific emotions?

      c. Once we have experienced an emotion, what are the consequences of reflecting upon it in different ways?

B. Unconscious Processing in Split-Brain Patients

   1. Gazzaniga and Sperry studied patients who had their epileptic seizures reduced or eliminated by the severing of their corpus callosum, the bundle of nerve fibers allowing the left and right hemispheres to communicate; although after surgery their two hemispheres could no longer pass information back and forth, their intelligence and personality remained virtually unaffected.

   2. Research suggests that there is a difference in the functions of the right and left hemispheres:

   _____

   _____

   _____

   _____

      a. In one study, Gazzaniga showed a split-brain woman a scary film such that only the right hemisphere could process it; the left hemisphere (which produces language and conscious recognition) remained unaware of it.

b. Without knowing why, the woman reported feeling scared and jumpy.

c. Needing an explanation, she guessed that Dr. Gazzaniga was somehow making her nervous.

C. Automatic Processing and the Generation of Emotion

1. Zajonc (pronounced ZIE- ahnce; rhymes with science) proposed that we have two systems that respond to stimuli: one that produces an automatic and unconscious evaluation, and another that allows for more conscious and deliberate assessment of elements like size, category, aesthetic properties, etc.

2. Murphy and Zajonc (1993) demonstrated the existence of automatic evaluations by showing participants a series of unfamiliar Chinese ideographs.

a. Independent variable #1:

_____
_____
_____

b. Independent variable #2:

_____
_____
_____

c. Dependent variable: how favorably participants rated each ideograph.

d. Findings:

_____
_____
_____
_____

e. Subsequent research showed that emotion primes were the only primes that influenced ratings of the ideographs (size and shape primes did not change perceptions of size or shape).

3. Dimberg and Ohman (1996) found that

_____
_____
_____
_____

D. Complex Appraisal and the Generation of Emotion

1. Appraisal theorists can be defined as

_____
_____
_____
_____

2. Stress can be defined as

_____
_____
_____
_____

a. In the short term, stress is adaptive, allowing people to deal with emergencies.

b. Chronic stress is produced by enduring sources of tension and can contribute to health problems, including ulcers, high blood pressure, heart disease, cancer, memory loss, and cell loss in the hippocampus.

c. Social threats (e.g., being the victim of prejudice) can lead to similar health problems.

3. Lazarus proposed that there are different kinds of stress, produced by different emotions and resulting from different appraisal processes.

a. The primary appraisal stage can be defined as

_____
_____
_____
_____

(1) Goal-congruent events tend to produce positive emotions.

(2) Goal-incongruent events tend to produce negative emotions.

b. The secondary appraisal stage can be defined as

_____
_____
_____
_____

c. The core-relational theme can be defined as

_____
_____
_____
_____

(1) Fear is defined by the theme that one is in danger.

(2) Anger is defined by the theme that one's self is offended.

(3) Sympathy is defined by the theme that a vulnerable individual needs help.

E. Dealing with Emotions

1. Pennebaker and his colleagues have conducted dozens of studies in which participants write about traumatic events (ranging from the Holocaust to earthquakes or floods or divorce) and have found that participants who write about their emotions associated with the trauma are healthier and have increased life satisfaction and school or job performance.

2. Research has offered explanations for why writing about emotions associated with a trauma helps victims:

a. _____
_____
_____
_____

b. _____
_____
_____
_____

c. _____
_____
_____
_____

3. Rumination can be defined as

_____
_____
_____
_____

4. Nolen-Hoeksema's research has found that depressed people are more likely to ruminate than nondepressed people, and those instructed to ruminate in laboratory studies experience prolonged negative affect.

V. The Rationality of Emotions

A. It is common to view emotions as irrational and disruptive, but some emotions may actually be rational and may aid in adaptive responding.

B. Emotions and the Maintenance of Social Bonds

1. The experience of embarrassment is profoundly negative, as evidenced by the lengths people will go to avoid potentially embarrassing situations, but embarrassment serves a social function by signaling regret for social transgressions and, in turn, promoting forgiveness and reconciliation.

2. Indications of the social function of embarrassment include:

a. _____
_____
_____
_____

b. _____
_____
_____
_____

3. In many ways, love may seem irrational, but love serves a vital social function, protecting long-term commitments against attractive alternatives or financial or health problems.

4. There is empirical evidence that love is adaptive:

a. _____
_____
_____
_____

b. _____
_____
_____
_____

c. _____
_____
_____
_____

C. The Effects of Emotion on Social Cognition

1. Research suggests that emotions (as long as they are not extreme) have systematic effects on our cognitions and generally lead to reasonable judgments.

2. People who are fearful are more attentive to potential threats, better remember potential threats, and judge the likelihood of threat to be higher, which is helpful in a dangerous situation but dysfunctional in a situation that does not really pose a threat.

D. Accounts of the Influence of Emotion on Cognition

1. The emotion-congruence perspective can be defined as

_____
_____
_____
_____

a. Bower et al. (1981) tested the hypothesis that it is easier to learn and remember information that is congruent with our current emotion because such information is more easily integrated into the memory structure that is already activated.

(1) Independent variable #1:

_____
_____
_____
_____

(2) Independent variable #2: the participants read a story about a student who was doing well or doing poorly (this is still an independent variable even though all participants read both stories).

(3) Dependent variable: memory for facts in the story.

(4) Finding:

_____
_____

_____

_____

b. Other research shows that emotions influence particular social judgments.
   (1) Anger triggers blame and sensitivity to unfair actions and makes unfair outcomes seem more likely in the future.
   (2) Sadness triggers situational attributions and makes loss seem more likely in the future.

2. The feelings-as-information perspective can be defined as

   _____

   _____

   _____

   _____

   a. Schwarz and Clore (1983) tested the feelings-as-information perspective by studying the effects of bright, sunny days and gloomy, overcast days on how happy and satisfied with their lives people were.
      (1) Independent variable #1: the weather was either cloudy or sunny on the days the participants were called.
      (2) Independent variable #2:

      _____

      _____

      _____

      _____

      (3) Dependent variable: happiness and life satisfaction ratings.
      (4) Findings:

      _____

      _____

      _____

      _____

   b. The feelings-as-information perspective proposes that people often rely directly on their feelings to make complex judgments.

3. The processing style perspective can be defined as

   _____

   _____

   _____

   _____

   a. Bodenhausen and colleagues have found that people are more likely to use stereotypes as shortcuts when they are experiencing positive moods or feeling angry compared to when they are feeling sad.

b. Isen suggests that happiness makes people think in creative, flexible, and integrative ways, as shown by:
   (1) _____

   _____

   _____

   _____

   (2) _____

   _____

   _____

   _____

   (3) People in positive moods are more likely to reach integrative compromises to a conflict they are negotiating.

c. Fredrickson (1998) suggests that the overall function of positive emotions is to broaden our intellectual and interpersonal resources.

VI. Happiness
    A. The Determinants of Pleasure
       1. Kahneman and Fredrickson have studied pleasurable experiences by having participants watch a pleasant film and rate their second-by-second pleasure using a ratings dial, and they have found that the following most influence pleasure ratings:
          a. _____

          _____

          _____

          _____

          b. _____

          _____

          _____

          _____

       2. They have found that people have a bias called duration neglect, which means that

          _____

          _____

          _____

          _____

    B. Knowing What Makes Us Happy
       1. Affective forecasting can be defined as

          _____

          _____

          _____

       2. Gilbert et al.'s research has found a number of ways in which we inaccurately predict what will make us happy:
          a. _____

          _____

          _____

          _____

b. _____

_____

_____

_____

3. Immune neglect can be defined as

_____

_____

_____

_____

4. Focalism can be defined as

_____

_____

_____

_____

   a. You may think you will be truly and forever happy once you have finished your GREs, but you underestimate the stress final exams will cause.
   b. You may think a vacation in the tropics will make you happy, but you underestimate the difficulties of getting there, the heat, sunburn, and daily hassles.

C. The Happy Life

1. Diener and his colleagues (2003) integrated studies involving over 1 million people and found that most people are "happy" (i.e., the modal response was 7 on a 10-point scale).
2. Brickman et al. (1978) found that

_____

_____

_____

_____

3. Gender and age have very little effect on happiness.
4. Money affects life satisfaction more in less wealthy countries.
   a. Myers (2000) found that

_____

_____

_____

_____

   b. Money does influence happiness for those who struggle with lack of jobs, poor nutrition, and disease.
5. Relationships matter a great deal to happiness, as shown by the following empirical evidence:
   a. _____

_____

_____

_____

   b. _____

_____

_____

_____

6. Diener (2000) has found that people are happier in cultures where individuals have more rights (e.g., the right to vote) and greater economic equality.

TESTING YOUR BASIC KNOWLEDGE

After studying the information in the chapter by filling in the outline above, test your basic knowledge with the following multiple-choice test. Answers are provided in the Answer Key section at the end of the chapter. If you find that you have gotten an answer wrong, it is important that you understand why it is wrong (as well as understanding why the correct answer is the better choice). Talk with peers, your tutor, or your professor if you need help.

Multiple-Choice Questions

1. Mandi had a sharp, physiologically arousing reaction to a news report showing children dying from hunger in Africa which faded after a few minutes. Danielle experienced a generally unpleasant feeling that lasted all day. Which woman felt an emotion (as defined by your textbook)?
   a. Mandi
   b. Danielle
   c. Both women felt emotions.

2. What system in the body prepares us for action by increasing our heart rate, increasing sweating, and inhibiting digestive activity?
   a. the amygdala
   b. the sympathetic autonomic nervous system
   c. the parasympathetic autonomic nervous system

3. According to the encoding and decoding hypotheses,
   a. the expression of emotions is universal.
   b. the expression of emotions is different across different cultures.
   c. emotions are the same across cultures, but the expression of those emotions differs.

4. Ekman and Friesen's famous 1971 study with the Fore in Papua, New Guinea, demonstrated that
   a. the Fore could accurately identify the emotions Western faces were displaying in photographs.
   b. college students from Western countries could accurately identify the emotions the Fore expressed in photographs.
   c. Both A and B are correct.

5. Which of the following is *not* a critique of the Ekman universality of facial expression studies?
   a. Ekman should have allowed participants to come up with their own words to identify the expressions.

b. Ekman's research included only a limited number of emotions.

c. Ekman did not include enough cultures to generalize his results.

6. When Jordan fell flat on her back after slipping on some ice, Lucy thought it was hysterical. But, out of concern for her friend's feelings (and her well-being), she suppressed her laughter and merely smiled quickly to herself. Lucy's attempt to de-intensify her emotion is an example of
   a. a display rule.
   b. misattribution of arousal.
   c. secondary appraisal.

7. Ekman and Friesen's research suggests that, when viewing a disgusting film in the presence of an authority figure, American participants will _____ their disgust, while Japanese participants will _____ their disgust.
   a. de-intensify; neutralize
   b. intensify; mask
   c. neutralize; intensify

8. There is no one word in English that can adequately translate the German word "schadenfreude." This is one piece of evidence suggesting that
   a. people tend to engage in ritualized displays of emotion.
   b. there are cultural variations in emotion.
   c. emotion is universal.

9. What is a major conclusion of the Boucher and Brandt (1981) findings?
   a. Boucher and Brandt's work suggested that, across cultures, similar situations evoke the same emotions.
   b. Boucher and Brandt found similarities in the facial expressions of humans and other species.
   c. Boucher and Brandt's study was the first to note the importance of studying non-Western cultures.

10. A student was listening to a politician deliver a speech about how important it is to help the poor and underprivileged. When asked to report on what the politician said, the student had a hard time remembering the details of the speech because the politician's vaguely disgusted tone of voice clashed so completely with the actual words he was saying. According to research discussed in your textbook, the student is probably
    a. a woman.
    b. American.
    c. Japanese.

11. As part of a research study, Jerome walks out to the middle of a rickety footbridge suspended over a deep ravine. He meets the experimenter in the middle of the bridge, and the experimenter asks Jerome what emotion he is feeling. Jerome looks around and says "I'm frightened!" According to Schachter and Singer's two-factor theory of emotion, how did Jerome arrive at that conclusion?
    a. Jerome felt a pattern of physiological arousal that is uniquely associated with fear.
    b. Jerome felt general physiological arousal and, since he was on a high bridge that would be frightening for most people, he labeled that arousal as fear.
    c. Jerome's primary appraisal identified his negative feelings, and his secondary appraisal labeled the feeling as fear.

12. Stanley is led to believe that he is late for a research study and rushes up two flights of stairs. When he arrives at the top, he is met by an extremely attractive research assistant. Stanley immediately feels a strong attraction and wonders if this person could be his true soul mate. Before proposing marriage, Stanley should probably check and see if
    a. he feels just as strongly attracted to the assistant after his heightened ANS activity calms down.
    b. the weather is cloudy or sunny.
    c. Neither of the above is consistent with social psychological research.

13. Which of the following supports the hypothesis that there are patterns of ANS activation that are specific to particular emotions?
    a. There is no such evidence.
    b. People who are asked to configure their facial muscles into an expression that conveys anger subsequently report feeling more angry.
    c. Heart rate is faster when people are experiencing fear than when they are experiencing disgust.

14. Gazzaniga's research on split-brain patients suggests which of the following?
    a. The right hemisphere is especially sensitive to emotional stimuli.
    b. The left hemisphere will generate a verbal explanation for an experienced emotion, even if the source of the emotion in unknown.
    c. Both A and B are correct.

15. Murphy and Zajonc conducted a study in which they showed participants Chinese ideographs. Each ideograph was preceded by a prime of a face expressing an emotion. What were the findings of this study?
    a. People who were exposed to a smiling face prime rated the ideograph more favorably when the prime was presented at subliminal speeds.
    b. People who were exposed to a smiling face prime rated the ideograph more favorably when the prime was presented at optimal speeds.
    c. Chinese participants were affected by the face primes, but American participants were not.

16. Phoebe, who wants to be a psychology major, fails her psychology test. According to Lazarus's description of the two stages of appraisal, what is Phoebe's reaction likely to be after the primary appraisal stage?
    a. "I can do better next time if I study harder and focus more on the information in the textbook."
    b. "I failed the test because the professor made the exam too hard."
    c. "I feel terrible! I want to be a psychology major and need to pass my psychology classes."

17. According to James Pennebaker, one of the best things you can do after experiencing a traumatic event is to
    a. write in a journal about how you are feeling.
    b. put the experience out of your mind and distract yourself with something pleasant.
    c. allow yourself to cry as hard as you can to let out your negative emotions.

18. While attending his first day of college, Asa is trying to maintain his "cool" as a calm, relaxed young man. But after his very first class, he crashes into Leah in the hallway and knocks all her books to the ground. Asa helps her pick up her books, but carefully neutralizes his embarrassment. What advice would a social psychologist give?
    a. Asa did the right thing because neutralizing his embarrassment is a good way to follow the display rules of American culture.
    b. Asa should show his embarrassment because that emotion demonstrates regret and prompts forgiveness.
    c. Leah should refuse Asa's help in picking up her books so that she can show her strong, independent side.

19. According to the emotion-congruence perspective,
    a. a negotiation will be more likely to end in a mutually satisfying compromise if the negotiators are feeling happy.
    b. participants are likely to report greater happiness on sunny days compared to cloudy days.
    c. it will be easier to remember sad information if you are already in a sad mood.

20. According to the processing style perspective,
    a. a negotiation will be more likely to end in a mutually satisfying compromise if the negotiators are feeling happy.
    b. participants are likely to report greater happiness on sunny days compared to cloudy days.
    c. it will be easier to remember sad information if you are already in a sad mood.

21. Which of the following is *not* a major determinant of whether an experience is pleasurable or not?
    a. the duration of pleasurable feelings during the event
    b. the amount of pleasure felt during the peak moment of the event
    c. the amount of pleasure felt at the end of the event

22. In what way does focalism interfere with accurate affective forecasting?
    a. if we focus too much on only one aspect of an experience, we may overlook or underestimate the extent to which other aspects will shape our overall emotional reaction
    b. if we focus on one event for too long, we are likely to slip into rumination
    c. because we tend to focus on negative aspects of an event, we usually underestimate our ability to deal with and overcome painful setbacks

23. According to the research findings, is there a correlation between money and happiness?
    a. No, there is no correlation.
    b. Yes, but it is a negative correlation.
    c. Yes, but only among people in relatively impoverished countries.

24. Mario gets plastic surgery on his nose, confident that he will be much, much happier once his physical appearance is improved. According to Phillip Brickman and his colleagues, what might Mario discover after the surgery?
    a. He would have been happier spending the money on something more tangible like a house, car, or boat.
    b. His happiness hasn't increased as much as he thought it would.
    c. The negative effects of having major surgery offset any positive feelings associated with an improved appearance.

25. According to a _____ perspective, emotions are biologically based and contributed to humans' ability to survive and reproduce.
    a. cultural
    b. evolutionary
    c. immunity neglect

Essay Questions

After you have mastered the multiple-choice questions, try testing your basic understanding by thoroughly answering each of the broad essay questions below. Because it is critical that you think through this information on your own, we have not provided any answers to these questions. Your learning and retention of this material will be greatly enhanced if you do one or more of the following to check your answers: carefully review the textbook information; compare your responses to your class lecture notes; talk over your answers with a peer; ask your professor to review your answers or review any information that is unclear to you.

1. Define an emotion, making sure you clarify how it is different from a mood. Also, be sure to discuss the different components of emotions.

2. Present the basic premises of the evolutionary and cultural perspectives on emotion. Discuss the research evidence supporting each perspective, and explain how the evolutionary perspective can be regarded as accurate given the evidence for cultural variations.

3. Discuss the research findings that describe how our physical bodies are involved in our emotions. Compare and contrast that research to Schachter and Singer's two-step theory of emotion.

4. Can emotion be generated unconsciously? What evidence can you provide that supports your answer?

5. Discuss the role of cognitive appraisal in understanding our emotions.

6. What advice can you derive from James Pennebaker's and Susan Nolen-Hoeksema's research about dealing with your emotions?

7. Do emotions serve any adaptive function? In what ways do emotions influence our thinking? Be sure to review each of the three accounts of the influence of emotion on cognition.

8. Describe the determinants of pleasure, the barriers to accurately predicting what will make us happy, and what the research evidence says about what actually does make us happy.

TESTING YOUR IN-DEPTH UNDERSTANDING

Test your in-depth understanding of the material by working through the Critical Thinking Exercises provided at the end of each textbook chapter. To maximize this learning opportunity, work together with a tutor, study group, or your professor. Alternatively, write down your thoughts and responses.

Guided questions for one of the exercises are provided below. The "answers" provided in the Answer Key section are not hard and fast "correct" responses. You are encouraged to talk over your responses with your classmates, tutor, and/or professor keeping in mind that there may not be just one "correct" answer to each question. That being said, however, there are ways to answer these questions that indicate more or less reflective thought and more or less understanding and integration of the material from the chapter.

Guided Questions for Critical Thinking Exercise #3

Do we know what makes us happy? Why is it that we often seem to have little knowledge about what will make us

happy or not? In a related vein, what insights did you glean from this chapter regarding living a more satisfying life?

1. If you look at the first two questions, you can intuit that the answer to the first question is, no—we often don't know what will make us happy. So, move on from there and try to answer the second question, which asks why we don't know what makes us happy. As a basis for your answer, refer to the second subsection of the chapter's discussion of happiness, and be sure to use the following concepts: affective forecasting, immune neglect, and focalism.

2. What insights have you gained about being happier and more satisfied, or, at least, about having a better handle on your own emotions and those of others? Start with the concepts you reviewed in #1 (immune neglect and focalism) and extract advice about living your life from those concepts. Then, you might also want to review the following concepts and see what advice you can extract from these ideas:

   display rules
   ritualized displays
   duration neglect
   determinants of pleasure
   emotion congruence
   feelings-as-information
   processing style
   hypercognize
   two-factor theory of emotion
   misattribution of arousal
   rumination
   writing about traumatic feelings
   stress

Enhance your understanding of the chapter by thinking about and doing the remaining two Critical Thinking Exercises. Discuss your answers with your peers, study group, tutor, or professor.

Critical Thinking Exercise #1

Knowing what you now know about emotion, if you were to redo the Ekman study of facial expression in a culture that had had no contact with Western culture, how would you redo the study? What methodological pitfalls of Ekman's study would you avoid? Where would you expect to document universality of expression? And where would you expect to find cultural variation?

Critical Thinking Exercise #2

Are emotions rational? Define what you mean by rational, and provide evidence arguing for the claim that emotions are rational.

SOCIAL PSYCHOLOGY IN THE POPULAR MEDIA

You might be interested in the following popular media references, each of which relates in some way to information in this chapter.

Film

Eternal Sunshine of the Spotless Mind (2004; directed by Michel Gondry; starring Jim Carrey, Kate Winslet). Jim Carrey's character decides he will be happier if he has the memories of his ex-girlfriend, played by Kate Winslet, erased. His affective forecasting proves to be quite wrong, and he struggles to hang on to the memories, even as they slip away. Rated R.

Song

Barenaked Ladies. (1992). "If I Had a Million Dollars." From the album *Gordon*. A silly, fun song about what the guys in the band would do with a million dollars, reminding us that money probably won't make someone more happy or change their taste for Kraft macaroni and cheese.

Book

Dalai Lama and Cutler, Howard C. (1998). *The Art of Happiness: A Handbook for Living*. New York: Riverhead Books. It would be interesting to read this best-selling book and compare it to the research from the chapter. From the front flap: "Through conversations, stories, and meditations, the Dalai Lama shows us how to defeat day-to-day anxiety, insecurity, anger, and discouragement. Together with Dr. Cutler, he explores many facets of everyday life, including relationships, loss, and the pursuit of wealth…. Based on 2,500 years of Buddhist meditations mixed with a healthy does of common sense. . . ."

ANSWER KEY

Annotated Chapter Outline

I. Characterizing Emotion
  A. Defining Emotion
    1. Emotions can be defined as brief psychological and physiological responses that are subjectively experienced as feelings and that prepare a person for action.
    2. Emotions are brief (moods last longer).
      a. Facial expressions of emotion typically last between one and five seconds.
      b. Physical responses (for example, elevated heart rate) last only dozens of seconds.
    3. Emotions are reactions to specific people and events (moods can be a result of unspecified stimuli).
    4. Emotions motivate behavior toward certain objectives, or goals.
    5. Emotions serve a social function; for example, gratitude, love, and anger all support formation and maintenance of friendships.
  B. The Components of Emotion
    1. Physiological responses
      a. Different brain regions and neurotransmitters are involved in different emotions; for example, the amygdala plays a central role in evaluative reactions.
      b. Emotions are associated with changes in the autonomic nervous system (ANS), which consists of glands, organs, muscles, arteries, and veins throughout the body that are controlled by nerve cells originating in the spinal cord, and that help the individual deal with emergency situations.
        (1) The sympathetic autonomic nervous system (SANS) prepares the body for action.
        (2) The parasympathetic autonomic nervous system (PANS) restores the body's resources.
    2. Emotions involve cognitive processes; for example:
      a. Language labels our emotions.
      b. Emotion shapes memory, attention, and judgment.
    3. Emotions involve expressive behaviors; for example, we communicate with:
      a. Facial expressions
      b. Voice
      c. Posture
      d. Touch

II. Universality and Cultural Specificity in Emotion
  A. Both the evolutionary approach and the cultural approach contribute to our understanding of emotion.
    1. The evolutionary approach contends that emotions are biologically based adaptations that contribute to the likelihood that our genes will be passed on to the next generation.
    2. The cultural approach assumes that emotions are strongly influenced by values, roles, institutions, socialization, and construal, and that these vary in different cultures.

B. Darwin and Emotional Expression
  1. Darwin linked human expressions of emotion to animal displays.
  2. Displays are nonverbal expressions that signal emotion, attitudes, or intentions.
C. Studies of the Universality of Facial Expression
  1. The encoding hypothesis can be defined as the hypothesis that the experience of different emotions is associated with the same distinct facial expressions across cultures.
  2. The decoding hypothesis can be defined as the hypothesis that people of different cultures can interpret distinct facial expressions for different emotions in the same ways.
  3. Ekman et al. (1969) took photos of actors displaying each of six emotions (anger, disgust, fear, happiness, sadness, and surprise), and then showed the photos to participants in Japan, Brazil, Argentina, Chile, and the U.S. to see which emotion they identified with which emotion.
     a. Findings: across each of the five different cultures, all participants showed high accuracy rates in labeling the emotions in the photographs.
     b. Critique: all the cultures chosen had high exposure to Western media, and participants may have learned about the expressions instead of innately knowing them.
  4. Ekman and Friesen (1971) studied the remote Fore tribe in Papua, New Guinea, where there was no Western or outside influence at all.
     a. Findings: the Fore had high accuracy rates in matching a photograph of a facial expression with a story about someone having such an emotion.
     b. Findings: U.S. college students had high accuracy rates in interpreting the expressions on the faces of Fore who had been photographed displaying the emotion they would feel if they had been the person in the story.
  5. Because of these studies and many others, facial expressions of emotion are considered to be universal in all people.
D. Critiques of the Universality Studies
  1. The free-response critique can be defined as a critique of Ekman and Friesen's emotion studies based on the fact that researchers provided the terms with which participants labeled facial expressions rather than allowing the participants to label the expressions with their own words.
     a. Participants might have chosen "happiness" when another, more specific, positive emotion (such as "gratitude" or "pride") was more true for them.
     b. Studies have subsequently asked participants to use their own words, and the results have indicated that participants across cultures do choose similar words to describe the six different facial expressions.
  2. The forced-choice critique can be defined as a critique of Ekman and Friesen's emotion study that holds that accuracy rates in judgments of emotional expressions may have been inflated by allowing participants to make educated guesses about expressions they may not have known how to label.
     a. Subsequent research has added "none of the above" as a response option.
     b. Such research indicates that accuracy rates are still very high.
  3. Ekman and Friesen only studied six different emotions.
     a. It would be wrong to conclude that only these six emotions have universally recognizable facial expressions.
     b. Embarrassment, shame, and sympathy have all also been shown to have facial expressions that are recognizable across cultures.
E. Cultural Specificity of Emotion
  1. Cultural Variation in Emotional Expression
     a. Researchers have found great cultural variation in the expression of emotion.
     b. Cultures may have different display rules, which are culturally specific rules that govern how and when and to whom we express emotion, and may include these ways of altering emotional expression:
        (1) People may de-intensify the expression of an emotion.
        (2) People may intensify the expression of an emotion.
        (3) People may mask or hide the expression of an emotion.
        (4) People may neutralize the expression of an emotion.
     c. Ekman (1992) and Friesen (1972) found support for this hypothesis by videotaping students while they were watching a disturbing videotape that typically evoked disgust.
        (1) Independent variable #1: Japanese or American college student participants.
        (2) Independent variable #2: the room was dark or illuminated.

(3) Independent variable #3: an authority figure was present or absent.

(4) Dependent variable: how coders rated the facial expressions the participants displayed.

(5) Findings: when in the dark, all participants displayed expressions that were judged to be "disgust," but in the light and in the presence of an authority figure, American participants intensified their expressions of disgust (consistent with cultural norms), while Japanese participants masked their disgust with polite smiles (consistent with a cultural norm that people should hide negative emotion because it disrupts social harmony).

d. Matsumoto and Ekman (1989) found that Japanese college students attribute more intense emotion to the same facial expressions than do American college students.

e. Ritualized displays can be defined as highly stylized ways of expressing particular emotions; for example, the expression of emotion by Indian participants.

2. Culture and the Language of Emotion

a. Based on reading hundreds of ethnographies written by anthropologists, Russell found that almost all languages have words for anger, fear, happiness, sadness, and disgust.

b. Cultures vary in the number of words they have to represent emotions; for example:

(1) 2,000 in English.

(2) 750 in Taiwanese.

(3) 8 among the Chewong of Malaysia.

c. Cultures vary in which emotions they have words for; for example:

(1) Aboriginal Australians use the same word for fear and shame.

(2) Japanese use the same word for shame and embarrassment.

(3) Germans have a word for a unique emotion of finding pleasure in seeing the suffering of another *(Schadenfreude)*.

d. Cultures vary according to whether they hypercognize a given emotion.

(1) Hypercognize can be defined as representing a particular emotion with numerous words and concepts.

(2) Tahitians have forty-six different words that refer to anger.

3. Cultural Similarities and Differences in the Elicitors of Emotion

a. Boucher and Brandt (1981) asked participants to describe events in which someone was feeling each of several different emotions and found that Americans could identify the emotions triggered by Malaysian incidents and vice versa.

b. Kitayama and colleagues showed that cultures can differ in terms of which emotions are triggered by which events, particularly along the dimension of engagement or disengagement with other people.

(1) People in interdependent cultures tend to have positive emotions triggered in social situations.

(2) People in independent cultures tend to have positive emotions triggered during activities that are more self-relevant (e.g., a personal achievement).

4. Cultural Differences in the Construal of Events

a. Cultures vary in how they construe the same particular event and, thus, in what emotions are elicited by the event.

b. Mesquita and Ellsworth (2001) found that middle-class Europeans construe being alone as a pleasant state for private reflection, while many interdependent peoples construe being alone as a sad state of isolation.

c. In a nomadic tribe from Egypt, being dependent on others triggers shame because being in the presence of a more powerful person is construed as a reminder of weakness; in contrast, in Japan, there is a positive feeling associated with dependence because it is construed as a manifestation of social harmony.

5. Cultural Differences in the Attentiveness to Emotional Cues: Ishii et al. (2003) presented spoken words to participants and asked them to make judgments about the meaning of the words and also the tone with which the words were spoken.

a. Independent variable #1: participants were Japanese or American.

b. Independent variable #2: word meanings were either pleasant or unpleasant.

c. Independent variable #3: tone of voice saying the words was either pleasant or unpleasant.

d. Dependent variable: how quickly participants identified the meaning and tone.

e. Finding: Japanese participants, for whom tone of voice was an important cue to social harmony, took longer to judge meaning when the tone contradicted the meaning, compared to judgments of tone with conflicting meanings; Americans, who generally think people say what they mean, took longer to judge tone when meaning contradicted the tone, compared to judging meaning when tone conflicted.

f. Japanese participants were attending more closely to tone, and American participants were attending more closely to meaning.

III. Emotion in the Mind and Body

A. William James and Emotion-Specific Physiology

1. In seeking to understand the experience of emotion, James theorized that we first have particular bodily reactions to emotional stimuli, and then we truly experience the emotion when we perceive and identify the physiological state, which is unique for each emotion.

2. James's thesis raised two questions:

a. To what extent does emotion reside in the body (ANS), and to what extent does emotion reside in the mind (cognitive interpretation)?

b. Are there distinct ANS patterns for the different emotions?

B. Schachter and Singer's Two-Factor Theory of Emotion

1. The two-factor theory of emotion can be defined as a theory that says that there are two components to emotional experience: undifferentiated physiological arousal and our construal of our state of undifferentiated arousal.

2. Emotion is experienced when a person in a state of general physiological arousal attributes that arousal to a specific emotional stimulus.

3. To test this theory, Schachter and Singer (1962) conducted a study in which they led participants to believe that they were testing a vitamin compound's effects on vision.

a. Independent variable #1: participants were given an injection of epinephrine or a placebo.

b. Independent variable #2 (only for those in the epinephrine-informed condition): half of the participants were informed that the shot would make them jittery and physiologically aroused; half were not told this information.

c. Independent variable #3: half of the participants were joined by a confederate who exhibited "euphoria" (great happiness); half were joined by a confederate who exhibited great anger about the survey questions.

d. Dependent variables: self-reported feelings of anger and happiness, and angry or happy behaviors.

e. Findings: participants who were aroused by the epinephrine, but were unaware that it was the cause of their arousal, labeled their arousal as anger when in the presence of the angry confederate, and labeled their arousal as happiness when in the presence of the happy confederate; those who knew that the shot would produce arousal experienced even less anger or happiness than participants in the control condition.

4. Misattribution of arousal can be defined as attributing emotional arousal produced by one cause (for example, exercise) to another stimulus in the environment.

a. People find cartoons funnier and erotica sexier when they view it after engaging in physiologically arousing exercise.

b. Some people fall asleep faster when given a placebo they think will make them jittery because they can attribute anxiety about life to the pill and feel more relieved and able to sleep.

C. Emotion in the Body: Evidence for ANS Specificity in Emotion

1. Schachter and Singer's research suggests that there are no emotion-specific ANS responses.

2. Levenson et al. (1990) believe that these are emotion-specific ANS responses and had participants deliberately manipulate their facial muscles according to very specific guidelines created after thousands of hours of observing real facial expressions of emotion.

a. They asked participants to move their facial muscles to conform to the expressions of the six basic emotions, and measured their ANS activity as they held the expressions for ten seconds.

b. Findings: there were different patterns of ANS activity for each emotion, including these patterns:

(1) Heart rate is greater for fear, anger, and sadness than for disgust.

(2) Sweat activity in the hands is greater for fear and disgust than for anger or sadness.

(3) Finger temperature is greater for anger than for fear (suggesting blood flow differences).

3. Research suggests that blushing (increased blood flow to the face) is unique to situations involving negative, self-focused attention.

IV. Unconscious and Conscious Elicitation of Emotion

A. Appraisal Processes

1. Appraisal processes can be defined as the ways whereby we evaluate events and objects in our environment according to their relation to our current goals.

2. There are three questions that arise in relation to processing emotions:

a. How can we study automatic, unconscious emotional responses to stimuli?

b. How do we appraise the environment in ways that give rise to specific emotions?

c. Once we have experienced an emotion, what are the consequences of reflecting upon it in different ways?

B. Unconscious Processing in Split-Brain Patients

1. Gazzaniga and Sperry studied patients who had their epileptic seizures reduced or eliminated by the severing of their corpus callosum, the bundle of nerve fibers allowing the left and right hemispheres to communicate; although after surgery their two hemispheres could no longer pass information back and forth, their intelligence and personality remained virtually unaffected.

2. Research suggests that there is a difference in the functions of the right and left hemispheres: the left hemisphere interprets stimuli using language, and the right hemisphere responds more readily to emotional stimuli and nonverbal cues.

a. In one study, Gazzaniga showed a split-brain woman a scary film such that only the right hemisphere could process it; the left hemisphere (which produces language and conscious recognition) remained unaware of it.

b. Without knowing why, the woman reported feeling scared and jumpy.

c. Needing an explanation, she guessed that Dr. Gazzaniga was somehow making her nervous.

C. Automatic Processing and the Generation of Emotion

1. Zajonc (pronounced ZIE- ahnce; rhymes with science) proposed that we have two systems that respond to stimuli: one that produces an automatic and unconscious evaluation, and another that allows for more conscious and deliberate assessment of elements like size, category, aesthetic properties, etc.

2. Murphy and Zajonc (1993) demonstrated the existence of automatic evaluations by showing participants a series of unfamiliar Chinese ideographs.

a. Independent variable #1: before each ideograph, the participants saw either a smiling or an angry face.

b. Independent variable #2: the faces were either shown at suboptimal (fast, unconscious) speeds or optimal (conscious identification was possible) speeds.

c. Dependent variable: how favorably participants rated each ideograph.

d. Findings: the unconsciously activated positive evaluation of the suboptimally presented smiling faces carried over and led to more favorable evaluations of the ideographs; the suboptimally presented angry faces carried over and led to the less favorable evaluations of the ideographs; optimal presentations of the faces did not influence the judgments because participants were consciously aware of the emotional stimuli.

e. Subsequent research showed that emotion primes were the only primes that influenced ratings of the ideographs (size and shape primes did not change perceptions of size or shape).

3. Dimberg and Ohman (1996) found that suboptimally presented smiling faces led participants to smile, while suboptimally presented frowning faces led participants to frown and show elevated arousal.

D. Complex Appraisal and the Generation of Emotion

1. Appraisal theorists can be defined as researchers who investigate how the complex appraisals of a stimulus or situation influence which emotion is experienced.

2. Stress can be defined as heightened SANS activity, ruminative thought, and vigilant attention based on a sense that one's challenges and demands surpass one's capacities, resources, and energies.

a. In the short term, stress is adaptive, allowing people to deal with emergencies.

b. Chronic stress is produced by enduring sources of tension and can contribute to health problems, including ulcers, high blood pressure, heart disease, cancer, memory loss, and cell loss in the hippocampus.

c. Social threats (e.g., being the victim of prejudice) can lead to similar health problems.

3. Lazarus proposed that there are different kinds of stress, produced by different emotions and resulting from different appraisal processes.

a. The primary appraisal stage can be defined as an initial, quick positive or negative evaluation of ongoing events based on whether they are congruent or incongruent with the person's goals.

(1) Goal-congruent events tend to produce positive emotions.

(2) Goal-incongruent events tend to produce negative emotions.

b. The secondary appraisal stage can be defined as a subsequent evaluation in which people determine why they feel the way they do about an event, possible ways of responding to the event, and future consequences of different courses of action.

c. The core-relational theme can be defined as distinct themes like danger or offense or fairness that define the essential meaning for each emotion.

(1) Fear is defined by the theme that one is in danger.

(2) Anger is defined by the theme that one's self is offended.

(3) Sympathy is defined by the theme that a vulnerable individual needs help.

E. Dealing with Emotions

1. Pennebaker and his colleagues have conducted dozens of studies in which participants write about traumatic events (ranging from the Holocaust to earthquakes or floods or divorce) and have found that participants who write about their emotions associated with the trauma are healthier and have increased life satisfaction and school or job performance.

2. Research has offered explanations for why writing about emotions associated with a trauma helps victims:

a. Pennebaker et al. (1997) found that writing about their emotions gives insight and perspective, which helps victims cope.

b. Suppressing negative emotions increases SANS activity; expressing such emotions can help to normalize SANS activity.

c. Labeling emotions identifies what the emotion is about, thus reducing the extent to which the emotion is misattributed.

3. Rumination can be defined as the tendency to think about some event over and over again, including thinking of all its ramifications, causes, and implications. It does not actively lead to insight, perspective, or change, but keeps bringing to mind negative emotions.

4. Nolen-Hoeksema's research has found that depressed people are more likely to ruminate than nondepressed people, and those instructed to ruminate in laboratory studies experience prolonged negative affect.

V. The Rationality of Emotions

A. It is common to view emotions as irrational and disruptive, but some emotions may actually be rational and may aid in adaptive responding.

B. Emotions and the Maintenance of Social Bonds

1. The experience of embarrassment is profoundly negative, as evidenced by the lengths people will go to avoid potentially embarrassing situations, but embarrassment serves a social function by signaling regret for social transgressions and, in turn, promoting forgiveness and reconciliation.

2. Indications of the social function of embarrassment include:

a. Nonverbal displays of embarrassment in humans resemble appeasement displays in other species.

b. Semin and Manstead (1982) found that participants gave a target who had knocked over a supermarket display more favorable evaluations if he showed embarrassment rather than appearing unbothered.

3. In many ways, love may seem irrational, but love serves a vital social function, protecting long-term commitments against attractive alternatives or financial or health problems.

4. There is empirical evidence that love is adaptive:

a. Love has a distinct facial expression and a distinct display, which is difficult to produce voluntarily and communicates the partners' feelings to others.

b. Research shows that partners who display and experience love in one interaction engage in more commitment-related behaviors like reassurance and kindness in a subsequent conflict conversation.

   c. The nonverbal display of love correlates with levels of oxytocin, a neuropeptide that promotes affiliation and commitment.

C. The Effects of Emotion on Social Cognition

   1. Research suggests that emotions (as long as they are not extreme) have systematic effects on our cognitions and generally lead to reasonable judgments.

   2. People who are fearful are more attentive to potential threats, better remember potential threats, and judge the likelihood of threat to be higher, which is helpful in a dangerous situation but dysfunctional in a situation that does not really pose a threat.

D. Accounts of the Influence of Emotion on Cognition

   1. The emotion-congruence perspective can be defined as a theory that maintains that moods and emotions are connected nodes, or areas, in the associative networks of the mind, and that the content of the mood or emotion influences judgments of other events or objects.

      a. Bower et al. (1981) tested the hypothesis that it is easier to learn and remember information that is congruent with our current emotion because such information is more easily integrated into the memory structure that is already activated.

        (1) Independent variable #1: participants were hypnotized to feel happy or sad.

        (2) Independent variable #2: the participants read a story about a student who was doing well or doing poorly (this is still an independent variable even though all participants read both stories).

        (3) Dependent variable: memory for facts in the story.

        (4) Finding: participants remembered more about the story that was consistent with their hypnotized state.

      b. Other research shows that emotions influence particular social judgments.

        (1) Anger triggers blame and sensitivity to unfair actions and makes unfair outcomes seem more likely in the future.

        (2) Sadness triggers situational attributions and makes loss seem more likely in the future.

   2. The feelings-as-information perspective can be defined as a theory that assumes that, since many judgments are often too complex for us to thoroughly review all the relevant evidence, we rely on our emotions to provide us with rapid, reliable information about events and conditions within our social environment.

      a. Schwarz and Clore (1983) tested the feelings-as-information perspective by studying the effects of bright, sunny days and gloomy, overcast days on how happy and satisfied with their lives people were.

        (1) Independent variable #1: the weather was either cloudy or sunny on the days the participants were called.

        (2) Independent variable #2: half of the participants were also asked, just prior to the life satisfaction question, "how's the weather down there?"

        (3) Dependent variable: happiness and life satisfaction ratings.

        (4) Findings: people who were NOT asked about the weather were happier and more satisfied with their lives on sunny than cloudy days (thus, the good mood effects of sunshine or bad mood effects of rainy days figured into their judgment); people who were first asked about the weather were able to discount that information and gave happiness and satisfaction judgments that were independent of the weather.

      b. The feelings-as-information perspective proposes that people often rely directly on their feelings to make complex judgments.

   3. The processing style perspective can be defined as a theory that holds that different emotions lead people to reason in different ways—for example, that positive moods facilitate use of preexisting heuristics and stereotypes, whereas negative moods facilitate more careful attention to situational details.

      a. Bodenhausen and colleagues have found that people are more likely to use stereotypes as shortcuts when they are experiencing positive moods or feeling angry compared to when they are feeling sad.

      b. Isen suggests that happiness makes people think in creative, flexible, and integrative ways, as shown by:

        (1) People feeling positive moods are more likely to find novel word associations (e.g., carpet and texture versus carpet and rug).

        (2) People feeling positive moods categorize more flexibly (e.g., allowing a "cane" to be an item of clothing), whereas those in neutral moods are more rigid in categorizing objects.

(3) People in positive moods are more likely to reach integrative compromises to a conflict they are negotiating.

c. Fredrickson (1998) suggests that the overall function of positive emotions is to broaden our intellectual and interpersonal resources.

VI. Happiness

A. The Determinants of Pleasure

1. Kahneman and Fredrickson have studied pleasurable experiences by having participants watch a pleasant film and rate their second-by-second pleasure using a ratings dial, and they have found that the following most influence pleasure ratings:

    a. The peak moment of pleasure strongly predicts overall pleasure ratings.

    b. Pleasure ratings at the end of the event strongly predict overall pleasure ratings.

2. They have found that people have a bias called duration neglect, which means that the length of an emotional experience, be it pleasurable or unpleasant, in judging the overall experience is relatively unimportant.

B. Knowing What Makes Us Happy

1. Affective forecasting can be defined as predicting our future emotions—for example, whether an event will make us happy or angry or sad.

2. Gilbert et al.'s research has found a number of ways in which we inaccurately predict what will make us happy:

    a. People who had not experienced a romantic breakup overestimated the extent to which such an event would diminish their life satisfaction.

    b. Assistant professors overestimated the extent to which getting tenure would make them happy and being denied tenure would make them unhappy.

3. Immune neglect can be defined as the tendency to underestimate our capacity to be resilient in responding to difficult life events, which leads us to overestimate the extent to which life's difficulties will reduce our personal well-being.

4. Focalism can be defined as a tendency to focus too much on a central aspect of an event, while neglecting to consider the impact of ancillary aspects of the event or the impact of other events.

    a. You may think you will be truly and forever happy once you have finished your GREs, but you underestimate the stress final exams will cause.

    b. You may think a vacation in the tropics will make you happy, but you underestimate the difficulties of getting there, the heat, sunburn, and daily hassles.

C. The Happy Life

1. Diener and his colleagues (2003) integrated studies involving over 1 million people and found that most people are "happy" (i.e., the modal response was 7 on a 10-point scale).

2. Brickman et al. (1978) found that good events (like winning the lottery) or bad events (like losing one's legs in an accident) have only slight effects on overall happiness.

3. Gender and age have very little effect on happiness.

4. Money affects life satisfaction more in less wealthy countries.

    a. Myers (2000) found that most college students state that earning a lot of money is the primary reason to go to college, but he found that actually earning more money is not a primary source of satisfaction (for students in relatively wealthy countries like the U.S.).

    b. Money does influence happiness for those who struggle with lack of jobs, poor nutrition, and disease.

5. Relationships matter a great deal to happiness, as shown by the following empirical evidence:

    a. People who are married are twice as likely as unmarried people to say they are "very happy."

    b. Contact with friends consistently predicts life satisfaction.

6. Diener (2000) has found that people are happier in cultures where individuals have more rights (e.g., the right to vote) and greater economic equality.

Testing Your Basic Knowledge

ANSWERS TO MULTIPLE-CHOICE QUESTIONS

1. a	14. c
2. b	15. a
3. a	16. c
4. c	17. a
5. c	18. b
6. a	19. c
7. b	20. a
8. b	21. a
9. a	22. a
10. c	23. c
11. b	24. b
12. a	25. b
13. c	

Testing Your In-Depth Understanding

EXAMPLE ANSWERS TO THE GUIDED QUESTIONS FOR
CRITICAL THINKING EXERCISE #3

1. Immune neglect and focalism make it hard for us to predict what will make us happy. We underestimate our own resilience, and we play up certain angles of future events too much, while forgetting about other relevant aspects of the event. The research about the actual correlates of happiness also reveals a potential problem—as Myers found, most college students think making more money is the primary reason to go to college. Many Americans in general believe that more money, status, prestige, and more STUFF will make them happier. Even if they consciously reject that sort of materialistic ideology, most people will be familiar with the tug of desire to get the latest technology (iPod), the latest hot fashion item, etc., etc. The research in the text demonstrates that, once a certain basic standard of living (being well-fed, having a home, not having a disease) is reached, having greater income (and being able to spend it on whatever one likes) does not correlate with greater happiness. What does correlate with greater happiness is having strong, satisfying relationships.

2. You can review the meanings of the concepts by looking back at your textbook and/or at other parts of this Study Guide chapter. Below, see some examples of advice for living more calmly and happily based on the concept. See if you can complete the list, add in the information from #1, and create a narrative (paragraph form) mini advice book about how to be happy.

   display rules: your relationships will go more smoothly if you learn and follow the display rules for your culture or subculture, and learn how emotional displays influence others (e.g., embarrassment, although we often try to hide it, can work in your favor).

   ritualized displays: same as above; be sure to learn the specific expressions of specific emotions relevant to the culture you are living in.

   duration neglect: you should go for the activity or experience that seems like it will be most pleasurable, even if it won't last as long as another event, because the research shows that the length of the experience isn't related to pleasure.

   determinants of pleasure: really throw yourself into any experience you are having and try to have one high point and try to end on a good note.

   emotion congruence: don't try to force yourself to absorb information that is contrary to a specific emotion you are having at the moment; for example, if you just had a fight with a significant other and are feeling highly negative emotions, you will not be able to study your happiness research articles effectively, so don't try.

   feelings-as-information: let yourself use your feelings as information; don't try to deny them entirely, but be aware that feelings that are unrelated to the current decision can sneak in and affect your judgment; writing your feelings down can help you deal with them better (see below).

   processing style: be aware that the emotion you are feeling can lead you to be more or less systematic about your decision making; to make good decisions and maintain positive social bonds, try to think about things when you are in a neutral mood.

   hypercognize: be aware of the multiple words people may use to describe an emotion; in this way, you can better understand the feelings of your relationship partners.

   two-factor theory of emotion: realize that you sometimes label generalized arousal according to the cues that are in your environment.

   misattribution of arousal: be sure you are accurate in your labels of your arousal, and that you don't misattribute your arousal to the wrong source.

   rumination: try to catch yourself when you start thinking in circles, as that kind of thinking can lead to depression.

   writing about traumatic feelings: think about your feelings (without dwelling on them) and write them down, aiming for insight about what you felt and why.

   stress: be aware of the negative impact of stress and try to find ways that work for you to reduce your stress.

CHAPTER 13 | Aggression and Altruism

The goal of this chapter is to review the social psychological research from two important areas: aggression and altruism. For aggression, the chapter examines situational determinants of aggression and then reviews a major theoretical approach to aggression (frustration-aggression theory and the more recent neo-associationist theory). The chapter also reviews the cultural and evolutionary underpinnings of aggressive behavior. The review of altruism research follows a similar path: situational determinants like diffusion of responsibility are first discussed, followed by the influence of construal processes on helping. The chapter reviews the perspective of evolutionary theory on helping, empathy-based helping, and briefly reviews one type of cultural difference—helping in urban versus rural environments.

ANNOTATED CHAPTER OUTLINE

After first reading through the chapter quickly, create a comprehensive framework for the information in the chapter by reading the outline below and filling in the missing information. Instead of simply re-copying information from the textbook, try to use your own words wherever possible; you can check your answers against the completed outline in the Answer Key section at the end of the chapter.

I. Aggression
  A. Explanations for aggression vary, depending on whether it is hostile aggression or instrumental aggression.
    1. Hostile aggression can be defined as
    _____
    _____
    _____
    _____

    2. Instrumental aggression can be defined as
    _____
    _____
    _____
    _____

  B. Gender and Aggression
    1. Boys and men are more physically aggressive than girls and women.
      a. The vast majority of people arrested for rape, murder, robbery, or assault are men.
      b. Men are overwhelmingly the victims of violence.
    2. Girls and women are more likely to engage in relational aggression, which is a form of aggression in which
    _____
    _____
    _____
    _____

    3. The gender difference in aggression may exist for any of several reasons:
      a. Socialization
      b. Biological predispositions
      c. Evolution
        (1) In our evolutionary past, men were hunters and protectors, and they used violence to fulfill these roles and to obtain mates.
        (2) Physical aggressiveness increased men's inclusive fitness, which can be defined as
        _____
        _____
        _____
        _____

d. All behavior, even that predisposed by genetics, is highly changeable.

C. Situational Determinants of Aggression
1. Factors that affect the body may produce aggression:
   a. Alcohol consumption
   b. Biochemical factors like testosterone
   c. Genetic factors
2. Media violence may lead to aggressive behavior.
   a. Twelve-year-olds have seen (on average) 100,000 acts of violence on American television, and high school graduates have seen (on average) 13,000 people killed on television.
   b. There is considerable evidence that exposure to media violence increases violent behavior.
      (1) Huesmann et al. (2003) conducted a longitudinal study and found that

      _____
      _____
      _____

      (2) Leyens et al. (1975) found that watching aggressive films versus control films made juvenile delinquents in a minimum security prison more aggressive.
      (3) Leyens and Picus (1973) found that

      _____
      _____
      _____
      _____

      (4) Berkowitz (1965) found that people are more likely to be aggressive after watching films that show "justified" violence.
      (5) Leyens et al. (1976) found that directing people's attention away from the violence to other aspects of the film decreased the likelihood of subsequent aggressive behavior.
3. Playing violent video games may be correlated with aggressive thoughts and behavior.
   a. About 85 percent of American teens play video games regularly, and eight- to thirteen-year-old boys play on average of more than 7.5 hours per week.
   b. Contrary to the claims of the video game industry, there is substantial evidence that watching violent video games is associated with aggressive behavior.

(1) In one study of the effects of playing violent video games, researchers found that undergraduates who had previously played Mortal Kombat versus a control, nonviolent video game were much more aggressive with a competitor in a subsequent game involving blasting one another with loud static over headsets.
(2) Anderson and Bushman (2001) reviewed thirty-five similar studies and noted that they all reached the same conclusions for children, women, and men:
   (a) _____
   _____
   _____
   (b) _____
   _____
   _____
   (c) _____
   _____
   _____
   (d) _____
   _____
   _____
   (e) _____
   _____
   _____

4. Heat
   a. The number of hot days (above 90 degrees Fahrenheit) was a strong predictor of

   _____
   _____
   _____

   b. Violent crime increases during the hot, summer months.
   c. Reifman et al. (1991) found that

   _____
   _____
   _____

   d. Heat may increase aggression through misattribution of arousal.
      (1) Heat causes physiological arousal.
      (2) We may not realize that heat is the cause of arousal.

(3) When encountering a potentially angering situation, we may mistakenly believe our arousal is anger.

(4) This anger may lead to other thoughts and feelings that make aggression more likely.

D. Construal Processes and Aggression

1. The Frustration-Aggression Hypothesis

a. Miller and Dollard proposed that frustration causes aggression and all aggression is caused by frustration.

(1) Frustration can be defined as

_____

_____

_____

(2) Refinements to the basic theory suggest aggression increases in direct proportion to:

(a) _____

_____

_____

(b) _____

_____

_____

(c) _____

_____

_____

(d) _____

_____

_____

b. Harris (1974) tested several of these propositions by having a confederate "cut" into a line of people waiting to buy tickets to see a movie.

(1) Independent variable:

_____

_____

_____

(2) Dependent variable: observed aggressive reactions of the person on line toward the person who cut into the line.

(3) Finding:

_____

_____

_____

2. Critiques of the Frustration-Aggression Account

a. There are exceptions to the claim that all aggressive behavior follows from the thwarting of goals.

(1) Heat, shock, pollution, crowding, and pain may lead to aggression, but they do not seem to be a direct consequence of frustration.

(2) Bullying may be aggression to raise status or show off, but not a result of frustration.

b. Frustration can lead to responses other than aggression, such as learned helplessness, which can be defined as

_____

_____

_____

3. A Neo-Associationistic Account of Aggression

a. Construal of events is an important element leading to aggression; actions that are seen as intentionally harmful are more likely to lead to aggression than those seen as unintentional.

b. Berkowitz's neo-associationistic account of aggression suggests that

_____

_____

_____

(1) Anger involves several elements:
(a) Blame
(b) Physical arousal
(c) Feelings of injustice and revenge

(2) Berkowitz and Troccoli (1990) found that

_____

_____

_____

(3) Shame often triggers anger and aggression.

4. Weapons and Violence

a. There are 638 million guns in the world in the hands of private citizens, and 200 million of them (31 percent) belong to Americans.

b. Berkowitz and LePage (1967) conducted a study in which participants thought they were taking turns evaluating one another's problem-solving skills.

    (1) Independent variable #1:

_____

_____

_____

_____

    (2) Independent variable #2:

_____

_____

_____

_____

    (3) Dependent variable: the number of shocks delivered by the participant to the confederate.

    (4) Finding:

_____

_____

_____

_____

E. Culture and Aggression

   1. The United States has a higher rate of gun-related homicides than Canada, despite the fact that there are a similar number of guns per capita.

     a. The United States is the most violent industrialized country except for Russia.

     b. The difference between homicide rates in Canada and the U.S. may lie in income inequality.

        (1) Daly et al. (2001) proposed that

_____

_____

_____

_____

        (2) Income inequality is far greater in the U.S. than in Canada and many other Western countries, which may account for the higher homicide rate in the U.S.

   2. The cultural perspective argues that there is dramatic cultural variation in levels of aggression, and that this may be because

_____

_____

_____

_____

   3. The Culture of Honor

     a. The culture of honor identified by Nisbett and Cohen is

_____

_____

_____

_____

     b. This culture gives rise to firm rules of politeness as a way of recognizing the honor of others, thereby promoting social stability, but also leading to strong reactions when those rules are broken.

     c. Research suggests that people in the U.S. South possess more of a culture of honor than those in the North.

        (1) Nisbett et al. (1995) looked at archival research on argument-related homicides and felony-related homicides among white males and found that

_____

_____

_____

_____

        (2) Cohen et al. (1996) conducted experimental studies looking at the effects of an insult on participant's thoughts, feelings, and behaviors, and found:

           (a) _____

_____

_____

_____

           (b) _____

_____

_____

_____

           (c) _____

_____

_____

_____

           (d) _____

_____

_____

_____

        (3) Warmer temperatures cannot explain higher homicide rates in the South because the highest rates of homicide are in the cool mountain areas.

        (4) Nisbett and Cohen (1996) argue that the culture of honor arose anywhere people made their living by herding animals, an occupation in which the theft of the animals can quickly and easily result in total loss of income.

           (a) The American South was settled largely by herders, while the North was settled largely by farmers.

           (b) Vulnerability to theft leads to the adoption of a tough, honor-driven exterior to demonstrate that one will not tolerate infractions.

   4. Rape-Prone Cultures

     a. Reeves-Sanday examined anthropological and historical records from 156 cultures across hundreds of years to uncover the cultural determinants of rape.

    (1) Rape-prone cultures can be defined as

_____

_____

_____

_____

    (2) The incidence of rape was unrelated to the extent to which a society was sexually repressed.

    (3) Rape-prone cultures tended to be characterized by

_____

_____

_____

_____

    (4) Women in rape-prone cultures had

_____

_____

_____

_____

    (5) An example of a rape-free culture is that of the Mbuti Pygmies: women and men participate equally in political decision making, there is minimal interpersonal fighting, and women's contributions to society are highly valued.

F. Evolution and Violence

   1. Wilson and Daly suggest that evolution has favored those who devote resources to the care of their own genetic offspring, and they note that stepparents do not receive inclusive fitness benefits when raising another person's children.

    a. In regard to child abuse, Daly and Wilson (1996) found that

_____

_____

_____

_____

    b. The death rate for children raised by stepparents in a South American foraging society was twice that of children raised by genetic parents.

   2. Given the cost associated with raising a child, inclusive fitness concerns led men to be highly distressed by female infidelity (because it potentially led to uncertainty about the identity of a child's father).

    a. Wilson and Daly (1996) found that lethal violence against wives in Australia, Canada, and the United States is

_____

    b. Wilson et al. (1995) report that lethal violence is eight times more likely in relationships that do not have legal status, suggesting concerns about infidelity.

    c. Daly and Wilson (1988) found that men killing men was twenty times more common than women killing women, often for what began as a trivial disagreement, because:

      (1) _____

_____

_____

      (2) _____

_____

_____

II. Altruism

A. Altruism can be defined as

_____

_____

_____

_____

B. Situational Determinants of Altruism

   1. Darley and Batson's (1973) "Good Samaritan" study demonstrates the powerful influence of situational forces on our tendency to help.

    a. Independent variable #1: seminary students were asked to give a talk about common careers for seminary students or a talk about the parable of the Good Samaritan.

    b. Independent variable #2:

_____

_____

_____

    c. Dependent variable:

_____

_____

_____

    d. Findings:

_____

_____

_____

_____

   2. Audience Effects

    a. Bystander intervention can be defined as

_____

_____

_____

_____

b. Diffusion of responsibility can be defined as

_____

_____

_____

c. Darley and Latané (1968) conducted a study inspired by the Kitty Genovese incident in which college students sat in separate cubicles and had a discussion via an intercom system.
  (1) Independent variable: participants were led to believe their group consisted of just one other person, two other people, or five other people.
  (2) Dependent variables:

  _____

  _____

  _____

  (3) Finding:

  _____

  _____

  _____

d. Many other studies with various setups have found similar results: 75 percent of people helped when they were alone, but only 53 percent helped when others were present.

3. Victim Characteristics
  a. Piliavin and Piliavin (1972) found that

  _____

  _____

  _____

  b. People (and nonhuman primates) are more likely to help similar others (e.g., people from their own racial or ethnic group), and others to whom they are attracted.
  c. Helping is more likely if the need for help is completely unambiguous.
  d. Women tend to receive more help than men, especially attractive and feminine women, presumably because

  _____

  _____

  _____

C. Construal Processes and Altruism
  1. A first step in helping is that observers construe a situation as one in which help is required.
    a. A screaming victim gets more help than a silent one.

b. When participants see vivid events leading up to the situation, they are more likely to help than if they only see the situation once help is necessary.
c. Pluralistic ignorance occurs when

_____

_____

_____

_____

d. Latané and Darley (1968) tested the effects of pluralistic ignorance in an experiment in which they asked participants to fill out a packet of questionnaires in a lab.
  (1) Independent variable: participants were alone, with two other real participants, or were with two confederates trained to remain calm throughout the session.
  (2) Dependent variable:

  _____

  _____

  _____

  (3) Findings:

  _____

  _____

  _____

  (4) Students who reported the smoke said they construed it as indicating true danger; students who did not report the smoke construed it as intentional (e.g., "truth gas") or harmless (e.g., air conditioning ventilation).
e. Darley et al. (1973) demonstrated that pluralistic ignorance is less likely to occur when other people's concerns are clearly visible.
  (1) Independent variable:

  _____

  _____

  _____

  (2) Dependent variable: percentage of participants who came to the aid of a nearby workman who could be heard moaning that his leg hurt after a loud crash.
  (3) Finding:

  _____

  _____

  _____

f. Two pieces of advice to overcome pluralistic ignorance and diffusion of responsibility when you need help:

(1) _____

_____

_____

(2) _____

_____

_____

D. Evolutionary Approaches to Altruism

1. Because natural selection favors behaviors that increase survival, altruism was initially puzzling to evolutionary researchers.

2. Kin Selection

a. Kin selection can be defined as

_____

_____

_____

b. Kin selection theory hypothesizes that we should have a highly developed ability to recognize kin; mothers can recognize their new babies from photographs and smells on T-shirts, even if they have had little contact with the newborn.

c. Kin selection theory hypothesizes that we should direct more of our helping behavior toward kin than toward nonkin.

(1) Across numerous cultures, people report being more willing to help and receiving more help from close relatives versus more distant relatives or nonrelatives.

(2) Borgida et al. (1992) found that

_____

_____

_____

(3) Segal (1984) found that

_____

_____

_____

_____

3. Reciprocity

a. Reciprocal altruism is an evolutionary explanation for why we help nonrelative friends and strangers.

b. Reciprocal altruism can be defined as

_____

_____

_____

(1) It reduces the likelihood of dangerous conflict.

(2) It reduces the dangers of scarce resources.

(3) It allows alliance formation.

c. de Waal (1996) found that primates are more likely to share, groom, and "babysit" for other primates who do the same for them.

d. The impulse to return favors may be a human universal.

(1) Kunz and Woolcott (1976) found that

_____

_____

_____

_____

(2) Berkowitz and Daniels (1964) found in a lab study that people who had received help from a confederate were more helpful to others in a subsequent interaction.

4. Reputational Advantages and Social Rewards

a. Social rewards can be defined as

_____

_____

_____

_____

b. Note that the desire to gain reputational advantage or rewards may be unconscious.

E. Empathy-Based Altruism: A Case of Pure Altruism?

1. Batson argues that there are two egoistic motives for helping, and one altruistic motive:

a. Social rewards—egoistic.

b. Experienced distress—egoistic—which is

_____

_____

_____

c. Empathy—altruistic.

(1) Empathy can be defined as

_____

_____

_____

(2) When we empathize with another's distress, we are motivated to reduce their distress, even at our own expense, for their sake, not ours.

2. Batson et al. (1983) created an experimental paradigm to differentiate between the three types of motives.

a. Independent variable #1:

_____

_____

_____

_____

b. Independent variable #2: participants'
reactions to the confederate's discomfort
were divided into egoistic distress reactions
and empathetic reactions.

c. Dependent variable:

_____

_____

_____

d. Finding:

_____

_____

_____

_____

e. Critiques
(1) Empathy was not manipulated.
(2) A social rewards account cannot be
eliminated.

3. Fultz et al. (1986) led participants to believe
that they were the "listeners" in an impression
formation study with a participant named
Janet.

a. Independent variable #1:

_____

_____

_____

b. Independent variable #2:

_____

_____

_____

c. Dependent variable: how much time
participants volunteered to spend with Janet
in a subsequent interaction (given Janet's
note saying that she was lonely).

d. Finding:

_____

_____

_____

4. Eisenberg et al. (1989) evaluated the facial
expressions, heart rate, and self-reported
emotions of children as they watched a moving
video about young children who couldn't
attend school because they were injured in an
accident; they also measured likelihood of
helping by taking homework to the children.

a. Finding for participants who felt empathy:

_____

_____

_____

_____

b. Finding for participants who felt distress:

_____

_____

_____

_____

F. The Culture of Altruism

1. Steblay (1987) reviewed thirty-five studies that
included seventeen different kinds of helping
behaviors and found that strangers were more
likely to be helped in rural areas.

a. You're more likely to be helped in a town
of 1,000 than 5,000, in a town of 5,000 than
10,000, and so on.

b. Once the population rises above 50,000, the
likelihood of helping remains about the
same.

c. People's current context was a better
predictor of helping that the type of area
they grew up in.

2. Milgram (1970) suggested that helping is less
likely in larger cities because

_____

_____

_____

3. Smaller environments are typically less
diverse, increasing the chances that someone
who is similar to you will be the one needing
help, as opposed to urban environments, which
are made up of more diverse populations.

4. Since larger urban areas have more people
around to help, there may be more diffusion of
responsibility.

TESTING YOUR BASIC KNOWLEDGE

After studying the information in the chapter by filling in the
outline above, test your basic knowledge with the following
multiple-choice test. Answers are provided in the Answer
Key section at the end of the chapter. If you find that you
have gotten an answer wrong, it is important that you understand why it is wrong (as well as understanding why the correct answer is the better choice). Talk with peers, your tutor,
or your professor if you need help.

Multiple-Choice Questions

1. Luke reluctantly aims a pistol and shoots Anakin in
order to prevent Anakin from hurting an innocent
person. What type of aggression is Luke engaging in?
a. hostile
b. instrumental
c. frustrated

2. Girls are less aggressive than boys.
   a. This is true.
   b. This is false.
   c. This is true for physical aggression, but not true for relational aggression.

3. Huesmann and Eron's research (Huesmann et al., 2003) suggests which of the following conclusions about the influence of media violence on actual violence?
   a. The amount of violent television viewed at age eight predicts the likelihood of being involved in serious criminal activity at age thirty.
   b. The likelihood of being involved with serious criminal activity at age thirty was predicted solely by the amount of dispositional aggression children showed at age eight.
   c. Violent television does predict aggressive behavior among children, but this effect does not extend into adulthood.

4. Playing violent video games
   a. increases aggressive thoughts and emotions.
   b. increases blood pressure and heart rate.
   c. Both A and B are accurate.

5. Higher temperatures may lead people to be more aggressive because
   a. heat inhibits a person's ability to think rationally.
   b. heat causes arousal which, in turn, can lead a person to misattribute that arousal to an anger-eliciting stimulus, increasing the chances that aggression will occur.
   c. cooler temperatures have been shown to have a calming effect on physiological aggression systems.

6. According to the frustration-aggression hypothesis,
   a. frustration leads to aggression, and aggression is always a consequence of frustration.
   b. frustration only leads to aggression when the perpetrator can identify with the target.
   c. frustration will lead to either aggression or learned helplessness.

7. In which of the following conditions would Berkowitz's neo-associationistic account of aggression predict the highest likelihood of aggression?
   a. when a confederate cuts into a line in front of the twelfth person from the front
   b. when a person is engaging in a physically arousing sport, like football
   c. when a participant is angry and in the presence of an aggression cue, like a gun

8. Leonard argues with his wife and becomes very angry with her. In which of the following situations is Leonard most likely to slap his wife?
   a. He leaves the room and goes into his study where he unloads his gun and begins cleaning it. His wife comes in a few moments later to continue their argument.
   b. He leaves the room and goes into his study where he pulls out a user's manual for his computer and begins reading it. His wife comes in a few moments later to continue their argument.
   c. Leonard is equally likely to engage in physical violence in either case; A and B could both be correct answers.

9. According to your textbook, what is one explanation for why, despite having a similar number of guns per capita, the homicide rate is so much higher in the United States than in Canada?
   a. Americans have shorter tempers than Canadians.
   b. There is greater income inequality in the U.S. compared to Canada.
   c. American law is harsher with respect to homicide than Canadian law.

10. Wayne calls Keith a "jerk" and accuses Keith of being dishonest. Keith responds by immediately becoming wildly angry and punching Wayne. According to the research on the culture of honor, which of the following is most likely?
    a. Keith is from the southern United States.
    b. Keith has old-fashioned values.
    c. Keith watched a large number of "western" movies about cowboys when he was young.

11. Which of the following is *not* a characteristic of a rape-prone culture?
    a. a history of frequent warfare
    b. political and educational dominance of men over women
    c. cultural repression of sexuality

12. According to an evolutionary account of violence,
    a. physical aggression to protect their children promotes inclusive fitness for men.
    b. stepparents are more likely to abuse their children than genetic parents.
    c. Both A and B are true.

13. Marta falls in love with another man, but she does not have sex with him. Christine has sex with another man, but she does not love him. According to an evolutionary account of violence, which woman's husband is more likely to express his jealousy with aggression?
    a. Marta's husband, because being in love with someone else is a greater emotional betrayal.
    b. Christine's husband, because of concerns about raising another man's child.
    c. Because men are more likely to be violent than women, aggression is equally likely in both cases.

14. Darley and Batson's famous "Good Samaritan study" revealed what results?
    a. Even seminary students on their way to deliver a lecture about the Good Samaritan overlooked a man needing help when they were in a hurry to get to the lecture on time.
    b. Participants were more likely to help a stranger when they were primed with the Good Samaritan parable than when they were not.
    c. Whether or not they were in a hurry had no impact on the likelihood of a seminary student helping a stranger.

15. According to social psychological research, if someone fell and sprained her ankle on a city street, under which of the following conditions would this person be *most* likely to receive quick and immediate help?
    a. if there are only two people present
    b. if there are fifteen or more people present
    c. if the victim remains calm and quiet

16. Batson's empathy-altruism hypothesis states that we will help a victim of misfortune regardless of whether helping is in our best interests if
    a. the costs of helping are minimal.
    b. the victim is unable to control his or her situation.
    c. we relate to the victim's pain and suffering.

17. How does a social rewards perspective on helping differ from a kin selection perspective?
    a. Only the social rewards perspective maintains that helping is motivated by evolutionary concerns.
    b. Only the social rewards perspective explains why we would help people we are not related to.
    c. Only the kin selection perspective has supporting empirical evidence.

18. The day before your social psychology exam, your teacher asks the class if there are any questions. You are confused about the bystander effect, but feel that you must be the only person who is confused, since the rest of the class does not appear to have any questions. Since no one else is asking questions, you decide to keep your question to yourself. After the exam, you learn that everyone missed the question about the bystander effect. What phenomenon accounts for this widespread mistake?
    a. diffusion of responsibility
    b. pluralistic ignorance
    c. reciprocal altruism

19. Which of the following *best* illustrates the kind of thinking influenced by diffusion of responsibility?
    a. "Everyone seems to be reacting calmly. Maybe there's no real problem."

    b. "I hope I don't make things worse than they already are by trying to help."
    c. "There are plenty of other people here; one of them will help."

20. Annie is participating in a research study in which she has to watch another subject, Elaine, receive shocks. Annie is told that she is free to leave the study and go home after seeing Elaine receive two uncomfortable shocks. Alternatively, Annie could choose to take Elaine's place for the remaining eight shocks. Under what conditions is Annie most likely to volunteer to take Elaine's place?
    a. if Annie is experiencing distress watching Elaine receive the shocks
    b. if Annie is able to identify with Elaine and understand what Elaine is going through
    c. if Annie looks around and sees that no one else seems concerned with Elaine's well-being

21. Helping strangers is more likely in a rural environment compared to an urban environment. Which of the following explanations has been proposed by social psychologists?
    a. There is less diversity in small towns than in larger cities, and people are more likely to help those who are similar to themselves.
    b. People who are raised in small towns develop more of a sense of civic responsibility than people who are raised in large, urban environments.
    c. People living in large, urban cities have chosen to live there because they are more callous and uncaring than people who choose to live in small towns.

22. According to reciprocal altruism,
    a. people are more likely to help those who are genetically related than to help strangers.
    b. people are more likely to help others who have, in the past, helped them.
    c. people are more likely to help another person if there is some sort of reward for doing so.

23. John is filling out a survey in a room with four other people. Suddenly, smoke starts entering the room from underneath a door. According to research by Latané and Darley, what is John's likely response?
    a. John will look around the room at the other people and follow their cue.
    b. John will report the problem and/or investigate the smoke.
    c. John will immediately jump up and run out of the building to safety.

24. Women are more likely to receive help than men, especially if
    a. they seem to be independent and self-sufficient.
    b. they are dressed in more feminine clothing.
    c. they smile while requesting the help.

25. During the warm-up for an ice skating competition, Tanya has her boyfriend run out on the ice and hit Nancy in the leg so that Nancy (who would have been likely to beat Tanya) can't participate in the competition. The boyfriend's aggressive action *best* illustrates
    a. hostile aggression.
    b. instrumental aggression.
    c. reciprocal altruism.

Essay Questions

After you have mastered the multiple-choice questions, try testing your basic understanding by thoroughly answering each of the broad essay questions below. Because it is critical that you think through this information on your own, we have not provided any answers to these questions. Your learning and retention of this material will be greatly enhanced if you do one or more of the following to check your answers: carefully review the textbook information; compare your responses to your class lecture notes; talk over your answers with a peer; ask your professor to review your answers or review any information that is unclear to you.

1. Discuss gender differences in aggression.

2. Provide examples of situational determinants of aggression and, where possible, provide empirical evidence.

3. Compare and contrast the frustration-aggression hypothesis and the neo-associationistic account of aggression. What evidence does the neo-associationistic account provide that can speak to the issue of gun control?

4. Explain the culture of honor and discuss the characteristics of rape-prone cultures.

5. Discuss the evolutionary underpinnings of aggression.

6. Define and discuss the ways in which diffusion of responsibility, pluralistic ignorance, and victim effects can influence helping behavior.

7. Explain and discuss empathy-based altruism. Fully describe one study that illustrates empathy-based altruism.

8. Why is help more likely to occur in rural versus urban environments?

TESTING YOUR IN-DEPTH UNDERSTANDING

Test your in-depth understanding of the material by working through the Critical Thinking Exercises provided at the end of each textbook chapter. To maximize this learning opportunity, work together with a tutor, study group, or your professor. Alternatively, write down your thoughts and responses.

Guided questions for one of the exercises are provided below. While there are multiple ways to answer these questions, short answers are given in the Answer Key at the end of the chapter. Note that the valuable part of this exercise is not simply knowing the answer but working with the material to come up with the answer.

Guided Questions for Critical Thinking Exercise #2

Do you think that knowing about the Darley and Latané findings on bystander intervention would affect bystanders' behavior when they see someone who suddenly appears to be seriously ill or is involved in an accident? (To find out if it really does, see Beaman, Barnes, Kleentz, and McQuirk, 1978.)

1. In research not reviewed in this chapter, Latané and Darley have proposed that there are five steps that lead to helping behavior: (a) Notice that something is happening, (b) interpret the situation as one in which help is needed, (c) assume responsibility for providing the help, (d) decide on the appropriate way in which to help, (e) decide to give the help. For each of those steps, brainstorm how situational factors and/or construal processes could encourage or discourage helping.

2. Now go through and do a thought experiment. For each of the barriers to helping that you listed in #1, try to reason through whether that barrier could be eliminated through education.

3. Finally, actually go to PSYCHINFO and look up the study indicated.

Enhance your understanding of the chapter by thinking about and doing the remaining three Critical Thinking Exercises. Discuss your answers with your peers, study group, tutor, or professor.

Critical Thinking Exercise #1

Think of a situation in which aggression is likely to be both hostile and instrumental. Do you think people would be more likely to perceive the hostile motives or the instrumental ones?

Critical Thinking Exercise #3

Who would be more likely to give altruistic aid—a member of an independent culture or a member of an interdependent culture? Would it make a difference whether the victim was a member of an ingroup or an outgroup?

Critical Thinking Exercise #4

Think of some ways you might reduce hostile aggression in some setting. Think of some ways you might increase altruism in some setting.

SOCIAL PSYCHOLOGY IN THE POPULAR MEDIA

You might be interested in the following popular media references, each of which relates in some way to information in this chapter.

Films

Bowling for Columbine (2002; directed by Michael Moore). In this Oscar-award winning documentary, Michael Moore explores the culture of violence that exists in the United States.

Hotel Rwanda (2004; directed by Terry George; starring Don Cheadle). This movie tells the story of Paul Rusesabagina, the Rwandan hotel manager described at the beginning of the textbook chapter. A highly praised film, rated by many as a "must see" movie.

Mean Girls (2004; directed by Mark Waters; starring Lindsay Lohan, Tina Fey). A funny and smart mainstream movie exploring the topic of "relational aggression." Lindsay Lohan plays a teenager who had been home schooled but is now attending high school for the first time. She falls in with a clique of snobby "mean girls" and gets an insider's look at relational aggression.

Books

Aronson, Elliot. (2001). *Nobody Left to Hate: Teaching Compassion after Columbine.* New York: Owl Books. In this very readable popular press book, Aronson, also a social psychologist, examines youth violence. In particular, he explores the Columbine High School massacre. From the front cover: "Elliot Aronson brings to bear the power of social psychology to offer a road map for changing the social environment of the school from competition to cooperation. . . ."

Wiseman, Rosalind. (2004). *Queen Bees and Wannabes: Helping Your Daughter Survive Cliques, Gossip, Boyfriends, and Other Realities of Adolescence.* New

York: Three Rivers Press. The movie *Mean Girls* was based on research from this book about adolescent female friendship. From the front flap of the hardcover edition: "Wiseman has spent more than a decade listening to thousands of girls talk about the powerful role cliques play in shaping what they wear and say, how they respond to boys, and how they feel about themselves. . . . She takes readers into "Girl World" to analyze teasing, gossip, and reputations; beauty and fashion; alcohol and drugs; boys and sex and more. . . ."

ANSWER KEY

Annotated Chapter Outline

I. Aggression
   A. Explanations for aggression vary, depending on whether it is hostile aggression or instrumental aggression.
      1. Hostile aggression can be defined as behavior intended to harm another, either physically or psychologically, and motivated by feelings of anger and hostility.
      2. Instrumental aggression can be defined as behavior intended to harm another in the service of motives other than pure hostility (for example, to attract attention, to acquire wealth, and to advance political and ideological causes).
   B. Gender and Aggression
      1. Boys and men are more physically aggressive than girls and women.
         a. The vast majority of people arrested for rape, murder, robbery, or assault are men.
         b. Men are overwhelmingly the victims of violence.
      2. Girls and women are more likely to engage in relational aggression, which is a form of aggression in which gossip, alliance formation, and exclusion are used to intentionally hurt others.
      3. The gender difference in aggression may exist for any of several reasons:
         a. Socialization
         b. Biological predispositions
         c. Evolution
            (1) In our evolutionary past, men were hunters and protectors, and they used violence to fulfill these roles and to obtain mates.
            (2) Physical aggressiveness increased men's inclusive fitness, which can be defined as an evolutionary tendency to

look out for oneself, one's offspring, and one's close relatives together with their offspring so that one's genes will survive.

    d. All behavior, even that predisposed by genetics, is highly changeable.

C. Situational Determinants of Aggression

    1. Factors that affect the body may produce aggression:

        a. Alcohol consumption

        b. Biochemical factors like testosterone

        c. Genetic factors

    2. Media violence may lead to aggressive behavior.

        a. Twelve-year-olds have seen (on average) 100,000 acts of violence on American television, and high school graduates have seen (on average) 13,000 people killed on television.

        b. There is considerable evidence that exposure to media violence increases violent behavior.

            (1) Huesmann et al. (2003) conducted a longitudinal study and found that exposure to violent television at age eight was a significant predictor of criminal activity at age thirty, above and beyond the influence of dispositional aggressiveness as measured at age eight.

            (2) Leyens et al. (1975) found that watching aggressive films versus control films made juvenile delinquents at a minimum security prison more aggressive.

            (3) Leyens and Picus (1973) found that people tend to be more aggressive after watching films in which they can "identify" with the violent perpetrator.

            (4) Berkowitz (1965) found that people are more likely to be aggressive after watching films that show "justified" violence.

            (5) Leyens et al. (1976) found that directing people's attention away from the violence to other aspects of the film decreased the likelihood of subsequent aggressive behavior.

    3. Playing violent video games may be correlated with aggressive thoughts and behavior.

        a. About 85 percent of American teens play video games regularly, and eight- to thirteen-year-old boys play on average of more than 7.5 hours per week.

        b. Contrary to the claims of the video game industry, there is substantial evidence that watching violent video games is associated with aggressive behavior.

            (1) In one study of the effects of playing violent video games, researchers found that undergraduates who had previously played Mortal Kombat versus a control, nonviolent video game were much more aggressive with a competitor in a subsequent game involving blasting one another with loud static over headsets.

            (2) Anderson and Bushman (2001) reviewed thirty-five similar studies and noted that they all reached the same conclusions for children, women, and men:

                (a) Playing violent games increases aggressive behavior.

                (b) It reduces helping behavior.

                (c) It increases aggressive thoughts.

                (d) It increases aggressive emotions.

                (e) It increases heart rate and blood pressure.

    4. Heat

        a. The number of hot days (above 90 degrees Fahrenheit) was a strong predictor of violent but not nonviolent crime.

        b. Violent crime increases during the hot, summer months.

        c. Reifman et al. (1991) found that major league pitchers were more likely to hit batters during hotter weather.

        d. Heat may increase aggression through misattribution of arousal

            (1) Heat causes physiological arousal.

            (2) We may not realize that heat is the cause of arousal.

            (3) When encountering a potentially angering situation, we may mistakenly believe our arousal is anger.

            (4) This anger may lead to other thoughts and feelings that make aggression more likely.

D. Construal Processes and Aggression

    1. The Frustration-Aggression Hypothesis

        a. Miller and Dollard proposed that frustration causes aggression and all aggression is caused by frustration.

            (1) Frustration can be defined as the internal state that accompanies the thwarting of an individual's attempts to achieve some goal.

(2) Refinements to the basic theory suggest aggression increases in direct proportion to:
    (a) The amount of satisfaction the goal would have provided if it had not been blocked.
    (b) The more completely the goal is blocked.
    (c) The more frequently the person's goal has been blocked.
    (d) The closer a person is to achieving the goal.

b. Harris (1974) tested several of these propositions by having a confederate "cut" into a line of people waiting to buy tickets to see a movie.
    (1) Independent variable: cutting in front of the twelfth person in a line, or cutting in front of the second person in line.
    (2) Dependent variable: observed aggressive reactions of the person on line toward the person who cut into the line.
    (3) Finding: the person who was closer to the goal, second in line, responded more aggressively than the person who was twelfth in line.

2. Critiques of the Frustration-Aggression Account
  a. There are exceptions to the claim that all aggressive behavior follows from the thwarting of goals.
    (1) Heat, shock, pollution, crowding, and pain may lead to aggression, but they do not seem to be a direct consequence of frustration.
    (2) Bullying may be aggression to raise status or show off, but not a result of frustration.
  b. Frustration can lead to responses other than aggression, such as learned helplessness, which can be defined as passive and depressed responses that individuals show when their goals are blocked and they feel that they have no control over their outcomes.

3. A Neo-Associationistic Account of Aggression
  a. Construal of events is an important element leading to aggression; actions that are seen as intentionally harmful are more likely to lead to aggression than those seen as unintentional.

b. Berkowitz's neo-associationistic account of aggression suggests that any aversive event can lead to aggression if it produces anger.
    (1) Anger involves several elements:
      (a) Blame
      (b) Physical arousal
      (c) Feelings of injustice and revenge
    (2) Berkowitz and Troccoli (1990) found that making people raise their arms for six minutes (which causes pain) can make them subsequently behave more aggressively.
    (3) Shame often triggers anger and aggression.

4. Weapons and Violence
  a. There are 638 million guns in the world in the hands of private citizens, and 200 million of them (31 percent) belong to Americans.
  b. Berkowitz and LePage (1967) conducted a study in which participants thought they were taking turns evaluating one another's problem-solving skills.
    (1) Independent variable #1: whether, in the first phase of the study, the confederate administered one "feedback" shock (neutral condition) or seven "feedback" shocks (anger condition).
    (2) Independent variable #2: whether, in the second phase of the study, the participant saw no object, a neutral object, or a gun on the table next to the shock generator.
    (3) Dependent variable: the number of shocks delivered by the participant to the confederate.
    (4) Finding: consistent with the neo-associationistic perspective, participants in the angry condition and the gun prime condition delivered more shocks than any other group; note that the prime (the gun) only had an impact when the participant was angry.

E. Culture and Aggression
1. The United States has a higher rate of gun-related homicides than Canada, despite the fact that there are a similar number of guns per capita.
  a. The United States is the most violent industrialized country except for Russia.
  b. The difference between homicide rates in Canada and in the U.S. may lie in income inequality.

(1) Daly et al. (2001) proposed that homicide rates are sensitive to income inequality because such inequality promotes competition between males for marriage partners and economic resources (roots of violence).

(2) Income inequality is far greater in the U.S. than in Canada and many other Western countries, which may account for the higher homicide rate in the U.S.

2. The cultural perspective argues that there is dramatic cultural variation in levels of aggression, and that this may be because there are certain values and habitual ways of construing the self and others that can lead to a greater propensity for violence in some cultures.

3. The Culture of Honor

   a. The culture of honor identified by Nisbett and Cohen is a culture that is defined by strong concerns about one's own and others' reputations, leading to sensitivity to slights and insults and a willingness to use violence to avenge any perceived wrong or insult.

   b. This culture gives rise to firm rules of politeness as a way of recognizing the honor of others, thereby promoting social stability, but also leading to strong reactions when those rules are broken.

   c. Research suggests that people in the U.S. South possess more of a culture of honor than those in the North.

      (1) Nisbett et al. (1995) looked at archival research on argument-related homicides and felony-related homicides among white males and found that felony-related homicide rates were about equally common in the South, North, and Southwest, but honor-related homicides were far more common in the South and Southwest than in the North.

      (2) Cohen et al. (1996) conducted experimental studies looking at the effects of an insult on participant's thoughts, feelings, and behaviors, and found:

         (a) Southerners showed more anger in their faces than did Northerners.

         (b) Southerners showed increased levels of testosterone and cortisol.

         (c) Southerners shook hands more firmly (to show strength, honor, power).

         (d) Southerners took longer to move out of the way than Northerners when meeting a confederate in the middle of a narrow hallway.

      (3) Warmer temperatures cannot explain higher homicide rates in the South because the highest rates of homicide are in the cool mountain areas.

      (4) Nisbett and Cohen (1996) argue that the culture of honor arose anywhere people made their living by herding animals, an occupation in which the theft of the animals can quickly and easily result in total loss of income.

         (a) The American South was settled largely by herders, while the North was settled largely by farmers.

         (b) Vulnerability to theft leads to the adoption of a tough, honor-driven exterior to demonstrate that one will not tolerate infractions.

4. Rape-Prone Cultures

   a. Reeves-Sanday examined anthropological and historical records from 156 cultures across hundreds of years to uncover the cultural determinants of rape.

      (1) Rape-prone cultures can be defined as cultures in which rape tends to be used as an act of war against enemy women, as a ritual act, and as a threat against women so that they will remain subservient to men.

      (2) The incidence of rape was unrelated to the extent to which a society was sexually repressed.

      (3) Rape-prone cultures tended to be characterized by high levels of cultural violence, warfare, machismo, and male toughness.

      (4) Women in rape-prone cultures had lower status relative to men (e.g., less participation in education and politics).

      (5) An example of a rape-free culture is that of the Mbuti Pygmies: women and men participate equally in political decision making, there is minimal interpersonal fighting, and women's contributions to society are highly valued.

F. Evolution and Violence

   1. Wilson and Daly suggest that evolution has favored those who devote resources to the care of their own genetic offspring, and they note that stepparents do not receive inclusive fitness benefits when raising another person's children.

a. In regard to child abuse, Daly and Wilson (1996) found that American stepchildren are 100 times more likely to suffer lethal abuse at the hands of a stepparent than a genetic parent, and Canadian stepchildren are 70 times more likely (controlling for other contributing factors to child abuse).

b. The death rate for children raised by stepparents in a South American foraging society was twice that of children raised by genetic parents.

2. Given the cost associated with raising a child, inclusive fitness concerns led men to be highly distressed by female infidelity (because it potentially led to uncertainty about the identity of a child's father).

a. Wilson and Daly (1996) found that lethal violence against wives in Australia, Canada, and the United States is three to five times higher when a couple is separated (implying opportunities for infidelity) than when they are together.

b. Wilson et al. (1995) report that lethal violence is eight times more likely in relationships that do not have legal status, suggesting concerns about infidelity.

c. Daly and Wilson (1988) found that men killing men was twenty times more common than women killing women, often for what began as a trivial disagreement, because:

(1) Evolution favored men who fought to achieve higher status and, thus, acquired more mates and more children.

(2) There is much greater variability in reproductive success (many children or none) for men versus women (more men remained single and childless than women).

II. Altruism

A. Altruism can be defined as unselfish behavior that benefits others without regard to the consequences for the self.

B. Situational Determinants of Altruism

1. Darley and Batson's (1973) "Good Samaritan" study demonstrates the powerful influence of situational forces on our tendency to help.

a. Independent variable #1: seminary students were asked to give a talk about common careers for seminary students or a talk about the parable of the Good Samaritan.

b. Independent variable #2: participants were either told there was no hurry to get across campus to the lecture room or told that they would need to moderately hurry, or told that they were already late (high hurry).

c. Dependent variable: the proportion of students in each condition who stopped to help a man slumped in a doorway who was in obvious distress.

d. Findings: while the topic of the talk had little effect, there was a large main effect for the other independent variable; participants who were not in a hurry were six times more likely to stop to help than participants who were in a hurry; only 10 percent of the participants who were in a hurry stopped to help.

2. Audience Effects

a. Bystander intervention can be defined as helping a victim of an emergency by those who have observed what is happening; it is generally reduced as the number of observers increases, as each individual feels that someone else will be likely to help.

b. Diffusion of responsibility can be defined as a reduction of a sense of urgency to help someone involved in an emergency or dangerous situation under the assumption that others who are also observing the situation will help.

c. Darley and Latané (1968) conducted a study inspired by the Kitty Genovese incident in which college students sat in separate cubicles and had a discussion via an intercom system.

(1) Independent variable: participants were led to believe their group consisted of just one other person, two other people, or five other people.

(2) Dependent variables: the percentage of participants who left their cubicles to help their fellow participant who was apparently having an epileptic seizure, and the length of time it took before they began to help.

(3) Finding: 85 percent of people who thought they were the only one available to help did help, 62 percent who thought there was one other person listening helped, 31 percent who thought there were four other people listening helped.

d. Many other studies with various setups have found similar results: 75 percent of people helped when they were alone, but only 53 percent helped when others were present.

3. Victim Characteristics
   a. Piliavin and Piliavin (1972) found that subway riders in Philadelphia were less likely to help a collapsed man when he had blood trickling from his mouth, presumably because the perceived cost of helping a bleeding victim was greater than the perceived cost of helping someone who was not bleeding.
   b. People (and nonhuman primates) are more likely to help similar others (e.g., people from their own racial or ethnic group), and others to whom they are attracted.
   c. Helping is more likely if the need for help is completely unambiguous.
   d. Women tend to receive more help than men, especially attractive and feminine women, presumably because of the perceived chance for romantic involvement and/or the perception of a feminine female as being dependent and in more need of aid.

C. Construal Processes and Altruism
   1. A first step in helping is that observers construe a situation as one in which help is required.
      a. A screaming victim gets more help than a silent one.
      b. When participants see vivid events leading up to the situation, they are more likely to help than if they only see the situation once help is necessary.
      c. Pluralistic ignorance occurs when people are uncertain about what is happening and assume that nothing is wrong because no one else is responding or appears concerned.
      d. Latané and Darley (1968) tested the effects of pluralistic ignorance in an experiment in which they asked participants to fill out a packet of questionnaires in a lab.
         (1) Independent variable: participants were alone, with two other real participants, or were with two confederates trained to remain calm throughout the session.
         (2) Dependent variable: how many and how quickly participants left the room and reported to the experimenter that it was filling up with smoke flowing in from underneath another door.
         (3) Findings: 75 percent of participants in the alone condition quickly left the room and reported the smoke; 38 percent of participants in the "real participant" condition left the room and reported the smoke; and the best

example of pluralistic ignorance occurred in the condition in which the participant was in the room with two confederates trained to look calm and unconcerned—only 10 percent of the participants left the room and reported the smoke.
         (4) Students who reported the smoke said they construed it as indicating true danger; students who did not report the smoke construed it as intentional (e.g., "truth gas") or harmless (e.g., air conditioning ventilation).
      e. Darley et al. (1973) demonstrated that pluralistic ignorance is less likely to occur when other people's concerns are clearly visible.
         (1) Independent variable: participants were alone, seated back-to-back so they could not see each other's faces, or seated face-to-face.
         (2) Dependent variable: percentage of participants who came to the aid of a nearby workman who could be heard moaning that his leg hurt after a loud crash.
         (3) Finding: 90 percent of participants who were alone helped; 80 percent of participants seated face-to-face helped; only 20 percent of participants seated back-to-back helped.
      f. Two pieces of advice to overcome pluralistic ignorance and diffusion of responsibility when you need help:
         (1) Make your need clear.
         (2) Ask a specific person.

D. Evolutionary Approaches to Altruism
   1. Because natural selection favors behaviors that increase survival, altruism was initially puzzling to evolutionary researchers.
   2. Kin Selection
      a. Kin selection can be defined as the tendency for natural selection to favor behaviors that increase the chances of survival of genetic relatives.
      b. Kin selection theory hypothesizes that we should have a highly developed ability to recognize kin; mothers can recognize their new babies from photographs and smells on T-shirts, even if they have had little contact with the newborn.
      c. Kin selection theory hypothesizes that we should direct more of our helping behavior toward kin than toward nonkin.

(1) Across numerous cultures, people report being more willing to help and receiving more help from close relatives versus more distant relatives or nonrelatives.

(2) Borgida et al. (1992) found that people were three times more likely to donate a kidney to a relative than to a nonrelative.

(3) Segal (1984) found that identical twins were more likely to cooperate than fraternal twins.

3. Reciprocity

a. Reciprocal altruism is an evolutionary explanation for why we help nonrelative friends and strangers.

b. Reciprocal altruism can be defined as the tendency to help other individuals with the expectation that they will be likely to help in return at some other time.

(1) It reduces the likelihood of dangerous conflict.

(2) It reduces the dangers of scarce resources.

(3) It allows alliance formation.

c. de Waal (1996) found that primates are more likely to share, groom, and "babysit" for other primates who do the same for them.

d. The impulse to return favors may be a human universal.

(1) Kunz and Woolcott (1976) mailed Christmas cards to strangers and found that 20 percent reciprocated and sent a card back.

(2) Berkowitz and Daniels (1964) found in a lab study that people who had received help from a confederate were more helpful to others in a subsequent interaction.

4. Reputational Advantages and Social Rewards

a. Social rewards are defined as benefits like praise, positive attention, tangible rewards, honors, and gratitude that may be gained from helping others.

b. Note that the desire to gain reputational advantage or rewards may be unconscious.

E. Empathy-Based Altruism: A Case of Pure Altruism?

1. Batson argues that there are two egoistic motives for helping, and one altruistic motive:

a. Social rewards—egoistic.

b. Experienced distress—egoistic—which is a motive for helping that may arise from a need to reduce one's own distress.

c. Empathy—altruistic.

(1) Empathy can be defined as identifying with another person and feeling and understanding what that person is experiencing.

(2) When we empathize with another's distress, we are motivated to reduce their distress, even at our own expense, for their sake, not ours.

2. Batson et al. (1983) created an experimental paradigm to differentiate between the three types of motives.

a. Independent variable #1: in an easy-escape condition, participants could simply leave after witnessing a confederate receive the first two of ten uncomfortable shocks; in a difficult-to-escape condition, participants were told they would have to watch all ten shocks being administered.

b. Independent variable #2: participants' reactions to the confederate's discomfort were divided into egoistic distress reactions and empathetic reactions.

c. Dependent variable: the number of participants who volunteered to trade places with the confederate and receive the remaining shocks for her.

d. Finding: those who felt empathy were more likely to volunteer to receive the shocks, even if they could easily escape; those who felt egoistic distress were only likely to volunteer to receive her shocks if they were in the difficult-to-escape condition.

e. Critiques

(1) Empathy was not manipulated.

(2) A social rewards account cannot be eliminated.

3. Fultz et al. (1986) led participants to believe that they were the "listeners" in an impression formation study with a participant named Janet.

a. Independent variable #1: low-empathy participants were asked to concentrate on the facts contained in the information Janet provided; high-empathy participants were asked to imagine how Janet must be feeling.

b. Independent variable #2: in the low-social-evaluation condition, all exchanges were conducted via sealed envelopes, and the experimenter(s) would be unaware of anyone's responses; in the high-social-evaluation condition, the experimenter reviewed all communications.

c. Dependent variable: how much time participants volunteered to spend with Janet in a subsequent interaction (given Janet's note saying that she was lonely).

d. Finding: high-empathy participants volunteered more time to spend with Janet, regardless of which social evaluation condition they were in.

4. Eisenberg et al. (1989) evaluated the facial expressions, heart rate, and self-reported emotions of children as they watched a moving video about young children who couldn't attend school because they were injured in an accident; they also measured likelihood of helping by taking homework to the children.

a. Finding for participants who felt empathy: a concerned gaze, lower heart rate, and greater likelihood of helping.

b. Finding for participants who felt distress: painful wince, higher heart rate, less likelihood of helping.

F. The Culture of Altruism

1. Steblay (1987) reviewed thirty-five studies that included seventeen different kinds of helping behaviors and found that strangers were more likely to be helped in rural areas.

a. You're more likely to be helped in a town of 1,000 than 5,000, in a town of 5,000 than 10,000, and so on.

b. Once the population rises above 50,000, the likelihood of helping remains about the same.

c. People's current context was a better predictor of helping that the type of area they grew up in.

2. Milgram (1970) suggested that helping is less likely in larger cities because they contain so many social stimuli that most people experience stimulus overload and are unlikely to attend as carefully to cues that would encourage helping.

3. Smaller environments are typically less diverse, increasing the chances that someone who is similar to you will be the one needing help, as opposed to urban environments, which are made up of more diverse populations.

4. Since larger urban areas have more people around to help, there may be more diffusion of responsibility.

Testing Your Basic Knowledge

ANSWERS TO MULTIPLE-CHOICE QUESTIONS

1.	b	14.	a
2.	c	15.	a
3.	a	16.	c
4.	c	17.	b
5.	b	18.	b
6.	a	19.	c
7.	c	20.	b
8.	a	21.	a
9.	b	22.	b
10.	a	23.	a
11.	c	24.	b
12.	c	25.	b
13.	b		

Testing Your In-Depth Understanding

EXAMPLE ANSWER TO THE GUIDED QUESTIONS FOR CRITICAL THINKING EXERCISE #2

1. Brainstorm how situational factors and/or construal processes could encourage or discourage helping for each of Latané and Darley's five steps.

a. Notice that something is happening: Milgram's stimulus overload hypothesis suggests that, in some circumstances, people may simply be too overloaded with input to notice events that are out of the ordinary.

b. Interpret the situation as one in which help is needed: as indicated in your textbook, a large problem here is with pluralistic ignorance. In emergency situations, people tend to look at one another for information and guidance. If you look around with a calm expression and see everyone else looking around with a calm expression, you (along with everyone else) may end up deciding the situation is one in which help is not required.

c. Assume responsibility for providing the help: as indicated in your textbook, a large problem here is with diffusion of responsibility. As the number of people present during an emergency increases, each person feels a diminished sense of responsibility to be the one to step forward and offer help.

d. Decide on the appropriate way in which to help: a practical concern here may be whether or not you have the skills or equipment required to help (e.g., someone is drowning and you can't swim, you don't have a cell phone, and the nearest person who could help is miles away). Research not reviewed in your textbook suggests that people who take a first aid course are more likely to offer medical assistance than those who do not.

e. Decide to give the help: this step involves making the actual decision to put your own welfare, time, resources on the line in order to offer assistance. As reviewed in your textbook, characteristics of the victim and the situation may influence your final decision. For example, helping a person who is bleeding may be perceived as too costly in terms of time or emotional investment. Your textbook also notes that we have more of a tendency to help (established via evolution) when there is an opportunity to receive some sort of social reward for helping.

2. For each of the barriers to helping, consider whether education could eliminate that barrier.
   a. Notice that something is happening: while learning about the possibility of stimulus overload may remind people to be more vigilant in those situations, most people have limited attentional resources and, thus, they would be unable to add much to their attention if they were overloaded in the first place.
   b. Interpret the situation as one in which help is needed: pluralistic ignorance could definitely be addressed with education. If you know that other people's reactions are a bad indicator of what they should do, then people can learn to not turn to that information and, instead, to use their own good judgment to evaluate the situation.
   c. Assume responsibility for providing the help: diffusion of responsibility, logically, seems to also be reasonably addressed with education. If you know that all the other people around are feeling the same way you are (i.e., "someone else will help"), then you should realize that no one else will help and, thus, you need to step forward.
   d. Decide on the appropriate way in which to help: while education in social psychology is unlikely to help in this instance, such education may motivate a person to take a first aid class.
   e. Decide to give the help: it is unlikely that learning about this research will make a person more altruistic if he is motivated strongly by social rewards. But learning about victim characteristics and the kind of cost-benefit analysis people go through may alter the thought processes of those who are truly empathetic. Such knowledge may lead empathetic people to be conscious of their cost-benefit analysis.

3. Finally, actually go to PSYCHINFO and look up the study indicated. For help doing this, see the PSYCHINFO section at the end of this Study Guide, or ask your tutor, professor, or a librarian for help.

CHAPTER 14 | Morality, Justice, and Cooperation

The goal of this chapter is to review the relevant research associated with three areas of social psychological research: morality, justice, and cooperation. The chapter reviews the evolutionary and cultural variations in morality and a two-system model of how moral decisions are made. Three different types of justice are discussed: distributive justice, procedural justice, and restorative justice. Finally, the chapter reviews cooperation in the context of a frequently used experimental paradigm: the prisoner's dilemma.

ANNOTATED CHAPTER OUTLINE

After first reading through the chapter quickly, create a comprehensive framework for the information in the chapter by reading the outline below and filling in the missing information. Instead of simply re-copying information from the textbook, try to use your own words wherever possible; you can check your answers against the completed outline in the Answer Key section at the end of the chapter.

I. The Evolution of Morality, Justice, and Cooperation
  A. Some suggest that our capacity for goodness developed spiritually; others believe that it developed through culture and education.
  B. The evolutionary view on our capacity for goodness argues that we

    _____
    _____
    _____
    _____

  C. Our capacity for selfless behavior has four evolutionarily developed elements:
    1. _____;
      de Waal's research with primates has found

_____
_____
_____
_____
    2. _____;
      de Waal found that

_____
_____
_____

    3. A sense of justice: de Waal found that chimpanzees share the meat of a kill only with those who helped with the hunt, and they punish chimps who steal.
    4. The capacity to cooperate: de Waal found that primates defuse aggression or conflict or avoid it entirely with submissive gestures, offers of food, grooming, intervention of third parties, and the like.

II. Morality
  A. Defining Morality and Moral Judgment
    1. Morality can be defined as

      _____
      _____
      _____
      _____

    2. General characteristics of actions judged as morally right or wrong:
      a. _____
      _____
      _____
      _____

b. _____

_____

_____

_____

c. _____

_____

_____

_____

B. Universality and Cultural Variation in Moral Judgment
   1. There is a great deal of similarity in what is judged to be moral or not across cultures.
      a. People in radically different cultures seem similarly appalled by

      _____

      _____

      _____

      _____

      b. Turiel (2002) found that

      _____

      _____

      _____

      _____

      c. Evolution may explain universal moral judgments in that our most successful ancestors lived together in groups and needed to be attuned to harm and violations of basic rights.
   2. There is also a great deal of cultural variation; what is accepted in one culture may seem outrageously wrong in another.
      a. People in different cultures make different moral judgments about polygamy, public beheadings, dancing, contact with people from different social positions.
      b. Our minds may be equipped with the ability to take on any emotion-based moral rules, but culture may emphasize some and de-emphasize others, leading us to take on some but not others.
   3. Moral Transgressions and Transgressions of Social Convention
      a. Moral transgressions can be defined as

      _____

      _____

      _____

      _____

      b. Social convention transgressions can be defined as

      _____

      _____

      _____

      _____

      c. Shweder et al. (1997) studied moral beliefs by asking participants to read scenarios about thirty-nine different inappropriate actions and to say whether they believed moral rules or social conventions had been violated.
         (1) Independent variable #1: participants were American or were from eastern India.
         (2) Independent variable #2:

         _____

         _____

         _____

         _____

         (3) Dependent variable: judgments of how serious the action was, how right or wrong it was, and whether it could be accepted under any circumstances.
         (4) Finding:

         _____

         _____

         _____

         _____

         _____

   4. Ethics of Moral Reasoning
      a. The ethic of autonomy can be defined as

      _____

      _____

      _____

      _____

      _____

      b. The ethic of community can be defined as

      _____

      _____

      _____

      _____

      c. The ethic of divinity can be defined as

      _____

      _____

      _____

      _____

         (1) To Westerners, the ethic of divinity may seem least relevant to morality because in many Western cultures bodily and spiritual purity are thought to be a matter of personal choice rather than moral obligation.
         (2) Westerners have an implicit concern with the ethic of divinity, as shown when they speak about "washing one's sins away" or perceive homeless people or HIV-positive people as being "dirty."

d. Vasquez et al. (2001) asked American and Filipino students to list moral rules and found that

_____

_____

_____

_____

5. Reciprocity and Moral Reasoning
   a. Reciprocity is the most basic social obligation, the foundation of communities, but also a constraint on an individual's rights and freedom.
   b. Miller and Bersoff (1994) tested the hypothesis that cultures that give more emphasis to community would attach greater significance to violations of reciprocity than cultures that emphasize individual rights.
      (1) Independent variable:

_____

_____

_____

_____

      (2) Dependent variable: whether the students rated an example of a reciprocity behavior as being a moral decision or a matter of personal choice.
      (3) Finding:

_____

_____

_____

_____

C. A Two-System View of Morality
   1. Haidt (2001) proposes that there are two systems of moral judgment: an intuitive system and a controlled system.
   2. When Each System Is Used
      a. The first system is

_____

_____

_____

_____

      (1) Harm-related emotions like sympathy and concern motivate helping behavior.
      (2) Self-critical emotions like shame, embarrassment, and guilt arise when we have violated moral codes about virtue or character.
      (3) Other-praising emotions like gratitude and awe signal our approval to others.
      (4) Other-condemning emotions like anger, disgust, and contempt are important to a sense of justice.

b. The second system is

_____

_____

_____

      (1) Young children use their own perspective to understand moral implications.
      (2) After about age ten, people begin to use society's perspective to make moral judgments.
      (3) A sophisticated approach that some people never reach is to take a universal perspective and consider implications, no matter what position people occupy in society.

3. Studies of the Two Systems of Moral Judgment
   a. Studies suggest that the two systems are separate and that often our careful moral reasoning is simply after-the-fact rationalization of emotion-based moral intuitions.
   b. Haidt et al. (1993) had Brazilian and American participants read a variety of scenarios and indicate whether they thought the people involved should be punished or not.
      (1) Independent variable #1:

_____

_____

_____

      (2) Independent variable #2: participants had a high or low socioeconomic status.
      (3) Independent variable #3:

_____

_____

_____

      (4) Dependent variables: inclination to punish offenders; emotional and more controlled reasoning reactions to stories.
      (5) Findings for punishment variable:

_____

_____

_____

_____

_____

_____

(6) Findings for affective reactions variable:

_____

_____

_____

c. Greene et al. (2001) asked participants to judge moral and nonmoral dilemmas and to decide whether the action depicted was appropriate or not.

  (1) Independent variable:

_____

_____

_____

  (2) Dependent variable: which areas of the brain were activated during this activity, as indicated by fMRI (functional magnetic resonance imaging).

  (3) Finding:

_____

_____

_____

  (4) Other findings: participants took longer to decide the appropriateness of moral actions when automatic, emotional intuitions (it is wrong to kill anyone) contradicted more controlled moral reasoning (it is better to kill one person to save five than to let five people die).

III. Justice

  A. Our sense of justice is our sense of what is fair, guiding our allocation of collective resources and punishment for violation of rules and norms.

    1. Our sense of justice is a safeguard against the unchecked pursuit of self-interest.

    2. Distributive justice can be defined as

_____

_____

_____

_____

    3. Procedural justice can be defined as

_____

_____

_____

_____

    4. Restorative justice can be defined as

_____

_____

_____

_____

B. Distributive Justice

  1. Distributive justice is concerned with whether you believe that your rewards or benefits are equal to your efforts or costs.

  2. Self-Interest and Distributive Justice

    a. We tend to allocate resources in ways that favor the self, although we look for ways of making that seem fair.

    b. One example of a case of perceived unfair allocation of resources is

_____

_____

_____

  3. Egocentric Construals and Distributive Justice

    a. We commonly believe that we contribute more than others and/or act more fairly than others.

    b. Messick et al. (1985) found that

_____

_____

_____

_____

    c. Ross and Sicoly (1979) found that both partners in a marriage indicated that they consistently contributed more to the household than their partner.

    d. Messick and Sentis (1979) conducted a study to examine sense of fairness and expectations of rewards.

      (1) Independent variable:

_____

_____

_____

      (2) Dependent variable: how much money they felt they or the other person should be paid for ten hours of work.

      (3) Finding:

_____

_____

_____

_____

  4. Self-Interest in the Ultimatum Game

    a. "Allocators" are given a fixed amount of money and told to save some for themselves and give the rest to their partner, a responder.

    b. "Responders" are allowed to accept or reject the money offered, although rejecting an offer means no one gets any money.

    c. Findings:

_____

_____

_____

_____

5. Relationship-Specific Principles of Distributive Justice
    a. Resources are allocated differently in different kinds of relationships.
    b. Three principles seem to govern how we distribute resources in relationships:
        (1) Equity (which typically governs in work relationships) can be defined as

    _____

    _____

    _____

        (2) Equality (which typically governs in friendships) can be defined as

    _____

    _____

    _____

        (3) Need (which typically governs in families) can be defined as

    _____

    _____

    _____

6. Social Comparisons and Distributive Justice
    a. Despite their relatively poorer objective outcomes, low SES individuals report being about as satisfied with their lives as higher SES individuals.
    b. One explanation may be that low SES individuals are comparing their life circumstances with nearby others who live under similar circumstances.
    c. Relative deprivation can be defined as

    _____

    _____

    _____

    _____

    d. Stouffer et al. (1949) found that

    _____

    _____

    _____

    _____

    e. People are most likely to feel that life is unfair and to protest when social comparisons indicate that they could be doing better.
        (1) Social protest typically is started by

    _____

    _____

    _____

    _____

    (2) Social protest typically is started after

    _____

    _____

    _____

    _____

C. Procedural Justice
    1. Procedural justice assesses the extent to which the criteria used to distribute rewards and punishments is fair.
    2. Three factors shape our sense of procedural justice:
        a. _____

    _____

    _____

    _____

        b. _____

    _____

    _____

    _____

        c. _____

    _____

    _____

    _____

    3. Tyler and his colleagues have conducted numerous studies looking at the rewards and punishments people receive from authority figures and the extent to which recipients thought the authority figure was neutral, trustworthy, and had treated them with respect, and have found:
        a. _____

    _____

    _____

    _____

        b. _____

    _____

    _____

    _____

D. Restorative Justice
    1. Belief in a just world can be defined as

    _____

    _____

    _____

    _____

    2. Because a belief in a just world is so cherished, we respond to injustice with a strong motivation to set things right through restorative action.
    3. Shifting Perceptions of Perpetrators and Victims
        a. We might shift our beliefs about perpetrators and victims of injustice by

    _____

    _____

    _____

    _____

    (e.g., stigmatizing rape victims).

b. We might rationalize society-wide injustices through system justification, which is

_____

_____

_____

(1) People tend to maintain positive stereotypes about high-status individuals and negative stereotypes about low-status individuals.

(2) People espouse ideologies (e.g., meritocracy beliefs) that assume people get what they deserve.

4. Punishment
   a. Retributive punishment can be defined as

   _____

   _____

   _____

   (1) Retributive punishment is preferred by people who are angry as a consequence of attributing the cause of a crime to the perpetrator's character.

   (2) This is the more vengeful form of punishment.

   b. Utilitarian punishment can be defined as

   _____

   _____

   _____

   (1) Utilitarian punishment is preferred by people who feel sympathy as a consequence of attributing the cause of the crime to situational forces.

   (2) This form of punishment assumes that the crime does not reflect a stable part of the defendant's character and that the likelihood of future crimes can be reduced.

5. Reconciliation
   a. Reconciliation involves apologies and forgiveness.
   b. Contrary to the dispersal hypothesis, de Waal has found that chimpanzees will engage in reconciling behaviors after unjust acts in order to restore cooperative relations.
   c. With apologies, the offender takes responsibility for the offense, expresses remorse, and thereby reduces the anger of the victim of the injustice.
   d. Ohbuchi et al. (1989) found that

   _____

_____

_____

e. Forgiveness involves the release of negative feelings and increased compassion and empathy toward the offender.

f. Ludwig and Vander Laan (2001) found that forgiveness had important health benefits, showing that participants who imagined themselves forgiving someone who had harmed them had lower blood pressure, less stress-related heart rate increases, and reduced brow furrowing associated with anger.

IV. Cooperation
A. In the last 100 years, the world has become a much more interconnected place and, although there are many examples of conflict and polarization, cooperation is still present and a central part of being a social species.

B. The Prisoner's Dilemma Game
   1. Explanation of the game:

   _____

   _____

   _____

   2. Looking only at one individual, it seems to make the most sense to defect since the $8 is the greatest reward, but looking at both players, cooperation is best since both players will get $5 instead of sometimes getting $2.

   3. This game mirrors some essential aspects of real-world conflicts.

   4. Primed to Cooperate or Defect
      a. Neuberg (1988) found that

      _____

      _____

      _____

      b. If people are exposed to competitive and aggressive stimuli in the media, video games, and films, it may foster a more competitive society.

   5. Cooperation on Wall Street and Main Street
      a. The way we explicitly label different situations may influence levels of competition and cooperation.
      b. Liberman et al. (2002) found that

      _____

      _____

      _____

6. Competition Begets Competition
   a. Some people are more inclined to interpret situations as opportunities for competition rather than cooperation.
   b. Kelley and Stahelski (1970) asked people what they thought the point of the game was and created three types of game pairs: two cooperators, two competitors, and one cooperator paired with one competitor, and found that:
      (1) _____
      _____
      _____
      _____
      (2) _____
      _____
      _____
      _____

C. Failure to Perceive Common Grounds for Cooperation
   1. We tend to construe our opponents as enemies, to view our own group as moral and the outgroup as amoral, and to construe opponents' interests as hostile to our own.
   2. People often overlook areas of agreement with their ideological opponents.
      a. Keltner, Robinson, and colleagues have found in a series of studies that opposing sides to various issues tend to overestimate their differences.
      b. In studies of negotiations, the negotiators tend to underestimate the amount of common ground and often settle for less-desirable outcomes than those that were possible.
      c. Opponents are often suspicious of each other's offers and concessions and tend to engage in reactive devaluation, which is
      _____
      _____
      _____
      _____
      d. Ross and Stillinger (1991) found that
      _____
      _____
      _____
      _____

D. Tit for Tat and the Elements of Cooperation
   1. Axelrod (1984) asked people to submit strategies for the prisoner's dilemma game; after having fourteen different strategies play out, the strategy with the best average was found to be the tit-for-tat strategy.

2. The tit-for-tat strategy can be defined as
   _____
   _____
   _____
   _____

3. This strategy is successful for five reasons:
   a. _____
   _____
   _____
   _____
   b. _____
   _____
   _____
   c. _____
   _____
   _____
   d. _____
   _____
   _____
   e. _____
   _____
   _____

TESTING YOUR BASIC KNOWLEDGE

After studying the information in the chapter by filling in the outline above, test your basic knowledge with the following multiple-choice test. Answers are provided in the Answer Key section at the end of the chapter. If you find that you have gotten an answer wrong, it is important that you understand why it is wrong (as well as understanding why the correct answer is the better choice). Talk with peers, your tutor, or your professor if you need help.

Multiple-Choice Questions

1. Behavior that is moral, just, and cooperative was initially puzzling for evolutionary theorists because
   a. it seems likely that amoral, unjust, and competitive individuals would take advantage of such behavior and thus be more likely to survive and reproduce.
   b. such behavior is too infrequent in human beings to be part of our evolutionary history.
   c. such behavior is found among human beings, but not among other animal species.

2. de Waal's research with chimpanzees found that, when distributing the meat from a kill, chimps are more likely to share the meat with those who helped with the hunt than those who did not. This research suggests that chimps may have
   a. a vengeful streak.
   b. a sense of justice.
   c. the ability to cooperate.

3. If you view "being kind" as a morally correct behavior, then you should
   a. feel an obligation to be kind even if you don't really want to.
   b. be rewarded when you are kind and punished when you are not.
   c. Both A and B are characteristics of actions judged to be moral.

4. Two groups of participants are reading a series of stories about morally questionable actions and deciding how serious each transgression was. When reading about a young woman who ate lunch with her husband's brother, the participants from India judged this more harshly than the participants from America. Why?
   a. because Indians believe in harsher punishments for moral transgressions
   b. because Americans view social convention transgressions as less serious than do Indians
   c. Both A and B are accurate.

5. Which of these three frameworks for moral reasoning is most commonly used among Americans?
   a. ethic of autonomy
   b. ethic of community
   c. ethic of divinity

6. In Haidt's two-system view of morality, the first system
   a. provides judgments based on controlled reasoning processes.
   b. provides quick, automatic moral intuitions.
   c. is usually overridden by the decisions of the second system.

7. We are most likely to feel self-critical emotions like shame or embarrassment when we
   a. have violated the ethic of community.
   b. have violated moral codes about virtue or character.
   c. discuss topics related to the ethic of divinity.

8. According to the research on perspective taking, children younger than ten years old typically
   a. use their own perspectives to make moral judgments.
   b. evaluate the morality of various actions by using society's perspective.
   c. use a universal perspective of right and wrong to make moral judgments.

9. Haidt et al. (1993) asked participants to read about various moral transgressions, including a family eating its dog after it was accidentally hit by a car. The researchers found that
   a. all participants, driven by their disgust, thought punishment was warranted.
   b. only those most concerned with the ethic of community thought punishment was warranted.
   c. none of the participants felt punishment was warranted for this action.

10. Functional MRI imaging was used in a study by Greene et al. (2001) to demonstrate that an impersonal moral decision was processed by the part of the brain responsible for _____, while a personally engaging moral decision was processed by the part of the brain involved in _____.
    a. emotion; working memory.
    b. working memory; emotion.
    c. Neither A nor B is correct.

11. Alex knows he is the teacher's favorite student and thus is not surprised when he gets a higher grade on his term project (which he worked very hard on) than his friend Molly—even though Molly's project was better than his. If Alex is angry about his grade and wishes it had been lower, then Alex is probably more concerned with which type of justice?
    a. distributive
    b. procedural
    c. restorative

12. An intriguing study by Messick and Sentis (1979) asked participants to consider how much money should be awarded for ten hours of work if seven hours of work garnered $25. What were the findings of the study?
    a. Participants paid both themselves and other people (on average) $35 for the ten hours of work.
    b. Participants paid other people more money for the ten hours of work than they paid themselves.
    c. Participants paid themselves more money for the ten hours of work than they paid other people.

13. How do "responders" react in the ultimatum game when they are offered an unfairly small amount of money?
    a. They accept the money and later give negative ratings to the allocator.
    b. They reject the money, knowing that doing so means neither player gets any money at all.
    c. They make a counteroffer that will improve their net income.

14. Morton is working with his best friend Jonathan on a new social psychology textbook. Morton does about 60 percent of the work, and Jonathan does the remaining

40 percent. They are paid $1,000 for the textbook. According to the principle of equality, Morton is most likely to give how much money to Jonathan?

a. $400, or 40%

b. $500, or 50%

c. however much money Jonathan needs to pay off his school loans since Morton's loans are already paid off

15. Coworkers are more likely than families or friends to follow which principle of distributive justice?

a. equity

b. morality

c. need

16. Women earn approximately 76 cents for every dollar a man earns doing the same job at the same level of expertise. According to your textbook, what might explain why these woman, nevertheless, report being satisfied with their salaries?

a. In evolutionary times, women were more likely to be mothers and so are now more nurturing and less competitive in the work environment.

b. Women are more concerned with the ethic of community and so are willing to accept a lower salary if it promotes a harmonious work environment.

c. Women are comparing their salaries to the people who are most similar and closest to them—typically other female workers.

17. Research on procedural justice has found that

a. in judging whether our outcomes are fair or not, we are more likely to care about the criteria used to make the reward decision than the size of the reward.

b. we tend to view rewards that are larger and more beneficial to us as being more fair than rewards that are smaller and less beneficial.

c. unjustly small rewards motivate us to punish those who gave the reward.

18. How neutral an authority figure is, how much we can trust the system the authority figure represents, and how much respect the authority figure treats us with are all indications of the extent to which we sense an outcome is fair in the sense of

a. distributive justice.

b. procedural justice.

c. restorative justice.

19. A belief in a just world can lead people to

a. judge criminals more harshly and recommend harsher prison sentences.

b. blame the victim of a crime, suggesting that the person got what he or she "deserved."

c. engage in cooperative and altruistic behaviors.

20. One reason why we may maintain positive stereotypes about high-status people and negative stereotypes about low-status people is that such stereotypes serve to

a. justify a system in which wealth and opportunities are distributed unequally.

b. punish those who are at the lowest end of the economic ladder.

c. reduce the amount of cognitive resources needed to process social stimuli.

21. According to Axelrod's research, the strategy that yields the best average results in the prisoner's dilemma game is

a. consistent cooperation.

b. tit-for-tat.

c. a pattern of cooperation followed by defection.

22. After pairing people who tended to cooperate with people who tended to compete in a game of prisoner's dilemma, Kelley and Stahelski (1970) found that the competitors were likely to view the cooperators

a. as worthy opponents.

b. as being cooperative.

c. as being competitive.

23. Isabelle and her daughter, Amy, have a long history of disagreeing about financial issues. After getting her first job, Amy considers her options for starting an investment account. Amy is leaning toward investing half of her money in a socially responsible mutual fund and the other half in a regular fund that has a higher yield. But after Isabelle suggests that exact strategy to Amy, Amy finds herself arguing with her mother and fiercely defending the need to put all of her money in socially responsible funds. Amy's change in attitude may be the result of

a. the ethic of divinity.

b. reactive devaluation.

c. relative deprivation.

24. According to the textbook, if you make a mistake and harm or offend another person, the best way to defuse their anger is to

a. take responsibility for your wrongdoing and express remorse.

b. do nothing and allow the person to express their anger.

c. offer a utilitarian reconciliation.

25. Bill and Al have been long-time enemies. One day Al calls Bill a bad name. In an effort to punish Al for that action, Bill calls Al an even worse name. What kind of punishment is this?

a. utilitarian

b. restorative

c. retributive

Essay Questions

After you have mastered the multiple-choice questions, try testing your basic understanding by thoroughly answering each of the broad essay questions below. Because it is critical that you think through this information on your own, we have not provided any answers to these questions. Your learning and retention of this material will be greatly enhanced if you do one or more of the following to check your answers: carefully review the textbook information; compare your responses to your class lecture notes; talk over your answers with a peer; ask your professor to review your answers or review any information that is unclear to you.

1. Discuss the evolutionary logic for why humans tend to engage in moral, just, and cooperative behavior.

2. Define morality and discuss the cultural similarities and differences in what is viewed as moral versus immoral. Also, describe the two-system view of morality and describe one research study supporting it.

3. Define and distinguish distributive, procedural, and restorative justice. Discuss the factors that influence our judgments of distributive and procedural justice, and describe the different ways in which people go about gaining restorative justice.

4. Explain the logic of the prisoner's dilemma game and discuss what the findings from studies on the game reveal about our tendency to cooperate.

TESTING YOUR IN-DEPTH UNDERSTANDING

Test your in-depth understanding of the material by working through the Critical Thinking Exercises provided at the end of each textbook chapter. To maximize this learning opportunity, work together with a tutor, study group, or your professor. Alternatively, write down your thoughts and responses.

Guided questions for one of the exercises are provided below. The "answers" provided in the Answer Key section are not hard and fast "correct" responses. You are encouraged to talk over your responses with your classmates, tutor, and/or professor, keeping in mind that there may not be just one "correct" answer to each question. That being said, however, there are ways to answer these questions that indicate more or less reflective thought and more or less understanding and integration of the material from the chapter.

Guided Questions for Critical Thinking Exercise #1

Use Shweder's three ethics of morality—autonomy, community, and divinity—to illuminate the views of individuals who oppose gay marriage, and those who support it.

1. First, review Haidt's two-system view of morality. Why might engaging in this type of Critical Thinking Exercise be beneficial?

2. Next, review the three ethics of morality.

3. Finally, answer the question posed by using your knowledge of contemporary society (and/or doing some research on the Internet) to articulate your own views and try to imagine the views of those on the opposing side of the issue.

Enhance your understanding of the chapter by thinking about and doing the remaining three Critical Thinking Exercises. Discuss your answers with your peers, study group, tutor, or professor.

Critical Thinking Exercise #2

Imagine that your professor decides to only give A's to those students who weigh between 135 and 156 pounds. What form of injustice are you most likely to experience?

Critical Thinking Exercise #3

What psychological principles that you have learned about in this course help explain the reactive devaluation phenomenon?

Critical Thinking Exercise #4

Can you think of situations in which the tit-for-tat strategy might not actually be the best strategy for negotiating with others?

SOCIAL PSYCHOLOGY IN THE POPULAR MEDIA

You might be interested in the following popular media references, each of which relates in some way to information in this chapter.

Film

Return to Paradise (1998; directed by Joseph Ruben; starring Anne Heche, Vince Vaughn, Joaquin Phoenix, David Conrad). A fictional story about one young man who is arrested in Malaysia for possession of a "stash" of hashish left over from a vacation with two of his friends. His friends unknowingly return to America and live happy lives for two years. During those two years, their friend has been in a small, dark, dirty cell in a harsh Malaysian prison. When he is sentenced to be hanged for his crime, an attorney (played by Heche) tries to convince his two friends to return to Malaysia and help. If they confess to owning part of the hashish, they will save their friend. But such a confession will lead to a prison sentence for them. Although this movie did not do well at the box office, it is an extremely good film and an excellent dramatic portrayal of the prisoner's dilemma.

Book

Lewis, Michael (1989). *Liar's Poker: Rising Through the Wreckage on Wall Street.* New York: Norton. A look back at the ethical and moral dilemmas on Wall Street in the 1980s. From the front flap of the hardcover edition: "In this shrewd and wickedly funny book, Michael Lewis describes an astonishing era and his own rake's progress through a powerful investment bank. . . . With the eye and ear of a born storyteller, Michael Lewis shows us how things *really* worked on Wall Street. . . ."

Web Sites

The Prisoner's Dilemma Game—http://www.iterated-prisoners-dilemma.net. This Web site allows you to play a version of the prisoner's dilemma game, as well as to manipulate several variables and examine the outcomes over numerous trials. The Web site also includes links to other related sites.

Untapped Potential: U.S. Science and Technology Cooperation with the Islamic World—http://www.brookings.edu/fp/saban/analysis/darcy20050419.htm. An article by Michael A. Levi and Michael B. d'Arcy discussing strategies to promote cooperation between the U.S. and the Islamic world.

ANSWER KEY

Annotated Chapter Outline

I. The Evolution of Morality, Justice, and Cooperation
  A. Some suggest that our capacity for goodness developed spiritually; others believe that it developed through culture and education.
  B. The evolutionary view on our capacity for goodness argues that we are better able to survive and reproduce if we have positive relationships and behave in a cooperative fashion with others.
  C. Our capacity for selfless behavior has four evolutionarily developed elements:
      1. Compassion: de Waal's research with primates has found that they become very upset when witnessing harm to other group members and take care of vulnerable group members.
      2. The tendency to act on moral principles: de Waal found that high-status monkeys share

food and break up conflicts among lower-status chimps.
      3. A sense of justice: de Waal found that chimpanzees share the meat of a kill only with those who helped with the hunt, and they punish chimps who steal.
      4. The capacity to cooperate: de Waal found that primates defuse aggression or conflict or avoid it entirely with submissive gestures, offers of food, grooming, intervention of third parties, and the like.

II. Morality
  A. Defining Morality and Moral Judgment
      1. Morality can be defined as a system of principles and ideals that people use as a guide to making evaluative judgments (good versus bad) of the actions or character of another person.
      2. General characteristics of actions judged as morally right or wrong:
          a. Obligation: the sense that a rule should be followed.
          b. Inclusive: the rule applies to all people and in all contexts.
          c. Sanctions: there are punishments for violations and praise for adherence.
  B. Universality and Cultural Variation in Moral Judgment
      1. There is a great deal of similarity in what is judged to be moral or not across cultures.
          a. People in radically different cultures seem similarly appalled by harm to children, genocide, and incest.
          b. Turiel (2002) found that children in different cultures agree that harming others or violating others' important rights is wrong.
          c. Evolution may explain universal moral judgments in that our most successful ancestors lived together in groups and needed to be attuned to harm and violations of basic rights.
      2. There is also a great deal of cultural variation; what is accepted in one culture may seem outrageously wrong in another.
          a. People in different cultures make different moral judgments about polygamy, public beheadings, dancing, contact with people from different social positions.
          b. Our minds may be equipped with the ability to take on any emotion-based moral rules, but culture may emphasize some and de-emphasize others, leading us to take on some but not others.

3. Moral Transgressions and Transgressions of Social Convention
    a. Moral transgressions can be defined as violations of others' rights, or harm to others.
    b. Social convention transgressions can be defined as violations of agreed-upon rules that govern such things as how we greet each other, whom we associate with, how we eat, the gender-based roles and identities we assume, and sexual behavior.
    c. Shweder et al. (1997) studied moral beliefs by asking participants to read scenarios about thirty-nine different inappropriate actions and to say whether they believed moral rules or social conventions had been violated.
        (1) Independent variable #1: participants were American or were from eastern India.
        (2) Independent variable #2: the inappropriate actions were either moral transgressions or social convention transgressions.
        (3) Dependent variable: judgments of how serious the action was, how right or wrong it was, and whether it could be accepted under any circumstances.
        (4) Finding: Indian and American participants judged moral transgressions as being equally wrong; Indians participants judged social convention transgressions as being more wrong than did American participants.
4. Ethics of Moral Reasoning
    a. The ethic of autonomy can be defined as a framework of moral reasoning that is centered on rights and equality, and is focused on protecting individuals' freedom to pursue their own interests (e.g., U.S. Constitution).
    b. The ethic of community can be defined as a framework of moral reasoning that revolves around duty, status, hierarchy, and interdependence, and whose goal is to protect relationships and roles within social groups to which one belongs (e.g., Confucianism).
    c. The ethic of divinity can be defined as a framework of moral reasoning that is defined by a concern for purity, sanctity, pollution, and sin.
        (1) To Westerners, the ethic of divinity may seem least relevant to morality because in many Western cultures bodily and spiritual purity are thought to be a matter of personal choice rather than moral obligation.
        (2) Westerners have an implicit concern with the ethic of divinity, as shown when they speak about "washing one's sins away" or perceive homeless people or HIV-positive people as being "dirty."
    d. Vasquez et al. (2001) asked American and Filipino students to list moral rules and found that U.S. students most often listed rules that were based on the ethic of autonomy, while Filipino students drew equally from all three ethics.
5. Reciprocity and Moral Reasoning
    a. Reciprocity is the most basic social obligation, the foundation of communities, but also a constraint on an individual's rights and freedom.
    b. Miller and Bersoff (1994) tested the hypothesis that cultures that give more emphasis to community would attach greater significance to violations of reciprocity than cultures that emphasize individual rights.
        (1) Independent variable: students were either American or Indian.
        (2) Dependent variable: whether the students rated an example of a reciprocity behavior as being a moral decision or a matter of personal choice.
        (3) Finding: Indian students were more likely to rate it as a moral matter than a personal choice; American students showed the opposite pattern.
C. A Two-System View of Morality
    1. Haidt (2001) proposes that there are two systems of moral judgment: an intuitive system and a controlled system.
    2. When Each System Is Used
        a. The first system is quicker, automatic, and emotional, and it yields moral intuitions (gut feelings) about right and wrong.
            (1) Harm-related emotions like sympathy and concern motivate helping behavior.
            (2) Self-critical emotions like shame, embarrassment, and guilt arise when we have violated moral codes about virtue or character.
            (3) Other-praising emotions like gratitude and awe signal our approval to others.

(4) Other-condemning emotions like anger, disgust, and contempt are important to a sense of justice.

b. The second system is slower and effortful and uses controlled reasoning processes to take into account logical and ethical principles and to debate consequences, as well as using perspective taking to make moral judgments.

　　(1) Young children use their own perspective to understand moral implications.

　　(2) After about age ten, people begin to use society's perspective to make moral judgments.

　　(3) A sophisticated approach that some people never reach is to take a universal perspective and consider implications, no matter what position people occupy in society.

3. Studies of the Two Systems of Moral Judgment

a. Studies suggest that the two systems are separate and that often our careful moral reasoning is simply after-the-fact rationalization of emotion-based moral intuitions.

b. Haidt et al. (1993) had Brazilian and American participants read a variety of scenarios and indicate whether they thought the people involved should be punished or not.

　　(1) Independent variable #1: participants were either American or Brazilian.

　　(2) Independent variable #2: participants had a high or low socioeconomic status.

　　(3) Independent variable #3: the scenarios involved situations that involved harm, violations of social convention, or harmless but offensive actions (e.g., eating the family dog after it was accidentally hit by a car and killed).

　　(4) Dependent variables: inclination to punish offenders; emotional and more controlled reasoning reactions to stories.

　　(5) Findings for punishment variable: members of both cultures wanted to punish those committing harmful acts and were less likely to punish those violating social convention; because the ethic of community was strong among Brazilians and low SES Americans, those groups endorsed

punishment for harmless but offensive actions, while high SES Americans (putting their feelings of disgust aside and considering individual rights) were less likely to endorse punishment for such actions.

　　(6) Findings for affective reactions variable: affective reactions to the stories strongly predicted the punishment ratings for Brazilian participants, but reasoned analysis predicted the judgments of high SES Americans.

c. Greene et al. (2001) asked participants to judge moral and nonmoral dilemmas and to decide whether the action depicted was appropriate or not.

　　(1) Independent variable: the moral dilemmas were impersonal (e.g., flip a switch so that one person is killed by a runaway trolley instead of five) or were emotionally evocative (e.g., push a stranger off a footbridge in order to save five other people).

　　(2) Dependent variable: which areas of the brain were activated during this activity, as indicated by fMRI (functional magnetic resonance imaging).

　　(3) Finding: areas of the brain involved with emotion were activated when participants were judging the emotionally evocative moral dilemmas; areas of the brain involved with working memory and reasoning were activated when processing the impersonal dilemmas.

　　(4) Other findings: participants took longer to decide the appropriateness of moral actions when automatic, emotional intuitions (it is wrong to kill anyone) contradicted more controlled moral reasoning (it is better to kill one person to save five than to let five people die).

III. Justice

A. Our sense of justice is our sense of what is fair, guiding our allocation of collective resources and punishment for violation of rules and norms.

1. Our sense of justice is a safeguard against the unchecked pursuit of self-interest.

2. Distributive justice can be defined as a type of justice that is based on whether people feel that the outcomes they receive are fair or unfair.

3. Procedural justice can be defined as a type of justice that is based on whether the processes by which rewards and punishments are being distributed are considered fair.

4. Restorative justice can be defined as the actions people take, from apologies to punishment, to restore justice.

B. Distributive Justice

1. Distributive justice is concerned with whether you believe that your rewards or benefits are equal to your efforts or costs.

2. Self-Interest and Distributive Justice
   a. We tend to allocate resources in ways that favor the self, although we look for ways of making that seem fair.
   b. One example of a case of perceived unfair allocation of resources is that of American salaries: in the past thirty-five years, the average annual American salary has gone from about $32,000 to about $36,000, while the average annual CEO salary in America has risen from $1.3 million to $37.5 million.

3. Egocentric Construals and Distributive Justice
   a. We commonly believe that we contribute more than others and/or act more fairly than others.
   b. Messick et al. (1985) found that participants rated themselves as more commonly behaving fairly than others.
   c. Ross and Sicoly (1979) found that both partners in a marriage indicated that they consistently contributed more to the household than their partner.
   d. Messick and Sentis (1979) conducted a study to examine sense of fairness and expectations of rewards.
      (1) Independent variable: in one scenario, participants were told to imagine that they had worked ten hours on a task and a partner had worked seven hours and been paid $25; in another scenario, participants were told to imagine that they had worked seven hours and been paid $25, while their partner worked ten hours.
      (2) Dependent variable: how much money they felt they or the other person should be paid for ten hours of work.
      (3) Finding: when paying themselves, participants suggested an average of $35; when paying the other person, they suggested an average of $30.

4. Self-Interest in the Ultimatum Game
   a. "Allocators" are given a fixed amount of money and told to save some for themselves and give the rest to their partner, a responder.
   b. "Responders" are allowed to accept or reject the money offered, although rejecting an offer means no one gets any money.
   c. Findings: studies show that although allocators generally keep more money for themselves than they give to their partners, they still typically make substantial offers to their partners; when an allocator does make a very small offer, responders usually reject it, implying a greater concern for fairness than for getting any money.

5. Relationship-Specific Principles of Distributive Justice
   a. Resources are allocated differently in different kinds of relationships.
   b. Three principles seem to govern how we distribute resources in relationships:
      (1) Equity (which typically governs in work relationships) can be defined as a principle of distributive justice that dictates that all individuals should receive rewards that directly correspond to their contributions.
      (2) Equality (which typically governs in friendships) can be defined as a principle of distributive justice that dictates that all individuals making contributions to some endeavor should receive equal rewards.
      (3) Need (which typically governs in families) can be defined as a principle of distributive justice that says that individuals with the greatest needs should be given priority for resources.

6. Social Comparisons and Distributive Justice
   a. Despite their relatively poorer objective outcomes, low SES individuals report being about as satisfied with their lives as higher SES individuals.
   b. One explanation may be that low SES individuals are comparing their life circumstances with nearby others who live under similar circumstances.
   c. Relative deprivation can be defined as a feeling of deprivation based on comparisons with relevant others who are seen as doing better than oneself.
   d. Stouffer et al. (1949) found that African-American soldiers stationed in the South

were more satisfied than those stationed in the North after World War II, presumably because the soldiers stationed in the North felt more relative deprivation when comparing their circumstances to the relatively good conditions enjoyed by their northern nonmilitary counterparts than soldiers stationed in the South when comparing themselves to nonmilitary southern African Americans, who were relatively worse off than those in the military.

   e. People are most likely to feel that life is unfair and to protest when social comparisons indicate that they could be doing better.

     (1) Social protest typically is started by the relatively advantaged members of a disadvantaged group (as they have had more contact with advantaged group members and compare their lives to those of the more advantaged).

     (2) Social protest typically is started after a small political or economic gain (as this leads members of disadvantaged groups to see what is possible, to feel the injustice of still being so far behind, and to adopt new standards and expectations).

C. Procedural Justice

  1. Procedural justice assesses the extent to which the criteria used to distribute rewards and punishments is fair.

  2. Three factors shape our sense of procedural justice:

   a. Neutrality of the authority figure.

   b. Trust in the system.

   c. Respect from the authority figure.

  3. Tyler and his colleagues have conducted numerous studies looking at the rewards and punishments people receive from authority figures and the extent to which recipients thought the authority figure was neutral, trustworthy, and had treated them with respect, and have found:

   a. The magnitude of reward or punishment was not correlated with perceptions of fairness (indicating that distributive and procedural justice are independent).

   b. People's ratings of neutrality, trust, and respect were stronger predictors of fairness than the reward or punishment.

D. Restorative Justice

  1. Belief in a just world can be defined as the conviction that people get what they deserve in life, that their outcomes match their actions and character.

  2. Because a belief in a just world is so cherished, we respond to injustice with a strong motivation to set things right through restorative action.

  3. Shifting Perceptions of Perpetrators and Victims

   a. We might shift our beliefs about perpetrators and victims of injustice by convincing ourselves that those who receive negative outcomes deserve those outcomes (e.g., stigmatizing rape victims).

   b. We might rationalize society-wide injustices through system justification, which is the tendency to justify differences in wealth and opportunity with beliefs that imply that such inequalities are deserved, just; and even natural and inevitable.

     (1) People tend to maintain positive stereotypes about high-status individuals and negative stereotypes about low-status individuals.

     (2) People espouse ideologies (e.g., meritocracy beliefs) that assume people get what they deserve.

4. Punishment

   a. Retributive punishment can be defined as punishment based on eye-for-an-eye justice in which the goal is to avenge a prior evil deed rather than prevent a future one.

     (1) Retributive punishment is preferred by people who are angry as a consequence of attributing the cause of a crime to the perpetrator's character.

     (2) This is the more vengeful form of punishment.

   b. Utilitarian punishment can be defined as punishment in which the goal is reducing the likelihood of future crimes committed by the criminal through such means as rehabilitation or isolation of the criminal.

     (1) Utilitarian punishment is preferred by people who feel sympathy as a consequence of attributing the cause of the crime to situational forces.

     (2) This form of punishment assumes that the crime does not reflect a stable part of the defendant's character and that the likelihood of future crimes can be reduced.

5. Reconciliation

   a. Reconciliation involves apologies and forgiveness.

b. Contrary to the dispersal hypothesis, de Waal has found that chimpanzees will engage in reconciling behaviors after unjust acts in order to restore cooperative relations.

c. With apologies, the offender takes responsibility for the offense, expresses remorse, and thereby reduces the anger of the victim of the injustice.

d. Ohbuchi et al. (1989) found that participants were more likely to like and trust partners who led them to fail at a task when those partners apologized than if they did not apologize.

e. Forgiveness involves the release of negative feelings and increased compassion and empathy toward the offender.

f. Ludwig and Vander Laan (2001) found that forgiveness had important health benefits, showing that participants who imagined themselves forgiving someone who had harmed them had lower blood pressure, less stress-related heart rate increases, and reduced brow furrowing associated with anger.

IV. Cooperation

A. In the last 100 years, the world has become a much more interconnected place and, although there are many examples of conflict and polarization, cooperation is still present and a central part of being a social species.

B. The Prisoner's Dilemma Game

1. Explanation of the game: there are two players, and each player has the choice to "cooperate" or "defect," with payoffs determined by their combined choices; both players cooperating gives both players $5 (for example), both players defecting gives both players $2, and the player who defects against a cooperating player gets $8.

2. Looking only at one individual, it seems to make the most sense to defect since the $8 is the greatest reward, but looking at both players, cooperation is best since both players will get $5 instead of sometimes getting $2.

3. This game mirrors some essential aspects of real-world conflicts.

4. Primed to Cooperate or Defect

a. Neuberg (1988) found that those subliminally primed with hostile words were more likely to defect on a majority of the game trials than those primed with neutral words.

b. If people are exposed to competitive and aggressive stimuli in the media, video games, and films, it may foster a more competitive society.

5. Cooperation on Wall Street and Main Street

a. The way we explicitly label different situations may influence levels of competition and cooperation.

b. Liberman et al. (2002) found that people played the game more cooperatively overall when it was described as "the community game" versus when it was described as "the Wall Street game."

6. Competition Begets Competition

a. Some people are more inclined to interpret situations as opportunities for competition rather than cooperation.

b. Kelley and Stahelski (1970) asked people what they thought the point of the game was and created three types of game pairs: two cooperators, two competitors, and one cooperator paired with one competitor, and found:

(1) The competitors led both competitors and cooperators to play the game competitively.

(2) The cooperators could accurately guess if they were playing with a competitor or cooperator, but the competitors inaccurately judged everyone as being competitive.

C. Failure to Perceive Common Grounds for Cooperation

1. We tend to construe our opponents as enemies, to view our own group as moral and the outgroup as amoral, and to construe opponents' interests as hostile to our own.

2. People often overlook areas of agreement with their ideological opponents.

a. Keltner, Robinson, and colleagues have found in a series of studies that opposing sides to various issues tend to overestimate their differences.

b. In studies of negotiations, the negotiators tend to underestimate the amount of common ground and often settle for less-desirable outcomes than those that were possible.

c. Opponents are often suspicious of each other's offers and concessions and tend to engage in reactive devaluation, which is considering an offer from an opposing side to be less attractive just because the other side made a concession.

d. Ross and Stillinger (1991) found that students at Stanford University who were protesting so administrators would divest from South African companies in the 1980s judged a partial divestment plan more favorably before they learned the administrators were proposing it and less favorably after they heard the administrators were advocating it.

D. Tit for Tat and the Elements of Cooperation

1. Axelrod (1984) asked people to submit strategies for the prisoner's dilemma game; after having fourteen different strategies play out, the strategy with the best average was found to be the tit-for-tat strategy.

2. The tit-for-tat strategy can be defined as a strategy in which one cooperates with one's opponent on the first round and then reciprocates whatever the opponent did on the previous round, meeting cooperation with cooperation, and defection with defection.

3. This strategy is successful for five reasons:
   a. It is cooperative.
   b. It is not envious.
   c. It is not exploitable.
   d. It forgives.
   e. It is easy to read.

Testing Your Basic Knowledge

ANSWERS TO MULTIPLE-CHOICE QUESTIONS

1. a	14. b
2. b	15. a
3. c	16. c
4. b	17. a
5. a	18. b
6. b	19. b
7. b	20. a
8. a	21. b
9. b	22. c
10. b	23. b
11. b	24. a
12. c	25. c
13. b	

Testing Your In-Depth Understanding

EXAMPLE ANSWER TO THE GUIDED QUESTIONS FOR CRITICAL THINKING EXERCISE #1

1. You can use the textbook or other portions of this chapter of the Study Guide to review the two-system view of morality. Engaging in exercises in which you consider the views of opposing sides should enhance your ability to engage in the second system of moral judgment—the controlled and reasoned system. Bolstering this system may make it more likely that initial "gut" moral reactions are reviewed in a more careful manner.

2. You can use the textbook or other portions of this Study Guide chapter to review the ethics of autonomy, community, and divinity.

3. Ethic of autonomy: Those in favor of gay marriage tend to argue that everyone should be free to marry the person of his or her choosing, even if that person is of the same sex. Those opposed to gay marriage generally argue that allowing gays to marry undermines the right of heterosexuals to observe a religious practice that is, by definition, exclusive to opposite-sex pairs.

Ethic of community: Those in favor of gay marriage might argue that marriage is a bedrock of modern society and that families—any kind of loving families—should be encouraged and can only improve society. Those opposed to gay marriage generally argue that allowing opposite-sex marriages would diminish the strength of marriage by diluting its meaning and would undermine the family because, according to this view, the most stable and societally useful relationships are those between two opposite-sex partners.

Ethic of divinity: Those in favor of gay marriage argue that being gay is a biological fact, not a choice and, as such, there is nothing "dirty" or "impure" about a gay marriage. Those opposed to gay marriage often argue that being gay is condemned in the Christian Bible and is a lifestyle choice that is sinful.

Avoiding Plagiarism:
About Inappropriate Paraphrasing

Most students are aware that directly copying from a source is plagiarism. Many students are aware that failing to provide a citation for any *ideas* from a source (even if not directly quoted) is plagiarism. But psychology professors often encounter students who innocently engage in inappropriate "paraphrasing" when using their sources. Students do not realize that, even when a source citation is provided, direct paraphrasing is usually considered plagiarism.

IDENTIFYING PLAGIARISM

"What do you mean by paraphrasing?"

Direct paraphrasing involves lifting sentences from the text and rephrasing them by substituting synonyms for the words that the author used. Occasionally this technique may be used for literary analysis. In these instances, the reader understands that you are paraphrasing. In psychological writing (and writing in many other disciplines), the reader assumes you are using your own words and sentence structures. Thus, even when discussing someone else's ideas (even if you include citations), the reader assumes that the sentences that are not in quotations are your own unique sentences. If they are not, you are implicitly trying to take credit for someone else's work. This is why many professors consider direct paraphrasing to be a form of plagiarism.

"But I learned that paraphrasing is the right way to use sources in a research paper!"

It is also important to avoid direct paraphrasing so that your paper will be clear and coherent. In psychological writing,

you are typically explaining or defending a point by using evidence reported in multiple sources. Because the ultimate point you want to make is not dependent on the particular wordings the authors used, the entire paper you write needs to be in your own words—even in those places where you are discussing someone else's research. If you paraphrase (or even quote excessively) in scientific writing, it typically interferes with the "flow" of your own work, and it is often difficult for the reader to see how the paraphrased ideas fit with your broader discussion. Thus, in psychological writing, paraphrasing is considered bad writing practice. If you reach a point where you feel the particular wording another author used is important to your point, then that is one of the rare places where you should use a direct quotation (and, as with all information that you learn from another source, include a citation).

"How else am I supposed to use sources in my paper?"

Avoid the common tendency to paraphrase by closing all books and sources before beginning to write your paper, or (more realistically) a small section of it. Refer only to your notes (and don't directly copy down phrases in your notes) and/or refer to what is in your memory about a source. After you have your own words on paper in draft form, you can then refer back to a source to get a detail, or double-check that you are accurately using the information. Thus, you are using your own words while writing the paper and double-checking your accurate use of your sources via revision of your own words. Remember, you still need to include source citations because you are using someone else's ideas.

A USEFUL EXAMPLE*

Below is an example of what constitutes inappropriate paraphrasing versus appropriate use of a source. The excerpt comes from *Establishing Authorship,* an essay by Paul C. Smith at Alverno College about how to identify and avoid plagiarism. Here is Smith's discussion of paraphrasing:

If correct citation and quotation practices are sciences, paraphrasing is a bit of an art. There are no hard-and-fast rules for paraphrasing. You must instead develop a "feel" for it. I'll try to provide some examples of what constitutes an adequate paraphrase and what constitutes an inadequate paraphrase. Here is a paragraph to be paraphrased:

> "Long-term memory, that immensely complex storehouse, has also been most extensively studied with the use of verbal materials, usually presented in the form of long lists. As we shall see, this approach has resulted in some extremely important findings, but it has also been a bit misleading. After all, remembering lists of words is somewhat different from remembering a conversation, a recipe, or the plot of a movie" (Klatsky, 1975, p.17).

Here is an inadequate paraphrase:

> Long-term memory is a complex storehouse that has been studied extensively using verbal materials presented in the form of long lists. While this approach has resulted in some important findings, it has been misleading. Remembering a list is not like remembering a discussion or a movie (Klatsky, 1975).

Here is an adequate paraphrase:

> We usually study long-term memory by having subjects attempt to recall aloud items from long lists. Because such a task is different in important ways from the kinds of tasks long-term memory is usually called upon to perform, our findings are somewhat questionable (Klatsky, 1975).

You should first notice that in both cases the reference was provided (Klatsky, 1975). This work is still the source of the ideas, even if not directly quoted. The inadequate paraphrase is not really the student's own words, but rather just Klatsky's words rearranged a bit (with a few words omitted). **If you were to turn in a paper containing this paragraph you would have committed an act of plagiarism.** It should be apparent that a person could write such a paragraph without really understanding the original paragraph at all. The author of the adequate paraphrase, on the other hand, must

have understood Klatsky's original paragraph. The meaning of that paragraph is captured in the paraphrase, but the words used to express that meaning are the author's own. An adequate paraphrase indicates to the reader that the author **understood** the original material. Authors should not include material that they do not understand. Rosnow and Rosnow refer to the inclusion of material the author does not understand as "lazy writing" (1992, p. 49).

In summary:

1. Whenever possible, paraphrase instead of quoting. Quotes are really only appropriate when the original source's exact words are important to the content of your paper. This is why you'll find so few quotes in psychological publications.

2. Paraphrasing means more than just changing a few words around here and there. A paraphrase is **your own words**—the kind of thing you could write two days after reading the original source, without having the original source in front of you. A paraphrase nonetheless requires a reference to the original source, for example, "Igor (1969) demonstrated that the brain has no effect on human behavior. . . ."

3. If you must quote, you must follow the appropriate format for quotations, giving the original source's exact words, and a reference to the original source.

References:

Klatsky, R. (1975). *Human memory: Structures and processes.* San Francisco: W.H. Freeman and Company.

Rosnow, R. L, & Rosnow, M. (1992). *Writing papers in psychology.* Belmont, CA: Wadsworth Publishing Company

FOR MORE INFORMATION ON PLAGIARISM AND HOW TO PROPERLY CITE SOURCES

FAQ's—http://www.muhlenberg.edu/mgt/provost/academic/plagiarismdef.html

List of Additional Resources—http://www.web-miner.com/plagiarism

Proper (APA) Style Guide—http://www.uwsp.edu/psych/apa4b.htm

Finding, Reading, and Citing Psychology Articles—http://www.muhlenberg.edu/depts/psychology/FindReadCite.htm

---

*The excerpt is included by permission of Paul C. Smith at Alverno College.

PSYCHINFO:
What It Is and How to Use It

PSYCHINFO is a database indexing articles that have been published in psychology journals. The search engine or "interface" used to search through PSYCHINFO is different at each college or university. For example, your institution may use the vendor "First Search," or your library may use "EBSCOHOST." To learn how to use your library's specific search engine, check with your instructor or a librarian. Below is general information about using PSYCHINFO.

COMMON TYPES OF ARTICLES INDEXED IN PSYCHINFO

Peer-reviewed articles: Peer-reviewed articles have been carefully reviewed by three or more experts in the field of psychology. Before these articles were published, these reviewers approved of the methods, conclusions, and other aspects of each article. The process is quite rigorous, and many articles are rejected for publication and/or sent back to the authors for substantial revision.

Empirical articles: Empirical articles are the most common type of reference found in the PSYCHINFO database. Each article contains a report of one or more experimental, correlational, archival, or observational studies conducted by the author(s). The article will provide background information in the Introduction, information about how the study was conducted in a Methods section, detailed statistical findings in the Results section, and a discussion of what the results mean in the context of previous studies in the Discussion section. These are peer-reviewed articles. It is often important to include empirical articles in your research process so that you learn the most recent research advances, typical methodologies in the area, and specific findings related to the variables you are studying.

Review articles: Literature review articles summarize and comment on a series of empirical studies conducted (typically by multiple authors) on related topics. These are peer-reviewed articles and can be very useful ways to gain general background information on a topic from a single source.

Book chapters: Book chapters typically either summarize an area of empirical research (similar to literature reviews) or propose new conclusions based on existing research. Book chapters are not typically peer-reviewed, but they are often written by topical experts at the request of the book's editor. Book chapters can also be useful ways to gain background information.

Dissertations: A dissertation is a long research paper that a graduate student must write in order to receive a Ph.D. Although all psychology dissertations are indexed in PSYCHINFO, they are often not appropriate sources for undergraduate class papers. First, dissertations are not peer-reviewed in the sense discussed above. Second, only one copy of the dissertation exists (at the institution that granted the student's degree). Because of this, it often takes too long to obtain a copy of the dissertation (weeks or months) and can be expensive for your college or university's library. If you find a dissertation that seems like it would be perfect for your research paper, try searching the author's name to see if he or she published a version of the same dissertation research in an established psychology journal.

ANATOMY OF A PSYCHINFO "RECORD"

PSYCHINFO itself does not provide you with the full text of the article (although your library may provide links to full text where available). Instead, PSYCHINFO provides a "record" for each article that has several key pieces of important information:

Title: The title of a psychology article is usually quite descriptive and can give you a quick sense of whether the article is relevant to your topic or not.

Year: The year the article was published.

Authors: It is important to keep track of all of the authors (not just the first) and the order in which the authors are listed. When you write your papers, you will use the authors and the year the article was published to cite your sources.

Source: This is the journal or book that the article or chapter was published in. It is important to know this so that you can find the article on the periodical shelves, in the "stacks," or elsewhere in your library.

Abstract: An abstract is an extremely short, dense summary of the article. It is designed to give you a sense of what the article will be about and is NOT designed as a stand-alone source. Professors can easily spot papers in which students have only read abstracts, rather than the actual article.

Subject terms: These are specific terms assigned by a professional librarian, designed to help people searching PSYCHINFO more easily find this article. Subject terms are often NOT everyday words or phrases; rather, they are more typically technical words or phrases. By analogy, if you were looking in a telephone book, you probably wouldn't search for the everyday word "car." Instead, you might try the more technical term "automobile." If you are uncertain of the technical terms that are relevant to your topic, you can use the PSYCHINFO Thesaurus and/or look at the subject terms listed in a record that does seem to be directly relevant and search for more articles with those subject terms.

SEARCHING PSYCHINFO

PSYCHINFO indexes thousands of articles in psychology. Virtually any topic you can think of has been studied in some way by some psychologist somewhere. Thus, the typical challenge is how to find just the right articles among the hundreds and hundreds that may emerge from a search. Below are some suggestions to get you started.

Examples of Types of Searches

Keyword or "Terms anywhere" searches: Keyword searches are the most general way to search PSYCHINFO and it is often best to start with a keyword search. This type of search finds the word you put in the search engine in any part of the entire record (abstract, title, etc.). The most common problem with a keyword search is that you end up with too many records (hundreds or thousands) to properly evaluate each article for its usefulness. *NOTE: PSYCHINFO search engines do NOT sort the results by relevance as do many Internet search engines. Thus, the perfect article or articles for your paper may be the 100th or 200th article on a long list, rather than the first or second.*

Subject Term searches: Subject searches look for the word you type in the search engine only in the subject term field of the record. As such, you may get more specific (and fewer) results with a subject term search. The caution here is that you need to know the specific language and terms for the subject search—everyday expressions will often yield too few or no records. See above for more information.

Title search: This is an uncommon type of search as it will look for the word you put in the search engine only in the title. This type of search is most useful when you want an article that is primarily about a common topic (e.g., self-esteem) rather than an article that simply uses or refers to the construct.

Author search: Searching for specific authors can be very useful if you identify a person or person(s) who seem to specialize in the topic you are interested in.

Search Tips and Strategies

Browsing: When you first sit down in front of PSYCHINFO a good goal is to simply learn a bit more about the topic you are interested in. What key terms or phrases do psychologists use to discuss this topic? What types of research have been done on this topic—research with humans or animals, children or adults, experimental or correlational research, field studies or laboratory studies. What authors seem to specialize in the topic? What subtopics more specifically define this general topic area. Spending a half hour to an hour "browsing" can improve the quality of your research ideas, your sources, and consequently your paper. When browsing, keyword searches are often most useful. Quickly review the results and make notes regarding the answers to the questions above. Of course, save the records for any articles that look especially useful.

Searching: After getting a "schema" for your topic, you are ready to dive in and really search for actual articles you will use in your paper. You might want to switch to the more specific subject term search, using the terms you gathered in the browsing phase. Keep modifying and building your search as you get more information. You will be trying lots of different searches to make sure you are zeroing in on all of the most relevant articles. When you start seeing the same records pop up over and over, you know that you have thoroughly investigated the literature.

Double-check: As you write your paper you might find holes in your research. This is very common. Be prepared to go back to PSYCHINFO to look for articles that may fill those holes. Once you start obtaining and reading the articles you find, another way of double-checking your work is following the paper trail that the authors have left for you. Look over the articles you have found: are there relevant papers cited in the introductions of articles that you are using? Also consider doing one last search before turning in your paper. After writing the paper you will be much more of an expert on the topic and may be able to conduct a more savvy search. At this stage it might make sense to do extremely specific searches in the title, author, source, or abstract fields.

Limiting Your Search to Reduce the Number of "Hits"

Most search engines for PSYCHINFO allow you to limit your search such that certain articles are automatically dropped from your search results. Limiting your search can be helpful, but also potentially damaging. Read the tips below to responsibly limit your searches. Speak with your librarian about how to limit searches using your library's interface with PSYCHINFO.

1. Limiting to "Full-text" or "References Available": My strong advice is to NEVER limit your search to full-text only articles. You will probably severely limit your results if you do so. While more and more articles are available full-text, MANY of your best resources may not be available online. Additionally, I strongly suggest you NEVER limit your search to articles only available in your library (unless you attend a very large university). Medium and smaller college/university libraries often have impressive collections of key journals available. However, few institutions can afford to subscribe to all of the 2,500+ psychology journals in existence. The quality of your paper will be determined in large part by the quality of your sources. Don't handicap yourself by overlooking sources you may have to obtain via interlibrary loan (see below).

2. Limiting by Language: So what limits are useful? Language is a safe bet. For example, you can limit your search to articles written only in English. Or, if you are fluent in a second language, choose that language also. Unfortunately, however, language alone will only be marginally helpful in narrowing your search results because many psychology articles are in English.

3. Limiting by "Publication Type": Students in lower-level psychology courses who are new to PSYCHINFO, may want to also limit by the types of documents your professor is allowing for the assignment. For example, your professor may ask that you use empirical articles, journal articles, peer-reviewed articles, and/or chapters only. Type of source limitation is especially helpful if you want to choose everything except the many dissertation hits you will get from your search. (See information above about the difficulty of using dissertations in your class research papers.) Do not limit yourself to too few resources, however. Again, always use this limit feature sparingly.

Tips for Increasing Number of "Hits"

If your searches are yielding few records (e.g., less than twenty) or no records at all, try the following tips to find more articles.

1. Review the browsing and searching options discussed above.

2. Be sure you are trying one search term at a time and making sure each individual term yields hits. The most common mistake for PSYCHINFO rookies is to put in three or four search terms all at once and then declare there "are no articles" on their topic when, in actuality, they just had one "bad" search term in their search.

3. Similarly, keep trying different search terms and try using the PSYCHINFO Thesaurus.

4. If you can find just one article that seems close to what you want, use that article's search terms or reference list to help you find more articles.

OBTAINING YOUR ARTICLES

As indicated above, you must obtain the articles that PSYCHINFO directs you to in order to use the information in your paper. A professor will easily spot a paper that is written on the basis of abstracts alone, and some professors may consider this a form of plagiarism and/or inappropriate source citation. Any given article listed in PSYCHINFO will be available from one of three sources:

1. On the shelves in your library: check periodicals shelves and/or the "stacks."

2. Via an interlibrary loan (ILL) request: almost all libraries share their resources with one another. If your library does not own a particular journal, you can probably obtain the article from another library by filling out an ILL request.

3. Online: an increasing number of psychology articles are available online. Check with your librarian to find out the best way to check and see if the article(s) you want are available in full-test form via the Internet.

Useful Web Links

ADVICE FOR PRESENTATIONS

- Designing Effective PowerPoint Presentations—http://www.ri.net/middletown/technologyhub/techreferences/effectivepowerpoint/points_files/frame.htm

- Tips for Giving an Effective Oral Presentation—http://www.business.umt.edu/faculty/herron/speaking_hints.htm

ADVICE FOR WRITING PAPERS

- General Writing Tips on Writing Psychology Papers—http://www.muhlenberg.edu/depts/psychology/WritingTips.htm

- Examples of APA Style Writing—http://www.uwsp.edu/psych/apa4b.htm

- Purchasing Your Own APA Style Manual—http://www.apa.org/books/4200061.html

- Stylistic Taboos: Common Writing Errors—http://www.sonic.net/~ideas/evr/toptab.html

- Writing *Empirical* Research Papers: Tips for Beginners—http://www.muhlenberg.edu/depts/psychology/EmpiricalPrimer.htm

PARAPHRASING, PLAGIARISM, AND USE OF QUOTATIONS

- Plagiarism, Quotations, and Paraphrasing—http://www.cc.colorado.edu/Dept/PY/Plag.html

- Several Great Examples of Inappropriate Paraphrasing—http://www.hamilton.edu/academics/resource/wc/AvoidingPlagiarism.html

- What Is Plagiarism—http://www.georgetown.edu/honor/plagiarism.html

- Avoiding Plagiarism—http://sja.ucdavis.edu/avoid.htm; http://owl.english.purdue.edu/handouts/research/r_plagiar.html

MORE INFORMATION ABOUT PSYCHOLOGY CAREERS AND MAJORING IN PSYCHOLOGY

- A Student's Guide to Careers in the Helping Professions—http://www.lemoyne.edu/OTRP/otrpresources/helping.html

- Tips for Students Thinking about Graduate School—http://www-personal.umd.umich.edu/~jsheldon/jsbrochure.html

- Links to Information on Graduate School and Careers—http://psych.hanover.edu/gradframe.html

- Graduate Studies in Psychology—the American Psychological Association (APA) annually publishes this useful guide that lists all North American programs, their specialties, and requirements. Search for this book on the APA books Web site—http://www.apa.org/books/

- Explore Areas of Psychology—http://psych.hanover.edu/Krantz/PsychScholar/explore.html

- Tipsheets on Various Psychology Topics—http://www.psychwww.com/tipsheet/index.html

- "What Can I Do With a Psychology Degree?" (requires Adobe Acrobat Reader)—http://www.muhlenberg.edu/ocdp/majors/information/psychology.pdf

MORE INFORMATION ABOUT SOCIAL PSYCHOLOGY

- Social Psychology Network—the largest social psychology database on the Internet—http://www.socialpsychology.org/